ALTERNATIVES TO PRISON
Community-Based Corrections, A Reader

Edited by
Gary R. Perlstein
Portland State University

and

Thomas R. Phelps
California State University, Sacramento

HV
9275
.A48

Goodyear Publishing Company, Inc.
Pacific Palisades, California

TO VERNON FOX WHO TAUGHT US
THAT PRACTICE WITHOUT THEORY
IS JUST AS STERILE AS THEORY
WITHOUT PRACTICE.

Library of Congress Catalog Card Number: 74-20318

Perlstein, Gary and Phelps, Thomas
    Alternatives to prison.
California   Goodyear Publishing Co., Inc.
Apr. 1975

                                                9-12-74

(Goodyear series in criminal justice)

Copyright © 1975 by
GOODYEAR PUBLISHING COMPANY, Inc.
Pacific Palisades, California

All rights reserved. No part of this book
may be reproduced in any form or by any means
without permission in writing from the
publisher.

Library of Congress Catalog Card Number: 74-20318

ISBN: 0-87620-036-6
Y-0366-8

Current printing (last digit):
10 9 8 7 6 5 4 3 2 1

Printed in the United States of America

CONTENTS

PREFACE v

part one
COMMUNITY-BASED CORRECTIONS AND THE PUBLIC 1

chapter one
FUTURE TRENDS IN JUVENILE AND ADULT COMMUNITY-BASED CORRECTIONS, Daniel Skoler 3
chapter two
THE DIVERSION OF OFFENDERS, Robert M. Carter 16
chapter three
IDEOLOGY AND CRIMINAL JUSTICE POLICY: SOME CURRENT ISSUES, Walter B. Miller 26
chapter four
CORRECTIONAL PROGRAMS, National Advisory Commission on Criminal Justice Standards and Goals 66
chapter five
MARSHALING CITIZEN POWER TO MODERNIZE CORRECTIONS, Chamber of Commerce of the United States 94

part two
IN LIEU OF INCARCERATION 113

chapter six
MAKING CORRECTION A COMMUNITY AGENCY, Wallace Mandell 115
chapter seven
CORRECTIONAL HISTORY, Lamar T. Empey 124
chapter eight
A QUIET REVOLUTION: PROBATION SUBSIDY, Robert L. Smith 136

part three
POST-INSTITUTIONAL COMMUNITY-BASED PROGRAMS   145

chapter nine
THE HALFWAY HOUSE MOVEMENT,
The Reverend J. T. L. James   147
chapter ten
SO YOU WANT TO OPEN A HALFWAY HOUSE,
Richard L. Rachin   161
chapter 11
POST-INSTITUTIONAL REHABILITATION OF THE PENAL
OFFENDER: A COMMUNITY REPORT, Reuben J. Margolin   175
chapter twelve
THE REINTEGRATION OF THE OFFENDER INTO THE
COMMUNITY: SOME HOPES AND SOME FEARS,
Frank P. Miller   183
chapter 13
CROFTON HOUSE: AN EXPERIMENT WITH A COUNTY
HALFWAY HOUSE, Bernard C. Kirby   195
chapter fourteen
INHERENT TREATMENT CHARACTERISTICS IN A HALFWAY
HOUSE FOR DELINQUENT BOYS, Robert C. Trojanowicz   205

part four
EDUCATION AND EMPLOYMENT PROGRAMS   221

chapter fifteen
NEWGATE: NEW HOPE THROUGH EDUCATION, National
Council on Crime and Delinquency   223
chapter sixteen
CHANGES IN CORRECTIONS: SHOW OR SUBSTANCE?,
Clyde E. Sullivan   228
chapter seventeen
EMPLOYMENT PROBLEMS OF RELEASED PRISONERS.
George A. Pownall   238
chapter eighteen
WORK-RELEASE: CONFLICTING GOALS WITH A
PROMISING INNOVATION, Elmer H. Johnson   247
chapter nineteen
STATE WORK-RELEASE PROGRAMS: AN ANALYSIS OF
OPERATIONAL POLICIES, Lawrence S. Root   258

**part five
JUVENILE OFFENDERS** 271

chapter twenty
COMMUNITY-BASED DELINQUENCY-PREVENTION
PROGRAMS: AN OVERVIEW, Irving A. Spergel 273
chapter twenty-one
YOUTH SERVICES BUREAUS, National Advisory
Commission on Criminal Justice Standards and Goals 289
chapter twenty-two
YOUTH SERVICE BUREAUS: A CONCEPT IN SEARCH OF
DEFINITION, Margaret K. Rosenheim 320
chapter twenty-three
RESOLUTIONS OF THE NATIONAL COUNCIL OF JUVENILE
COURT JUDGES 331
chapter twenty-four
A HANDBOOK FOR VOLUNTEERS IN JUVENILE COURT,
Vernon Fox 333

PREFACE

In 1790 a revolutionary idea became law. This idea, one that faced a great amount of resistance, was that imprisonment should be substituted for mutilation and other forms of cruel punishment. Unfortunately, the prison environment has not proved to be an effective means of changing behavior. This is perhaps most observable in the offender who returns to his home community no better able to cope than before.

One alternative to the traditional pattern of "arrest, trial, prison, and release" is community treatment. Most offenders do not require lengthy confinement either for their own protection or that of society. What is needed is the creation of varied programs which provide a bridge between prison and freedom. For others, programs are needed to divert offenders from the criminal justice system. The closed prison setting exists to help criminals who need medium or close security.

However, even though the treatment of offenders within the community appears to offer a more humane, less costly method of rehabilitation, we would offer a word of caution. The revolution won in 1790 naively congratulated itself on answering all the problems of corrections. But the community-based treatment of offenders should not be seen as a panacea for use with all prisoners.

The purpose of this book is not to provide all the answers or to present simple solutions to complex problems. However, it does present many of the new and important contributions in the area of community-based corrections. Hopefully, this will enable the reader to see where the field has been, where we are now, and, perhaps, even where we should go.

The book is divided into five parts: Community-based Corrections and the Public; In Lieu of Incarceration; Post Institutional Community-based Programs; Education and Employment Programs; and, Juvenile Offenders. This insures that the varied areas of community-based corrections are included.

We wish to thank the many people who contributed their time and energy to see this book become a reality. Special thanks are due Julia Robertson and Michael Clow.

part one:
COMMUNITY-BASED CORRECTIONS AND THE PUBLIC

Traditional prison programs are currently being subjected to serious criticism. The citizen fear of crime has to be answered with something new that works, for strident demands for longer confinement accomplish nothing. Correctional programs that involve communities are one response of great potential, which the following selections try to clarify.

Daniel Skoler identifies these innovative programs in the forefront of corrections: youth service bureaus, court diversion projects, expanded use of probation with full services, volunteer and paraprofessional services, community custody, community or regional correctional centers, foster care or substitute homes, and new uses for correctional manpower. Skoler also emphasizes the need for research and evaluation to determine the effectiveness of community-based programs. Robert Carter follows with his discussion of diversion as a means for processing offenders. He traces the origin of diversion and explores the philosophical and practical issues associated with the concept. Carter studies the effect large scale use of diversion has on criminal justice agencies. Both Skoler and Carter score the failure of traditional corrections and are optimistic about community-based programs.

Walter Miller provides a careful analysis of the ideological motivations of criminal justice agencies. Acceptance or rejection of community programs is shown to be influenced by established conservative or liberal philosophies. Concluding his remarks on a positive note he says: "... the purposes of effective policy and practice are not served when we are unable to recognize in opposing positions the degree of legitimacy, validity, and humane intent they may possess." Significance of community corrections as an alternative to institutionalization is discussed in the selection from the National Advisory Commission on Criminal Justice Standards and Goals. The commission suggests that each state correctional system develop a plan for implementing a range of community-based services. This should be accomplished by 1978. Reaction to this recommendation may be predicated on the ideological assumptions of criminal justice policy-makers. The interest of the public in alternatives to incarceration is found in the selection prepared by the Chamber of Commerce of the United States.

chapter one
FUTURE TRENDS IN JUVENILE AND ADULT COMMUNITY-BASED CORRECTIONS

Daniel Skoler

In recent years, we have seen study after study, report after report, and commission after commission criticize the failure of institutions in our correctional system—the jails, the prisons, the training schools, and the many other types of institutions that have been built and operated over the last two hundred years, ostensibly with rehabilitation in mind. As undependable as existing statistics are in the correctional field, or for that matter in criminal administration-at-large, they appear nevertheless to repudiate the effectiveness of institutional treatment in the rehabilitation of both adult and juvenile offenders.

It was perhaps unrealistic to expect that institutions could be effective. An institution, in itself, makes for an artificial situation, unrelated to circumstances which prevail in the outside society that either contribute to lawful behavior or produce delinquency and criminality. The typical institution is a substitute, forced into artificiality by the very circumstances of confinement.

This situation has been compounded by the fact that we commit to institutions all types of offenders—the first offender and the recidivist, the misfits, the alcoholics, the addicts, and, in the cases of juveniles, even those whose only offense may be that they were neglected by parents and families. It is further compounded by the fact that in most places we staff these institutions, and staff them skimpily, with less-educated and untrained personnel.

An institution, in sum, is not an inspiring place in which to be confined, and it is not an inspiring place in which to work. Ask an inmate. It may be true that institutions do not have to be as depressing and as destructive as they are. But the hard facts are that it will take many years—perhaps generations—and a good deal of money to make them significantly better. Some of the funds for this purpose are now becoming available through federal sources, but our most optimistic guess is that it will be many years before sufficient quantities have been infused to make much difference in the kind of institutions we have.

There are about 200,000 people in prison in this country, and perhaps 300,000 more in jails and juvenile institutions. Nearly all of these facilities are inadequate, merely from a physical point of view, for purposes of rehabilitation. With costs of construction now running nearly $25,000 per patient or inmate, it appears that even at today's prices, more than $12 billion would be required to rebuild our institutional system. By the time we actually got around to it, the costs would be much higher. And this does not take into consideration the money that would be required for more and better personnel and for new and improved institutional programs.

In economic terms alone, then, we have no alternative but to turn to the community and its resources if we are to do anything meaningful in the rehabilitation of offenders. This is not an undesirable prospect. It forces us to abandon outmoded ideas of punishment and retribution, and to focus squarely on rehabilitation. It also compels us to turn to a more promising setting in which rehabilitation can be accomplished. The average community in this nation possesses more resources that can be used for this purpose than the institutions which now serve it. In any event, it is only in the community that rehabilitation of the offender can ultimately take place. Here is where he must live, if he is to take his place in harmony with the rest of society, and here is where he must be adjusted to the habits and styles of life which will enable him to do so. These are hardly revelations to anyone familiar with contemporary corrections.[1] The insight has taken root and, today, community treatment is the "in-thing"—possibly a product of the conceptual revelations of the sixties linking delinquency inextricably with community, environment, and external opportunity as opposed to individual makeup or psychological deficiency.[2]

Under the Omnibus Crime Control and Safe Streets Act, today's largest grant-in-aid program directing federal resources toward criminal justice improvement, most of the states are emphasizing community programs in their planning and funding.[3] And if the Safe Streets Act and counterpart Juvenile Delinquency Prevention and Control Act are to accomplish the goal of reducing crime and delinquency, we think this priority offers the most promise. Let us examine some of the new thrusts.

YOUTH SERVICE BUREAUS

One of the major trends is toward the use of youth service bureaus. But we have noted no common agreement as to what a youth service bureau is, what services it should provide, or under whose auspices it should be operated. Some of them are operated by the police, others by probation departments, some by the courts, and others by the schools and a wide range of public and private social agencies. The prototype was, perhaps, defined in the 1967 reports of the President's Commission on Law Enforcement and Administration of Justice, where creation of "youth service bureaus" constituted one of the key action recommendations for delinquency control. There the bureau was conceptualized, with considerable latitude for flexibility, as a neighborhood youth service agency acting

> "as a central coordinator of all community services for young people
> ... and providing services lacking in the community or neighborhood, especially ones designed for less seriously delinquent juveniles."[4]

The agencies would be located, if possible, in comprehensive neighborhood community centers, receiving juveniles (delinquent and nondelinquent) referred by police, parents, schools, and other sources as well as the juvenile courts. Services would be voluntary, and thus, in the case of juvenile court referrals, the bureau was expected, ideally, to have the authority to refer back (30- to 60-day period) those juveniles it could not handle effectively. The major target was to get at the child-in-trouble/pre-delinquent/early delinquent group, not now adequately handled by criminal justice apparatus, with an agency having mandatory responsibility to develop treatment plans, voluntarily accepted, and superintend their execution by purchase of services, referral to helping agencies (mental health, vocational, counseling, etc.) and direct administration where necessary.

The services offered in bureau-type projects to date vary considerably. Some offer not much more than counseling. Others provide housing, support, training and education, and medical and psychiatric services. At this stage of development perhaps a diversity of approach is desirable. Different models can be tested and their effectiveness measured. But eventually some tried and proven standards should emerge. The Law Enforcement Assistance Administration, through both block grants and discretionary grants to state and local government, is funding large numbers of these projects. These projects will be observed carefully, and when it appears timely, appropriate professional organizations will be commissioned to distill the standards, guidelines, and alternate models that appear to be the most productive. The youth service bureau concept appears attractive, but as yet, little knowledge has been gained and little reliable guidance can be given on such questions as ideal residential/outpatient mixes; kind and quality of diagnostic services; balance of "purchase of service" and direct service inputs; size of caseloads; programming interface for adjudicated delinquents and, say, school problem referrals; extent of community and paraprofessional involvement; minimal and ideal staff needs; budgetary formats, etc. Yet these are inescapable issues for effective implementation of bureau efforts.

COURT DIVERSION PROJECTS

In the juvenile delinquency field, the past year has witnessed a particularly heavy funding of court diversion projects. Most of them appear to be modeled on the Vera Institute project in Manhattan. This effort stops the prosecution clock on less serious cases at the arraignment stage, offers counseling and job placement to the accused, and if he responds, provides dismissal of the case without trial and adjudication. As of June 1970, more than 1,000 offenders had been processed with a success rate (charges dropped) of about one in three individuals.[5]

The diversionary projects depend on the formulation of agreements between the police, the prosecutors, the courts, and the probation agencies. Again, the substance of these agreements varies considerably in the types of offenders who are eligible for diversion, and in the kinds of services that will be provided.

As with the youth service bureaus, we are in the trial-and-error process with the court diversion projects. Out of this diversity of experience should eventually come the data which will enable us to determine the most productive models.

One of the more successful diversion areas, collaterally related to corrections, is the detoxification centers which have been developed in the last five years to remove alcoholic offenders from the useless cycle of arrest, jail, trial, fine, release, and rearrest. Detoxification centers providing an opportunity to "dry out" in a medically supervised residential setting, with prosecution waived and some opportunity for counseling and referral to more intensive treatment, are operating effectively in such large cities as Washington, St. Louis, New York, Chicago, Houston, Wilmington, and Des Moines. The programs exhibit a healthy degree of variation in approach and techniques out of which may come sound specifications for standard diversionary mechanisms for the arrested alcoholic.

BROADENED PROBATION SCOPE

Probation by now is a commonly accepted technique, at least as far as the literature of corrections is concerned and the forms that have been adopted. But the comprehensive law enforcement plans submitted by the states over the past two years under the Safe Streets Act indicate a surprising absence of this service—both for adults and juveniles—in many areas of the country. In many jurisdictions it does not exist at all. In others, it exists only in law, and has never been implemented. In still others, probation is so rudimentary and unsupported that it cannot be said to have any effective existence. It has been said that probation has never really been tried in this country. The state plans suggest that this statement is substantially true.

Many experts are now even taking issue with the traditional concept of the probation officer as primarily a counselor, although it must be conceded that this role may have never had an adequate trial in most probation departments. The very size of caseloads and the responsibility for making pre-sentence investigations and preparing pre-sentence reports has commonly prevented officers from fulfilling the counselor role in any realistic sense.

But the offender needs more than counseling. An effort to educate and train the offender, to provide him with housing, medical services, and other support, should not wait until he has been committed to an institution. These resources all exist in the community, and it is the opinion of many experts that the probation officer should marshal and coordinate these community resources in the interests of his clients. The probation officer should also have the funds available with which to purchase a wide range of services, where needed.[6]

We often hear the economic argument that probation is much cheaper than institutionalization. It may cost only $250 a year per probationer under present circumstances, in contrast to institutional cost running as high as five or six thousand dollars a year for adults and as high as ten to twelve thousand for juveniles. But this begs the question. Probation should cost much more, if the full services needed by probationers are to be provided.

The economic argument, however, would still be valid. Certainly to provide needed rehabilitative services in the community would still cost much less than it would to confine offenders in institutions, where the services are largely absent or provided under circumstances that limit their possible usefulness.

Under the Safe Streets Act, plans are being laid this year for the beginning of a major effort to beef up probation, to make it truly a useful rehabilitation tool, rather than what it is in too many places today—a kind of suspended sentence. The most important trend in corrections over the next several years may well be the full development of probation, involving all possible community resources. Contrary to the situation that prevails with respect to institutions, this kind of thrust could be economically feasible. Substantial federal financial assistance has already been available from a number of sources, e.g., the HEW Youth Development and Delinquency

Prevention Administration (and its predecessor grant programs) and Vocational Rehabilitation Administration (the latter particularly with respect to purchase of services).

VOLUNTEER AND PARAPROFESSIONAL SERVICES

Associated with the development of various types of community-based programs, we find increasing utilization of volunteers, paraprofessionals, and ex-offenders. As noted in other aspects of community programs, there is yet no apparent consensus as to the extent of the roles these personnel can play, the kind of persons who should be selected, or the kind of training and supervision they should have. In some places there has been little attempt even at definition, although, as in the case of the youth service bureau, the general concept has found acceptance and stimulated new programs.

But out of this diversity should come some hard lessons on which to formulate soundly based and needed guidelines and standards. The Law Enforcement Assistance Administration is currently working on contractual arrangements for an evaluation of these programs over the next few years. Hopefully, this evaluation will be objective, realistic, and based on hard data rather than subjective evaluations. The old saw that if we "save even one offender" is not enough. The standard of cost-effectiveness must apply. The time has come to pierce the mystique of generality that has surrounded subprofessional utilization. Are indigenous residents the only group that can be effectively used? What about college students, middle-class volunteers, homemakers seeking a part-time challenge, and full professionals in one calling who may be willing to accept subprofessional status and service in another? Which groups do which tasks best, which require compensation, and which may be relied on for no-cost contributions? What roles may be properly assigned to these groups in determining program or agency policies?

A major and increasing contribution in this area, particularly with respect to indigenous and disadvantaged citizens, is coming from the manpower programs of the Department of Labor. Both the "new careers" program and the "public service careers" program, for example, have focused substantial resources on the development and training of paraprofessionals for meaningful roles in corrections and other criminal justice activities. Also, the Department of Labor, through its Concentrated Employment Program and the Job Opportunities in the Business Sector (JOBS) program, has experienced considerable success in using subprofessionals as job coaches in working with the offender population in training and job placement.

COMMUNITY CUSTODY

We have one problem of a particularly serious nature that must be resolved in the immediate future. That is the practice in at least thirty-six states of confining children in local and county jails along with adult criminals. The state law-enforcement plans submitted annually under the Omnibus Crime Control Act are graphic in their descriptions of this problem.

Under the Act, pursuant to both the "block grant" and "discretionary grant" authority,[7] literally hundreds of halfway houses, group homes, foster homes, and other types of shelter care are being funded. Funds are also available for this purpose from a number of federal aid programs. But the solution is not as easy as it sounds. Many of the halfway houses, for example, are operated on shoestrings, with a minimum of personnel and a lack of supporting services. Some of these places look not much better, and their atmosphere is not much better, than the jails themselves. Again, standards are needed, and a contract to produce such standards, under the auspices of a national professional organization, is about to be funded by the Law Enforcement Assistance Administration (LEAA).[8]

Another hard fact is that there are some youngsters and some adults who require confinement, at least for a time, and this cannot be provided by the types of shelter or residential care described. We need community detention centers for juveniles, and we need some type of community center to replace the jails for adults.

But there is no point in merely constructing additional detention facilities. Some juvenile detention facilities are merely jails for children, and new jails for adults can be, and frequently are, not much better than old jails.

COMMUNITY/REGIONAL CORRECTIONAL CENTERS

There has been much written recently, and a good deal of discussion, concerning the establishment of regional or community correctional centers for adults. A number of existing facilities have been given such designations, but upon examination, they are often found to be the same old jails. LEAA has searched the country and identified almost no facilities which have the range of programs needed to meet this designation. However, a number of jurisdictions are undertaking studies and making plans to create such centers, several with the support of federal funds.

To assist in what may be a major trend of the seventies, the Law Enforcement Assistance Administration has funded contracts to develop planning materials and designs for such facilities.[9] The emphasis in the planning phase is to minimize use of detention facilities in the first place, this by a review and examination of existing practices and how they might be improved. The second phase is to design facilities for those who must be held in detention and to provide these facilities with additional services beyond detention. These include diagnostic services, probation offices, classrooms, medical facilities, and even provision for educational and training opportunities. A key feature of these facilities will be the development of cooperative arrangements with other community agencies and services. The objective will be to get the individual out of detention as quickly as possible and involved in the community in a productive program.

The LEAA contracts include an effort to produce planning and design materials for community centers for juveniles. That project is now well underway, and it involves a considerable refinement of existing practice, with emphasis upon attention to the client from the moment of referral and the architectural realization of a truly therapeutic community setting. Since the average citizen and community are more receptive to innovation with respect to juvenile programs, this project may go farther than the adult project in producing break-throughs in community concepts and designs.

FOSTER CARE AND SUBSTITUTE HOMES

Community treatment means, above all, living and adjusting in the community. We have talked about group facilities, detention centers, and residential programs as alternatives to normal home life in a family setting. The closest substitute to normal family life in the disposition spectrum, particularly as regards juvenile or youthful offenders has been the traditional, perhaps, shopworn concept of "foster care."

As the economics of community treatment, in contrast to institutional care, command larger claim on our limited budgets, there may be room for vast expansion of the use of substitute parental homes as a string to our community corrections bow. This would not necessarily take the form of traditional "foster care" or child adoption. One need not look far to discern in our youth a new and laudable concern for the welfare of their fellow man outside the family circle and willingness to "share, clothe, and feed" in the best traditions of the Christian ethic.

In an affluent and problem-ridden society, where the best of the new generation will be seeking new personal challenges and "relevance," we may be able to divert commitment and interest, at least partially, from the rewards of a second home, a third car, and world travel to the challenge of adding troubled youths to the family circle for substantial stays. Instead of a limited, subsidized foster-care system, families who have "made it" (our nation has many) may, perhaps, be willing as volunteers to take on residential referrals of delinquent youths, both to assist rehabilitation of the delinquent and to enrich the lives and commitment of the volunteer family. If this kind of movement came about—admittedly a "Jules Verne" item in this examination of future trends—a remarkable correctional resource could be added to the community treatment concept, one with almost unlimited placement possibilities for the many delinquents who lack any home or family setting on which to build a rehabilitation program. Should we see the day when middle-class American families actually wanted, in large number, to bring juvenile and pre-delinquent youths into their homes as a service commitment, there would, of course, need to be maintained the full panoply of standards, guidance, training, and supportive resources needed to make the system work.

MANPOWER FOR THE NEW WAVE

These new trends in programs and facilities are encouraging and hopeful, but if they are to make a better showing than traditional methods, more is required. If they possess the potentiality for success, this potentiality can be realized only by commensurate improvements in personnel attracted to the field of corrections.

One need not review the findings of the Joint Commission on Correctional Manpower and Training in this respect. We know that correctional personnel are relatively uneducated and untrained. We know that the field is lacking in leadership, and that its rank-and-file workers are too often apathetic and unmotivated.

Some of these problems can be readily resolved. The money is at hand to raise salaries, to improve the education and training of personnel, and to hire large numbers of personnel. The motivation will be more difficult to bring about, but our society-at-large holds hope that this problem is not insurmountable. Increasing numbers of youths are unsatisfied with predominantly materialistic drives. Citizens of all ages are more and more concerned with the way we have polluted our physical environment. And the concern over law and justice that produced the Safe Streets Act is really a concern over pollution of our social environment.

There is awareness in all segments of society that we must improve the quality of American life and, in the process, undertake significant redefinition of national values. Certainly the objective of American corrections in the salvage and redirection of offenders is a high national goal. In any such redefinition, corrections should emerge as a more desirable and rewarding field to devote one's career to than its image has permitted in the past.

RESEARCH ROLE

In a "future trends" presentation of this kind, we cannot omit the subject of research. As a requirement for corrections, it has been talked about and written about for decades, but little has been done. Scientists in other fields have produced television, the supersonic transport, and the artificial kidney. But in corrections we have not progressed much beyond the days of the horse-drawn carriage.

In a country where annually we commit billions of dollars to research that produces more efficient military and space equipment, we must afford some fraction of that sum for research into techniques for changing lives from ways of criminality to patterns that will conform to minimum standards of lawful behavior. Fortunately, these priorities are beginning to find expression in federal policy and research-and-development support.[10]

We know that human behavior can be changed, however difficult the process may be. We know, for example, that jails and prisons can make individuals worse, insofar as criminal disposition is concerned. As discouraging as this knowledge may be, it demonstrates the malleability of the human personality. While the search for constructive ways of improving human behavior proceeds, we must also apply research techniques to evaluation of the corrections programs we have practiced for so many years and to the new community-based programs. We do not yet have assurance that the community-based programs will be more effective than penitentiaries and training schools. It has taken nearly 200 years to find that the traditional institutions are largely ineffective. We cannot await comparable time spans to evaluate the usefulness of the community programs.

The Critical Need for Evaluation

One of the deficiencies of past research has been the varying criteria by means of which to measure the effectiveness of programs. Usually evaluation has been effected by the persons administering the programs, a useful component, but not the only one, of a comprehensive evaluation research effort. It is, understandably, a rare experience to encounter among administrators operating experimental corrections programs those who will acknowledge that their programs are failures or who cannot produce some data purporting to demonstrate "success." Yet we know from the gross information available that the balance for American corrections, in its totality, falls on the side of failure.

A serious problem in prior years has been the inability of projects initially conceived as demonstration or experimental efforts to maintain this posture and produce a convincing showing one way or the other. This has been due to a number of constraints, including a lack of money and time, changes in personnel or operating conditions (impairing the integrity of the experiment), and an evaluation without sufficient controls or rigor to successfully measure results. Unfortunately, too many past demonstrations have been structured as independently designed, discrete experiments. In such cases, the significance of encouraging (or discouraging) results has been difficult to discern, at least until a number of successive efforts conducted over a period of years have been completed.

An alternative technique, receiving recognition in a few programs, is to conduct multiple efforts at the same time, or to promptly repeat in several locations a promising initial experiment, in each case under a commonly administered reporting and evaluation program. This is what is, in effect, happening with the intensification of experimental efforts and new approaches made possible by the infusion of Crime Control Act funds. Significant replication and joint evaluation offer a better picture of what a given demonstration can produce within a compressed period of time and tend to cancel out accidents of time, place, and people often operative in any single effort.[11]

Hopefully, LEAA and the correctional community will make the most of the rich opportunity for sound evaluation research which the seventies should offer to our field. Old shortcomings must be remedied. Definitions of "success" often involve relatively short periods of follow-up. Or they involve measures indicating "a reduction in the seriousness of further criminal behavior" or "a longer delay in the onset of further criminal behavior." Criminal careers often reflect that this is the normal course of events, as offenders learn to bargain for pleas involving lesser offenses or acquire the sophistication to avoid the law for longer periods of time. The public is entitled to more clear-cut measures of "success." Evaluation targets should hypothesize that after an offender has gone through a corrections program, he will stay out of significant trouble with the law indefinitely. That means more extended and more hard-headed approaches to research.

It has been characteristic of this country, in its search for ways and means of reducing crime and delinquency, to seek some "magic bullet," some solution that is quick, easy, and inexpensive. Yet, if there is anything that we have learned about crime and delinquency, it is that there are perhaps an infinite number of determinative variables, and that the causes of criminal behavior for one individual may be much different than for another. It follows, therefore, that amelioration and solution of the crime problem will be a complex undertaking. It will take a long time, it will be difficult to achieve, and it will be highly expensive.

All indicators show that we are witnessing the beginning of a new era and a new national commitment in corrections—one rooted in the increasingly accepted concept (mental health, special education, problems of the aged) that community responsibility and settings are an ultimate and necessary precondition for progress. Nevertheless, the prediction may be ventured a safe one—that we are not yet on the threshold of final solutions to the problems of offender rehabilitation. There is a long road to travel, and we have probably taken only the first step.

NOTES

1. For a good discussion of the rationale, history, and "elements of the community-centered" corrections movement in the United States, see *Trends in the Administration of Justice and Correctional Programs in the U.S.* (1956), chapters 2 and 3. See also *A Report on Developments in the United States—1965–1970*, prepared for the Fourth United Nations Congress on the Prevention of Crime and Treatment of Offenders; and *Administration of Justice in a Changing Society*, chapter on "Trends in the Administration of Justice and Correctional Programming" (95 pp.).
2. See, e.g., such landmark works as Cloward and Ohlin, *Delinquency and Opportunity: A Theory of Delinquent Gangs* (Glencoe, Illinois: Free Press, 1960); and Albert Cohen, *Delinquent Boys* (New York: Free Press, 1961).
3. Public Law 90–351 (1968). In the 1970 plans submitted under the Act for disposition of that year's $215-million action appropriation, approximately $23 million was focused in community correctional programs. See *Second Annual Report of the Law Enforcement Assistance Administration* (September 1970), pp. 5, 25, 44–5; and *LEAA Preliminary Program Division Analyses: 1970 State Law Enforcement Plans* (July 1970), pp. 13–21. For a statement of the LEAA community corrections priority, see pamphlet *Corrections Program—LEAA* (1970), pp. 13–14.
4. *The Challenge of Crime in a Free Society* (Washington, D.C.: Government Printing Office, 1970), p. 82.
5. *The Manhattan Court Employment Project* (New York Criminal Justice Coordinating Council, 1970), 12 pp.
6. In addition, private nonprofit organizations such as Jobs Now in Chicago, Illinois, and Jobs Therapy, Inc., of Seattle, Washington, have been successfully using professional businessmen as volunteers to establish one-to-one relationships in supporting the offender's adjustment on a job. For elaboration of the various Labor Department programs named, see *1970 Manpower Report to the President*, U.S. Dept. of Labor (Washington, D.C.: Government Printing Office).
7. These terms refer, respectively, to action funds granted to the states on the basis of population for redistribution in accordance with their approved, comprehensive criminal justice improvement plans ("block grants"—85 percent of action funds appropriated) and to action funds awarded by LEAA in its discretion for programs and projects deemed meritorious and consistent with national crime-control funding and supplementation priorities established by LEAA (Secs. 303–306, P.L. 90–306, P.L. 90–351). See also opening remarks by Richard W. Velde, Associate Administrator, Law Enforcement Assistance Administration, in *Outside Looking In*, a series of monographs assessing the effectiveness of corrections (Federal Prison Industries, Inc., 1971), 59 pp.
8. For an excellent "manual-in-brief" on halfway house planning from program through staffing, facilities, and budget, see *The Residential Center: Corrections in the Community* (Bureau of Prisons, 1969), 26 pp. See also *Guide for Youth Service Bureaus* (National Council on Crime and Delinquency, publication pending, 1971).
9. LEAA Contracts 70–TA–057 (regional and community correctional facilities for juveniles) and 70–TA–058 (regional and community correctional facilities for juveniles); *LEAA Second Annual Report* (September 1970), p. 202.
10. See *Presidential Memorandum to the Attorney General* (November 13, 1969) on national correctional policy, in which President Nixon, among other things, directed that the Department of Justice "institute a program of research, experimentation, and evaluation of correctional methods and practices so that successful techniques may be identified quickly and applied broadly in all correctional systems." As regards research and development support, in fiscal year 1970 the Law Enforcement Assistance Administration committed

approximately $10 million in research or discretionary funds for support of projects that would test and evaluate new techniques and practices, *LEAA Second Annual Report* (September 1970), pp. 51, 158–171.

chapter two
THE DIVERSION OF OFFENDERS

Robert M. Carter

Diversion is increasingly being suggested as a viable alternative to traditional processing of offenders through the criminal justice system. This article is in two parts. The first segment attributes the current emphasis on diversion to three factors: (1) increasing recognition of deficiencies in the nonsystem of justice, (2) rediscovery of the ancient truth that the community itself significantly impacts upon behavior, and (3) growing demands of the citizenry to be active participants in the affairs of government. The second section identifies major unresolved problem areas in the diversion process, such as the absence of guidelines for diversion, fiscal complexities, political and social issues, inadequate and uneven community resources, lack of assessment or evaluation of diversion programs, and the need for redefining traditional roles.

ORIGINS OF DIVERSION

Although there is considerable discussion and writing by academicians, administrators, and researchers about the system of criminal and/or juvenile justice, the United States does not have a single system of justice. Each level of government, indeed each jurisdiction, has its own unique system. These many "systems"—all established to enforce the standards of conduct believed necessary for the protection of individuals and the preservation of the community—are a collectivity of some 40,000 law enforcement agencies and a multiplicity of courts, prosecution and defense agencies, probation and parole departments, correctional institutions, and related community-based organizations. It is clear that our approach to criminal and juvenile justice sacrifices much in the way of efficiency

From *Federal Probation* 36, no. 4 (1972):31–36. Reprinted by permission.

and effectiveness in order to preserve local autonomy and to protect the individual.

The many systems of justice in existence in the United States in the early 1970s are not the same as those which emerged following the American Revolution. Indeed, this 200-year evolution has not been uniform or consistent; some of the innovations and changes in our systems have been generated by judicial decisions and legislative decrees, others have evolved more by chance than by design. Trial by jury and the principle of bail, for example, are relatively old and date back to our European heritage in general and the English Common Law in particular. Probation and parole began in the nineteenth century and the juvenile court is a twentieth-century innovation.

Coupled with the numerous criminal and juvenile justice arrangements in the United States and their uneven development is the separation of functions within the systems. There are similar components in all systems, ranging from apprehension through prosecution and adjudication to correction. Although in fact interwoven and interdependent, one with the other, these components typically function independently and autonomously. This separateness of functions, which on one hand prevents the possibility of a "police state," on the other leads to some extraordinary complex problems. Not the least of these is that the systems of justice are not integrated, coordinated, and effective entities, but rather are fragmented nonsystems with agencies tied together by the processing of an increasing number of adult and juvenile offenders. These nonsystems are marked by an unequal quality of justice; inadequate fiscal, manpower and training resources; shortages in equipment and facilities; lack of relevant research and evaluation to provide some measure of effectiveness; and, until recently, a general indifference and apathy on the part of the public which the systems were designed to serve.

Society Itself Contributes to Criminal Behavior

Society deals with crime in a manner which reflects its beliefs about the nature and cause of crime. Many centuries ago, for example, when crime was believed to be the product of the possession of the mind and body by an evil spirit, the primitive response was simple: drive the devil out of the body by whatever means were available for such purposes. The American tradition as relates to the etiology of crime has focused, until recently, upon the individual as a free agent—able to choose between good and evil and aware of the differences between right and wrong. Our "treatment" of crime accordingly reflected the simplistic notion that criminality was housed solely within the psyche and soma of the offender. Regardless of whether the prevalent philosophy was revenge, retaliation, retribution, or rehabilitation, the individual was seen as being of primary importance.

We have long assumed that the criminal or delinquent either willfully disregards legitimate authority by his illegal acts or suffers from some personal defect or shortcoming. There is much to learn, however, about the mysteries by which a society generates abnormal responses within its own circles. But this has become increasingly apparent: Society itself contributes significantly to such behavior. Indeed, it is the self-same social structure expressing its force and influence in an ambivalent manner which helps create on one hand the conforming individual—the person respectful of the social and legal codes—and on the other the deviant and lawbreaker who are disrespectful of the law. We have only recently become aware that crime and delinquency are symptoms of failures and disorganization of the community as well as of individual offenders. In particular, these failures may be seen as depriving offenders of contact with those social institutions which are basically responsible for assuring the development of law-abiding conduct.

Note, for example, that it has become increasingly common to discuss the "decline in respect for law and order." In every quarter, and with increasing intensity, we hear that the citizenry, for reasons as yet unclear, is not only failing to honor specific laws, but also displays a mounting disregard for the "rule of law" itself as an essential aspect of the democratic way of life. But even as this concern is echoed, it is not clear that we are all agreed as to what is meant by "decline in respect for law and order" or precisely to whom or to what we are referring. It may be that a large amount of what we observe and label as "disrespect for law" in a wide range and diversity of communities is in fact a normal reaction of normal persons to an abnormal condition or situation.

As knowledge expands to recognize the role of society in the creation of deviance, justice systems themselves will be modified. The implementation of knowledge, of course, always lags behind the development of knowledge.

Mass Disaffection by Large Segment of Population

Concurrent with the recognition that (1) the justice system is but a nonsystem, and (2) the community itself has an enormous impact upon the crime problem, there has been—particularly within the past decade—the emergence of mass disaffection of a large segment of our population. This disaffection with the American system is often described in terms which suggest that citizens are not involved in decision making and are acted upon by the government rather than impacting upon government. The disaffection has been manifested in many communities and in various ways.

We have, for example, been witness to mass civil disorder, unparalleled in recent times. We have seen our young people in revolt against the war in Vietnam, the grape industry, selective service, marijuana laws, prison administration, Presidential and Congressional candidates, Supreme Court nominees, and Dow Chemical. We have observed rebellion against "the establishment," ranging from burning ghettos and campuses everywhere to looters in the North, freedom riders in the South, and maniacal bombers from East to West. Young and old, black and white, rich and poor have withstood tear gas and Mace, billy clubs and bullets, insults and assaults, jail and prison, in order to lie down in front of troop trains, sit-in at university administration buildings, love-in in public parks, wade-in at nonintegrated beaches, and lie-in within legislative buildings. The establishment has been challenged on such issues as the legal-oriented entities of the draft, the rights of blacks to use the same restrooms and drinking fountains as whites, the death penalty, and free speech. Young people have challenged socially oriented norms with "mod" dress and hair styles, language, rock music, and psychedelic forms, colors, and patterns. We have seen the emergence of the hippy and yippy; the youthful drug culture; black, yellow, red, and brown power advocates; and organizations such as the Panthers, Women's Lib, the Third World Liberation Front, and the Peace and Freedom Party.

But this disaffection or unrest is not restricted to youth alone. Increasingly, adults are rebelling against the system. One need look no further than the recent slow-downs, work stoppages, and strikes of such tradition-oriented groups as police and fire officials, military personnel, social workers, schoolteachers, and indeed even prison inmates. Adult participation in protest has generally been more moderate than that of youth; some has been through membership in political organizations of a left-wing orientation; others have joined conservative right-wing organizations such as the Birch Society of Minutemen. Millions of Americans protested against the political establishment by voting for a third or fourth party or not voting at all in the last presidential election.

Movement Toward Diversion

These three phenomena—recognition that the community impacts significantly upon behavior, the uncertainty as to the effectiveness or quality of justice in the nonsystem of justice, and the growing desire of the citizenry for active, relevant and meaningful participation in every area of governmental affairs and community life—are moving the responses to the challenge of crime in a new direction. This direction is typically referred to as "diversion" and relates specifically to movement away from the justice system. It is most likely a prelude to "absorption" . . . a process in which communities engage in a wide variety of deviant behavior without referral to or only minimum interaction with the traditional establishment agencies.

Diversion is justice-system oriented and focuses upon the development of specific alternatives for the justice-system processing of offenders. The diversion model and its application have been generated from a belief that the control of crime and delinquency would be improved by handling criminals and delinquents outside the traditional system. Diversion is also predicated upon the reported effects of the "labeling" process and the impact of the "self-fulfilling prophecy." Whether diversion, at long range, is more effective than the established justice system and whether the "labeling" and "self-fulfilling" phenomena are operationally significant is unclear. These uncertainties do not dictate against diversion models, but rather should serve to restrain unbounded enthusiasm based upon belief and emotion rather than fact.

Absorption may be defined generally as the attempts of parents, peers, police, schools, and neighborhoods to address social problems—including those of crime and delinquency—by minimizing referral to or entry into one or more of the official governmental agencies designated to handle those manifesting deviant behavior. If there has already been a referral, absorption involves the removal of the transgressor from the official processes by offering solutions, techniques, or methods of dealing with him outside of the usual agency channels. Absorption is not restricted to the criminal offender or delinquent. It is, for example, equally applicable to deviants within the educational process. Absorption is adaptive behavior within the community in which alternative strategies are developed for coping with social problems. These involve the extensive use of community and personal resources.

DIVERSION: SOME PRACTICAL/OPERATIONAL ISSUES

There are issues about diversion—involving both philosophy and practice—which demand in-depth examination. Failure to address these completely interwoven issues is likely to result in diversion efforts which are every bit as fragmented and disjointed as those justice-system practices which, in some measure, led to the diversion movement. Rather clearly, there is a need to explore operational aspects of diversion, examine the community, its role and resources, and determine the latent and manifest impact of diversion on the justice system. These requirements are, in fact, mandates for assessment and evaluation. There is an explicit need to: (1) determine the guidelines and standards which define those eligible or ineligible for diversion, those agencies which are appropriate to receive those who are diverted, and programmatic activities of the agencies which receive diverted cases; (2) identify or develop, and mobilize, resources in a community, determine techniques for increasing community "tolerance" levels, enhance the delivery system for these resources, and make more equitable the availability of resources to diverse types of communities; (3) determine the impact of diversion practices on the justice systems overall, as well as their component parts, and examine the need for possible administrative, organizational, and legal changes; and (4) prepare a complete methodology for evaluating the effectiveness of diversion, keeping in mind that being "progressive" is not synonymous with being "successful."

The need for diversion guidelines is critical. Without some minimum standards for practice and procedure, and general consensus or agreement on philosophy, there is a distinct possibility that diversion may become the source of continuing and substantial inequities. Basic questions—such as who is (or is not) to be diverted, by whom, on what basis, and to what programmatic activities—should be answered by some shared understandings. Without such common understandings, the justice system—through increased use of nonsystematic diversion—may become more confused, autonomous, and fragmented.

Some minimum standards are needed, for example, to guide the *selection of individuals* for diversion. Diversion practices may be exclusionary and identify types of offenders who are deemed ineligible, such as those with a history of violence or felony offenders. Or practice may be permissive and allow that all offenders who will benefit from nonjustice-system treatment are to be considered eligible, regardless of other considerations. Diversion may be restricted to adjudicated offenders, or it may include nonadjudicated offenders. If the former, diversion is from the system after entry; if the latter, diversion is an alternative to entry into the system. Both raise substantial legal issues.

Determinations as to time frames are required; i.e., the optimum time for diversion, the length of time or duration of diversion, and so on. Guidelines are also needed as to actions to be taken if the person diverted fails to comply with the actual or implied conditions of diversion, or if it appears that the diversion plan is inappropriate.

Meaningful standards are necessary, for the *selection of agencies* to receive those who are diverted. Diversion need not necessarily be made to private agencies; it may be appropriate for there to be diversion to those public agencies which normally have been either minimally or not at all concerned with the offender population. And it may be appropriate for diversion to be to individuals rather than agencies. The selection of agencies requires community inventories, which in turn may indicate the need for new private and/or public agencies, or combinations/

consortiums/conglomerates of established agencies which address needs of offenders.

Of equal significance is the complex and politically sensitive problem of sifting through a wide variety of potential diversion agencies, including those with "unusual" or nontraditional characteristics—such as those with an ex-offender or ex-addict staff. Underlying many of these guidelines are fiscal considerations, including possible requirements for subsidies to agencies which handle those who are diverted. A delicate issue arises from public support of private agencies, in terms of performance objectives and standards, constraints, and expectations. The subsidy issue is made even more complex as the need arises to determine which public agency at what level of government pays the subsidies to those new partners in the justice system.

There is, of course, a requirement to examine the *programmatic activities* which receive diverted offenders. While an inventory of these various programs and some estimate of their effectiveness are essential to rational diversion practice, a basic question emerges as to whether offenders should be diverted if appropriate (or at least similar) programs exist within the justice system. And if such programs already exist in the justice system, the advantages, if any, which accrue by transfer of these programs and clientele to community-based, nonjustice-system organizations must be established.

The movement of programs and offenders to nonjustice-system organizations will require new roles for justice- and nonjustice-system personnel. As an example, the probation or parole officer realistically might be required to become a catalyst and seek to activate a community and its caretakers to absorb the offender as a member of that community. This would require a complete knowledge of community resources and diagnosis of clientele needs. There would be an emphasis on reducing the alienation of the offender from his community by impairing the continued maintenance of a criminal identity and encouraging a community identity. The officer would no longer find employment for the offender, but instead direct him into the normal channels of job seeking in the community. Residential, marital, medical, financial, or other problems would be addressed by assisting the offender engage those community resources which deal with these problem areas. This new role, then, might be one of insuring a process of community, not correctional, absorption. Again illustrating interrelationships of these issues, note that the "new role" phenomenon itself raises questions about training for and acceptance of the role and methods or techniques of implementation.

Imbalance in Community Resources a Problem

Other issues arise as one examines the role and resources of the community. Not at all insignificant is the complex issue of imbalance among communities to accept cases which are diverted and to provide necessary services and resources. Some communities have distinct economic advantages over others—and it is clear that diversion has an economic, as well as a motivational, base. Middle- and upper-class communities and their citizens, socially and economically secure, often have internal financial resources available to mobilize a wide range of agencies of diversion or specialized services, ranging from psychiatric care through private schools. The differences in resource levels need scrutiny, for it would be socially disastrous to deny diversion to those who are economically disadvantaged; diversion cannot be restricted to the affluent. Without action to balance resource requirements with the capacity of delivering services, the poor and the disadvantaged will continue to flow into and through the justice agencies.

A parallel community-based problem occurs where there is a low community tolerance for diversion. How is community tolerance to be increased? A simple demonstration of need may be insufficient. Numerous examples of low or nontolerance may be cited, ranging from open through latent resistance and hostility directed against self-help groups and agency halfway houses. And besides the very difficult "how," there is the related question of "who" is responsible for dealing with community fears and anxieties. Is every justice agency seeking to divert offenders responsible for its own resource development, or is some overall plan among cooperating justice agencies more rational? And again, as one question leads to another, if a plan is necessary, who designs and implements it, and how are activities financed and monitored?

Diversion Will Result in Significant Changes

Although changes in justice systems are inevitable consequences of an increased use of diversion, there is a distinct probability that the changes will be both unplanned and unsystematic. These changes may range from administrative and organizational restructuring, and modification in procedure and policy, on one hand, through major changes in the populations which are serviced by the justice systems on the other.

As justice agencies become partners with communities, there may be requirements in all agencies for organizational change to include new bureaus or divisions of "community service." This would require new personnel or reassignment of personnel; development acceptance of new roles, such as those of diagnostician and/or catalyst; innovative training; perhaps additional funding and different kinds of facilities; and new understandings within the agencies and communities themselves. Permanent linkages with community organizations may be required. Traditional pyramid, hierarchical organizational models may have to be flattened. New information systems will be required, and continuing involvement or monitoring of diverted cases may be desirable.

The large-scale diversion of offenders—either from or after entry into the justice system—may have other consequences for the justice agencies. If, for example, substantial numbers of offenders are diverted by local law enforcement to community-based agencies, there will be, in all likelihood, reduced inputs to prosecution, adjudication, and correctional agencies. Lessened inputs will alleviate some of the backlog in the judicial system and reduce caseload pressure in probation and parole and size of institutional population. While these occurrences are desirable, at some point in time the bureaucratic instinct for survival may be threatened. Reactions protective of the establishment may set in. Of greater significance, however, is that increased idversion may leave the justice system with a unique clientele of hardened, recalcitrant, difficult offenders who seem unlikely to "make it" in the community. These offenders may have complex problems requiring long-range treatment, and they may represent a major threat to and be rejected by their communities. In addition to creating major management problems, these offenders will require new and different programs, facilities, and staff for treatment. In short, extensive diversion may not only "threaten" the justice establishment, it may change the justice system population and alter the system itself.

Planning and Evaluation Necessary

There are yet other important aspects of diversion which require attention—planning and evaluation. A lack of mid-range and strategic planning and systematic evaluation has long been a major defect in justice operations from law enforcement through corrections. The movement toward diversion of offenders mandates that planning and evaluation not be "tacked on" to operational processes, but rather be built in, continually updated, constantly reviewed. The questions about planning and evaluation are familiar—criteria must be established; funds must be made available; personnel, software, and hardware must be obtained; methodologies developed; responsibilities delineated. Without such planning and evaluation, it appears certain that diversion practices will produce more confusion and chaos than clarity and consistency.

CONCLUSION

This article has explored the origins of diversion and identified some of the major operational and philosophical problems associated with the movement. Diversion is seen as an outgrowth of a fragmented justice system, which has been neither just nor efficient; the increasing demands of our citizenry to be participants in the affairs of government, including the justice system; and recognition that the community is an appropriate base for many justice operations. But even as there is increasing momentum toward diversion, there is a pressing need for guidelines, standards and shared understandings, examination of the role and resources of the community, study of the long-range impact of diversion on the justice system and society, and planning and evaluation.

Diversion is both a challenge and an opportunity. As a potentially major mechanism of the justice system, diversion requires considered attention. Although changes in our justice systems are indicated, rapid movement to untested and ill-defined alternatives is inappropriate.

chapter three
IDEOLOGY AND CRIMINAL JUSTICE POLICY: SOME CURRENT ISSUES

Walter B. Miller

There is currently in the United States a widespread impression that our country is experiencing a major transitional phase—a period in which long-established social arrangements and the moral and conceptual notions that undergird them are undergoing substantial change. Optimists see this process as a transition from one relatively effective social order to another; pessimists see it as a one-way passage to catastrophe.

It is hard to judge the validity of these conceptions. Few generations have been free from the conviction that the nation was in the throes of "the crisis of our times," and such perceptions have not always corresponded with judgments of later historians.[1]

Since criminal behavior, ways of thinking about crime, and methods of dealing with crime make up an intrinsic component of any social order, the notion of a transitional phase also affects the perceptions and actions of both criminals and criminal justice system personnel. As soon as one considers crime as one facet of a larger set of social and historical shifts, however, a paradox emerges. One gets an impression both of striking and substantial change, and of striking and substantial stability.

This paradox seems to apply equally to crime and to societal response to crime. On the one hand, patterns of contemporary criminal behavior reflect substantial shifts—e.g., a massive increase in drug use and drug-related crimes, a new dimension of political motivation affecting many adult prisoners. On the other hand, an impression of changelessness and stability is evident in the relatively unchanging nature of youth crime and periodic attention to youth gang violence.[2]

Reprinted by special permission of the Journal of Criminal Law and Criminology, Copyright © 1973 by Northwestern University School of Law, vol. 64, no. 2.

A similar paradox affects those responsible for making and implementing criminal justice policy. On the one hand, we seem to be in the midst of a radical shift in conceptualizing and coping with crime, indicated by a host of current slogans such as decentralization, decriminalization, deinstitutionalization, victimology, and others. On the other hand, there is a surprising sameness in the basic issues which these slogans reflect —issues such as free will versus determinism, individual rights versus state's rights, concentration versus diffusion of power. Do these concerns represent progressive movement or merely contemporary replays of ancient dramas?

Intriguing as it might be to explore these issues with respect to the behavior of both those who engage in crime and those who attempt to deal with it, I shall treat only the latter. The terms "criminologist" or "criminal justice personnel" will be used here to refer to those persons who maintain some consistent responsibility for dealing with criminals and their behavior.

One may seek to escape this paradox by employing the concept of "ideology." Ideology is also a central element in the complex patterns of change and stability, and a key to their understanding. A useful point of departure may be found in a quotation from Myrdal's *An American Dilemma:*

> The place of the individual scientist along the scale of radicalism-conservatism has always had strong influences on both the selection of research problems and the conclusions drawn from research. In a sense, it is the master scale of biases in social science.[3]

It is this master scale, and its influence on the field of criminal justice, which will be my major concern here.

The term "ideology" may be used in many ways.[4] It will be used here only to refer to a set of general and abstract beliefs or assumptions about the correct or proper state of things, particularly with respect to the moral order and political arrangements, which serve to shape one's positions on specific issues. Several aspects of ideology as used in this sense should be noted. First, ideological assumptions are generally pre-conscious rather than explicit, and serve, under most circumstances, as unexamined presumptions underlying positions taken openly. Second, ideological assumptions bear a strong emotional charge. This charge is not always evident, but it can readily be activated by appropriate stimuli, in particular by direct challenge. During the process of formation, ideological premises for particular individuals are influenced by a variety of informational inputs, but once established they become relatively impervious to change, since they serve to receive or reject new evidence in terms of a self-contained and self-reinforcing system.

The major contention of this presentation is that ideology and its consequences exert a powerful influence on the policies and procedures of those who conduct the enterprise of criminal justice, and that the degree and kinds of influence go largely unrecognized. Ideology is the permanent hidden agenda of criminal justice.

The discussion has two major aims. First, assuming that the generally implicit ideological basis of criminal justice commands strong, emotional, partisan allegiance, I shall attempt to state explicitly the major assumptions of relevant divergent ideological positions in as neutral or as nonpartisan a fashion as possible. Second, some of the consequences of such ideologies for the processes of planning, program, and policy in criminal justice will be examined.

I shall use a simple conceptual device for indicating ideological positions—a one-dimensional scale that runs from five on the right to zero in the middle to five on the left. Various ideological positions under consideration will be referred to this scale, using the terms "left" and "right" in an attempt to achieve neutrality. Although not all eleven possible distinctions will be made in every analysis, five scale distinctions on each side seem to be the minimum needed for present purposes. Later discussions will in some instances attribute considerable importance to differences as small as one scale degree.

The substance of ideologically divergent positions with respect to selected issues of current concern will be presented in three ways. Positions will be formulated first as "crusading issues"—shorthand catchwords or rallying cries that furnish the basic impetus for action or change in the criminal justice field. Such catch phrases are derived from a deeper and more abstract set of propositions as to desired states or outcomes. These will be designated "general assumptions." Third, differentiated positions will be delineated for all points along the full range of the scale—extreme right to extreme left—for three major policy issues.[5]

IDEOLOGICAL POSITIONS

Right: Crusading Issues

Crusading issues of the right differ somewhat from those of the left; they generally do not carry as explicit a message of movement toward new forms, but imply instead that things should be reconstituted or restored. However, the component of the message that says, "Things should be different from the way they are now," comes through just as clearly as in the crusading issues of the left. Current crusading issues of the right with respect to crime and how to deal with it include the following.

1. *Excessive leniency toward lawbreakers.* This is a traditional complaint of the right, accentuated at present by the publicity given to reform programs in corrections and policing, as well as to judicial activity at various levels.

2. *Favoring the welfare and rights of lawbreakers over the welfare and rights of their victims, of law enforcement officials, and of the law-abiding citizen.* This persisting concern is currently activated by attention to prisoners' rights, rehabilitation programs, attacks on police officers by militants, and in particular by a series of well-publicized Supreme Court decisions aimed to enhance the application of due process.
3. *Erosion of discipline and of respect for constituted authority.* This ancient concern is currently manifested in connection with the general behavior of youth, educational policies, treatment of student dissidents by college officials, attitudes and behavior toward law enforcement, particularly the police.
4. *The cost of crime.* Less likely to arouse the degree of passion evoked by other crusading issues, resentment over what is seen as the enormous and increasing cost of crime and dealing with criminals—a cost borne directly by the hard-working and law-abiding citizen—nevertheless remains active and persistent.
5. *Excessive permissiveness.* Related to excessive leniency, erosion of discipline, and the abdication of responsibility by authorities, this trend is seen as a fundamental defect in the contemporary social order, affecting many diverse areas such as sexual morality, discipline in the schools, educational philosophies, child-rearing, judicial handling of offenders, and media presentation of sexual materials.

Right: General Assumptions

These crusading issues, along with others of similar import, are not merely ritualized slogans but reflect instead a more abstract set of assumptions about the nature of criminal behavior, the causes of criminality, responsibility for crime, appropriate ameliorative measures, and, on a broader level, the nature of man and of a proper kind of society. These general assumptions provide the basic charter for the ideological stance of the right as a whole, and a basis for distinguishing among the several subtypes along the points of the ideological scale. Major general assumptions of the right might be phrased as follows.

1. The individual is directly responsible for his own behavior. He is not a passive pawn of external forces, but possesses the capacity to make choices between right and wrong—choices which he makes with an awareness of their consequences.
2. A central requirement of a healthy and well-functioning society is a strong moral order which is explicit, well-defined, and widely adhered to. Preferably the tenets of this system of morality should be derived from and grounded in the basic

precepts of a major religious tradition. Threats to this moral order are threats to the very existence of the society. Within the moral order, two clusters are of particular importance:
   a. Tenets which sustain the family unit involve morally derived restrictions on sexual behavior, and obligations of parents to maintain consistent responsibility to their children and to one another.
   b. Tenets which pertain to valued personal qualities include: taking personal responsibility for one's behavior and its consequences; conducting one's affairs with the maximum degree of self-reliance and independence, and the minimum of dependency and reliance on others, particularly public agencies; loyalty, particularly to one's country; achieving one's ends through hard work, responsibility to others, and self-discipline.
3. Of paramount importance is the security of the major arenas of one's customary activity—particularly those locations where the conduct of family life occurs. A fundamental personal and family right is safety from crime, violence, and attack, including the right of citizens to take necessary measures to secure their own safety, and the right to bear arms, particularly in cases where official agencies may appear ineffective in doing so.
4. Adherence to the legitimate directives of constituted authority is a primary means for achieving the goals of morality, correct individual behavior, security, and other valued life conditions. Authority in the service of social and institutional rules should be exercised fairly but firmly, and failure or refusal to accept or respect legitimate authority should be dealt with decisively and unequivocally.
5. A major device for ordering human relations in a large and heterogeneous society is that of maintaining distinctions among major categories of persons on the basis of differences in age, sex, and so on, with differences in religion, national background, race, and social position of particular importance. While individuals in each of the general categories should be granted the rights and privileges appropriate thereto, social order in many circumstances is greatly facilitated by maintaining both conceptual and spatial separation among the categories.

Left: Crusading Issues

Crusading issues of the left generally reflect marked dissatisfaction with characteristics of the current social order and carry an insistent message about the desired nature and direction of social reform. Current issues of relevance to criminal justice include:

1. *Overcriminalization.* This reflects a conviction that a substantial number of offenses delineated under current law are wrongly or inappropriately included, and applies particularly to offenses such as gambling, prostitution, drug use, abortion, pornography, and homosexuality.
2. *Labeling and stigmatization.* This issue is based on a conception that problems of crime are aggravated or even created by the ways in which actual or potential offenders are regarded and treated by persons in authority. To the degree a person is labeled as "criminal," "delinquent," or "deviant," will he be likely to so act.
3. *Overinstitutionalization.* This reflects a dissatisfaction over prevalent methods of dealing with suspected or convicted offenders whereby they are physically confined in large institutional facilities. Castigated as "warehousing," this practice is seen as having a wide range of detrimental consequences, many of which are implied by the ancient phrase "schools for crime." Signaled by a renewed interest in "incarceration," prison reform has become a major social cause of the left.
4. *Overcentralization.* This issue reflects dissatisfaction with the degree of centralized authority existing in organizations which deal with crime—including police departments, correctional systems, and crime-related services at all government levels. Terms which carry the thrust of the proposed remedy are local control, decentralization, community control, a new populism, and citizen power.
5. *Discriminatory bias.* A particularly blame-worthy feature of the present system lies in the widespread practice of conceiving and reacting to large categories of persons under class labels based on characteristics such as racial background, age, sex, income level, sexual practices, and involvement in criminality. Key terms here are racism, sexism, minority oppression, and brutality.

Left: General Assumptions

As in the case of the rightist positions, these crusading issues are surface manifestations of a set of more basic and general assumptions, which might be stated as follows.

1. Primary responsibility for criminal behavior lies in conditions of the social order rather than in the character of the individual.

Crime is to a greater extent a product of external social pressures than of internally generated individual motives, and is more appropriately regarded as a symptom of social dysfunction than as a phenomenon in its own right. The correct objective of ameliorative efforts, therefore, lies in the attempt to alter the social conditions that engender crime rather than to rehabilitate the individual.
2. The system of behavioral regulation maintained in America is based on a type of social and political order that is deficient in meeting the fundamental needs of the majority of its citizens. This social order, and the official system of behavioral regulation that it includes, incorporates an obsolete morality not applicable to the conditions of a rapidly changing technological society—and disproportionately geared to sustain the special interests of restricted groups—but which still commands strong support among working-class and lower-middle-class sectors of the population.
3. A fundamental defect in the political and social organization of the United States, and in those components of the criminal justice enterprise that are part of this system, is an inequitable and unjust distribution of power, privilege, and resources—particularly of power. This inequity pervades the entire system, but appears in its more pronounced forms in the excessive centralization of governmental functions and consequent powerlessness of the governed, the military-like, hierarchical authority systems found in police and correctional organization, and policies of systematic exclusion from positions of power and privilege for those who lack certain preferred social characteristics. The prime objective of reform must be to redistribute the decision-making power of the criminal justice enterprise rather than to alter the behavior of actual or potential offenders.
4. A further defect of the official system is its propensity to make distinctions among individuals based on major categories or classes within society, such as age, sex, race, social class, criminal or noncriminal. Healthy societal adaptation for both the offender and the ordinary citizen depends on maintaining the minimum separation—conceptually and physically—between the community at large and those designated as "different" or "deviant." Reform efforts must be directed to bring this about.
5. Consistent with the capacity of external societal forces to engender crime, personnel of official agencies play a predominantly active role, and offenders a predominantly reactive role, in situations where the two come in contact. Official

agents of behavioral regulation possess the capacity to induce or enhance criminal behavior by the manner in which they deal with those who have or may have engaged in crime. These agents may define offenders as basically criminal, expose them to stigmatization, degrade them on the basis of social characteristics, and subject them to rigid and arbitrary control.

6. The sector of the total range of human behavior currently included under the system of criminal sanctions is excessively broad, including many forms of behavior (for example, marijuana use, gambling, homosexuality) which do not violate the new morality, and forms which would be more effectively and humanely dealt with outside the official system of criminal processing. Legal codes should be redrafted to remove many of the behavioral forms now proscribed and to limit the discretionary prerogatives of local authorities over apprehension and disposition of violators.

AN IDEOLOGICAL SPECTRUM: DIFFERENTIATED POSITIONS OF LEFT AND RIGHT

The foregoing ideologically relevant propositions are formulated as general assumptions common to all those designated as "left" or "right." The present section will expand and differentiate these generalized propositions by distributing them along the ideological scale proposed earlier. Charts I, II, and III (see pp. 45–62) present thirty differentiated positions with respect to three major issues of relevance to criminal justice policy. Statements concerning each issue are assigned ten positions along scales running from right five through left five. The three issues are: conceptions as to the causes of crime and the locus of responsibility for criminality; conceptions of proper methods of dealing with offenders; conceptions of proper operating policies of criminal justice agencies. Not included in these tables is a theoretically possible "centrist" position.

Several features of the charts should be noted. Statements representing ideologically influenced positions on the scale are formulated in a highly condensed and simplified manner, lacking the subtleties, qualifications, and supporting arguments which characterize the actual stances of most people. The basic model is that of an "ideal type" analysis, which presents a series of simplified propositions formulated to bear a logical relationship to one another and to underlying abstract principles, rather than to reflect accurately the actual positions of real people.[6] Few readers will feel entirely comfortable with any of the statements exactly as phrased here; most will feel instead that given statements might reflect the general gist of their position, but with important qualifications, or that one can subscribe to selected parts of statements at several different points along the scale. On the other hand, few readers will fail to find some statements with which they disagree completely; it is most unlikely, for example, that one could support with equal enthusiasm the major tenets attributed here to positions at left four and right four.

In "placing" oneself with respect to the scaled positions outlined here, one should look for those statements with which one feels least uncomfortable rather than expecting to find formulations which correspond in all respects to his viewpoint. The process of ascertaining discrepancies between actual positions and those represented here as "pure" examples of rightist or leftist ideology serves one of the purposes of ideal-typical analysis; few are ideological purists, but this type of analysis makes it possible to identify positions which correspond more or less closely to ideological orthodoxy. Those whose positions are closer to the extremes will feel least comfortable with statements attributed to the opposing side of the spectrum; those closer to "centrist" positions will tend to find orientations congenial to their own at a larger number of scale positions, possibly including positions on both sides of the spectrum.

To say that the statements show some logical relationship to one another and to underlying principles is not to say that they are logically consistent; in fact, several obvious inconsistencies appear in the charts. For example, right five maintains that criminals are unwitting puppets of a radical conspiracy and, at the same time, holds that they are responsible for their own behavior. Left four calls for maximum access to information concerning the inner workings of criminal justice agencies and, at the same time, advocates minimum access by employers, personnel departments, and others to criminal records of individuals. If one fails to find in internal consistency the "logical" basis for these propositions, where do the logical relationships lie?

Although some degree of logical inconsistency is likely in almost any developed set of propositions about human behavior, the consistency in the above propositions lies largely in the degree to which the interests of particular classes of persons are supported, defended, and justified. The inconsistencies often lie either in the means advocated to achieve such ends or in the rationales used to defend or exculpate favored interests and condemn opposing ones. In the above examples, if one assumes that a basic interest of left four is maximum protection of and support for actual or putative offenders, then these ends are served in the one instance by maximum access to information which might reveal errors, inequities, or violations in their treatment by criminal justice officials, and in the other by denying to potential employers and others access to information that might jeopardize their welfare. Similarly, in attempting to reconcile the apparent contradiction in assertions that offenders are pawns of a radical conspiracy and also that they are directly responsible for their behavior, a rightist could argue that offenders are indeed responsible for their behavior, and that they make a deliberate personal choice to follow the crime-engendering appeals of the radicals.

While statements at different scale positions frequently present differing orientations to the same subissue (e.g., scope of criminal law, appropriate degree of restraint of offenders, extent to which "rehabilitation" should be an objective), not all of the statements on each major issue treat all of the included subissues. The positioned statements are defective with respect to "dimensionality," the possibility of full scalability across all issues. Each of the included subissues represents an independently scalable dimension. The "cause" issue incorporates approximately 14 distinguishable dimensions or subissues, the "offender" issue 15, and the "agencies" issue 18. To include a separate statement for each dimension at each scale position for all three issues would require a minimum of 470 statements—an impractical number for a presentation at this level. Selection of subissues and their assignment to given positions was guided by an attempt both to produce internally coherent statements and to cover a fairly broad range of subissues.

One often finds convergences at the extremes of a distribution of ideological positions. Several instances can be found in the charts; for example, both right five and left five attribute criminality to deliberate or systematic efforts or policies of highly organized interest groups, although of differing identities (radicals, the ruling class). If quantifiable weights can be assigned to the scalable dimensions of the chart, two major types of distribution are included—"opposition" and "convergence" distributions. "Opposition" distributions occur where the maximum weight or magnitude is found at one extreme of the scale and the minimum at the other, with intermediate positions showing intermediate values. Examples may be found in the subissues "degree of coercive power to be exercised by official agencies" (left five espouses the minimum degree, right five the maximum, with others occupying intermediate positions), and "degree of personal culpability of offenders" (right five maximum, left five minimum, others in between). Policy disputes involving this type of distribution tend to be most difficult to resolve.

In "convergence" distributions similarities or partial similarities are found in the positions of those at opposing ends of the spectrum. One instance is found in attitudes toward rehabilitation of offenders—an objective strongly opposed by partisans at both left four and right four, although for different reasons. A rather complex but crucial instance is found in the statements concerning "localized" versus "centralized" authority. Both left four and right four call for increased local autonomy, whereas the more "moderate" of both left and right favor continued or increased federal authority and support for criminal justice programs and operations. The apparent convergence of the extremes is, however, complicated by a number of factors. One relates to which branch of government exercises authority, another relates to the particular policy area at issue. Those at left four are not adverse to strong federal initiatives to improve social-service delivery capacity of local welfare agencies. Those at right four, while decrying the iron grip of federal bureaucrats over local affairs, are not adverse to strong federal initiatives to improve technological capacity of local police forces. The more extreme leftists seek greatly increased local autonomy for citizen control over police and correctional operations, but welcome strong federal power in formulating and enforcing uniform civil rights measures. The more extreme rightists adamantly oppose the use of centralized power to enforce "mixing" of racial and other social categories or to compel uniform operations of local police, courts, and corrections—but welcome strong federal power in the development and maintenance of military forces, or a strong federal investigatory branch with the power to probe corruption and collusion in local programs, particularly those of left-oriented agencies.

The unifying principle behind these apparent contradictions is the same as that noted for intra-position inconsistencies; ideologically derived objectives are supported despite possible discrepancies involving the means to achieve them or the identity of sources of support. An additional dimension of considerable importance is also involved—that of time. Ideological positions of left and right are delineated on the basis of a given point in time, earlier designated as "current." But specific stances of the left and right can change rapidly in response to changing circumstances, or they can even reverse themselves. Moreover, some of the "crusading issues" currently fashionable will become passé in the near future.

The "decentralization" issue again provides a good example. Whether one favors more or less power for "centralized" or federal agencies depends on the current ideological complexion of the several federal departments or branches. Viewed very broadly, in the early 1930s the left looked to the executive branch as a prime source of support for policies they favored, and the right to the judicial and legislative; in the 1960s the left viewed both the executive and judicial as allies, the legislature as a potential source of opposition, and sought more power for the High Court and the Presidency. At present the right views the executive as supportive, and the left looks to the legislature as an ally in an attempt to curb the power of the Presidency. Reflecting these shifts have been changes in attitudes of the left and right toward "local control." While traditionally a crusading issue of the right (state's rights), the banner for community control was taken up in the 1960s by the left as an effective method of bypassing entrenched political power at the local level—primarily with respect to civil rights. Recently the trend has begun to reverse because of a resurgence of the right's traditional "anti-big-government" stance and an increasing resort to local control by community groups pursuing rightist causes (e.g., exclusion of blacks from white schools).

Further detailed analyses of convergences and divergences, consistencies and contradictions, and past, present, and future fashions of both these issues and others could be developed. It might be useful at this point, however, to briefly consider a more fundamental level—the basic philosophical underpinnings of the two sides—and to compress the variety and complexity of their varied positions into a single and simple governing principle.

For the right, the paramount value is order—an ordered society based on a pervasive and binding morality—and the paramount danger is disorder—social, moral, and political. For the left, the paramount value is justice—a just society based on a fair and equitable distribution of power, wealth, prestige, and privilege—and the paramount evil is injustice—the concentration of valued social resources in the hands of a privileged minority.

Few Americans would quarrel with either of these values, since both are intrinsic aspects of our national ideals. Stripped of the passion of ideological conflict, the issue between the two sides could be viewed as a disagreement over the relative priority of two valuable conditions: whether *order with justice,* or *justice with order* should be the guiding principle of the criminal justice enterprise.

These are ancient philosophical issues, and their many aspects have been argued in detail for centuries. Can both order and justice be maximized in a large, heterogeneous, pluralistic society? Can either objective be granted priority under all circumstances? If not, under what circumstances should which objective be seen as paramount? It might appear that these issues are today just as susceptible to rational discussion as they have been in the past; but this is not so, because the climate militates against such discussion. Why this is so will be considered shortly—after a brief discussion of the ideologies of the formal agencies of criminal justice.

IDEOLOGICAL COMPLEXION OF CRIMINAL JUSTICE AGENCIES

The ideological positions of four major professional fields will be discussed—academic criminology, the police, the judiciary, and corrections. Rather than complex analysis or careful delineation, tentative impressions will be offered. Each system will be characterized on a very gross level, but it is important to bear in mind the possibility that there is as much ideological variability within each of the several systems as there is among them. Of particular importance within these systems are differences in age level, social class and educational level, and rank.

Academic criminologists. This group is included not out of any presumption about the importance of the role they play, but rather because academic criminology provides the platform from which the present analysis is presented. Probably the most important point to make here is that the day-to-day ideological environment of the average academic criminologist, viewed within the context of the total society, is highly artificial; it reflects the perspectives of a deviant and unrepresentative minority. Academic criminology, reflecting academic social science in general, is substantially oriented toward the left, while the bulk of American people are oriented toward the right.[7] Furthermore, the members of the large liberal academic majority do proportionately more writing and speechmaking than those of the small conservative minority, so that their impact on the ideological climate exceeds even their large numbers. If the proportion of right-oriented persons in academic criminology comes close to being just the reverse of that in the general population, then this marked ideological divergence certainly has implications for those situations in which academicians come in contact with the public, particularly where they interact with representatives of other criminal justice branches. It also has an important impact on their own perceptions of the ideological positions of the public and other criminal justice professionals.

Police. The bulk of police officers have working-class backgrounds, and the contemporary working class is substantially rightist. Archie Bunker is a caricature, but the reality he exaggerates is a significant one. Rightist ideology in one of its purest versions may be found in the solemn speeches of Officer Joe Friday to temporarily discouraged young police officers or disgruntled citizens. Among police departments, differences in ideological complexion are found in different regions (for example, West Coast departments generally have higher proportions of college-trained personnel), different sized communities, and departments with different personnel policies. Within departments, age differences may be important (some younger officers are less rightist), as well as differences in rank and function (some departments have more liberally oriented chiefs or research and planning personnel). The majority of working police professionals, however, subscribe to the ideological premises here designated as "rightist."

Judiciary. The legal and judicial field is probably characterized by greater ideological diversity than either the police or corrections. One reason is that leftist positions are more common among those with college degrees than among those with less education. Since college education is a prerequisite to formal legal training, lawyers are more likely to have been exposed to the leftward orientation characteristic of most academic faculties, particularly those of the larger and more prestigious universities.[8] Judges show enormous variation in ideological predilections, probably covering the full range from right five to left four. Variation is related to factors such as the law school attended, size of jurisdiction, social status of jurists and their clientele, region, level of the court. While public attention is often directed to the actions of highly moralistic, hard-line judges at right four and five positions, such jurists are probably becoming less common.

Ideological orientations of the legal profession have recently been subject to public attention, particularly in connection with two developments. First, the Supreme Court has in the recent past been associated with a series of decisions that reflect basic tenets of the left. Included have been such issues as increased protection for the rights of suspected and accused persons, inadmissibility of illegally obtained evidence, minimization of distinctions based on race, reduction of discretionary powers of law-enforcement personnel, and reduction of judicial discretion in juvenile proceedings.[9] These decisions and others were perceived by the right as posing a critical threat to an established balance of power and prerogatives between law-enforcement personnel and offenders, seriously endangering the law-enforcement process and the security of the public.

The second development is the emergence during the past ten years of a group of young left-oriented lawyers whose influence is probably disproportionate to their small numbers. Able, dedicated, active on a variety of fronts, many representing low-income or black clients, their activities became best known in connection with Federal Anti-Poverty programs. Many of these lawyers have assumed positions along the ideological scale as far left as the left three and left four positions.

Despite these well-publicized manifestations of leftward orientations in some sectors of the legal profession, it is unlikely that a substantial proportion of the profession consistently espouses the tenets of the left, particularly those of left three and beyond. The more liberal judges are generally found in federal and higher-level state courts, but conservative views are still common among jurists of the lower level courts, where the great bulk of day-to-day legal business is transacted. Moreover, as part of the ideological shifts noted earlier, the Burger court is regarded by the right with considerably less antipathy than the Warren court.[10]

Corrections. Corrections, the current hot spot of the criminal justice field, probably contains a mixture of ideological positions, with the bulk of correctional personnel ranged along the right. The average lower-echelon corrections employee has a working-class background similar to that of the average patrolman, and thus manifests the rightist orientation characteristic of that class. As in the case of police, age may be an important basis for differentiation, with older officials more likely to assume right-oriented positions. Among other bases are size of the institution and age level of the bulk of inmates. Juvenile corrections tends to have a higher likelihood of left-oriented staff, both at administrative and lower-echelon levels.

Prison reform is currently one of the most intense crusading issues of the left. While most reform efforts are exerted by persons not officially part of the correctional system, there has been some influx of left three and four persons into the official system itself, particularly among younger staff in juvenile correction facilities.

CONSEQUENCES OF IDEOLOGY

If, as is here contended, many of those involved in the tasks of planning and executing the major policies and procedures of our criminal justice system are subject to the influence of pervasive ideological assumptions about the nature of crime and methods of dealing with it—assumptions which are largely implict and unexamined—the question then arises: What are the consequences of this phenomenon?

While both the crusading issues and graded ideological positions presented earlier were phrased to convey the tone of urgent imperatives, the assumptions from which they arise were phrased in relatively neutral terms as a set of general propositions about the nature, causes, and processes of coping with crime. So phrased and so regarded, these assumptions are susceptible to rational considerations. Their strengths and weaknesses can be debated, evidence can be employed to test the degree of validity each may possess, contradictions among them can be considered, and attempts made to explain or reconcile differences among them. Formulated and used in this manner, the question arises: Why are they characterized here as "ideological?"

The scale of ideology presented comprises a single major parameter—substantive variation along a left-right scale with respect to a set of issues germane to crime and the criminal justice process. But there is an additional important parameter which must also be considered: that of intensity—the degree of emotional charge which attaches to the assumptions. It is the capacity of these positions to evoke the most passionate kinds of reactions and to become infused with deeply felt, quasi-religious significance that constitutes the crucial element in the difference between testable assumptions and ideological tenets. This dimension has the power to transform plausibility into ironclad certainty, conditional belief into ardent conviction, the reasoned advocate into the implacable zealot. Rather than being looked upon as useful and conditional hypotheses, these assumptions, for many, take the form of the sacred and inviolable dogma of the one true faith, the questioning of which is heresy and the opposing of which is profoundly evil.

This phenomenon—ideological intensification—appears increasingly to exert a powerful impact on the entire field. Leslie Wilkins has recorded his opinion that the criminal justice enterprise is becoming progressively more scientific and secularized;[11] an opposite, or at least concurrent, trend is here suggested—that it is becoming progressively more ideologized. The consequences are many. Seven will be discussed briefly: polarization, reverse projection, ideologized selectivity, informational constriction, catastrophism, and distortion of opposing positions.

Polarization. Polarization is perhaps the most obvious consequence of ideological intensification. The more heavily a belief takes on the character of sacred dogma, the more necessary it becomes to view the proponents of opposing positions as devils and scoundrels, and their views as dangerous and immoral. Cast in this framework of the sacred and the profane, of virtuous heroes and despicable villains, the degree of accommodation and compromise that seems essential to the complex enterprise of criminal-justice planning becomes, at best, enormously complicated, and at worst, quite impossible.

Reverse projection. This is a process whereby a person who occupies a position at a given point along the ideological scale perceives those who occupy any point closer to the center than his own as being on the opposite side of the scale. Three aspects of this phenomenon, which appears in its most pronounced form at the extremes of the scale, should be noted. First, if one grants the logical possibility that there can exist a "centrist" position—not a position which maintains no assumptions, but one whose assumptions are "mixed," "balanced," or not readily characterized—then this position is perceived as "rightist" by those on the left, and "leftist" by those on the right.

A second aspect concerns the intensity of antagonism often shown by those occupying immediately adjacent positions along the ideological scale. Perhaps the most familiar current manifestation of this is found in the bitter mutual denunciations of those classified here as occupying the positions of left four and left five. Those at left four are often taken by those at left five as far more dangerous and evil than those seen as patent fascists at right four and five. Left fours stand accused as dupes of the right, selling out to or being coopted by the establishment, and blunting the thrust of social activism by cowardly vacillation and compromise.

A third aspect of reverse projection is that one tends to make the most sensitive intrascale distinctions closest to the point that one occupies. Thus, someone at right four might be extremely sensitive to differences between his position and that of an absolute-dictatorship advocate at right five, and at the same time cast left four and five into an undifferentiated class of commies, communist dupes, and radicals—quite oblivious to the distinctions that loom so large to those who occupy these positions.

Ideologized selectivity. The range of issues, problems, areas of endeavor, and arenas of activity relevant to the criminal justice enterprise is enormous. Given the vastness of the field relative to the availability of resources, decisions must be made as to task priorities and resource allocation. Ideology plays a paramount but largely unrecognized role in this process, to the detriment of other ways of determining priorities. Ideologized selectivity exerts a constant influence in determining which problem areas are granted greatest significance, which projects are supported, what kinds of information are gathered, and how research results are analyzed and interpreted. Divergent resource allocation policies of major federal agencies can be viewed as directly related to the dominant ideological orientation of the agency.

Only one example of ideologized selectivity will be cited here. The increasing use of drugs, soft and hard, and an attendant range of drug-related crime problems is certainly a major contemporary development. The importance of this problem is reflected in the attention devoted to it by academic criminologists. One major reason for this intensive attention is that explanations for the spread of drug use fit the ideological assumptions shared by most academicians (drug use is an understandable product of alienation resulting from the failure of the system to provide adequate meaning and quality to life). Also one major ameliorative proposal, the liberalization of drug laws, accords directly with a crusading issue of the left—decriminalization.

Another contemporary phenomenon, quite possibly of similar magnitude, centers on the apparently disproportionate numbers of low-status urban blacks arrested for violent and predatory crimes, brought to court, and sent to prison. While not entirely ignored by academic criminologists, the relatively low amount of attention devoted to this phenomenon stands in sharp contrast to the intensive efforts evident in the field of drugs. Important aspects of the problem of black crime do not fit the ideological assumptions of the majority of academic criminologists. Insofar as the issue is studied, the problem is generally stated in terms of oppressive, unjust, and discriminatory behavior by society and its law-enforcement agents—a formulation that accords with the tenet of the left which assumes the capacity of officials to engender crime by their actions, and the parallel assumption that major responsibility for crime lies in conditions of the social order. Approaches to the problem that involve the careful collection of information relative to such characteristics of the population itself as racial and social status run counter to ideological tenets that call for the minimization of such distinctions both conceptually and in practice, and thus are left largely unattended.

Informational constriction. An attitude which is quite prevalent in many quarters of the criminal-justice enterprise today involves a depreciation of the value of research in general, and research on causes of crime in particular. Several reasons are commonly given, including the notion that money spent on research has a low payoff relative to that spent for action, that past research has yielded little of real value for present problems, and that research on causes of crime in particular is of little value, since the low degree of consensus among various competing schools and theorists provides little in the way of unified conclusions or concrete guidance. Quite independent of the validity of such reasons, the anti-research stance can be seen as a logical consequence of ideological intensification.

For the ideologically committed at both ends of the scale, new information appears both useless and dangerous. It is useless because the basic answers, particularly with respect to causes, are already given, in their true and final form, by the ideology; it is dangerous because evidence provided by new research has the potential of calling into question ideologically established truths.

In line with this orientation, the present enterprise, that of examining the influence of ideology on criminal justice policy and programs, must be regarded with distaste by the ideologically intense—not only because it represents information of relevance to ideological doctrine, but also because the very nature of the analysis implies that ideological truth is relative.

Catastrophism. Ideological partisans at both extremes of the scale are intensely committed to particular programs or policies they wish to see effected, and recurrently issue dire warnings of terrible castastrophes that will certainly ensue unless their proposals are adopted (Right: Unless the police are promptly given full power to curb criminality and unless rampant permissiveness toward criminals is halted, the country will surely be faced with an unprecedented wave of crime and violence. Left: Unless society promptly decides to provide the resources necessary to eliminate poverty, discrimination, injustice, and exploitation, the country will surely be faced with a holocaust of violence worse than ever before.) Such predictions are used as tactics in a general strategy for enlisting support for partisan causes: "Unless you turn to us and our program . . ." That the great bulk of catastrophes so ominously predicted does not materialize does not deter catastrophism, since partisans can generally claim that it was the response to their warnings that forestalled the catastrophe. Catastrophism can thus serve to inhibit adaptation to real crises, by casting into question the credibility of accurate prophets along with the inaccurate.

Magnification of prevalence. Ideological intensification produces a characteristic effect on perceptions of the empirical prevalence of phenomena related to areas of ideological concern. In general, targets of ideological condemnation are represented as far more prevalent than carefully collected evidence would indicate. Examples are estimates by rightists of the numbers of black militants, radical conspirators, and welfare cheaters;

and by leftists of the numbers of brutal policemen, sadistic prison personnel, and totally legitimate welfare recipients.

Distortion of the opposition. To facilitate a demonstration of the invalidity of tenets on the opposite side of the ideological scale, it is necessary for partisans to formulate the actual positions of the opposition in such a way as to make them most susceptible to refutation. Opposition positions are phrased to appear maximally illogical, irrational, unsupportable, simplistic, internally contradictory, and, if possible, contemptible or ludicrous. Such distortion impedes the capacity to adequately comprehend and represent positions or points of view which may be complex and extensively developed—a capacity that can be of great value when confronting policy differences based on ideological divergencies.

IMPLICATIONS

What are the implications of this analysis for those who face the demanding tasks of criminal justice action and planning? It might first appear that the prescription would follow simply and directly from the diagnosis. If the processes of formulating and implementing policy with respect to crime problems are heavily infused with ideological doctrine, and if this produces a variety of disadvantageous consequences, the moral would appear to be clear: work to reverse the trend of increased ideological intensification, bring out into the open the hidden ideological agenda of the criminal justice enterprise, and make it possible to release the energy now consumed in partisan conflict for a more direct and effective engagement with the problem field itself.

But such a prescription is both overly optimistic and overly simple. It cannot be doubted that the United States in the latter twentieth century is faced with the necessity of confronting and adapting to a set of substantially modified circumstances, rooted primarily in technological developments with complex and ramified sociological consequences. It does not appear too far-fetched to propose that major kinds of necessary social adaptation in the United States can occur only through the medium of ardently ideological social movements—and that the costs of such a process must be borne in order to achieve the benefits it ultimately will confer. If this conception is correct, then ideological intensification, with all its dangers and drawbacks, must be seen as a necessary component of effective social adaptation, and the ideologists must be seen as playing a necessary role in the process of social change.

Even if one grants, however, that ideology will remain an inherent element of the policy-making process—and that while enhancing drive, dedication, and commitment it also engenders rigidity, intolerance, and distortion—one might still ask whether it is possible to limit the detrimental consequences of ideology without impairing its strengths. Such an objective is not easy, but steps can be taken in this direction. One such step entails an effort to increase one's capacity to discriminate between those types of information which are more heavily invested with ideological content and those which are less so. This involves the traditional distinction between "fact" and "value" statements.[12] The present delineation of selected ideological stances of the left and right provides one basis for estimating the degree to which statements forwarded as established conclusions are based on ideological doctrine rather than empirically supportable evidence. When assertions are made about what measures best serve the purposes of securing order, justice, and the public welfare, one should ask, "How do we know this?" If statements appear to reflect in greater or lesser degree the interrelated patterns of premises, assumptions, and prescriptions here characterized as "ideological," one should accommodate one's reactions accordingly.

Another step is to attempt to grant the appropriate degree of validity to positions on the other side of the scale from one's own. If ideological commitment plays an important part in the process of developing effective policy, one must bear in mind that both left and right have important parts to play. The left provides the cutting edge of innovation, the capacity to isolate and identify those aspects of existing systems which are least adaptive, and the imagination and vision to devise new modes and new instrumentalities for accommodating emergent conditions. The right has the capacity to sense those elements of the established order that have strength, value, or continuing usefulness, to serve as a brake on over-rapid alteration of existing modes of adaptation, and to use what is valid in the past as a guide to the future. Through the dynamic clash between the two forces, new and valid adaptations may emerge.

None of us can free himself from the influence of ideological predilections, nor are we certain that it would be desirable to do so. But the purposes of effective policy and practice are not served when we are unable to recognize in opposing positions the degree of legitimacy, validity, and humane intent they may possess. It does not seem unreasonable to ask of those engaged in the demanding task of formulating and implementing criminal justice policy that they accord to differing positions that measure of respect and consideration that the true ideologue can never grant.

Chart 1
SOURCES OF CRIME: LOCUS OF RESPONSIBILITY

LEFT	RIGHT
5. Behavior designated as "crime" by the ruling classes is an inevitable product of a fundamentally corrupt and unjust society.	5. Crime and violence are a direct product of a massive conspiracy by highly organized and well-financed radical forces seeking

Chart 1 (Continued)
SOURCES OF CRIME: LOCUS OF RESPONSIBILITY

LEFT	RIGHT
True crime is the behavior of those who perpetuate, control, and profit from an exploitative and brutalizing system. The behavior of those commonly regarded as "criminals" by establishment circles in fact represents heroic defiance and rebellion against the arbitrary and self-serving rules of an immoral social order. These persons thus bear no responsibility for what the state defines as crime; they are forced into such actions as justifiable responses to deliberate policies of oppression, discrimination, and exploitation.	deliberately to overthrow the society. Their basic method is an intensive and unrelenting attack on the fundamental moral values of the society, and their vehicle is that sector of the populace sufficiently low in intelligence, moral virtue, self-control, and judgment as to serve readily as their puppets by constantly engaging in those violent and predatory crimes best calculated to destroy the social order. Instigators of the conspiracy are most often members of racial or ethnic groups that owe allegiance to and are supported by hostile foreign powers.
4. Those who engage in the more common forms of theft and other forms of "street crime" are essentially forced into such behavior by a destructive set of social conditions caused by a grossly inequitable distribution of wealth, power, and privilege. These people are actually victims, rather than perpetrators of criminality; they are victimized by discrimination, segregation, denial of opportunity, denial of justice and equal rights. Their behavior is thus a perfectly understandable and justified reaction to the malign social forces that bring it about. Forms of crime perpetrated by the wealthy and powerful—extensive corruption, taking of massive profits	4. The bulk of serious crime is committed by members of certain ethnic and social class categories characterized by defective self-control, self-indulgence, limited time-horizons, and undeveloped moral conscience. The criminal propensities of these classes, which appear repeatedly in successive generations, are nurtured and encouraged by the enormous reluctance of authorities to apply the degree of firm, swift, and decisive punishment which could serve effectively to curb crime. Since criminality is so basic to such persons, social service programs can scarcely hope to affect their behavior, but their low capacity for discrimination

Chart 1 (Continued)
SOURCES OF CRIME: LOCUS OF RESPONSIBILITY

LEFT	RIGHT
through illicit collusion, outright fraud, and embezzlement—along with a pervasive pattern of marginally legal exploitative practices—have far graver social consequences than the relatively minor offenses of the so-called "common" criminal. Yet these forms of crime are virtually ignored and their perpetrators excused or assigned mild penalties, while the great bulk of law-enforcement effort and attention is directed to the hapless victims of the system.	makes them unusually susceptible to the appeals of leftists who goad them to commit crimes in order to undermine the society.
3. Public officials and agencies with responsibility for crime and criminals must share with damaging social conditions major blame for criminality. By allocating pitifully inadequate resources to criminal justice agencies, the government virtually assures that they will be manned by poorly qualified, punitive, moralistic personnel who are granted vast amounts of arbitrary coercive power. These persons use this power to stigmatize, degrade, and brutalize those who come under their jurisdiction, thus permitting them few options other than continued criminality. Society also manifests enormous reluctance to allocate the resources necessary to ameliorate the root social causes of crime—poverty, urban deterioration, blocked	3. The root cause of crime is a massive erosion of the fundamental moral values which traditionally have served to deter criminality, and a concomitant flouting of the established authority which has traditionally served to constrain it. The most extreme manifestations of this phenomenon are found among the most crime-prone sectors of the society—the young, minorities, and the poor. Among these groups and elsewhere there have arisen special sets of alternative values or "countercultures," which actually provide direct support for the violation of the legal and moral norms of law-abiding society. A major role in the alarming increase in crime and violence is played by certain elitist groups of left-oriented media

Chart 1 (Continued)

SOURCES OF CRIME: LOCUS OF RESPONSIBILITY

LEFT	RIGHT
educational and job opportunities—and further enhances crime by maintaining widespread systems of segregation—separating race from race, the poor from the affluent, the deviant from the conventional, and the criminal from the law-abiding.	writers, educators, jurists, lawyers, and others who contribute directly to criminality by publicizing, disseminating, and supporting these crime-engendering values.
2. Although the root causes of crime lie in the disabling consequences of social, economic, and educational deprivation concentrated primarily among the disadvantaged in low-income communities, criminal behavior is in fact widely prevalent among all sectors of the society, with many affluent people committing crimes such as shoplifting, drunkenness, forgery, embezzlement, and the like. The fact that most of those subject to arrest and imprisonment have low-income or minority backgrounds is a direct consequence of an inequitable and discriminatory application of the criminal justice process—whereby the offenses of the more affluent are ignored, suppressed, or treated outside of a criminal framework, while those of the poor are actively prosecuted. A very substantial portion of the crime dealt with by officials must in fact be attributed to the nature of the criminal statutes themselves. A wide	2. A climate of growing permissiveness and stress on immediate personal gratification is progressively undermining the basic deterrents to criminal behavior.—self-discipline, responsibility, and a well-developed moral conscience. The prevalent tendency by liberals to attribute blame for criminality to "the system" and its inequities serves directly to aggravate criminality, by providing the criminal with a fallacious rationalization which enables him to excuse his criminal behavior, further eroding self-discipline and moral conscience.

Chart 1 (Continued)
SOURCES OF CRIME: LOCUS OF RESPONSIBILITY

LEFT	RIGHT
range of commonly pursued forms of behavior such as use of drugs, gambling, sexual deviance—are defined and handled as "crime," when in fact they should be seen as "victimless" and subject to private discretion. Further, a substantial portion of these and other forms of illegal behavior actually reflect illness—physical or emotional disturbance rather than criminality.
1. Crime is largely a product of social ills such as poverty, unemployment, poor quality education, and unequal opportunities. While those who commit crimes out of financial need or frustration with their life conditions deserve understanding and compassion, those who continue to commit crimes in the absence of adequate justification should in some degree be held accountable for their behavior; very often they are sick or disturbed persons who need help rather than punishment. Officials dealing with crime are often well-meaning, but they sometimes act unjustly or repressively out of an excessively narrow focus on specific objectives of law enforcement. Such behavior in turn reflects frustration with the failure of society to provide them adequate resources to perform their tasks	1. The behavior of persons who habitually violate the law is caused by defective upbringing in the home, parental neglect, inadequate religious and moral training, poor neighborhood environment, and lack of adequate role-models. These conditions result in a lack of proper respect for the law and insufficient attention to the basic moral principles which deter criminality. The federal government also contributes by failing to provide local agencies of prevention and law enforcement with sufficient resources to perform adequately the many tasks required to reduce or control crime.

Chart 1 (Continued)
SOURCES OF CRIME: LOCUS OF RESPONSIBILITY

LEFT	RIGHT
for which they are responsible, as it also fails to provide the resources needed to ameliorate the community conditions which breed crime.	

Chart II
MODES OF DEALING WITH CRIME: POLICIES WITH RESPECT TO OFFENDERS

LEFT	RIGHT
5. Since the bulk of acts defined as "crime" by the ruling classes simply represents behavior which threatens an invalid and immoral social system, those who engage in such acts can in no sense be regarded as culpable, or "criminal." There is thus no legitimate basis for any claim of official jurisdiction over, let alone any right to restrain, so-called offenders. Persons engaging in acts which help to hasten the inevitable collapse of a decadent system should have full and unrestrained freedom to continue such acts, and to be provided the maximum support and backing of all progressive elements. The vast bulk of those now incarcerated must be considered as political prisoners, unjustly deprived of freedom by a corrupt regime, and freed at once.	5. Habitual criminals, criminal types, and those who incite them should bear the full brunt of social retribution, and be prevented by the most forceful means possible from further endangering society. Murderers, rapists, arsonists, armed robbers, subversives, and the like should be promptly and expeditiously put to death. The more vicious and unregenerate of these criminals should be publicly executed as an example to others. To prevent future crimes, those classes of persons who persistently manifest a high propensity for criminality should be prevented from reproducing, through sterilization or other means. Those who persist in crimes calculated to undermine the social order should be completely and permanently removed from the society, preferably by deportation.
4. All but a very small proportion of those who come under the jurisdiction of criminal justice agencies pose no real danger to	4. Dangerous or habitual criminals should be subject to genuine punishment of maximum severity, including capital

Chart II (Continued)
MODES OF DEALING WITH CRIME:
POLICIES WITH RESPECT TO OFFENDERS

LEFT	RIGHT
society, and are entitled to full and unconditional freedom in the community at all stages of the criminal justice process. The state must insure that those accused of crimes, incarcerated, or in any way under legal jurisdiction be granted their full civil rights as citizens, and should make available to them at little or no cost the full range of legal and other resources necessary to protect them against the arbitrary exercise of coercive power. Criminal justice processing as currently conducted is essentially brutalizing—particularly institutional incarceration, which seriously aggravates criminality and which should be entirely abolished. "Rehabilitation" under institutional auspices is a complete illusion; it has not worked, never will work, and must be abandoned as a policy objective. Accused persons, prisoners, and members of the general public subject to the arbitrary and punitive policies of police and other officials must be provided full rights and resources to protect their interests—including citizen control of police operations, full access to legal resources, fully developed grievance mechanisms, and the like.	punishment where called for, and extended prison terms (including life imprisonment) with airtight guarantees that these be fully served. Probation and parole defeat the purposes of public protection and should be eliminated. Potential and less-habituated criminals might well be deterred from future crime by highly visible public punishment, such as flogging, the stocks, and possibly physical marking or mutilation. To speak of "rights" of persons who have chosen deliberately to forfeit them by engaging in crime is a travesty, and malefactors should receive the punishment they deserve without interference by leftists working to obstruct the processes of justice. "Rehabilitation" as a policy objective is simply a weakly disguised method of pampering criminals and has no place whatever in a proper system of criminal justice. Fully adequate facilities for detection, apprehension, and effective restraint of criminals should be granted those police and other criminal-justice personnel who realize that their principal mission is swift and unequivocal retribution against wrongdoers and their permanent removal from society to secure the full protection of the law-abiding.

Chart II (Continued)
MODES OF DEALING WITH CRIME:
POLICIES WITH RESPECT TO OFFENDERS

LEFT

3. Since contacts with criminal justice officials—particularly police and corrections personnel—increase the likelihood that persons will engage in crime, a major objective must be to divert the maximum number of persons away from criminal justice agencies and into service programs in the community—the proper arena for helping offenders. There should be maximum use of probation as an alternative to incarceration, and parole as an alternative to extended incarceration. However, both services must be drastically overhauled, and transformed from ineffective watchdog operations manned by low-quality personnel to genuine and effective human services. Institutionalization should be the alternative of last resort, used only for those proven to be highly dangerous or for whom services cannot be provided outside of an institutional context. Those confined must be afforded the same civil rights as all citizens, including full access to legal resources and to officially compiled information, fully operational grievance mechanisms, right of petition, and appeal from official decisions. Every attempt must be made to minimize the separation between institution and

RIGHT

3. Rampant permissiveness and widespread coddling of criminals defeat the purposes of crime control and must be stopped. Those who persist in the commission of serious crime and whose behavior endangers the public safety should be dealt with firmly, decisively, and forcefully. A policy of strict punishment is necessary, not only because it is deserved by offenders but also because it serves effectively to deter potential criminals among the general public. A major effort must be directed toward increasing the rights and resources of officials who cope with crime, and decreasing the rights and resources—legal, statutory, and financial—of those who use them to evade or avoid deserved punishment. Predetention measures such as bail, suspended sentences, and probation should be used only when it is certain that giving freedom to actual or putative criminals will not jeopardize public safety, and parole should be employed—sparingly and with great caution—only in those cases where true rehabilitation seems assured. The major objective both of incarceration and rehabilitation efforts must be the protection of law-abiding society, not the welfare of the offender.

Chart II (Continued)
MODES OF DEALING WITH CRIME:
POLICIES WITH RESPECT TO OFFENDERS

LEFT

community by providing frequent leaves, work-release furloughs, full visitation rights, full access to citizen's groups. Full rights and the guarantee of due process must be provided for all those accused of crimes—particularly juveniles, minorities, and the underprivileged.

2. Since the behavior of most of those who commit crimes is symptomatic of social or psychological forces over which they have little control, ameliorative efforts must be conducted within the framework of a comprehensive strategy of services which combines individually oriented clinical services and beneficial social programs. Such services should be offered in whatever context they can most effectively be rendered, although the community is generally preferable to the institution. However, institutional programs organized around the concept of the therapeutic community can be most effective in helping certain kinds of persons, such as drug users, for whom external constraints can be a useful part of the rehabilitative process. Rehabilitation rather than punishment must be the major objective in dealing with offenders. Treatment in the community—in group homes,

RIGHT

2. Lawbreakers should be subject to fair but firm penalties, based primarily on the protection of society but taking into account as well the future of the offender. Successful rehabilitation is an important objective, since a reformed criminal no longer presents a threat to society. Rehabilitation should center on the moral re-education of the offender, and instill in him the respect for authority and basic moral values which are the best safeguards against continued crime. These aims can be furthered by prison programs which demand hard work and strict discipline, for these serve to promote good work habits and strengthen moral fiber. Sentences should be sufficiently long as to both adequately penalize the offender and insure sufficient time for effective rehabilitation. Probation and parole should not be granted indiscriminately but reserved for carefully selected offenders, both

Chart II (Continued)
MODES OF DEALING WITH CRIME: POLICIES WITH RESPECT TO OFFENDERS

LEFT	RIGHT
halfway houses, court clinics; on probation or parole—must incorporate the maximum range of services, including vocational training and placement, psychological testing and counseling, and other services which presently are either unavailable or woefully inadequate in most communities. Where imprisonment is indicated, sentences should be as short as possible, and inmates should be accorded the rights and respect due all human beings.	to protect society and because it is difficult to achieve the degree of close and careful supervision necessary to successful rehabilitation outside the confines of the institution.
1. Effective methods of dealing with actual or putative offenders require well-developed and sophisticated methods for discriminating among varying categories of persons and gearing treatment to the differential needs of the several types thus discriminated. A major goal is to insure that those most likely to benefit from psychological counseling and other therapeutic methods will receive the kinds of treatment they need, rather than wasting therapeutic resources on that relatively small group of offenders whose behavior is essentially beyond reform, and who are poor candidates for rehabilitation. All those under the jurisdiction of criminal justice agencies should be treated equitably and humanely. Police in particular should treat their clients with	1. An essential component of any effective method for dealing with violators is a capability for making careful and sensitive discriminations among various categories of offenders and tailoring appropriate dispositional measures to different types of offenders. In particular the capacity to differentiate between those with a good potential for reform and those with a poor potential will ensure that the more dangerous kinds of criminals are effectively restrained. Probationers and parolees should be subject to close and careful supervision, both to make sure that their activities contribute to their rehabilitation and that the community is protected from repeat violations by those under official jurisdiction. Time spent in prison should be

Chart II (Continued)
MODES OF DEALING WITH CRIME: POLICIES WITH RESPECT TO OFFENDERS

LEFT	RIGHT
fairness and respect—especially members of minority groups and the disadvantaged. Careful consideration should be given before sentencing offenders to extended prison terms to make sure that other alternatives are not possible. Similarly, probation and parole should be used in those cases where these statutes appear likely to facilitate rehabilitation without endangering public safety. Prisoners should not be denied contact with the outside world but should have rights to correspondence, visiting privileges, and access to printed and electronic media. They should also be provided with facilities for constructive use of leisure time, and program activities aimed to enhance the likelihood of rehabilitation.	used to teach inmates useful skills so that they may re-enter society as well-trained and productive individuals.

Chart III
MODES OF DEALING WITH CRIME: POLICIES WITH RESPECT TO CRIMINAL JUSTICE AGENCIES

LEFT	RIGHT
5. The whole apparatus of so-called "law enforcement" is in fact simply the domestic military apparatus used by the ruling classes to maintain themselves in power and to inflict harassment, confinement, injury, or death on those who protest injustice by challenging the arbitrary regulations devised by the militarists and monopolists to protect	5. Maximum possible resources must be provided those law-enforcement officials who realize that their basic mission is the protection of society and maintenance of security for the law-abiding citizen. In addition to substantial increases in manpower, law-enforcement personnel must be provided with the most modern, efficient, and lethal weaponry

Chart III (Continued)
MODES OF DEALING WITH CRIME: POLICIES WITH RESPECT TO CRIMINAL JUSTICE AGENCIES

LEFT

their interests. To talk of "reforming" such a system is farcical; the only conceivable method of eliminating the intolerable injustices inherent in this kind of society is the total and forceful overthrow of the entire system, including its so-called law-enforcement arm. All acts which serve this end, including elimination of members of the oppressor police force, serve to hasten the inevitable collapse of the system and the victory of progressive forces.

4. The entire American system of criminal justice must be radically reformed. Unless there is a drastic reduction in the amount of power now at the disposal of official agencies—particularly the police and corrections—a police state is inevitable. In particular, unchecked power currently possessed by poorly qualified, politically reactionary officials to deal with accused and suspected persons as they see fit must be curtailed; their behavior brutalizes and radicalizes the clients of the system. To these officials, "dangerous" usually means "politically unacceptable." Increasing concentration of power in entrenched bureaucracies must be checked, and the people given maximum rights to local

RIGHT

available, and the technological capacity (communications, computerization, electronic surveillance, aerial pursuit capability) to deliver maximum force and facilities possible to points of need—the detection, pursuit, and arrest of criminals, and in particular the control of terrorism and violence conducted or incited by radical forces.

4. The critical crime situation requires massive increases in the size of police forces and their technological capacity to curb crime—particularly in the use of force against criminals and radical elements. It is imperative that police command full freedom to use all available resources, legal and technical, without interference from leftist elements seeking to tie their hands and render them impotent. The power of the courts to undermine the basis of police operations by denying them fundamental legal powers must be curbed. The nation's capacity for incarcerating criminals—particularly through maximum security facilities—must be greatly expanded, and prison security strengthened. The

Chart III (Continued)
MODES OF DEALING WITH CRIME: POLICIES WITH RESPECT TO CRIMINAL JUSTICE AGENCIES

LEFT	RIGHT
control of their own lives, including the right to self-protection through associations such as citizens' councils and security patrols, to counter police harassment and brutality and to monitor the operations of local prisons. Means must be found to eliminate the extensive corruption which pervades the system—exemplified by venal criminality within police departments and the unholy alliance between organized crime, corrupt politicians, and those who are supposedly enforcing the laws. Most of the criminal offenses now on the books should be eliminated, retaining only a few truly dangerous crimes such as forceful rape, since most of the offenses which consume law-enforcement energies have no real victims and should be left to private conscience. However, statutes related to illegality by business interests, bureaucrats, corporations, and the like should be expanded, and enforcement efforts greatly increased. Virtually all prisons should be closed at once, and the few persons requiring institutional restraint should be accommodated in small facilities in local communities.	"prison reform" movement rests on a mindless focus on the welfare of convicted felons and a blind disregard for the welfare of law-abiding citizens. Particularly pernicious in the movement now underway to unload thousands of dangerous criminals directly into our communities under the guise of "community corrections" (halfway houses, group homes, etc.). The local citizenry must unite and forcefully block this effort to flood our homes and playgrounds with criminals, dope addicts, and subversives. Increasing concentration of power in the hands of centralized government must be stopped, and basic rights returned to the local community —including the right to exclude dangerous and undesirable elements, and the right to bear arms freely in defense of home and family. Strict curbs must be imposed on the freedom of the media to disseminate materials aimed to undermine morality and encourage crime.
3. The more efficiency gained by law enforcement agencies through improvements in	3. Law-enforcement agencies must be provided all the resources necessary to deal

Chart III (Continued)
MODES OF DEALING WITH CRIME: POLICIES
WITH RESPECT TO CRIMINAL JUSTICE AGENCIES

LEFT	RIGHT

technology communications, management, and so on, the greater the likelihood of harassment, intimidation, and discrimination directed against the poor and minorities. Improvements in police services can be achieved only through fundamental and extensive changes in the character of personnel, not through more hardware and technology. This should be achieved by abandoning antiquated selection and recruitment policies which are designed to obtain secure employment for low-quality personnel and which systematically discriminate against the minorities and culturally disadvantaged. Lateral entry, culture-free qualification tests, and other means must be used to loosen the iron grip of civil-service selection and tenure systems. The outmoded military model with its rigid hierarchical distinctions found among the police and other agencies should be eliminated and a democratic organizational model put in its place. The police must see their proper function as service to the community rather than in narrow terms of law enforcement. As part of their community responsibility, law-enforcement agencies should stringently

promptly and decisively with crime and violence. Failure to so act encourages further law breaking, both by those who are subject to permissive and inefficient handling and by those who become aware thereby how little risk they run of being caught and penalized for serious crimes. The rights of the police to stringently and effectively enforce the law must be protected from misguided legalistic interference —particularly the constant practice of many judges of granting freedom to genuine criminals laboriously apprehended by the police, often on the basis of picayune procedural details related to "due process" or other legalistic devices for impeding justice. The scope of the criminal law must be expanded rather than reduced; there is no such thing as "victimless" crime. The welfare of all law-abiding people and the moral basis of society itself are victimized by crimes such as pornography, prostitution, homosexuality, and drug use, and offenders must be vigorously pursued, prosecuted, and penalized. Attempts to prevent crime by pouring massive amounts of tax dollars into slum communities are worse than useless, since such people

Chart III (Continued)
MODES OF DEALING WITH CRIME: POLICIES WITH RESPECT TO CRIMINAL JUSTICE AGENCIES

LEFT	RIGHT
limit access to information concerning offenders, especially younger ones, and much of such information should be destroyed. There must be maximum public access to the inner operations of police, courts, and prisons by insuring full flow of information to the media, full accountability to and visitation rights by citizens and citizen groups, and full public disclosure of operational policies and operations. The major burden of corrections should be removed from the institutions, which are crime-breeding and dehumanizing, and placed directly in the communities, to which all offenders must at some point return.	can absorb limitless welfare "benefits" with no appreciable effect on their criminal propensities. Communities must resist attempts to open up their streets and homes to hardened criminals through halfway houses and other forms of "community corrections."
2. A basic need of the criminal justice system is an extensive upgrading of the quality of personnel. This must be done by recruiting better-qualified people—preferably with college training—in all branches and at all levels, and by mounting effective in-service training programs. Higher quality and better-trained personnel are of particular importance in the case of the police, and training must place more stress on human relations studies such as psychology and sociology, and relatively less stress on purely technical aspects of	2. There should be substantial increases in the numbers and visibility of police, particularly in and around schools, places of business, and areas of family activity. Although a few bad apples may appear from time to time, the bulk of our police are conscientious and upstanding men who deserve the continued respect and support of the community, and who should be granted ample resources to do the job to which they are assigned. Some of the proposed prison reforms may be commendable, but the burden to the taxpayer must never be lost

Chart III (Continued)
MODES OF DEALING WITH CRIME: POLICIES
WITH RESPECT TO CRIMINAL JUSTICE AGENCIES

LEFT	RIGHT

police work. Quality must be maintained by the development and application of performance standards against which all personnel must be periodically measured, and which should provide the basis for promotion. Sentencing procedures must be standardized, rationalized, and geared to specific and explicit rehabilitative objectives rather than being left to the often arbitrary and capricious whims of particular judges. Corrections as well as other criminal justice agencies must be made more humane and equitable, and the rights of prisoners as individuals should be respected. Attempts should be made to reduce the degree of separation of prison inmates from the outside world. Changes in both legislation and law-enforcement policies must be directed to reducing the disparities in arrest rates between richer and poorer offenders, so that commensurately fewer of the poor and underprivileged, and more of the better-off, are sought out, convicted, and imprisoned. Promising programs of humane reform must not be abandoned simply because they fail to show immediate measurable results, but should receive continued or increased federal support.

sight of: most of the reforms suggested or already in practice are of dubious benefit or yield benefits clearly not commensurate with their costs. More effort should be directed to prevention of crime; in particular, programs of moral re-education in the schools and communities, and the institution of safeguards against the influence of those in the schools, media, and elsewhere who promote criminality by challenging and rejecting the established moral values which serve to forestall illegal and immoral conduct.

Chart III (Continued)
MODES OF DEALING WITH CRIME: POLICIES WITH RESPECT TO CRIMINAL JUSTICE AGENCIES

LEFT	RIGHT
1. There must be better coordination of existing criminal justice facilities and functions so as to better focus available services on the whole individual, rather than treating him through disparate and compartmentalized efforts. This must entail better liaison between police, courts, and corrections, and greatly improved lines of communication, to the end of enabling each to attain better appreciation, understanding, and knowledge of the operational problems of the others. Coordination and liaison must also increase between the criminal justice agencies and the general welfare services of the community, which have much to contribute both in the way of prevention of crime and rehabilitation of criminals. Local politicians often frustrate the purposes of reform by consuming resources in patronage, graft, and the financial support of entrenched local interests, so the federal government must take the lead in financing and overseeing criminal justice reform efforts. Federal resources and standards should be utilized to substantially increase the level and quality of social service resources available to criminal justice enterprises, promulgate standardized and rationalized	1. The operations of the police should be made more efficient, in part through increased use of modern managerial principles and information-processing techniques. Police protection should focus more directly on the local community, and efforts should be made to restore the degree of personal moral integrity and intimate knowledge of the local community which many older policemen had but many younger ones lack. Prison reform is important, but innovations should be instituted gradually and with great caution, and the old should not be discarded until the new is fully proven to be adequate. There should be much better coordination among law enforcement agencies, to reduce inefficiency, wasteful overlap, and duplication of services. The federal government must assume a major role in providing the leadership and financial resources necessary to effective law enforcement and crime control.

Chart III (Continued)
MODES OF DEALING WITH CRIME: POLICIES WITH RESPECT TO CRIMINAL JUSTICE AGENCIES

LEFT	RIGHT

modes of operation in local communities, and bring administrative coherence to the host of uncoordinated efforts now in progress.

NOTES

1. A few examples of perceptions that "our times" are witnessing radical or unprecedented changes are found in selected excerpts from statements published in 1874, 1930, and 1939, respectively:

"Society has grave charges to answer in regard to its influence on the present and rising generation. . . . The social conditions of the present age are such as to favor the development of insanity. The habits inculcated by . . . growing wealth . . . among individuals of one class and the stinging poverty . . . of another . . . nurture dispositions which might . . . under more equitable distributions . . . have died out. Have we not seen [youth] emerging from the restraints of school, scoffing at the opinions of the world, flouting everything but their own conceit . . . ?" Dickson, *The Science and Practice of Medicine in Relation to Mind, and the Jurisprudence of Insanity* (1874), quoted in M. Altschule, *Roots of Modern Psychiatry* (1957), pp. 122, 133.

"In our nineteenth century polity, the home was a chief reliance . . . discipline was recognized as a reality . . . the pressure of the neighborhood . . . was strong . . . in the urban industrial society of today there is a radical change. . . . This complete change in the background of social control involves much that may be easily attributed to the ineffectiveness of criminal justice. . . ." Pound, *Criminal Justice in America* (1930), quoted in F. Tannenbaum, *Crime and the Community* (1938), p. 29.

"Men's ways of ordering their common lives have broken down so disastrously as to make hope precarious. So headlong and pervasive is change today that . . . historical parallels are decreasingly relevant . . . because so many of the variables in the situation have altered radically. . . . Professor James T. Shotwell recently characterized 'the anarchy we are living in today' as 'the most dangerous since the fall of Rome.'" R. Lynd, *Knowledge for What* (1939), pp. 2, 11.

2. An analysis involving long-term trends in youth gang violence and periodically recurrent representations of such violence as a new phenomenon engendered by contemporary conditions is included in Miller, "American Youth Gangs: Past and President," in A. Blumberg, *Issues in Criminology* (in preparation).

3. G. Myrdal, *An American Dilemma: The Negro Problem and Modern Democracy* (1944), p. 1038. Myrdal's citation of the "radicalism-conservatism" scale is part of an extended discussion of sources of bias in works on race relations, appearing as Appendix 2, "A Methodological Note on Facts and Valuations in Social Science," pp. 1035–64. His entire discussion is germane to issues treated in this chapter.

4. A classic treatment of ideology is K. Mannheim, *Ideology and Utopia (1936)*; see chapter II.1, "Definition of Concepts." See also G. Myrdal, *supra* note 3, pp. 1035–64. There is an extensive literature, much of it sociological, dealing with ideology as it relates to a wide

range of political and social phenomena, but the specific relation between ideology and criminal justice has received relatively little direct attention. Among more recent general discussions are E. Shils, *The Intellectuals and the Powers* (1972); Orlans, "The Political Uses of Social Research" (*Annals of the American Academy of Political and Social Science*, ser. 28, 1971), p. 393; Kelman, "*I.Q., Race, and Public Debate*," Hastings Center Report, No. 8 (1972). Treatments more specific to crime and criminal justice appear in L. Radzinowicz, *Ideology and Crime* (1966); Andanaes, "Punishment and the Problem of General Prevention," *International Annals of Criminology*, No. 8 (1969), p. 285; Blumberg, "The Adversary System," in C. Bersani, *Crime and Delinquency* (1970), p. 435; Glaser, "Criminology and Public Policy," *American Sociologist*, VI (1971), p. 30.

5. The substance of ideologically relevant statements formulated here as crusading issues, general assumptions, or differentiated positions was derived from examination and analysis of a wide range of materials appearing in diverse forms in diverse sources. Materials were selected primarily on the basis of two criteria: that they bear on issues of current relevance to criminal justice policy, and that they represent one possible stance with respect to issues characterized by markedly divergent stances. With few exceptions, the statements as formulated here do not represent direct quotes but have been generalized, abstracted, or paraphrased from one or more sets of statements by one or more representatives of positions along the ideological scale. A substantial portion of the statements thus derived were taken from books, articles, speeches, and media reporting of statements by the following: Robert Welch, writer; John Schmitz, legislator; Gerald L. K. Smith, writer; Meyer Kahane, clergyman; Edward Banfield, political scientist; William Loeb, publisher; George Wallace, government; Julius Hoffman, jurist; L. Patrick Gray III, lawyer; William Rehnquist, jurist; William Buckley, writer; Spiro Agnew, government; Robert M. McKiernan, police; Howard J. Phillips, government; Lewis F. Powell, Jr., jurist; Andrew Hacker, political scientist; Kevin Phillips, writer; Victor Reisel, labor; Albert Shanker, educator; Fred P. Graham, lawyer/writer; Warren Burger, jurist; James Q. Wilson, political scientist; Hubert H. Humphrey, legislator; James Reston, writer; Jacob Javits, legislator; Ramsey Clark, lawyer; Tom Wicker, writer; Earl Warren, jurist; James F. Ahearn, police; Henry Steele Commager, historian; Alan Dershowitz, lawyer; Julian Bond, legislator; Herbert J. Gans, sociologist; Ross K. Baker, political scientist; Russell Baker, writer; William Kunstler, lawyer; Benjamin Spock, physician; Noam Chomsky, anthropologist; Richard Cloward, sociologist; Herman Schwartz, lawyer; Richard Korn, sociologist; Michael Harrington, writer; Richard Quinney, sociologist; Frank Reissman, sociologist; Tom Hayden, writer; Eldridge Cleaver, writer; H. Bruce Franklin, professor; Abbie Hoffman, writer; Phillip Berrigan, clergyman; Jerry Rubin, writer. Among a range of nonacademic reports, pamphlets, and periodicals which served as sources for statements by these and other persons were: *John Birch Society Reprint Series*; *Ergo: The Rational Voice of Libertarianism*; *New Solidarity: National Caucus of Labor Committees*; *The Hastings Center Reports*; *S.D.S. New Left Notes*; *Guardian*; *Ramparts*; *National Review*; *The Nation*; *The New Republic*; *The New York Review*; *Commentary*; *Fortune*; *Time*; *Life*; *Newsweek*; *New York Times*; *New York Times Magazine*; *The Washington Post*; *The Manchester Union Leader*. It should be noted that the substance of materials appearing in published sources represents the publicly taken positions of the individuals involved. The relation between public positions and "actual" or private positions can be very complex, ranging from "close" to "distant" along a "degree of correspondence" axis, and with variation involving changes over time, differences according to the subissue involved, nature of audience addressed, and other factors.

6. The classic application of ideal-type method is that of Max Weber. See, e.g., the discussion of Weber's method and typology of authority and coordination in A. Henderson and T. Parsons, *Max Weber: The Theory of Social and Economic Organization* (1947) pp. 98, 329. In the field of criminology, MacIver applies ideal-type analysis to discussions of

social causality in general and crime causality in particular. See R. MacIver, *Social Causation* (1942), p. 174 *passim*. Neither of these applications directly parallels present usage, but underlying principles are similar.

7. Several recent studies provide indirect evidence of differences between academics and the general public in the likelihood that one will characterize his ideological positions as "right" or "left." Of 60,000 professors surveyed by the Carnegie Commission, approximately 70 percent characterized themselves as "left" or "liberal," and fewer than 25 percent as "conservative" or "midle-of-the-road." A survey of social science professors by Everett Ladd and Seymour Lipset showed that approximately 70 percent voted against the "conservative" Presidential candidate in 1972, compared with approximately 75 percent against four years before. These studies were reported in Hacker, "On Original Sin and Conservatives," *New York Times Magazine* (February 25, 1973), p. 13, § 6. Henry Turner and Carl Hetrick's survey of a systematic sample of members of the American Political Science Association showed that approximately 75 percent characterized themselves as Democrats (among academics "Democratic" almost invariably means "liberal," whereas it generally means "conservative" in blue-collar populations), a percentage which had remained stable for ten years. Those designating themselves as "Republicans" had declined to about 10 percent at the time of the survey. Turner and Hetrick's survey also showed that the Democratic majority was significantly more active in publication and political activity than the non-Democratic minority. H. Turner and C. Hetrick, "Political Activities and Party Affiliations of American Political Scientists" (paper delivered at the 1971 meetings of the American Political Science Association).

By comparison, a Gallup survey conducted in 1972 found that 71 percent of a systematically selected sample of voters designated themselves as "conservative" (41 percent) or "middle-of-the-road" (30 percent), with 24 percent characterizing themselves as "liberal." A survey by Daniel Yankelovich during the same period found that 75 percent of the voters surveyed viewed themselves as "conservative" (37 percent) or "moderate" (38 percent); and 17 percent as "liberal" (15 percent) or "radical" (2 percent). See Rosenthal, "McGovern Is Radical or Liberal to Many Polls," *New York Times* (August 27, 1972), p. 34, col. 3. An earlier poll by Yankelovich of American college students, seen by many as among the most liberal of large population categories, showed that approximately 70 percent reported themselves as holding "mainstream" positions and that among the remainder, conservatives outnumbered left-wing radicals by two to one. D. Yankelovich, *The Changing Values on Campus: Political and Personal Attitudes of Today's College Students* (1972).

8. Hacker states that ". . . the higher one climbs on the prestige ladder [of American colleges and universities] the less likely are conservatives to be found on the faculty." Hacker, *supra* note 7, p. 71.

9. Issues involved here fall into two general clusters: those affecting the rights and resources available to law-enforcement officials relative to those available to persons suspected, accused, or convicted of crimes; those relating to the conceptual or physical separation or combining of major population categories. Stands of the right and left with respect to the first cluster have been delineated in several places (right crusading issue 2, left general assumptions 3, 5; right policies respecting offenders 3, 4, and respecting agencies 3, 4; left policies respecting offenders 3, 4, and respecting agencies 3, 4). Major decisions of the U.S. Supreme Court during the 1960s which appear to accord with ideological stances of the left and to run counter to those of the right include: *Mapp* v. *Ohio*, 367 U.S. 643 (1961), which reduced resources available to law enforcement officials and increased resources available to the accused, by extending limitations on the admission of illegally obtained evidence; *Escobedo* v. *Illinois*, 378 U.S. 478 (1964), and *Miranda* v. *Arizona*, 384 U.S. 436 (1966), which reduced the power of law enforcement officials to proceed with criminal processing without providing suspects with knowledge of and recourse to legal rights and resources; *in re Gault*,

387 U.S. 1 (1967), which reduced the power of judges to make dispositions in juvenile proceedings and increased the legal rights and resources of defendants; *Katz* v. *United States,* 389 U.S. 347 (1967), which reduced prerogatives of law enforcement officials with respect to the gathering of evidence, by increasing protection of suspects against intrusions of privacy; *Gilbert* v. *California,* 388 U.S. 263 (1967), and *United States* v. *Wade,* 388 U.S. 218 (1967), which decreased the freedom of law enforcement officials to seek identification of suspects and increased the legal rights and resources available to suspects.

With respect to the second cluster—separation of population categories—stands of the right are delineated under general assumption 5, sources of crime 4, policies respecting criminal justice agencies 4; and of the left under crusading issue 5 and general assumption 4. The landmark decision here was *Brown* v. *Board of Education,* 347 U.S. 483 (1954), which held that racially segregated public education was per se discriminatory. While preceding the above-cited decisions by about a decade, *Brown* set a precedent for later court actions which provided support for the diminution of categorical segregation, as favored by the left, and reduced support for the maintenance of such separation, as espoused by the right.

10. It has been widely held that the Burger Court, reflecting the influence of the right-oriented Nixon appointees such as Justices Rehnquist and Powell, would evince marked support for rightist ideological premises, stopping or reversing many of the initiatives of the Warren Court in areas such as equal protection and due process. This viewpoint is articulated by Fred P. Graham, who writes, "Mr. Nixon's two new justices are strikingly like his first two appointments in conservative judicial outlook, and . . . this cohesion is likely to produce a marked swing to the right—particularly on criminal law issues. . . ." Graham, "Profile of the 'Nixon Court' Now Discernible," *New York Times* (May 24, 1972), p. 28, col. 3. See also Graham, "Supreme Court, in Recent Term, Began Swing to Right that Was Sought by Nixon," *New York Times* (July 2, 1972) p. 18, col. 1; "Nixon Appointees May Shift Court on Obscenity and Business," *New York Times* (October 2, 1972) p. 16, col. 4. However, Gerald Gunther, in a careful review of the 1971 term of the Burger court, characterizes the court essentially as holding the line rather than moving to reverse the directions of the Warren Court or moving in new directions of its own. Gunther writes, "There was no drastic rush to the right. The changes were marginal. . . . The new Court . . . has shown no inclination to overturn clear, carefully explained precedent." Gunther, "The Supreme Court 1971 Term; Foreword—In Search of Evolving Doctrine on a Changing Court: A Model for Newer Equal Protection, *Harvard Law Review,* LXXXVI (1972) pp. 1–3. Cf. Goldberg, "Supreme Court Review 1972; Foreword—The Burger Court 1971 Term: One Step Forward, Two Steps Backward?" *Journal of Criminal Law, Criminology and Police Science,* LXIII (1972) p. 463. Although the court has shown an inclination to limit and specify some of the broader decisions of the Warren court—e.g., limiting rights to counsel at line-ups as dealt with in Gilbert and Wade (see Graham, July 2, 1971, *supra*)—there does not appear at the time of writing any pronounced tendency to reverse major thrusts of Warren Court decisions relevant to presently considered ideological issues, but rather to curb or limit momentum in these directions.

11. Wilkins, "Crime in the World of 1990," *Futures,* IV (1970) p. 203.

12. The classic formulations of the distinction between "factual" and "evaluative" content of statements about human behavior are those of Max Weber. See, e.g., A. Henderson and T. Parsons, *supra* note 6, p. 8 *passim.* See also G. Myrdal, *supra* note 3.

chapter four
CORRECTIONAL PROGRAMS

National Advisory Commission on Criminal
Justice Standards and Goals

CORRECTIONS AND THE COMMUNITY

Revised public and professional expectations of corrections have brought about a transformation in its means and ends during the last several years. Tradition required institutions merely to hold prisoners until ordered to release them. Now both the public and the correctional staff expect prisoners to be, at least, no worse for the correctional experience and, at most, prepared to take their places in society without further involvement with the law. Tradition required probation and parole merely to provide some form of nominalk supervision. Now it is expected that the experience of probation and parole will provide the offender with positive assistance in making a better adjustment to his circumstances.

These revised expectations have led to an awareness that corrections must be linked to the community in every phase of operations. These links are hard to forge because correctional agencies of all kinds traditionally have maintained an isolation from other human service agencies.

In a sense, this entire report is a discussion of what is conveniently referred to as community-based corrections. The Commission considers community-based corrections as the most promising means of accomplishing the changes in offender behavior that the public expects—and in fact now demands—of corrections.

Dissatisfaction with incarceration as a means of correction has grown to a point where some states have almost completely abolished incarceration for

From *Report of the Task Force on Corrections*, National Advisory Commission on Criminal Justice Standards and Goals (Washington, D.C.: U.S. Government Printing Office, 1973), pp. 221–236.

some classes of offenders. In other states, experimental programs have been successful enough that once-overcrowded prisons and reformatories now are unused. Clearly, the future lies with community-based corrections. The institution model for corrections has not been successful in curbing potential crime. But at least it exists, with its physical plant and identified processes of reception, classification, assignment, custody, work, academic and vocational training, religion, and recreation.

The substitute models are talked about and are occasionally used. But community-based corrections is not well organized, planned, or programmed. This task is the challenge of the future. Required is a complicated interplay among judicial and correctional personnel, those from related public and private agencies, citizen volunteers, and civic groups. This interplay of the correctional system with other parts of the public sector and greater involvement of the private sector, including civic participation in dimensions not foreseen in the correctional world just a few years ago, requires leadership in the entire criminal justice field to collaborate in the exploitation of all possibilities for successfully changing repression to reintegration. Policy-makers must understand the essential elements of a sound community-based correctional system as well as they now understand the orderly management of the prison.

DEFINITION

As used in this chapter, the term "community-based corrections" includes all correctional activities that take place in the community. The community base must be an alternative to confinement of an offender at any point in the correctional process.

At the beginning of his experience as a subject of criminal justice decision making, the offender has not even been defined as such. A police officer decides whether to arrest or give him a summons. A magistrate rules on his eligibility for release on his own recognizance or on bail. Released in either of these ways, he may or may not receive correctional attention. Some communities have court employment projects. Some have informal probation for certain types of juvenile offenders. More have diversion programs for alcoholics and narcotics addicts.

After conviction and commitment to the control of the corrections agency, the now officially defined offender may be placed in the oldest community-based correctional program, supervision under probation.

Most persons confined to custodial control are potential participants in community-based corrections through work- and study-release programs, family visiting furloughs, and re-entry programming. Finally, well-established parole services constitute the community-based programming core for offenders released from relatively lengthy custody.

This enumeration of major program components does not exhaust the potential of community correctional services, but the central principle of the definition is clear. Community-based correctional programs embrace any activity in the community directly addressed to the offender and aimed at helping him to become a law-abiding citizen. Such a program may be under official or private auspices. It may be administered by a correctional agency directly or by a noncorrectional service. It may be provided on direct referral from a correction agency or on referral from another element of the criminal justice system (police or courts). It may call for changing the offender through some combination of services, for controlling him by surveillance, or for reintegrating him into the community by placing him in a social situation in which he can satisfy his requirements without law violation. A community-based program may embrace any one or any combination of these processes.

The use of control and surveillance is basic to a sound community-corrections system. Both policy-makers and the public must understand that the elimination of incarceration does not eliminate control.

SIGNIFICANCE OF COMMUNITY-BASED CORRECTIONS

The significance of community-based corrections will be assessed from three aspects: humanitarian, restorative, and managerial. The criteria of success in each differ markedly.

The *humanitarian* aspect of community-based corrections is obvious. To subject anyone to custodial coercion is to place him in physical jeopardy, to narrow drastically his access to sources of personal satisfaction, and to reduce his self-esteem. That all these unfavorable consequences are the outcome of his own criminal actions does not change their reality. To the extent that the offender can be relieved of the burden of custody, a humanitarian objective is realized. The proposition that no one should be subjected to custodial control unnecessarily is a humanitarian assertion. The key question is the definition of neccessity, which must be settled by the criterion of public protection.

The *restorative* aspect concerns measures expected to achieve for the offender a position in the community in which he does not violate the laws. These measures may be directed at change, control, or reintegration. The failure of offenders to achieve these goals can be measured by recidivism, and their success is defined by reaching specific objectives set by correctional decision-makers.

The *managerial* goals are of special importance, because of the sharp contrast between the per capita costs of custody and any kind of community program. Any shift from custodial control will save money. But the criterion of correctional success is not fiscal. A major object of correctional programs is to protect the public. Therefore, any saving of public funds must not be accompanied by a loss of public protection. When offenders can be shifted from custodial control to community-based programming without loss of public protection, the managerial criteria require that such a shift be made. Otherwise public funds will have been spent without satisfying a public objective.

It is necessary here to note that public protection is not always the sole objective of correctional programming. Some kinds of offenders, especially the most notorious, often could perfectly well be released without jeopardizing public safety. But their release will not be countenanced, because public demands for retribution have not been satisfied. Offenders in custody should be there predominantly because public protection seems to require it. Decision-makers must disentangle these objectives to assure that use of community-based correctional programs is not denied for irrelevant reasons.

RATIONALE FOR CORRECTIONS IN THE COMMUNITY

The movement toward community-based corrections is a move away from society's most ancient responses to the transgressor. For thousands of years, society relied mainly on banishment, physical punishment, or the death penalty to accomplish the goals of criminal justice. The world is now too small for any society to eject anyone. Our culture has so changed that we no longer consider imposing capital penalties on the sweeping scale that seemed appropriate to our ancestors.

Out of the realization that the old ways were unacceptable there emerged the prison, a place for artificial banishment or civil death. Nearly two centuries of experience with the penitentiary have brought us to the realization that its benefits are transient at best. At its worst, the prison offers an insidiously false security as those who were banished return to the social scene of their former crimes. The former prisoner seldom comes back the better for the experience of confinement. The effectiveness of the prison as a school for crime is exaggerated, for the criminal can learn the technology of crime far better on the streets. The damage the prison does is more subtle. Attitudes are brutalized, and self-confidence is lost. The prison is a place of coercion where compliance is obtained by force. The typical response to coercion is alienation, which may take the form of active hostility to all social controls or later a passive withdrawal into alcoholism, drug addiction, or dependency.[1]

Mitigating Damages Done by Prisons

One of the tasks of corrections is to mitigate alienation. For generations this task has been attempted mainly by placing some offenders on probation instead of sending them to prison. When offenders have been incarcerated, parole has made it possible for them to serve part of their terms in the community, in the belief that assistance of a parole officer will help them to choose a law-abiding course.

There has been a growing realization that prison commitments for most offenders can be avoided or at least abbreviated without significant loss of public protection.[2] If the committed offender eventually returns to the community, it is best that his commitment removes him for as short a time as possible. The principle has evolved: incarcerate only when nothing less will do, and then incarcerate as briefly as possible. The services provided by probation and parole should strengthen the weak, open new channels to the erratic, and avoid openly reinforcing the intimidation that is latent in the relationship between the offender and the state.

The objective is to motivate each offender by the incentives that motivate most citizens toward orderly social life. In large parts, these incentives derive from an economic philosophy in which a day's pay for a day's work forms a unit in a prospect of lifetime security. Such employment is the necessary, if not sufficient, basis for conventional life in America. Emphasis on the employment of the offender is a response to the common-sense awareness that the unemployed offender is a probable recidivist.

But community-based corrections cannot be limited to the services of an employment office. A man who has committed a crime and been caught and convicted has suffered a blow to his self-esteem that may be masked by bravado or indifference. He has good reason to believe that conventional persons will reject him, and he therefore seeks out the unconventional. In the prison he has no choice; he must associate with the unconventional. In the community, probation and parole resources should make accessible a whole range of social support services as needed.

The difficulty of the task is obvious. Far more is required than the one-to-one contact between probation or parole officer and the offender. The offender's predicament stems from the combination of personal deficits and social malfunctions that produced a criminal event and a social status. Most personal deficits characterizing offenders are also commonly found in nonoffenders. The social malfunctions of unemployment, discrimination, economic inequity, and congested urban living affect most citizens. The offender, like other citizens, must find a way to live with his deficits and with the disorder around him. If corrections is to mitigate alienation, it must mobilize the community services that can make such an outcome possible.

To a much larger extent than has been realized, social support services must be given outside the official correctional apparatus and inside the community. Schools must accept and help reintegrate the delinquent instead of exiling him to reform schools. Unions and employers must open doors to adult offenders instead of restricting their employment to the most menial and insecure labor.[3]

Corrections cannot continue to be all things to the offender. The correctional structure must change from a second-class social system consisting of a correctional bureaucracy and a dependent population of offenders subject to official control and service. Although the pattern of the future is not yet clear, it seems to consist of a brokerage service in which the agency opens up to the offender community services where such services exist, or helps create new services for the entire community where none existed before. This enlarged theory of corrections will be unfamiliar to many correctional and community agency personnel, but it offers the only reasonable prospect for dealing more successfully with the serious problem of the recidivist offender.

Community-Based Corrections as Deterrents

There remain two additional public policy considerations in the rationale for community-based corrections: the deterrence of intimidation of the offender who is caught and the deterrence of potential offenders. It may be legitimately argued that the milder punishment aspects of community-based programs will not sufficiently deter either the actual or potential offender.

For the offender who has been under control, deterrence can be measured by whether he commits further crimes. Current measurements hardly support the contention that incarceration deters. But, regardless of this finding, no one should minimize the deterrent effect of noninstitutional control by the correctional system. Indeed, the deterrent effect of proper control within the community, coupled with realistic opportunities for the offender to make an adjustment there, may be expected to be considerable, not only on the basis of theoretical assumptions but also as indicated by preliminary studies which offer suggestive findings.[4] And the experience of simply being under official jurisdiction constitutes a punitive experience for nearly all offenders.

The deterrence of potential offenders has not been supported by evidence. Despite many attempts, especially in the controversies over capital punishment, no one has ever proved that the threat of severe punishment actually deters crime. Indeed, there is evidence that swiftness and certainty have much greater deterrent effect than a long prison sentence.[5] This raises the serious question of how just it is to adhere to a policy that can be supported only by assumption.

But even if we allow that some crime is deterred by the criminal-justice system, the deterrent potentiality of the prison is grossly exaggerated. The argument should be framed properly in terms of the statistical chances of getting caught. In the case of most crimes other than homicide, the chances are much less than even. In most communities a criminal can reasonably assume that, even with repeated law violations, his chances of getting caught are relatively slight. The prospect of incarceration or other punishment is distant.

Documentation of the foregoing is available, particularly with reference to the failure of imprisonment in primary deterrence; that is, the discouragement of further criminal activity by those punished at least once. Available studies suggest strongly that jurisdictions making extensive use of probation instead of prison do not experience increased recidivism.[6]

Similarly, studies of confinement length do not establish that lengthier prison terms result in decreased recidivism.[7]

Secondary deterrence—the discouragement of first-time criminal behavior by persons who may fear punishment—is a more elusive subject. However, the available statistical studies and analyses on varying punishment and prison confinement practices in different localities offer some basis for comparison.

We can conclude that, at the least, there is no established statistical base relating crime rates to the severity of dispositions imposed by courts in different locales. Sophisticated studies of this problem are currently being conducted by Solomon Kobrin at the University of Southern California. Using complex mathematical models, he has arrayed different jurisdictions according to the degrees of severity of criminal sanctions imposed. The studies also take cognizance of known variables that may be related and that otherwise could account for differences. In general, the summary of the study indicates that again there is no known relationship between severity of punishment and the deterrence of nonoffenders.[8]

ROLE OF THE COMMUNITY IN CORRECTIONS

The recent shift in our nation's values—particularly in corrections' views of criminality—helps explain the rationale and current emphasis on citizen involvement and community programs. Within this general context, the various roles citizens play and corrections' responsibility to involve the public can be understood better.

Circumstances of the past decade have had dramatic impact on corrections. The poverty programs of the 1960s, which failed to win the war on poverty but made strong impressions on the nation, are of particular import for corrections. The ideology underlying those programs suggested that persons of minority origin and low socioeconomic status systematically are denied access to higher status in American society. They thus are persistently over-represented among those who experience mental and physical illness, educational failure, unemployment, and crime and delinquency.

Programs that attacked such systematic exclusion from higher status used varied techniques. Emphasis on cultural awareness attempted to promote dignity and pride among minority groups, inserted minority history into America's records, and resulted in new group cohesion, political clout, and often militant reactions with newly discovered strength. The "maximum feasible participation" emphasis of poverty programs, although ultimately failing to achieve what it called for, made official the acknowledged but often ignored rights of all Americans to have a say in their own destiny.

The disadvantaged began to assume positions on boards of public and private agencies designed to serve them but formerly run for them by persons of more affluent status. "New careers" provided alternative routes for low-income persons to social and economic mobility through revised employment and training schemes. The pervasive ideology proclaimed to the formerly powerless that "you, too, have power, if you choose to exercise it."

This trend, visible in civil rights concerns, in welfare activism, and in student unrest, has its counterpart in correctional systems, and for the first time the voices of the inmate and the ex-offender are being heard. There are prisoners' unions and racial and ethnic ex-offender groups in all American cities. This as yet undocumented movement offers powerful new allies for correctional reform, if professionals in corrections choose to take that view instead of frequent defensive reaction to exclude.

Today American prisons contain, for almost the first time in our history, substantial numbers of young persons of middle and upper socioeconomic levels, largely through prosecution of the nation's youth for drug use. Another new set of allies for correctional reform thus exists today: concerned parents and friends of such youths, along with a vast body of parents who fear that their children might be among those jailed or imprisoned in the future.

This group is perceived by correctional staffs as less threatening than minority group ex-offenders. The reforms they urge may be listened to with greater attention. But coalitions are to be expected. These young persons learn militant and disruptive techniques very quickly and will employ them if they observe that rational discussion does not accomplish the desired reform.

Corrections has a unique opportunity to enlist such potential supporters and to organize their widespread concern into constructive aid for improving the correctional system. This audience is a prime source for volunteers. These citizens have political influence and know-how about influencing policy at local and state levels. The corrections system must design and implement public information systems to present facts and interpretations. If the potential of this group in aiding the correctional cause is to be realized, agencies must inform the public of their needs and welcome participation.[9]

SOCIAL SERVICE AGENCIES

Other social services agencies also have an impact on corrections. As community-based treatment programs increase in number and variety, correctional personnel and offenders will interact increasingly in formal and informal ways with professionals from other human service areas such as welfare, education, health, and employment. As institutional walls disintegrate, figuratively speaking, the boundaries between the various human service areas will disappear as well—and correctional problems will come to be the problems of a range of professionals serving communities.

Another group of allies thus is identified: colleagues in related fields, many of whom have had relatively limited contact with the world of corrections. While there has been some professional mobility between welfare and corrections, or corrections and rehabilitation work, such relationships will become closer and more common as community-based programs develop. Concerns for meeting human needs are shared; common problems are faced in various settings. Social welfare personnel, broadly defined, clearly are allies of corrections. Their special talents and experiences will add enormously to the strength of correctional reform movements.

EDUCATION

In similar vein, greater interest and concern for all correctional issues can be fostered among educators. Corrections is related to education on many levels. Schools are a frequent point of contact for direct services, particularly with juveniles. Universities are training and recruiting grounds for future correctional personnel and increasingly are involved in in-service education. Various high school and college programs are part of the services offered in correctional settings. And, perhaps most importantly of all, the nation's schools provide citizens with their basic knowledge of the community they live in: its problems, its government, its criminal justice concerns. Correctional personnel should make conscious attempts to relate effectively to educational personnel, to insure that the public is informed fully about correctional issues. Such efforts will be repaid many times over.

A final word must be said about American citizens in general. The nation recovered from the wartime traumas of the 1940s and entered the 1950s, an era of apathetic affluence, in which many persons thought America finally had realized her goals and could rest on her laurels in comfortable unconcern. The 1960s, however, challenged that assumption and generated a national concern with issues of race, poverty, violence, and international responsibilities. The nation, now into the 1970s, is bruised and shaken in confidence but hopefully prepared to set its house in order in quieter, more rational ways than in the frenzied 1960s. Few houses require ordering more than the nation's prisons.

Corrections and Correctional Personnel

In addition to increased public concern, corrections' view of how to solve the problem of criminal behavior has contributed to acceptance of citizen participation and community programs. Since the 1920s, research concerning crime and delinquency has undergone a gradual shift from the individual per se as the object of study to the environment in which he has his origins. Clifford Shaw, who discussed individual criminals from a social point of view in the 1920s and 1930s,[10] and Richard Cloward and Lloyd Ohlin, who provided a sophisticated theoretical framework for the understanding of crime causation in the 1960s,[11] illustrate this shift spanning the last 50 years.

In that period, the view of social as opposed to individual causation of human behavior has come to represent a majority opinion. Crime is conceived as linked more to social factors than to factors in the individual. This concept does not ignore psychological, physical, or other individual characteristics, but considers them as they occur in a particular setting.

This change in concept supports a somewhat different correctional thrust: if the social milieu to a substantial degree causes criminal behavior, the social milieu itself must be attacked and changed. This rationale suggests that the correctional system must involve itself in social reform to control and prevent crime. Further, it requires an understanding that, if behavior is related to events and circumstances in the offender's milieu, changing his behavior in isolation from that world will not solve the problem. Evidence of behavioral change in the isolation of the total institution is meaningless. It is behavior at home, on the job, and on the streets that matters.[12]

The shift in correctional thought that underlies the change to community-based correctional programming also can be understood by considering empirical evidence as to the effectiveness of current programs in controlling crime and the promise of new patterns. Corrections is a large, uncoordinated set of subsystems, with large gaps in service, irrational resource allocation, inadequate information, and a range of treatment modes that lacks a consistent and workable rationale. The confusion about individual vs. social causation underlies some of the lack of coherence. Contemporary corrections has not integrated its theoretical base and its practice. Despite the shift in social science theory, notions of intervening in community circumstances have not been applied widely. Rather, the emphasis has been on changing the individual—on a "treatment" philosophy that largely ignores the enormous potential of the community as the place for reduction of criminal behavior.

It already seems clear that substantial numbers of offenders can be treated in the community safely, effectively, and at substantially lowered cost to the taxpayer.[13] These are sufficient reasons to justify use of community programs and facilities in preference to institutions with their well-documented personal costs to individuals and social and financial costs to communities. Experimentation accompanied by adequate research and documentation increasingly will aid correctional systems in allocating resources more effectively.

Many correctional leaders feel a sense of optimism regarding the future. Problems of the field are more visible than ever before instead of being hidden behind high walls and locked gates. Some correctional administrators may object to public airing of their problems, but they are aware that old programs are not working and that new insights and methods are needed.

Perhaps the greatest significance of the move toward community corrections is the implicit consequence that communities must assume responsibility for the problems they generate. The failure of prisons to rehabilitate was blamed unfairly on correctional personnel; responsibility for community programs is shared widely. Corrections must be increasingly conceived as part of the larger social system. Problems and person, crime and criminal, are imbedded in community life and must be dealt with there—this is the thrust of corrections for the future.

Community programs have two operating (as opposed to programmatic) objectives: to use and coordinate existing community service agencies offering resources in areas such as family planning, counseling, general social service, medical treatment, legal representation, and employment; and to involve other agencies in the mission of corrections. The varying and changing nature of communities limits the feasibility of setting precise standards for community participation. Implementation of community programs involves consideration of geographic area to be covered, number of individuals required from the community, which persons must become involved, availability of programs from other agencies, etc. A general discussion of citizens' varied roles and the correctional administrator's responsibility for involving them should provide overall guidance in assessing what is available and possible.

RESPONSIBILITY OF CITIZENS

In a democratic nation, responsibility for provision of necessary public services is shared broadly by the citizenry. Decisions are made directly by public interest and demand for services, or indirectly by public neglect. In the case of correctional services, as with education, health care, and welfare needs, the decision regarding type and quality of service is determined ultimately by the public's will. An objective, therefore, in considering ways to improve criminal justice standards and goals must be attainment of an informed and concerned public, willing to insist on exercising its right to make informed decisions concerning correctional services.

Historically this objective has not been realized, and a massive public information campaign to bring about citizen involvement will be required to reverse the patterns of the recent past. In an earlier era, the community directly exercised law-enforcement and correctional responsibilities: for example, the religious tribunals of New England, with punishments of banishment, public pillories, and even executions; and the citizen posses of the frontier West, with their "out of town by sunset" sentence or execution by hanging. These are well-documented examples of citizens acting to maintain public order and safety.

As the nation developed in size and complexity, these functions were delegated to public servants, supposed experts with specialized knowledge and certain personal characteristics. The sheriff's staff and the police force replaced the posse; the court system replaced church tribunals and posse justice; jails, workhouses, and prisons replaced the public pillory, banishments, and summary executions. A professional criminal justice system came into being.

Nowhere in modern times has a public information program to bring about citizen involvement in the criminal justice system been fully implemented and documented. In some areas, however, the involvement of citizens in correctional decisions and community-based experiments has been described by the correctional unit responsible for recruiting and utilizing volunteers.[14]

Over the years, the public has come to feel little sense of responsibility for these services. To a considerable extent it has come to view the criminal justice system as an adversary—an institution to be outwitted and opposed rather than a service controlled by and organized to serve the interests of individual citizens and the general public. One has only to listen as the young discuss the police and their elders talk of circumventing tax laws or traffic regulations to realize the extent to which the American public views the criminal justice system as "them" and not as "us."

The citizenry must be involved again, in more constructive ways than in the past, in determining the policies of the entire criminal justice system. The participating public should be able to exert a real influence on the shape of any community program, not only in the planning stages but at all crucial junctures involving actual operations. Because of their representative status, citizens must be considered as a resource on which the eventual success of a program heavily depends. Opinions and reactions of citizen participants can provide a useful index to levels of public tolerance, insights into ways of affecting certain attitudes, and suggestions for new techniques to generate further public participation.

The immediate aim of administrators should be to consult as many public representatives as possible, during all stages of a program from planning through operation. This should not be token participation for the sake of appearance, or confined to individuals and organizations representing a single community sector. It is especially important not to limit participation to persons associated with the power centers of the community or with whom corrections officials have closest rapport and can expect to be in least conflict.

The correctional administrator launching new programs faces a conflict that may be inherent in any effort to offer services for convicted persons: the limit on innovation beyond existing levels of public acceptance. The easiest programs to launch are those that do not require adjustment of attitudes toward the offender.

The correctional administrator cannot abdicate his responsibilities for the custody and activities of offenders committed to his care. Nor can he give only lip service to community involvement while actually ignoring public fears and wishes. Complex decisions are required—determinations of initial eligibility, conditions for participation, selection of activities, extent of custody and supervision, revocation proceedings, standards for evaluation, and program changes. These decisions must be made while keeping legal rights of offenders, legitimate community concerns, and administrative prerogatives in balance.

But programs cannot be geared toward existing attitudes with the assumption that attitudes never change. The ability of corrections to make an increasing impact on the problem of crime reduction must not be limited by unwillingness to risk uncharted territory, even when it appears potentially hostile or politically undesirable. Community support or opposition leading to achievement or frustration is related directly to the manager's skills in mediating among the variety of forces represented and his understanding of the varying roles citizens play.

The Community as Policy-Maker

A variety of specialized policy-making roles currently are undertaken by citizens, often at the request of criminal justice officials. In such situations, lay citizens function in task forces or study groups and serve a general advisory role to the government. A by-product, perhaps more important than this advisory objective, is the creation of an ever-larger pool of citizens who have in-depth knowledge of corrections issues. They provide much-needed feedback to corrections, especially regarding lay thought and opinion.

It is important that meaningful roles be assigned without expecting the advisory body merely to rubber-stamp the decisions that the correctional administrator has made. Community involvement that is only a façade will be discovered quickly. Therefore, administrators should carefully analyze, in advance of creating citizen committees, the areas in which their input is desirable, if not essential. Decisions to be left to the agency should be specified and communicated to the committee.

Frequently, advisory bodies are comprised of "leading citizens" representing only one element of the community rather than a cross-section. In recent years, the necessity of broad representation has been recognized, and most groups seek appropriate membership of minorities, ex-offenders, women, and special community interest groups.

A somewhat different model is the citizen organization that is not sponsored governmentally but is a voluntary association of private citizens with shared concerns. The state citizen councils on crime and delinquency affiliated with the National Council on Crime and Delinquency are examples of this type of citizen participation. They are characterized frequently by "blue-ribbon" opinion leaders, wide membership, and support from voluntary contributions. They usually confront only problems of specifically local concern. Sometimes they provide service functions in the "prisoner's aid" tradition. Frequently such councils have strong, if informal, and mutually supportive links to state correctional systems.

In the past few years, all states have created instrumentalities of one kind or another for developing and administering state plans for utilization of funds from the Law Enforcement Assistance Administration. These agencies have taken a variety of forms but invariably involve citizen participation, often in concert with professionals from law enforcement, the judiciary, and corrections. This involvement represents another model of citizens serving in advisory roles.

In some cases, special boards have been created with advisory and policy-making objectives for subparts of the criminal justice system, such as juvenile courts, local correctional agencies, or branches of state systems or institutions. At the local level, a broad spectrum of citizenry can be involved, in contrast to the "important person" membership of the state and federal commissions. No data exist on how widely this mechanism is employed, but where used, as in the county juvenile justice commissions in California, it is viewed as effective in interpreting correctional issues and enlisting local community support.

The Citizen as Reformer

The penal and correctional reform groups springing up in recent years are yet another model of citizen participation. They may have no formal or informal links with the correctional system, may even be organized to oppose correctional programs and to attack current practices. Such groups vary widely in philosophy and are characterized by extremely diverse membership patterns in different areas of the nation.

Church memberships, radical political entities, a range of ethnic organizations, counter-culture youth movements, and ex-inmate associations have taken up the cause of penal and correctional reform. The scope of this reformist movement is undocumented but represents a ground swell to be observed with interest by the public and by professionals in the criminal-justice system. In the tradition of the great reform movements of American history, such as abolition of slavery and child labor, penal reform groups of today have ample evidence of wrongs to be righted, of underdogs to be aided, and of inequities to be restored to balance.

This involvement of many citizens in penal reform clearly is an important way in which citizens relate to policy-making for the criminal justice system. The correctional administrator—so long removed from any public scrutiny and vested with unquestioned discretion—probably has great difficulty in responding constructively to some of these groups. For example, some of them oppose any improvements in corrections, in the belief that they will serve only to perpetuate an inherently bad system. Yet the goal of the administrator and penal reformer is the same: protection of society through protection of individual rights. With common cause, the efforts of both should be directed toward solution of problems rather than toward quarrels with each other. Professionals in corrections long have decried public apathy and lack of knowledge.

When the public cries out in protest against inadequacies of the system, expressing concern and seeking fuller knowledge, administrators have tended to close the doors more tightly, feeling that criticism reflects personally on them. Correctional personnel react with hostility to accusations, confrontations, and adverse publicity, despite the fact that the reformers are saying only what professionals have said to themselves for decades.

To be criticized publicly is painful. The challenge to correctional administrators is to utilize constructively the public concern lying behind the criticism. Appropriate strategies must be planned and implemented. The almost unprecedented public concern for improving correctional services can be put to constructive use. Dissipating energy and resources by reacting defensively can only delay progress. Courageous and enlightened correctional leaders (with very tough skin) are needed to accomplish this difficult task.

Citizens in Direct Service Roles

Involvement of citizens in direct service roles with correctional clientele is not a new phenomenon but a revived one. All students of elementary criminology and penology know of probation's origins in the good-hearted endeavors of the Boston shoemaker John Augustus, in the mid-nineteenth century. His willingness to take responsibility for an alcoholic who had been sentenced to incarceration and was released into his care was step. Gradually more citizens were enlisted to follow his example, but in time their work was assigned to hired professionals. In the century following Augustus' invention, use of the volunteer in direct service fell away, to be revived only in the mid-twentieth century.

Use of volunteers in corrections today is massive. Estimates of the National Information Center on Volunteers in Courts suggest that citizen volunteers outnumber professionals four or five to one and that, exclusive of law-enforcement agencies and above the misdemeanant court level, approximately 70 percent of correctional agencies have some sort of volunteer program.[15] The varieties of such programs are impressive, including one-to-one big brothers, pen pals, aviation training for delinquent boys, group programs of many kinds, basic and continuing education offerings, and legal services.

Some of these roles supplement professional responsibilities (teaching services and supervisory roles), while others are roles unique to volunteers (friendship situations). Other citizens play less direct service roles, serving as fund raisers or organizers of needed services, goods, and facilities. In recent years, institution doors that were formerly closed have been opened to groups of citizens in volunteer roles, including Alcoholics Anonymous and other self-help groups, ethnic culture programs, and church organizations. Such programs have the double effect of enhancing citizen involvement with the correctional system and providing needed services to correctional clients.

Correctional administrators must define roles in which volunteers can serve.[16] They must recruit, train, and properly supervise volunteers across the entire range of programs, from intake to discharge, from highly skilled roles to simpler relationships, from group social events to intensive casework, including library work, teaching, legal service, and cultural activities. The range seems endless. It is a mistake to conclude that volunteer services are entirely free. Constructive use of volunteers requires careful analysis of needed tasks, exhaustive searching out of resources, and careful guidance.

Much attention in recent years has been given to the role of the volunteer, and a growing amount of literature is available to aid administrators. The National Information Center on Volunteers in Courts, located at Boulder, Colorado; the National Council on Crime and Delinquency, Hackensack, New Jersey; the Commission on Voluntary Service and Action, New York, New York; and the National Center for Voluntary Action, Washington, D.C. —all further volunteerism. Each has substantial material to assist correctional agencies, such as research information, organization and management aids, training guides, and audiovisual materials. The literature in this area is richer than in most other suggested areas for citizen involvement.

The interested reader should also refer to this [National Advisory on Criminal Justice Standards and Goals] Commission's *Report on Community Crime Prevention*. The chapter on citizen action in that report contains an extensive discussion and listing of citizen-initiated and citizen-organized activities in preventing and reducing crime.

Volunteer roles increasingly are played by a wider range of citizens. Formerly a province of the middle- or upper-class person desiring to perform useful services for those less fortunate, volunteer services now are provided in increasing amounts by youths, minority groups, organized labor, university students and staff, and local community groups of all kinds.

There are many ways in which community involvement has been elicited or suggested. Some, such as tax credits for employers, require statutory authorization. Trade advisory councils have been formed to oversee training techniques, procure equipment, and establish links between corrections and the public in connection with industrial programs.[17] Volunteer counselors have been used successfully as institutional counselors and parole aides.

Professional persons in education, religion, medicine, psychology, law, and other fields have donated services. University departments have established institutional field placements in which interested students are supervised jointly by correctional and academic officials in work-study programs. Aid organizations concerned with specialized problems such as alcoholism, drug abuse, family breakdown, and prisoner rights have set up units within institutions.

The two main roles for citizen participation—policy-making and direct service—directly interact with one another, each making the other increasingly effective. The person who works as a volunteer can have a more effective voice in policy-making by his increased understanding, and the informed citizen will be more willing to undertake volunteer activities as he understands the need for bridges between community and correctional client.

RESPONSIBILITY OF CORRECTIONAL SYSTEMS FOR COMMUNITY PARTICIPATION

Correctional systems themselves must assume responsibility for enlisting broad community support for correctional programs. Despite the above descriptions, it still must be said that very little public involvement has yet been permitted or realized.

Agencies generally are responsible to administrative branches of government and only indirectly to the legislature and public. An unconcerned public has been relatively unaware of correctional issues. Correctional agencies have operated with little public scrutiny and in general have enjoyed that autonomy, while simultaneously complaining about the lack of public support for their endeavors. Given the realities of rising community concern and citizen involvement, these circumstances are likely to be altered drastically in the years ahead. It is in the general interest of correctional programs for citizens to exercise their prerogatives as participants in a democratic society. The correctional systems of today bear a heavy burden of responsibility for the lack of involvement with the community in past decades and should expend extra effort to make amends.

Corrections' Information and Change-Agent Role

Correctional agencies must provide a continuous flow of information to the public concerning issues and alternatives involved in implementing correctional programs, so that citizens may participate intelligently in the major decisions involved. For example, a major difficulty in instituting various types of community-based treatment centers is communities' refusal to have centers located in their territory. Such resistance will not be overcome immediately, but involvement of many citizens can be expected to bring success eventually.[18]

Similarly, experience has shown that simply being able to prove that new techniques can be efficient in reducing crime or costs of crime control does not guarantee their acceptance. Bail reform measures, for example, have been carefully evaluated and have demonstrated beyond question that costs of jail incarceration can be reduced without increasing the risk to society.[19] In addition to such cost effectiveness, bail reform substantially reduces the inequities of a jailing system that systematically discriminates against the poor. Still, release-on-recognizance projects have been instituted in only a fraction of the nation's courts.

The information program should go beyond the usual press releases and occasional public hearings. Corrections must assume an educational role, a change-agent role, for it is clear that drastic changes are required to bring the community-based correctional process into being.

The change-agent role also involves working with private agencies that too often have offered services in a way that favors other groups in the general population over inmates or former inmates. By selectively serving individual clients who are not as problem-ridden or difficult to deal with, these agencies have burdened governmental agencies with a disproportionate number of offenders. It is reasonable and appropriate to seek a redistribution of caseloads, so that the private sector assumes a greater share of responsibility for those with the major social disabilities of conviction and imprisonment.

It goes without saying that corrections officials should also work actively with private agencies and organizations that are concerned with such matters as prisoner aid, police, probation, or parole. These groups usually have specialized units that provide either direct services or access to sources for job placement, treatment for alcoholics and drug users, residential counseling facilities, foster homes, emergency housing, hospitalization, vocational and therapeutic counseling, and similar services.

The change-agent model should include massive public education efforts through the communications media and intensive educational-organizational efforts with the many subcommittees—ethnic, racial, special interest groups—for support of general community corrections and specific projects. This concept of correctional responsibility to educate and serve as a catalyst for change requires a sophisticated understanding of society as a system and of criminal justice, including corrections, as an integral part of the larger society.

Perhaps most of all it involves commitment on the part of correctional personnel, from top administrator to line worker, to the new role of change agent. The commitment extends to efforts to change those aspects of society that are related to crime causation—poverty, racism, and other inequities.

However, the step from recognizing a problem to implementing its solution is difficult. For the most part, the community alternatives that have been developed to date simply are minor variations on some older ideas. For example, the phrase "alternatives to incarceration" still is used, reflecting corrections' preoccupation with institutions. As the National Council on Crime and Delinquency points out, the emphasis should be reversed—"imprisonment must be viewed as an alternative to community treatment.[20] Work-release usually is still limited to the last few weeks before release from an institution; some halfway houses resemble small penitentiaries rather than open community residences. Implementation of the fundamentally different set of assumptions implied by community corrections is the challenge for this decade.

IMPLEMENTATION OF COMMUNITY-BASED CORRECTIONS

A basic principle underlying the philosophy of community-based corrections is that all efforts consistent with the safety of others should be made to reduce involvement of the individual offender with the institutional aspects of corrections. The alienation and dehumanization engendered in jails, work-houses, prisons, even probation services, is to be avoided wherever possible. The less penetration into the criminal justice system the better.

A second basic principle is the need for extensive involvement with the multiple aspects of the community, beginning with the offender and his world and extending to the larger social system.

As a final basic principle, it is apparent that community-based programs demand radically new roles for inmates, staff, and citizens. This must be made explicit in altered job descriptions, new patterns of training, different performance expectations.

The principle implies changes in recruitment. Since corrections needs to relate increasingly with the various facets of the community, its work force must increasingly represent those facets. This means greatly expanded recruitment from minority and economically disadvantaged groups, with all that implies for location of services (such as prisons), for innovative training, and for new kinds of staffing patterns.

Community Alternatives to Confinement

Nonresidential programs. Structured correctional programs, which supervise a substantial part of an offender's day but do not include "live-in" requirements, are another community-based necessity. The clients are persons who need more intensive services than probation usually can offer, yet are not in need of institutionalization. School and counseling programs, day treatment centers with vocational training, and guided group interaction programs are among the treatment modes used—many with related services to families.

Many such programs are described substantially in corrections literature.[21] Essexfields and Collegefields, community descendants of the Highfields residential program, were based on group dynamics theory and utilized peer-group pressures to modify behavior. The Provo experiment in Utah used similar theoretical approaches. The programs, in brief, involved intensive daily programs of work or school and counseling sessions. Essexfields, in Newark, New Jersey, used employment in a county mental hospital; Collegefields, a short-term project, used an academic program adopted for individual student needs as the heart of the program.

Each of these projects has demonstrated success in treatment outcomes sufficient to warrant further experimentation. Each clearly showed that intensive programs in communities are at least as effective as, and usually somewhat better than, institutionalization and that offenders who otherwise would be in penal settings can be treated safely in the community. To date, these types of programs have been used most extensively with adolescent populations.

Foster and group homes. Juvenile judges frequently have felt it necessary to commit youngsters to an institution when circumstances in the parental home were totally unsuitable. Foster home development and more recently the group home, when used for aiding delinquent youths, are attempts to prevent unnecessary institutionalization.

Foster homes, also extensively used to meet child dependency needs, are operated under a range of administrative arrangements, public and private, state and local, court and correctional. A project conducted by the Merrill Palmer Institute[22] of Detroit sought information concerning the nature of supportive services required for successful foster home care of disturbed and delinquent young persons and applied the information on an experimental basis. Particular attention was given to the need for training foster parents, an area usually neglected, and appropriate psychiatric and educational support was developed.

In most jurisdictions, foster care has been far less intensively aided than in the Merrill Palmer experiments. Foster care appears to be considered a less useful tool than the more recently developed group homes. These quasi-institutions often are administered by agencies with house parents as paid staff, in contrast to foster homes where a monthly or daily room-and-board fee is customarily made to foster parents. The theoretical assumptions underlying the group home are related to child development stages. Most delinquency occurs in adolescence when family ties are loosening as adulthood approaches. Transfer to a new family situation, as in the foster home, is felt to be less desirable than the semi-independence from family that is possible in the group home, along with a supportive environment and rewarding experiences with adults.

The group home model usually has six to ten young people living in a home owned or rented by agencies and staffed by employed "parents" or counselors, supplemented by other necessary professional services obtained mostly through existing community resources. Correctional agencies in Minnesota and Wisconsin use such group homes extensively. California has systematized the use of group homes through a classification related to particular types of youth. A group home variant in Boulder, Colorado, the Attention Home, is supported mainly by volunteer contributions of funds and personnel.[23]

Evaluation of such efforts generally is positive. Costs are high relative to nonresidential treatment, but not as high in most cases as institutional care and, in the case of Boulder where community resources are extensively used, considerably less.

The community correctional center. The popularity of the "community correctional center" concept in recent years has led to a bandwagon effect, with rapid growth of a wide variety of programs. Definition, therefore, becomes increasingly difficult. For purposes of this report, the term is used to mean a relatively open institution located in the neighborhood and using community resources to provide most or all of the services required by offenders. The degree of openness varies with offender types, and use of services varies with availability and offender needs. Such institutions are used for multiple purposes—detention, service delivery, holding, and pre-release.

The lines between community-based and institutional programs are blurring substantially. Because of their newness, projects of this nature have generated little evaluation, minimum descriptive material, and few guidelines. They do, however, provide a flexible and theoretically sound design with potential for meeting varied correctional needs.

The Institute for the Study of Crime and Delinquency, Sacramento, California, has undertaken a lengthy study to develop a model community-based treatment program for young adults, with attention to architectural design as well as services and management concerns.[24] The project, originally planned to develop a model prison, eventually came to envision a blurring of lines between institution and community. This was done intentionally to tailor the amount of "freedom" to the needs of each individual. An offender progresses from secure facility to open community residence gradually, in systematic phases. Decisions on individual programs are shared by offenders, staff, and citizens. The model represents a kind of amalgam of institution and community-based programs.

A comprehensive project undertaken by the Department of Architecture, University of Illinois, and supported by Law Enforcement Assistance Administration funds, has developed "Guidelines for Planning and Design of Regional Community Correctional Centers for Adults."

Many types of community correctional centers are in existence today, using such facilities as jails, parts or all of hotels or motels, floors or wings of YMCA's, surplus army barracks, and former fraternity houses. Some are used as alternatives to penal service, others as adjuncts to institutionalization. They serve many types of offenders, usually in separate facilities. An interesting variant in Minnesota is a "restitution" home where offenders live while working to earn funds to compensate victims.

Community Adjuncts to Institutions

The program activities discussed so far have been designed generally to serve as alternatives to the use of the institution. A major assumption throughout this report is that most persons committed to correctional authority can be served effectively and economically in community settings. The implications require a brief review.

It seems obvious that institutional populations will be made up increasingly of hard-core criminals and persons difficult to control. Prison will become the final resort. However, all but a very small fraction of institutionalized individuals ultimately return to the community, and it is therefore essential that institutional programs also involve the community.

The notion that isolating individuals from the community influences that made them engage in crime and that exposing them to the influences of prison will reform them is no longer accepted.[25] Instead, as this report so often notes, prisons have proved to be criminogenic in themselves. For this reason, administrators have been seeking alternative experiences for inmates.

Many of the programs in use today favor the traditional values of work, training, and education. While reintegration efforts must encompass standards that society accepts and endorses, correctional administrators should not impose their own value systems on the potential range of community programs. To do so may restrict the breadth and innovative character of what is offered.

Instead, the range of activities permitted in the larger community should be considered. For example, some offenders might participate with nonoffenders in private group therapy, consult with their own lawyers, conduct investigations in connection with their own trials, negotiate with community institutions, participate in school activities, attend social functions, and engage in athletics in the community.

Some of these ideas may seem unrealistic and foreign to today's conception of the inmate's role. However, the hypothesis is that the benefit to be derived when an offender's feelings of hopelessness and powerlessness are dissipated by virtue of his having a measure of control over his own destiny will far outweigh administrative anxieties and burdens.

The institutional custodial climate that so clearly separates the keeper from the kept should be replaced in significant measure by one of mutuality as staff and offenders work together in responsible citizen roles that are meaningful to both parties.

The concept of "bridging" is used to denote programs that establish lines between imprisoned inmate, institution, and free society, to afford the inmate experiences expressly intended to maximize his reintegration potential. Inmates participate in training, work, education, or other activities that provide as many normal transactions and experiences with community persons and organizations as possible. The number and variety of community resources that can be developed for these purposes is virtually unlimited.

The bridging concept contains the reciprocal notions of inmates relating outward to the community and of opening the institution to community access. As bridging from the prison to the outside is intended to normalize interactions with community resources, so bridging into the prison is intended to transform traditional prison activities into more normal patterns of life. Families and neighbors, employers and teachers, ministers and counselors enter the prison, participate in its life, and bring the ongoing community life into the formerly insulated institution.

Bridging activities provide much-needed diversification of options for inmates. Staff and program can be augmented significantly by utilizing more fully the opportunities available outside the walls or by bringing them inside. Inmates have the opportunity to try out socially acceptable roles in a planned transitional process.

The dependence fostered by institutionalization can be reduced. Inmates are allowed to discharge a measure of social and personal responsibility by assuming financial obligations and a larger measure of control over their destinies, thus contributing to their self-esteem and an awareness of their stake in the community.

Citizens who participate in bridging activities become involved in correctional services and decision making. Greater public participation should result in increased understanding of and support for these programs. Such public involvement also will prepare communities for a certain amount of conflict and failure, for bridging concepts imply risk of an unassessed nature. Expectations of total success will lead only to disillusionment, but realistic optimism for potential gains must be retained.

Work release. Work-release programs began to be used extensively in the 1950s. The practice permits selected inmates to work for pay outside the institution, returning each night. Prisoner employment is not new; the work gang for hire is a well-known feature in penal history. The work-release concept differs markedly, however, in allowing regular civilian employment, under specified circumstances, for selected low-risk inmates. Initially used mainly with misdemeanants, work release now is used widely with felons and youth offenders.[26] Other versions, similar in intent, provide for weekend sentences, furloughs, and release for vocational training or educational programs. All help to reestablish links to the community for the incarcerated.

In a few instances, commercial manufacturing operations have been introduced into prisons. Honeywell, Inc., has loaned a computer to a Massachusetts prison for use by inmates to do programming and data processing for various departments of state government, an up-to-date version of "state use." Union involvement in such efforts is crucial; it will add a much needed dimension to employment programs and represent a further potential resource for correctional programs.

Family visits. Prisons are attempting in a variety of ways to assist the reintegration of offenders into family circles, as well as the work world. Prison visiting always has been allowed, frequently under less-than-favorable circumstances, with minimum opportunities for privacy and personal communication. Conjugal visits long have been the practice in Mississippi institutions[27] but have not been allowed elsewhere in this country until recently. A relatively new California scheme allows entire families to spend up to two days in cottage-like houses on prison grounds.[28]

Family counseling programs for inmates and families are available in many states. A family life education program in Hennepin County, Minnesota, is used with adult inmates, their families, and with juvenile probation caseloads.[29] Adlerian group counseling methods, with involvement of even very young children, underlie this attempt to assist the offender and his family. Volunteers of America programs for youth involve families in somewhat similar ways, with special Sunday events such as picnics or parties to which families are invited for socializing.

In the Swedish penal system, where family visitation is taken for granted, some institutions even permit husband and wife to live together if both are institutionalized. Most interesting is their "holiday" policy—inmates, like other citizens, are entitled to a two-week vacation at the beach accompanied by families.[30] Such programs seem startling to American observers but are sensible if assisting families through difficult days and preparing them for stable relationships and desirable goals.

Educational programs. An educational bridging program is the Newgate model, in which mini-universities are established within prison walls to serve higher educational needs of inmates. Newgate programs are located across the country in state and federal institutions.[31] Each uses different procedures, but the common thread is use of education as the major tool.[32] Opportunities for continuation of college on release are arranged, and extensive support given. Evaluation evidence developed thus far is positive; a serious limitation of the program, however, is its very high cost.

Students from Augsburg College, Minneapolis, as part of their regular curriculum attend classes held in a penal institution with inmates and prison officers as fellow students.[33] While a range of courses is taught in this "co-learner" model, the criminology course is of most interest—as a living laboratory with mutual benefits to all students.

Ethnic programs. In recent years, with heightening cultural and ethnic awareness, various minority consciousness groups have formed in the nation's prisons, many involving extensive contact with similar groups outside. Enriching in many ways and clearly of potential assistance to the reintegration of inmates with their community, such programs are sensitive issues in correctional circles. Prisons mirror the racial unrest of the nation in aggravated form associated with the tensions of anxiety and fear, close quarters, lack of privacy, and hours of idleness. Cultural groups, strengthening the individual's awareness of his group identity and raising questions of discrimination, are potential sources of discord. But they are nonetheless vital links to the self-help potential of such groups on the outside.

Pre-release Programs

The federal prison system pioneered in the development of pre-release programs in the early 1960s. In several cities small living units were organized, usually in leased quarters, to which individuals could be transferred for the final months of a sentence as part of preparation for release. Special orientation programs and employment assistance were provided, with gradually increasing opportunities to exercise decision making. The purpose was to phase inmates into community life under supervision, with assistance as needed. Such centers are used increasingly in state programs.

The California system has reorganized its services to give its field staff (parole personnel) greater responsibility for inmate programming during the last six months of confinement, in essence converting that period into a release-planning phase. Arrangements have been made to permit temporary release at any time in the last sixty days before the official release date, thus permitting more flexible timing as plans are developed. Inmates within ninety days of release may make unescorted trips to home communities on three-day passes to facilitate release plans, another way of easing into the often difficult post-release period.[34]

Short-Term Return of Parolees

Related closely to pre-release planning is recent development in many states of programs permitting the short-term return of parolees who have made a misstep that is potential cause for parole revocation and return to the prison. Frequently, pre-release facilities are used for this function. The return to a relatively open institution allows the parolee a breather, more supervision than in the community, and time to plan a new and hopefully more effective reentry into the community. Research indicates that short-term returnees in California do as well on second release as those released after a long period of re-imprisonment.[35]

NOTES

1. Although these views are too well-known to require detailed documentation, those seeking a recent and persuasive brief are referred to Hans W. Mattick, "The Prosaic of Prison Violence," *University of Chicago Law School Occasional Paper* (1972).
2. See, for example, Herman G. Stark, "Alternatives to Institutionalization," *Crime and Delinquency* 13 (1967): 323.
3. See Jewett T. Flagg, "A Businessman's Interest in Corrections," *Crime and Delinquency* 6 (1960): 351, for the employers' views.
4. See District of Columbia Department of Corrections, *In-Program and Post-Release Performance of Work-Release Inmates: A Preliminary Assessment* (Washington, 1969); and Gordon P. Waldo, Theodore G. Chiricos, and Leonard E. Dobrin, "Community Contact and Inmate Attitudes," unpublished study, Florida State University, Tallahassee, (ca. 1970). For a tentative assessment of community-oriented programs, see LaMar T. Empey, *Alternatives to Incarceration* (Washington, D.C.: U.S. Department of Health, Education and Welfare, 1967).
5. See Franklin E. Zimring, *Perspectives on Deterrence* (Rockville, Maryland: National Institute of Mental Health, Center for Studies of Crime and Delinquency, 1971), p. 89.
6. See Frank R. Scarpitti and Richard M. Stephenson, "A Study of Probation Effectiveness," *Journal of Criminal Law, Criminology, and Police Science* 59 (1968): 361–69; and *Superior Court Probation and/or Jail Sample: One-Year Followup for Selected Counties* (California Criminal Statistics Bureau, 1969).

7. LaMar T. Empey, *op. cit.* note 4, p. 2. See also Carol Crowther, "Crimes, Penalties, and Legislatures," *Annals of the American Academy of Political and Social Science* 381 (1969): 147–158.

8. Solomon Kobrin, "The Deterrent Effectiveness of Criminal Justice Sanctioning Strategies," unpublished paper, University of Southern California School of Public Administration, Los Angeles (1972).

9. This involvement has already begun on many fronts. For a typical report, see "Citizen Involvement," *Criminal Justice Newsletter* (March 13, 1972), p. 46.

10. See, for example, Clifford R. Shaw, *The Natural History of a Delinquent Career* (University of Chicago Press, 1931).

11. Richard A. Cloward and Lloyd E. Ohlin, *Delinquency and Opportunity* (Glencoe, Illinois: Free Press, 1960).

12. A consideration of some of the issues raised here from the viewpoint of corrections may be found in Milton Burdman, "Realism in Community-Based Correctional Services," *Annals of the American Academy of Political and Social Sciences* 381 (1969): 71.

13. The final word on costs and effectiveness must await full implementation of community-based correctional variants. See, however, two publications of the District of Columbia Department of Corrections: "Costs, Benefits, Recidivism in Work Release, Prison College Program," *Newsletter* (January-February 1972), p. 2; and *Cost Analysis of the D.C. Work Release Program.*

14. See, for example, Bucks County (Pennsylvania) Department of Corrections, *Citizen Volunteer Program*, Fact Sheet (January 1972), p. 2.

15. Ivan H. Scheier, *et. al., Guidelines and Standards for the Use of Volunteers in Correctional Programs* (Washington, D.C.: Law Enforcement Assistance Administration, 1972), pp. iii, 5.

16. For one scheme of classifying these roles, see Vincent O'Leary, "Some Directions for Citizen Involvement in Corrections," *Annals of the American Academy of Political and Social Science* 381 (1969): 99. The paper also presents possibilities for expanding these roles.

17. Jude P. West and John R. Stratton, eds., *"The Role of Correctional Industries"* (Iowa City: University of Iowa Press, 1971), p. 3.

18. See, for example, Marshall Fels, *The Community: Site and Source of Correctional Rehabilitation* (Olympia: Washington Department of Social and Health Services, 1971).

19. See *The Manhattan Bail Project* (Criminal Justice Coordinating Council of New York City and Vera Institute of Justice, 1970); David McCarthy and Jeanne J. Wahl, "The District of Columbia Bail Project," *Georgetown Law Journal* 53 (1965): 675; and Gerald Levin, "The San Francisco Bail Project," *American Bar Association Journal* 55 (1969): 135.

20. *Policies and Background Information* (Hackensack, New Jersey: National Council on Crime and Delinquency, 1972), p. 15.

21. Saul Pilnick, Robert F. Allen, and Neale W. Clapp, "Adolescent Integrity from Highfields to Essexfields and Collegefields," paper presented to the National Conference on Social Work (1966). See also LaMar T. Empey and Maynard L. Erickson, *The Provo Experiment* (Boston: D. C. Heath, 1972).

22. "The Detroit Foster Homes Project of the Merrill Palmer Institute," unpublished report.

23. See John E. Hargardine, *The Attention Home of Boulder, Colorado* (Washington, D.C.: U.S. Department of Health, Education and Welfare, 1968); Andrew W. Basinas, "Foster Care for Delinquents" (*Social Service in Wisconsin*, 1968) pp. 7–9; Niels Christiansen, Jr., and William Nelson, *Juveniles in Group Homes* (Minneapolis: Minnesota Department of Corrections, 1969); John W. Pearson and Ted Palmer, *The Use of Group Homes for Delinquents* (Sacramento: California Youth Authority, 1968).

24. See Harold B. Bradley, *et al., The Non-Prison: New Approach to Treating Youthful Offenders* (Sacramento, California: Institute for the Study of Crime and Delinquency, 1970).

25. For a history of this function of the institution, see David J. Rothman, *The Discovery of the Asylum: Social Order and Disorder in the New Republic* (Boston: Little, Brown, 1972).

26. The problem of predictability in these endeavors may pose specific burdens on the administrator which are not posed by programs confined largely to institutions or others carried on in the community with more control and surveillance. However, some scientific certitude may be introduced into the selection process. See, for example, Isaac Fair, Inc., *Development of a Scoring System to Predict Success on Work Release, Final Report* (Washington: D.C. Department of Corrections, 1971).

27. Described in Columbus B. Hopper, *Conjugal Visiting at the Mississippi State Penitentiary* (privately printed); and Hopper, *Sex in Prison: The Mississippi Experiment with Conjugal Visiting* (Baton Rouge: Louisiana State University Press, 1969). See also *NCCD News*, April 1972, "Conjugal Visits: More to Them than Sex."

28. See, for example, "The Family Visiting Program at the California Correctional Institution, Tehachapi, July 1968," *Annual Research Review* (Sacramento: California Department of Corrections, 1970, p. 43.

29. See Richard E. Ericson and David O. Moberg, *The Rehabilitation of Parolees* (Minneapolis: Minnesota Department of Corrections, 1969), p. 42.

30. *Kriminalvarden*, 1968 (Stockholm: Swedish Correctional Administration, 1969). Has summary in English.

31. See William L. Claiborne, "Special Course at American University: Lorton Inmates Learn About Outside Life," *Washington Post* (February 19, 1972).

32. There remains some disagreement among professionals as to the most effective approaches to be adopted in the education area. See *New York Times* (March 26, 1972), p. 54, "Prison Officials Back Reform of Education for Inmates but Differ on Details."

33. Connie Schoen, "Things Volunteers Do," *American Journal of Correction* (1969), pp. 26–31.

34. Norman Holt, *California Prerelease Furlough Program for State Prisoners: An Evaluation* (Sacramento: California Department of Corrections, 1969).

35. *Short-Term Return Unit Program* (Sacramento: California Department of Corrections, 1969).

chapter five
MARSHALING CITIZEN POWER TO MODERNIZE CORRECTIONS

Chamber of Commerce of the United States

CORRECTIONS TODAY: AN OVERVIEW

Although the nation has neglected its criminal justice system as a whole, there is growing evidence of a new interest on the part of the public to improve the entire system, especially corrections. For example, the Congress has begun to allocate additional monies for corrections through the Law Enforcement Assistance Administration of the Department of Justice.

The President has indicated a direct interest in the improvement of corrections and demonstrated this interest by convening the recent National Correctional Conference in Williamsburg, Virginia. Attorney General John Mitchell announced at that correctional conference that a federal program is being initiated to assist state and local governments in modernizing their correctional systems. The program calls for a National Corrections Academy to train federal, state and local corrections personnel, a National Clearinghouse for Criminal Justice Architecture and Design, and a National Clearinghouse for Correctional Education.

The Attorney General, Secretary of Labor, and Secretary of Health, Education and Welfare recently communicated with the fifty governors, emphasizing that the highest priority be placed on the importance of correctional reform and the key role to be played by the individual states.

All these efforts indicate that we can look forward to a better correctional system in the future. However, we must realize that much more needs to be done now, for the following reasons.

From *Marshaling Citizen Power to Modernize Corrections* (1972). Reprinted by permission of the Chamber of Commerce of the United States.

Beyond any rational dispute, the nation's correctional system is ineffective.

In reality it is a "non-system"—a potpourri of facilities and programs which handles about 1.3 million offenders on an average day. Correctional operations are administratively fragmented among federal, state, county and local governments.

By any standard, correctional facilities, programs and personnel are badly overburdened.

Legacy of Neglect

Correctional improvement efforts are mired in two centuries of neglect and, too often, face open hostility by the public and legislators.

Overloaded, antiquated, underfunded correctional institutions have created problems of near desperation for the administrators and personnel who man them. The degree of this desperation has been intensified by the recent wave of disturbances and inmate rebellions in institutions across the country. Of approximately 460 state and federal institutions for offenders sentenced to long terms, there are 25 over 100 years old and 61 that opened before 1900.

State institutions are often expected to be largely self-supporting through their farming and prison industries, most of which involve only repetitive and underproductive work with obsolete equipment. Few correctional industrial programs provide skill-development opportunities or training experience relevant to the industrial requirements of the community. In many states, prisons are prohibited from training inmates or making products that will compete on the market with local industry.

Juvenile Offenders

Most crime in the United States is committed by youth.

Over 350,000 children, or about 30 percent of all offenders, are under the custody and supervision of juvenile correctional institutions or agencies on any given day.

Although 70 percent of all funds spent on juvenile corrections now goes toward supporting juvenile institutions rather than juvenile probation, these institutions are still inadequate. For example, standards recommended for the size of juvenile institutions call for facilities to accommodate 150 or less, with individual living units housing no more than 20 youngsters. Yet, according to survey data collected by the Task Force on Corrections of the President's Commission on Law Enforcement and the Administration of Justice, only 24 percent of all institutions meet this living unit standard, and the traditional feeling is toward building larger units.

Probation and Parole—Unfulfilled Promises

A person who is found guilty of a crime will often receive a suspended sentence, provided that he remain on good behavior and that he be placed under special supervision. Such a person is said to be on "probation."

A person who has served part of a given sentence in prison may be released under certain conditions, including special supervision. Such a person is termed to be on "parole."

Though the effectiveness of properly implemented parole and probation programs has been demonstrated many times, their full cost/benefit potential is yet to be achieved on a nationwide basis. A major weakness in probation and parole services is that they have never received adequate funds for the number of offenders under supervision. Two-thirds of all offenders are under probation or parole supervision, but these services receive less than one-third of the monies allocated for correctional efforts.

The President's Commission on Law Enforcement and the Administration of Justice notes that "probation and parole services are characteristically poorly staffed and often poorly administered." Of the 250 counties surveyed by the commission, one-third provided no probation services at all. Average probation and parole caseloads vastly exceed the recommended standards of 35 cases per officer. Over 76 percent of all persons convicted of a minor offense, and 67 percent of all those convicted of a major offense, who are on probation are in caseloads of 100 or more. Less than 4 percent of the probation officers in the nation carry caseloads of 40 or less.

Despite the far-from-ideal conditions existing in the probation and parole fields, studies indicate that roughly 55 to 65 percent of parolees are not returned to prison during the period of their parole supervision. Of those that are, about two-thirds are returned for parole violations, not for new crimes. Sixty to ninety percent of probationers complete their probation terms without revocations.

The Jail Mess

County and local jails are the first contact with the correctional world for most offenders. Most people in jails are awaiting trial and have not been sentenced or convicted of any crime. Some are serving short sentences for minor offenses. The need for the rights of inmates to be considered and protected in all levels of correctional facilities is evident, but the situation in jails is particularly poor. Yet, the initial and often lasting impressions toward corrections and our system of criminal justice are formed in these institutions.

In most city and county jail facilities for adult offenders (with a few outstanding exceptions), inmates are kept under maximum security, and general services and conditions are considered to be the worst of all penal institutions. The National Crime Commission's Task Force on Corrections states that: "In the vast majority of city and county jails . . . no significant progress has been made in the last fifty years."

Correctional Planning: By Guess and By Golly

Correction in the past has suffered from piecemeal and patchwork programming and crisis-oriented planning.

Plagued with a lack of resources and adequate planning for handling present and future problems, correction has too often operated on the basis of coping with problems as they arise, reacting to situations rather than planning ahead for them.

New federal funding programs, and the emerging emphasis on comprehensive criminal justice planning by the Law Enforcement Assistance Administration of the U.S. Department of Justice, should help improve the long-range planning and management of the nation's correctional system.

Correctional Personnel: Manpower Development and Training Programs

Surveys conducted by the Joint Commission on Correctional Manpower and Training in 1967–68 revealed widespread personnel recruitment and retention problems created by low pay, heavy workloads, insufficient training, and lack of merit-system employment in the correctional field. These problems have deprived the system of essential professional services and have resulted in programs often manned by personnel with little or no educational preparation for correctional work.

The Joint Commission also revealed that minority groups, females, and young people are under-represented in the nation's correctional work force. The commission urged a comprehensive nationwide recruitment program with particular emphasis on enlisting more qualified young people, women, blacks, Spanish-surnamed Americans, and other minority group members.

The recent availability of federal funds for college and university programs designed to prepare students for careers in corrections (and other areas of criminal justice) could help provide the kind of correctional personnel the country needs.

Contradictory Goals and Public Uncertainty

The average citizen does not know what is to be expected of correctional services. This attitude has created a paradox in handling offenders. Confusion over whether corrections should be punishment-oriented, rehabilitation-oriented, or both, brings public accusations that the system brutalizes offenders, on the one hand, or coddles them on the other. Manifestation of this confusion is the existence, side-by-side, of correctional facilities intended primarily for punishment and detention, and others designed to help rehabilitate offenders.

The conditions within many prisons achieve nothing but an increase in the number of recidivists (those released from institutions who commit additional crimes). Eighty percent of all felonies are committed by repeaters. These conditions may result also in the loss of self-respect and human dignity and lead to increased sophistication in criminal behavior through contact with hardened offenders.

The negative impact of imprisonment, coupled with the lack of acceptance by the community following release, often creates more bitterness and a desire to get back at society.

COMMUNITY CORRECTION: A CHEAPER AND MORE HUMANE APPROACH

There is growing evidence that new programs making use of community approaches to corrections as alternatives to incarceration, and also as a means of facilitating reintegration of the offender back into the community following release from an institution, can be more successful and less costly to society. Community-based correction recognizes the failure of massive, impersonal institutions far removed from population centers. It recognizes the importance of working with the offender in his home community, or near it, where his ties with family and friends can be used to advantage in his rehabilitation.

There are many types of community and transitional release programs that have demonstrated value in rehabilitating the offender and reducing the social costs of recidivism. Among these are:

> *Pre-trial intervention.* A program designed to provide a rapid rehabilitation response for young first-offenders following arrest but prior to trial, conviction, and sentencing. The court suspends prosecution for a 90-day period and places young offenders into a program of counseling, training, and employment assistance. Successful participation results in dismissal of charges and thus avoids the stigma of a criminal record.
>
> *Probation.* A court action which permits the convicted offender to retain his freedom in the community, subject to court control and the supervision and guidance of a probation officer. Probation sustains the offender's ability to continue working and to protect his

family's welfare, while avoiding the stigma and possible damaging effects of imprisonment.

Halfway houses. Small, homelike residential facilities located in the community for offenders who need more control than probation or other types of community supervision can provide. Halfway houses are used also for gradual readjustment to community life for those who have come out of institutions. Halfway-house programs usually offer supervised living, counseling services, and draw upon the community for education, training, jobs and recreation to aid in the rehabilitation process.[1]

Work-release. Under this alternative, the offender is confined in an institution only at night or on weekends but is permitted to pursue his normal life the remainder of the time. Such a program makes possible a greater degree of control than is possible under probation or other types of community supervision, but avoids total disruption of family life and employment.

Pre-release centers. Supervised programs designed to ease the transition from total confinement to freedom by involving people from the community who come to the prison to provide information in areas of vital interest to the inmate who is about to be released. Subjects covered include such topics as employment, finances, family life, community services, and legal resources.[2]

Parole. A procedure by which prisoners are selected for release and a service by which they are provided with the controls, assistance, and guidance they need as they serve the remainder of their sentences within the free community.

The report of the President's Task Force on Prisoner Rehabilitation concluded that "perhaps the greatest obstacle to improvement in the correctional system always has been the tendency of much of the public to regard it and treat it as a rug under which to sweep difficult and disagreeable people and problems . . . after all, the overwhelming majority of offenders do not stay under the correctional rug. . . . As a matter of fact, the two-thirds of the correctional population . . . on probation or parole are in the community right now. . . . 'Community-based corrections' is no visionary slogan, but a hard contemporary fact."

With increasing funding available—about a quarter of a billion dollars for Fiscal 1972—the Law Enforcement Assistance Administration has set a number of goals for its expanded corrections program. They include: community-based programs, with emphasis on youthful offenders; improvement of probation and parole; marshaling resources of the private sector; expanded use of halfway houses; replacement of outmoded jails with regional corrections facilities; new training centers for corrections personnel; more effective research.

Community Corrections Reduce the Need for Expensive Facilities

The shift to community-based corrections will eventually reduce the need for maximum security institutions. Experts agree that only 20 to 30 percent of present inmates represent a danger to society and must be securely confined. If the remaining 70 percent can be rehabilitated in less restrictive local institutions, or under supervision in the community, few facilities will be needed for those considered dangerous and least responsive to correctional treatment.

The cost of keeping an adult offender in a state institution is about six times as great as that to keep him under parole supervision, and fourteen times as great as that required to supervise him on probation. Based on current per-capita cost, it is estimated that it takes $11,000 a year to keep a married man in prison. This figure includes the inmate's loss of earnings, the cost to taxpayers if his family has to go on relief, and the loss of taxes he would pay. Compare this to the national average cost of 38 cents and 88 cents per day for probation and parole supervision, respectively, or an average of less than $365 a year, as reported by the President's Commission on Law Enforcement and the Administration of Justice.

In its 1967 *Task Force Report: Corrections*, the Commission projected that construction of institutions planned for completion by 1975 would cost more than a billion dollars, with construction estimated conservatively at $10,000 per bed. More recent data gathered by the Law Enforcement Assistance Administration indicate that institutional building costs currently average $15,000 to $20,000 per bed. When completed, the cost of the new space, based on 1969 estimates, would add over $200 million annually to the operating cost of the institutions. This amount would be considerably increased in the light of current costs.

Community Correction Is More Humane

Experience has shown that, as opposed to isolation and punishment, community-based correction which permits a person to live in his own community and maintain normal social relationships, while providing control, guidance, and access to rehabilitative resources and services, is a more efficient, economic, and more humane approach to the treatment of the offender. A considerable and impressive body of evidence has been accumulated indicating that correction in the community is more effective in reducing recidivism than severe forms of punishment.

Because the community-oriented approach is almost always more economical, it enjoys a substantial cost/benefit advantage. Experience has revealed that if one-third of the offenders currently held in institutions were transferred to probation along with their share of the correctional budget, they could be placed in caseloads of ten or less. This would provide the opportunity for more individual attention and enhance chances for probation to succeed. Under present circumstances, however, judges face the dilemma of having to choose between the worse of two worlds: whether to utilize already overburdened probation services, or whether to commit the offender to an institution which is ill-equipped to rehabilitate at all.

Examples of Successful Community-Based Correctional Programs

The Saginaw Project, the California Probation Subsidy Program, the Sacramento and Stockton Community Treatment Project, and the pre-trial intervention program have demonstrated that community correction is a more effective way to use public funds than imprisonment.

The Saginaw Project. A three-year experiment conducted between 1957 and 1960 in Michigan's Saginaw County illustrates the benefits which can accrue from a well-planned and adequately funded community corrections program. In this experiment, probation was the method of correction used. Probation staffs and facilities were strengthened to provide an adequate level of services through small caseloads and intensive supervision. The proportion of convicted felons (those convicted of a major offense) put on probation was raised from 59.5 percent to 67.1 percent. As a result of this type of intensive and highly individualized treatment, the proportion of probation failures experienced a decline from 32.2 percent during the three prior years, to 17.4 percent during the three experimental years. Estimated savings to taxpayers over the period was almost half a million dollars, because of reductions in costs of institutional care, costs of welfare for prisoners' families and parole expenditures.

The California probation subsidy program. The California subsidy program provides an outstanding example of how corrections can be made less costly and more effective. Under this program, California gives a grant to a county for every convicted offender who, by being placed in a community-based correctional program, helps to reduce the average number of people from that county who were formerly placed in state prisons.

For example, if a county that, over the years, averaged 25 inmates in state prisons for every 100,000 population cuts this down to 15 by using community-based programs, it can receive up to $4,000 for each of the 10 offenders *not* sent to state institutions, or a maximum of $40,000. These funds are to be used to improve the local services. The $4,000 state payment to counties reduces workloads and helps those who are already under local supervision, as well as those for whom the money was received.

Experience during the first two years of this program demonstrated that improved probation services can be given to five or six persons at the local level for each individual grant.

During the first two years, 3,814 offenders were supervised locally who might otherwise have entered California's state institutions. This represents a gross savings of $15.2 million for the state, and a net of $9.8 million after subsidy payments to the counties. This program has resulted in the indefinite postponement of scheduled construction of several state institutions.

The $9.8 million in state savings does not indicate a shift in state institutional costs to the county or city facilities. As has been earlier indicated, costs for probation-type programs are considerably less than for imprisonment in a state institution. The rate of local incarceration has also slowed significantly, which has further reduced costs.

Most people on probation under this program have responded positively to supervision and have not violated the rules of probation or committed other crimes. This finding supports the contention that good probation practices can reduce commitments to state institutions, while offering substantially increased protection to citizens through improved supervision of probationers.

Sacramento and Stockton Community Treatment Project. Another experiment in community-based corrections conducted in California has yielded noteworthy results. This experiment involves a parole plan with intensive community treatment for the individuals involved. Part of the motivation for the experiment resulted from budgetary squeezes. The state was looking for alternatives to building more and more institutions for growing numbers of juveniles committed to its Youth Authority, which runs correctional facilities for serious offenders up to age 21.

All those involved in the experiment were confirmed delinquents with histories of car theft, grand larceny, burglary, and robbery. All had served terms in county institutions for their offenses.

Some 56 percent of those committed to the Youth Authority were deemed suitable for the experiment. Youths were assigned on a random basis either to an experimental or control group. Those in the experimental group were returned to the community and received intensive counseling and supervision under specially trained parole agents in caseloads of ten or twelve. Youths in the control group were assigned to California's regular institutional treatment program, and then paroled under the usual parole program. As is the case in most experiments in community-based corrections, offenders with a record of seriously assaultive behavior or with attributes that would cause strong objections by the community were not in the experiment.

After the first two years of the experiment, studies showed that 41 percent of the experimental group had their paroles revoked, as opposed to 61 percent of the control group.

The savings in public money for the intensive parole program is certainly substantial. The cost of the project per youth is less than half the average cost of putting an offender in an institution. Moreover, the program is now handling a group larger than the population of one of the new juvenile institutions. Some $6 to $8 million, therefore, does not have to be spent for a building to house these offenders. At the same time, the program offers much more effective protection to the public than the traditional method, because fewer youths commit additional crimes.

Pre-trial intervention. Another low-cost, high-yield program recently developed is that of pre-trial intervention, which was designed primarily through the leadership of the Manpower Administration, U.S. Department of Labor, to help break up the backlog in court processing and to offer the court yet another alternative to imprisonment.

The pre-trial program explores methods of diverting young first-offenders from prosecution and imprisonment. Following successful experiments with two demonstration programs, it is now being tested in Atlanta, Boston, Cleveland, Minneapolis, San Antonio, Baltimore, and San Francisco, and will eventually have an enrollment of over 4,000 participants.

In cooperation with the courts and police authorities, carefully selected persons, primarily younger offenders, are offered an opportunity to participate in a specifically designed manpower program after arrest but prior to trial, conviction, and sentencing.

If a youth agrees to enter the program, a delay of generally three months is obtained before the case is processed by the courts. The youth is then directed to counseling, training, and jobs. If the youth reacts positively, charges are dismissed. So far the results have been encouraging. The courts, after reviewing the progress of participants during a ninety-day period, have dismissed charges in 70 percent of the cases.

This program, which is to be expanded to other cities in the near future, was built on two earlier efforts: The *Manhattan Court Employment Project*, operated by the Vera Institute of Justice in New York; and *Project Crossroads*, operated by the National Committee for Children and Youth in Washington, D.C.

The Washington project proved so successful that it has been incorporated into the court system as a continuing element of its practices, with the enthusiastic endorsement of the U.S. Attorney General and the Chief Judge. The recidivism rate for adult participants in Project Crossroads over a 15-month period was 22.2 percent; that of the control group (not receiving project services) was 45.7 percent. Program costs totaled approximately $500 per enrollee, and the project exhibited a benefit/cost ratio of at least two to one.

EX-OFFENDERS AND EMPLOYMENT: THE HIGH COST OF THE REVOLVING DOOR

Most authorities agree that the lack of meaningful employment opportunities has been a major contributing cause to the rising crime rate and the high rate of recidivism, and, in turn, to the increasing cost of crime. Unless assimilation into communities is facilitated by the availability of suitable jobs, corrections will continue to be a wasteful and high cost "revolving door" system under which nondangerous offenders serve what is virtually a life sentence on the installment plan—largely because of the obstacles in the way of stable, worthwhile employment.

Experience in vocational training and placement programs for public offenders (sponsored by the Manpower Administration, U.S. Department of Labor) since 1964 reveals that:

> Ex-offenders can be trained and placed in employment, regardless of previous education or the nature of their crime.
>
> When ex-offenders are placed in appropriate jobs, their rate of recidivism is two to three times less than that of ex-offenders who do not receive job assistance.
>
> Ex-offenders with better paying jobs are much less likely to be recidivists than those with no jobs, part-time jobs or lower-paying jobs.
>
> Independent of work experience in prison, if the released offender gets a remunerative job on release and is able to keep it for at least six months, the probability of recidivism declines.

Bars to Employment

Public and employer attitudes, laws, and licensing regulations bar ex-offenders from employment. Too often, the government which urges the ex-offender to pursue a normal law-abiding life is the same government that bars the way to that pursuit. By reason of various state statutes, certain manufacturers cannot employ convicted felons. An official of the Law Enforcement Assistance Administration testifying before the Senate Judiciary Penitentiaries Subcommittee told of a man with a misdemeanor record (for minor offenses) being denied a taxi driver's license, and of a federal court upholding a city's refusal to hire an ex-convict as a tree trimmer.

Employer attitudes toward ex-offenders remain the most difficult to counter because they are not written in any formal guidelines, such as those found in bonding, union or license requirements.[3] Since employment opportunities for the rehabilitated offender are an effective tool in the national effort to prevent crime, policies governing company employment practices should be reviewed and revised to encourage the hiring of such offenders, especially when they are qualified by education and training for the jobs available. For example, employers may want to consider eliminating questions regarding prior criminal records (particularly arrest records, as contrasted to conviction records) from job applications.

If, upon examining this aspect of the job application, company policy dictates that such questions are necessary, confidentiality of the information should be assured in all cases, and the applicant should be informed that such information does not mean he will not be considered for the job if he is otherwise qualified. Probation and parole officers can be extremely helpful in discussing the background and overall adjustment needs of the ex-offender with the prospective employer. Maximum benefit from the work experience can be derived for both the employer and the employee when these things are taken into consideration.

Bonding Assistance Program

The experimental Bonding Assistance Program, administered by the U.S. Department of Labor, has done much to open new doors for employment and has also documented the low risk to business in hiring ex-offenders.

In this project, fidelity bonds were posted in order to protect the prospective employer from loss due to theft or acts of dishonesty. The Department of Labor provided bonding assistance to more than 3,400 persons, most of whom were ex-offenders. Included were inmates released after completing skill training programs conducted in correctional institutions under the Manpower Development and Training Act.

Less than 2 percent have defaulted over a five-year period, and a state official administering this program declared that nationwide statistics regarding the programs' loss experience indicate that the average ex-offender is a better risk than some company employees. This program has motivated many employers to review their normal requirements for subsequent hiring, and in some cases to drop the bonding requirement.

The program has been so successful that bonding assistance is now available to all institutions where skill training under the Manpower Development and Training Act is provided. In 1971, the experimental effort was expanded nationwide on a pilot basis. Through more than 2,200 local public employment service offices, special assistance is given to ex-offenders and others who apply and who can demonstrate that they are barred from a specific job offer solely because of the inability to secure a commercial bond.

HOW THE PUBLIC CAN HELP OR HINDER

Chief Justice Warren Burger, speaking before the National Conference on Corrections, stated: ". . . it is my deep conviction that when society places a person behind walls, we assume a collective moral responsibility to try to change and help that person. The law will define legal duties, but I confess I have more faith in what a moral commitment of the American people can accomplish than I have in what can be done by the compulsion of judicial decrees."

Concerned citizens can do much to promote and support correctional programs that really correct. On the other hand, public uncertainty and lack of consensus on what constitutes an effective approach will result in weak and inconsistent legislative support for correctional programs. Citizen opposition through lack of understanding can also block implementation of desirable programs even with strong legislative backing.

Almost all studies and experts agree on the changes needed: more in-community facilities like halfway houses, more academic and vocational training in institutions, more work-release programs whereby local business and industry cooperate by providing job opportunities and follow-up counseling services, more separation of offenders not only by type of offenses but by amenability to rehabilitation, and more pooling of state and local facilities.

An informed and active citizenry can do much to bring these about.

BUSINESS LEADERSHIP ESSENTIAL

Training and Employment

The importance of employment in the rehabilitation process puts a tremendous responsibility—and opportunity—in the laps of the business community. Businessmen should take the initiative in opening doors to jobs for ex-offenders by:

> Providing post- and pre-release employment opportunities in meaningful positions.
>
> Giving appropriate guidance to correctional administrators regarding job trends and anticipated employment openings.
>
> Mobilizing business and public support for improved industrial and vocational training programs in institutions.

Providing volunteer management expertise to advise on curriculum and equipment needed for realistic training.

Informing the memberships of business associations about the manpower resources available from correctional institutions.

An outstanding example of how businessmen can assist materially in reducing the chances of an ex-offender having to return to crime is *Project Transition*, a program conducted by the South Carolina Department of Corrections.

In June of 1971, this project began capitalizing on the excellent organizational structure of state and local Chambers of Commerce. The State Chamber, together with several of the local chambers in Columbia, Spartanburg, and Greenville, was actively interested and involved in exploring the possibility of sponsoring a "Safer Communities" project. The project draws upon existing programs, such as the National Alliance of Businessmen and the Jobs in the Business Sector (JOBS) program. Project Transition representatives, in cooperation with a number of Chamber of Commerce committees, approached business leaders with the idea of employing ex-offenders under established contractual arrangements of the JOBS program. The proposal has been received with interest and encouragement. Several contracts have been entered into between Project Transition and JOBS to hire and train ex-offenders.

In another dimension to the cooperative efforts between the South Carolina Department of Corrections and the chamber activities, the state Jaycees are assisting with the department's job development programs by surveying local job markets in many cities in the state on a monthly basis for the best opportunities available for placing ex-offenders.

A similar forward-looking program involving collaboration between the state corrections department, businessmen, and Chambers of Commerce has been developed in the state of Illinois and is producing excellent results.

Advice and Guidance in Employee-Management Relations

Unions and employee associations are organizing growing numbers of people who work in the field of corrections. Business leaders experienced in collective bargaining negotiations with organized labor can provide helpful guidance and direction to correctional administrators who lack experience and sophistication in labor negotiations and employee-management relations.

Developing Positive Public Attitudes

Citizen groups, with leadership from the business community, can become a powerful force in promoting public interest in, and support for, community-based correctional programs for nondangerous offenders.

An active and involved citizens group can:

Mobilize public and legislative support for diversified treatment services and alternatives to incarceration.

Stimulate the development of detoxification centers to divert alcoholic offenders out of the correctional system and into facilities with medical services.

Support the establishment of halfway houses and undertake a program to educate the community to the need for these facilities.

Organize volunteers to participate in tutoring programs for offenders.

Initiate a volunteer probation aid program to provide troubled youth with adult guidance and assistance with school work and finding jobs.[4]

Initiate a similar program to provide persons in institutions periodic contacts with people from the community who can listen to their problems, advise them, and even develop special programs to take institutionalized offenders into their homes and into the community on a well-organized basis.

Support surveys of correctional facilities and services in terms of personnel requirements, standards for the buildings, food, sanitary conditions, treatment of prisoners, rehabilitation services, etc.[5]

Support improvement and innovation in existing local correctional services. Recommendations of the National Institute of Law Enforcement and Criminal Justice, (the research and development branch of the Law Enforcement Assistance Administration) to improve the quality of treatment and service in local jails and correctional agencies include the following:

1. Effective screening and diagnosis of inmates to determine medical treatment needs, and the improvement of medical services to meet those needs.
2. Classification of probationers in differentiated caseloads to meet special offender needs.
3. Use of volunteers, ex-offenders, and low income persons as probation and parole staff assistants.
4. Redefinition of the role of the probation and parole officer as community organizer and advocate for the offender as well as a link to the community service agencies which satisfy the offenders needs.

Encourage other community groups to become involved in corrections reform and to support new correctional programs. The imperfections in our knowledge of the causes of criminal behavior and methods of correcting that behavior will inevitably lead to mistakes and setbacks in our search for new ways to reclaim offenders. The goal must always be to develop or restore in the offender the capacity for lawful productive behavior in the community—a goal for which punishment alone, in our complex, fast-moving society, is clearly an inadequate prescription for success.

CONCLUSION

Meaningful jobs must be available to the ex-offender to assure his rehabilitation, or the correctional system will fail. *Equal employment opportunities should be extended to all citizens.*

Crime prevention and criminal rehabilitation are economically advantageous to the businessman who hires an ex-offender, as well as to the public, which does not have to pay the high cost of building and operating more prisons and which benefits from a reduction in recidivism.

Business and community leaders have a responsibility to learn about new correctional methods and to endorse and actively support correctional reform at all levels, state and federal, as well as in their own community.

All citizens, and particularly business leaders, should work toward a correctional system that really corrects. Such an effort can only serve to help make our communities safer and better places in which to live and work.

NOTES

1. A comprehensive directory of halfway house facilities operated under the auspices of various public and private agencies, both in the United States and abroad, is compiled annually by the International Halfway House Association, 2316 Auburncrest, Cincinnati, Ohio 45219.

2. A good example of a pre-release center program is that operated by the Texas Department of Corrections, Huntsville, Texas.

3. The American Bar Association's Commission on Correctional Facilities and Services has established a national clearinghouse and educational program focusing on disseminating information regarding unreasonable employment restrictions which impair the ability of the rehabilitated offender to obtain suitable job opportunities and measures that have been taken to remove these obstacles. This project, conducted under contract with the Manpower Administration, U.S. Department of Labor, will ultimately attempt to use the resources and influence of the legal community to overcome legal and licensing restrictions that discriminate against the ex-offender.

4. The National Research Center of Volunteers in Courts in Boulder, Colorado, has given national leadership to such programs.

5. The American Correctional Association has developed a self-evaluation procedure for use by correctional agency personnel and is in the final stages of implementing an accreditation plan—based on the Association's *Manual of Correctional Standards*—for institutions and services. The voluntary accreditation program will be governed by an autonomous

accrediting body and will field survey-teams to make outside objective evaluations to see if facilities meet correctional standards.

REFERENCES

A Review of the Pre-Release Programs. Huntsville, Texas: Institute of Contemporary Corrections and the Behavioral Sciences, 1969, p. 110.

A Time to Act. Washington, D.C.: Joint Commission on Correctional Manpower and Training, 1969, p. 69.

Bagdikian, Ben H., Series of eight articles on Corrections, *Washington Post,* January 30-February 6, 1972.

California's Community Treatment Project in 1969: An Assessment of Its Relevance and Utility to the Field of Corrections. Sacramento: California Department of Youth Authority, 1969, p. 67.

California's Probation Subsidy. Sacramento: California Department of Youth Authority, 1969, p. 32.

Community Work: An Alternative to Imprisonment. Washington, D.C.: Correctional Research Associates, 1967, p. 21.

Correctional Reform. Washington, D.C.: Advisory Commission on Intergovernmental Relations, 1971, p. 13.

Deskbook on Organized Crime (rev. ed.). Washington, D.C.: Chamber of Commerce of the United States, 1972, p. 76.

Differences That Make the Difference. College Park, Maryland: American Correctional Association, Joint Commission on Correctional Manpower and Training, 1967, p. 68.

Directory of Correctional Institutions and Agencies of the United States of America, Canada and Great Britain. Washington, D.C.: American Correctional Association, 1969, p. 101.

Doleschal, Eugene. "Graduated Release," *Information Review on Crime and Delinquency,* December 1969, pp. 1–36.

———. "The Deterrent Effect of Legal Punishment: A Review of the Literature." *Crime and Delinquency Literature,* June 1969, pp. 1–17.

Harlow, Eleanor. "Intensive Intervention: An Alternative to Institutionalization—A Review of the Literature." *Crime and Delinquency Literature,* February 1970, pp. 3–46.

Manpower Development and Training in Correctional Programs: MDTA Experimental and Demonstration Findings No. 3. Washington, D.C.: Manpower Administration, U.S. Department of Labor, 1969, p. 199.

Manual of Correctional Standards. Washington, D.C.: American Correctional Association, 1969, p. 642. With Study Guide (1968), 126 pp.

Morrison, June. *A Survey: The Use of Volunteers in Juvenile Courts in the United States.* Tucson: University of Arizona Press, 1971, p. 24.

Marshaling Citizen Power Against Crime. Washington, D.C.: Chamber of Commerce of the United States, 1971, p. 133.

New Roles for Jails. Washington, D.C.: Bureau of Prisons, Department of Justice, 1969, p. 32.

Pre-Release Center. Huntsville: Texas Department of Corrections, 1968, p. 196.

Pownall, George A. *Employment Problems of Released Prisoners.* Washington, D.C., 1969, p. 319.

Probation. Chicago: American Bar Association, 1970, p. 110.

Project Challenge. Washington, D.C.: National Committee for Children and Youth, 1969, p. 139.

Project Crossroads (four reports). Washington, D.C.: National Committee for Children and Youth, 1971.

Rosow, Jerome M. "The Role of Jobs in a New National Strategy Against Crime." *Federal Probation*, June 1971, pp. 14–18.

Standard Act for State Correctional Services. New York: National Council on Crime and Delinquency, 1966, p. 35.

Standards for Selection of Probation and Parole Personnel. New York: National Council on Crime and Delinquency, 1968, p. 5.

Struggle for Justice (Society of Friends). Philadelphia: Hill and Wang, 1971, p. 192.

Task Force Report: Corrections (President's Commission on Law Enforcement and the Administration of Justice). Washington, D.C.: Government Printing Office, 1967, p. 222.

The Criminal Offender: What Should Be Done? (President's Task Force on Prisoner Rehabilitation). Washington, D.C.: Government Printing Office, 1970, p. 24.

The Residential Center: Corrections in the Community. Washington, D.C.: Bureau of Prisons, Department of Justice, 1969, p. 26.

Using Volunteers in Court Settings (Department of Health, Education and Welfare). Washington, D.C.: Government Printing Office, 1929, p. 227.

FILMS

The Dangerous Years, 16-mm., black-and-white, sound, 30 minutes. Produced by Wolper Association for Kemper Insurance, distributed by Modern Talking Picture Service, Inc., New York, New York 10036.

The Odds Against, 16-mm., black-and-white, sound, 32 minutes. Produced and distributed by The American Foundation, Institute of Corrections, Philadelphia, Pennsylvania 19107.

The Revolving Door, 16-mm., black-and-white, sound, 29 minutes. Produced and distributed by The American Foundation, Institute of Corrections, Philadelphia, Pennsylvania 19107.

The Price of a Life, 16-mm., black-and-white, sound, 29 minutes. Produced and distributed by The American Foundation, Institute of Corrections, Philadelphia, Pennsylvania 19107.

part two
IN LIEU OF INCARCERATION

Community corrections must not be isolated from other social agencies. Wallace Mandell discusses the reasons for noncooperation between corrections and other public and private agencies. He explores the barriers to social agency cooperation with corrections and offers some solutions for their integration. LaMar Empey sees the corrections response to crime as successively historical identities that he terms revenge, restraint, reformation, and reintegration. Robert Smith discusses probation subsidy, which has reduced commitments to state institutions in the past decade. Its success continues even though many criminals are committing high-fear crimes that make them ineligible for this form of probation.

chapter six

MAKING CORRECTION A COMMUNITY AGENCY

Wallace Mandell

Correction, as an agency of state and local governments, greatly needs the cooperation of the other public and private agencies, for it too is responsible for the well-being of society. In many instances it deals with the same population that requires and uses services of other public agencies. Nevertheless, to date it has had few working relations with, and has not been accepted as a member of, the family of community agencies. Leaders in the field of correction have repeatedly pointed out that the correctional institutions are one segment of the health and welfare services of a community. They insist that correctional agencies cannot be effective in their mission if other social agencies do not cooperate in an integrated rehabilitation program extending beyond the prison walls.

The resources—such as health, education, and welfare—necessary to enhance correctional programs exist in every community but are under the control of independent social agencies. Although these agencies are generally committed, at a policy level, to helping with correctional problems, they do not do so. Many of the reasons for this isolation of correctional agencies are grounded in the historic views of prisons, jails, and reformatories long held by the community. Therefore, the correctional agency is unable to negotiate for the provision of services crucial to its rehabilitative goals.

Ultimately, the total community is penalized by the refusal of other agencies to cooperate with correction. The population held within correctional institutions comes from the same deprived groups now being

Reprinted, with permission of the National Council on Crime and Delinquency, from *Crime and Delinquency* 17 (1971):281–88.

served by many of the health and welfare agencies. Generally, an inmate has had a long career of deviant educational and social adjustment before incarceration; usually he is a school dropout without employable skills, and the product of a multiple-problem home situation. It can be predicted that he will be a major consumer of many costly welfare and social services throughout his lifetime and will repeatedly return to burden the correctional system.

No matter how effective the rehabilitative treatment carried on inside a correctional setting may have been, it is easily vitiated by the inmate's experiences upon release. Usually, he confronts both the lack of a job and the lack of supportive family relationships. Often he has no place to live. Such adverse conditions can easily overwhelm even the inmate released from a highly rehabilitative institution, influencing him to return to the slum environment and to a gang or criminal social life. If he is convicted of another crime, the ex-inmate is not returned to the school or the family service agency which might have served him; correction again becomes the recipient of these failures in social adjustment. The community agencies do not suffer any immediate consequences of their policy of rejecting ex-inmates since they do not appear on their caseloads, but the community continues to pay a heavy penalty. Repeatedly, correction becomes the sole agency dealing with these societal rejects, even though such individuals may require the skills and resources of many agencies for rehabilitation.

BLOCKS TO SOCIAL AGENCY COOPERATION

Stigma

Many of the social, health, and welfare agencies, particularly the public agencies, are caught between contradictory pressures—the requirements to help the needy and the protective regulations that dictate the refusal of aid to clients who do not conform to community standards and regulation. Moreover, each of these agencies, while subscribing to the larger societal aims, has at the same time assumed the attitude of a specialist dealing with only a segment of the societal corporate body, and this attitude frees it to reject unsuitable clients. Among the reasons correction has been isolated from the family of agencies is that as an agency it is in itself socially stigmatized because its clients are nonconforming. These views have affected the attitude and willingness of other public and private agencies to cooperate with correction. Since social stigma is attached to anything connected with prisons, jails, and their inmates, agencies fear that by dealing with any of these they too will be stigmatized, and this stigma impedes performance of their primary functions and services.

Low Success Rate in Dealing with Difficult Population

Correction deals with an extremely difficult population. By usual standards inmates tend to be aggressive, sullen, manipulative, and unpredictable. The younger ones, especially, tend to reject authority and view with suspicion all those who seem to represent it. Before an effective program can begin, professional staff who find it hard to empathize with criminality must cross certain cultural and class boundaries. Most agencies with limited staff prefer to concentrate on clients who "can be helped." The inmate population contains the manifest failures of education, welfare, and health agencies that may have tried to solve the inmates' problems. Many of the inmates are also failures of the so-called correctional institutions, as evidenced by a large percentage of recidivism. With this double brand of failure on them, ex-prisoners are not a readily acceptable clientele. Since agencies can refuse or terminate cases at will, they do not have information on the consequences or effectiveness of their techniques, and their experience reinforces their belief that they cannot help the criminal population. Cases with little promise of success have been eliminated. The agencies have drifted into a position where they can rationalize their satisfaction with the repeated application of a standard "successful" technique to a limited population.

Lack of Funds and Resources

Every agency must work to maintain a publicly acknowledged successful operation. Financial support depends, in part, on such an image. Although correction is given complete authority over the physical—and, indirectly, the psychological—being of the individuals entrusted to its care, the community does not really wish to pay to support those who disregard the laws of society. Consequently, with the community's ambivalence toward the role of correction, financial and professional support for this agency is indifferently and reluctantly given. Furthermore, the jail cannot financially support the agencies from whom it requests services unless it is well-financed and permitted to do so.

The prison is a residential care facility operating under the limitations imposed by law. Since it does not control its intake, this eliminates exchange of clientele, one of the most valuable bases for cooperation among agencies. Another crucial factor is the shortage of money and manpower in all agencies; hence, competition among the agencies for these resources leads to expediency of service rather than overall planned community services. As Kahn points out, agencies often rival one another for treatment resources.[1] Since staff members are evaluated in terms of their effectiveness with cases or with clients, there may be competition even within an agency for the resources that would be helpful to a specific case. Because referrals are often made by shopping among agencies to see what resources are available rather than through apportionment of available community resources on the bases of an overview of needs and public setting of priorities, the criminal population, which is of considerable public concern, is disregarded.

Self-Sufficient Orientation

The penal institution is necessarily compelled to be a multiple-service agency, responsible for the physical and mental health and the law-abiding behavior of the inmates. There is a continuing attempt by correctional agencies to become self-sufficient. They try to treat their population by making professional resources available within their own organization. But professional roles which utilize warmth, friendliness, and personal concern as a means of inducing change in the client are not easily integrated into an institution whose primary task is custody, and the maintenance of control over inmates.

In the hope of improving the efficiency of the system and providing services which could not be obtained through cooperation with other community agencies, educators, psychologists, counselors, social workers, and other professionals have been brought into correctional systems. One of the effects of this has been to reduce the pressure on correctional administrators to negotiate with other agencies in the community to obtain services for the inmates. Furthermore, this has reduced the pressure for cooperation with agencies outside the community.

Poor Staff

Another block to correction's exchange of resources with other agencies is the disparity between the training and status of correctional staff and that of other agency staffs. The educational background of correctional personnel is generally low. Job requirements are also low because it is difficult to recruit good staff. The professional noncustodial correctional personnel, therefore, are the key staff involved in interagency efforts. Such trained staff are handicapped because all rehabilitative efforts must be kept within the limitations imposed by the usual security and custody priorities in jails and prisons. The low priority given professional treatment because of the custodial function makes it difficult to adhere to professional standards within the institutions. This lowers the prestige of the professional among his colleagues. The enforced limitations imposed by civil service rather than professional standards also tend to reduce the agency staff's respect for the correctional professional's position. Therefore, the correctional institution does not attract professionals on a par with those in other community agencies. This difference in quality of correctional personnel reinforces a lack of respect for correction as an agency by other agencies, which negatively affects cooperative efforts.

Communication Difficulties

The dearth of professional training and a shared scientifically oriented language in correction leads to difficulty in developing a common language with other agencies. This gap in communication further blocks the development of plans to meet problems which should be of mutual concern in effectively furthering community goals.

Resentment Against Other Agencies

Some agencies have widened the gap between themselves and correction by using the correctional agency as a weapon. Welfare service agencies, for instance, may threaten clients with imprisonment for failure to make child support payments.

The correctional system is also the terminal point in a constellation of systems that includes the police, the district attorney, and the judiciary. Each of these systems in turn determines whether the accused will be passed on to the next, a decision which may move the individual into the correctional system. After an individual has been found guilty, the court becomes an independent judicial decision-making mechanism to determine whether or not he is likely to make a successful adjustment under alternative forms of service. Judges, professionally trained in the law, are expected to make decisions that involve educational, psychological, and employment issues and to decide on the alternative resources available in the community for a specific individual.

In the sentencing process, to evaluate problems presented in each case requires varied professional skills and trained advisers, which even the most highly motivated judges and courts seldom possess. Therefore, as the simplest—and frequently the only—available alternative, cases are routed to the correctional institution. (This is particularly well exemplified in cases where a child's family is inadequate, and the court which has the authority to remove the child from the unfortunate home may place the child in jail for his protection.)

There are many other instances where correctional institutions are recipients of persons who should be handled by other institutions. As Buell[2] points out, the juvenile bureau of police departments has "fallen heir to a community-wide role for which it is likely to be ill-equipped." In many instances, it becomes the point where behavior symptomatic of psychological difficulties is first discovered. Such cases might more appropriately have been referred to the noncorrectional community. Correctional agencies resent being forced to accept inmates for whom they are not primarily intended. They resent the agencies which coerce inappropriate use of their already overcrowded facilities.

Defensiveness About Criticism

Correctional institutions have rarely been subject to public supervision or review by civilian boards. They have been answerable to governmental, political, and administrative structures. In a desire to protect themselves against criticism, they have been unwilling to open their facilities to inspection. Inadequate financing has resulted in shocking jail conditions. Jail personnel, operating as best they can with limited financial resources, fear public observation and criticism as threats to their methods and management. Hence, short-sighted institutional self-interest retards public involvement and interagency activity.

INTEGRATING CORRECTION INTO THE FAMILY OF AGENCIES

If resources are to be efficiently used for the benefit of the total community, cooperation among the community's agencies is imperative. The *Manual on Correctional Standards* states that operating a correctional system, or any of its parts, in isolation from community agencies ought to be a thing of the past.[3] However, while probation and parole have a long history of using other community agencies, this practice is not well developed by the administrators of correctional institutions.

The common goal for all agencies is currently obscure because of the lack of cooperation and liaison. To overcome agency resistance to liaison and cooperation, correction must develop a realistic view of community agency interaction, a view that would consider not only the ideals about the welfare of clientele but also the immediate advantages to be gained by each community agency itself. This one essential ingredient, reciprocity of services, represents the key to agency coordination, for all relationships between agencies may be defined as a form of mutual aid in achieving each agency's goals. Correctional agencies do not seem to be in a position to offer funds, personnel, facilities, or prestige to other agencies. What solutions are there?

Removal of Stigma

If we are to establish a change in the public image of correction, public attention must be focused on the rehabilitative institutions, not merely on the custodial ones. To accomplish this, correction must mobilize public support for rehabilitation programs and stimulate the interest of well-known citizens who can lend their personal prestige and community status for the benefit of correction. This requires recruiting individuals who are respected and powerful members of the community. To attract them correction must give them a specific role in policy-making, since influential citizens will not permit their names or resources to be used by institutions in which they have no part to play. A technique used toward this end is to establish citizen correctional boards or advisory committees. In the few instances where they now exist, their function is unsatisfactory because they are used merely as window-dressing to ward off public disapproval. Boards guard against negative public opinion or unjustified criticism of an agency only when they are participating in a genuine effort to improve a situation.

Citizen groups have an opportunity to make alliances through which they benefit from correction. For example, among those whom such a mutual relationship can benefit are the labor unions, which draw their strength from working groups. In the unions, correction can and should find a strong ally.

The stigma attached to correction, the public indifference to neglect of the prisons, and correction's lack of success in reform of inmates make it difficult to attract powerful or even ordinary support for necessary resources. Nevertheless, there are specific groups which can be interested in correction if they are made aware of the immediate or long-range benefits obtainable through such participation. This involves opening the doors of the Department of Correction to review by civilians and will require a change in the attitudes of correctional personnel.

Support can also be recruited from among citizens deeply concerned with their own children's vulnerability to delinquency. This group has a stake in seeing to it that correction offers rehabilitative programs that will restore inmates to good citizenship.

Social change has antiquated the services of some agencies. Correction offers such agencies an opportunity to revitalize their programs in offering services essential for inmate rehabilitation. Such new programs can involve community leadership and arouse popular interest and community support for these agencies.

Increased Finances

The financial resources of correction are usually far below its needs, particularly in the field of rehabilitation. Many heavily populated urban centers do not have a tax-base structure with which to support essential services. Usually jail rehabilitation services are poorly financed because of the high cost of custody. Therefore, it is necessary not only to press local governments for the better care and rehabilitation of jail inmates but also to seek other possible financial resources.

Foremost among the potential sources of funds is the federal government. It is currently committed to supporting new programs for the betterment of all citizens—the poor, the ignorant, the handicapped, and those subjected to the correctional system. These programs are being introduced at regional and local levels. The jails have vast populations falling into the categories of every conceivable need. In just this respect, they offer a tremendous laboratory for sociological, psychological, medical, and educational research on those who have not made successful adjustments to society. The findings can be applied to problems of those outside the prison as well as to the techniques of rehabilitating inmates. Grants by the federal government to universities, to correction, and to recognized social agencies for research in jails can be a most rewarding undertaking.

Upgrading of Personnel

The qualifications of correctional personnel, currently low because of the low scale of financing, lack of prestige, and poor salaries, must be improved. Once qualifications are upgraded, an enormous step in the redefinition of correction will have been taken. However, there is a significant group of administrators who believe that raising salaries will, by itself, upgrade personnel. This is not true. When salary raises are not attached to new position descriptions and position requirements, the result is that existing personnel are reclassified under the new salary scales. They naturally understand these increments to be rewards for their past performance and are thus more reluctant than ever to change their patterns of performance. In addition, the raises put staff in a position where they are earning more than their educational background could bring them in any other employment. As a result, they become locked into the system, making it difficult to recruit younger, better-educated personnel. The upgrading of a system can be accomplished only through new position descriptions and requirements, not through better salary schedules.

The introduction of personnel not committed to the old system is one way an administrator can produce change. However, in institutions which operate under civil service rules it is difficult to change traditional habits and routines. There is no great turnover of staff which would make it possible to introduce radical changes through the newcomers. Moreover, senior personnel are apt to resist changes in customary attitudes and practices. Despite these handicaps, an administration committed to programs of rehabilitation can improve the quality of services through reorientation of personnel. In-service training as well as return to formal educational institutions for certificates and degrees must serve as the basis for promotion.

Evaluating the Success Rate

Correctional success has been judged by the most negative of standards; centered on custody, it has been measured according to the rate of escapes. By comparison, health and welfare agencies are judged by the success of their clients after completing the service program—e.g., educational and vocational success. Under the custodial definition, correction makes little effort to determine what happens to its clients upon their release.

The effect of this limited definition of success is evidenced by the energy expended to maintain a low rate of escapes as against that expended to reduce the rate of recidivism. If correction is to become a rehabilitative agency and to perform on a par with other social agencies, the criteria for success must be changed.

New Programs and Research

No single program can be effective in rehabilitating all segments of the correctional population; in fact, most of the principles now recommended as bases for programs have yet to be tested in a concrete situation. There must be a substantial investment in research on the principles of correctional rehabilitation and evaluation of the outcomes of programs. It is generally wasteful for single agencies to attempt evaluative research alone. They seldom have the resources to devote to research or the organizational capacity to undertake the manipulations required to reach conclusions about the effectiveness of programs. The practical solution to this problem must center in cooperative relationships between correctional agencies and universities, the assembling places of research and training personnel. The correctional institutions have resources attractive to universities—an important social problem, available subjects, and excellent laboratory facilities which lend themselves to research; together, correction and the universities have the potential to obtain funds for new programs. Another important advantage of such research activities to correctional systems is that the prestige of these affiliations will raise correction to the level of other agencies and give it some of the additional bargaining power it so badly needs.

NOTES

1. Alfred J. Kahn, *Planning Community Services for Children in Trouble* (New York: Columbia University Press, 1963), p. 443.
2. Bradley Buell, et al., *Community Planning for Human Services* (New York: Columbia University Press, 1952), p. 289.
3. American Correctional Association, *Manual of Correctional Standards*, Washington, D.C., 1969, p. 280.

chapter seven
CORRECTIONAL HISTORY

Lamar T. Empey

Current trends in reactions to crime are best understood in terms of an historical perspective. Correctional practices have been revolutionized twice in the past two centuries, and these revolutions have important implications for contemporary development.[1]

The first revolution occurred in the late eighteenth and early nineteenth centuries and was generated in part by the growth of Western democracy, and in part by the rational philosophers and legalists of that period. The latter had two objectives in mind. First, they wished to establish a more rational and equitable legal system. They reacted against the practice of basing penalties for crime on whether the offender and his victim were noblemen or commoners. All men, they believed, should be treated equally, not according to their stations in life but according to the crimes they had committed.

Second, they wished to make punishment more humanitarian. They believed that imprisonment should be substituted for the earlier forms of exile, execution, and corporal punishment. Imprisonment would serve as the means of eliminating the cruelties and excesses of that time. Accordingly, imprisonment became the predominant penalty for felonies in most of the Western world during the nineteenth century.[2]

The causation assumptions upon which these philosophers based their corrective policies were that men are rational beings who operate on a pleasure-pain principle, doing that which gives them pleasure and avoiding that which gives them pain. They believed, therefore, that reactions to crime should be rationally based on the same principle: light punishment for light crimes, heavy punishment for serious crimes, making sure in each case that the pain of punishment slightly exceeds

From *Alternatives to Incarceration* (Washington, D.C.: U.S. Government Printing Office, 1967), pp. 1–11.

the pleasure of the crime. By utilizing imprisonment and establishing, by statute, a prescribed punishment for each kind of offense, they believed that they could control crime effectively.

Given this conceptual framework, the objectives that were imposed upon correctional facilities were relatively clear and straightforward: the offender was to be punished and society was to be protected. Imprisonment would not only be more humane but would also help to deter other rational men from crime. It would be a lesson, teaching that crime does not pay.

This approach pervaded the legal practices of Western civilization and it has by no means been totally abandoned. It is still very much a part of our normative and legal structure today. Nevertheless, it has been shown to have several deficiencies.

Imprisonment has not worked out as an impartial and uniform reaction to crime. All criminals are not caught and legislatures cannot prescribe, like a pill, the way courts and correctional organizations should react to each offender, depending not upon situational or personal characteristics but upon the crime he committed. It is simply too mechanistic a procedure to deal with the complex problems that characterize crime and criminals.

Second, the desired deterrent and rehabilitative effect of imprisonment was not borne out by accumulated evidence. Crime did not decrease, especially where long and repeated imprisonment was involved. It seemed to increase rather than decrease the likelihood of further violations. Furthermore, punishment through imprisonment was not universally applicable or adequate for such offenders as drug addicts, sexual psychopaths, the mentally deficient, or the mentally ill.

Finally, the number of prisoners confined continued to increase, resulting in constantly overcrowded prisons. The result not only questioned whether imprisonment was a more humanitarian response to crime but made it clear that the cost of imprisonment would eventually be prohibitive. The cost of housing, guarding, and meeting all the needs of prisoners would eventually become too great for society to bear.

The late nineteenth and early twentieth centuries, therefore, were marked by a decline in this classical approach to corrections and a second revolution was introduced. In addition to the problems generated by the first revolution, the second revolution gained impetus through the growth of Freudian psychology and the social sciences. Freudian psychology, for example, suggested that crime is not always a deliberate defiance of social norms but may be an unconscious response to personal problems. The offender may be *sick* rather than *wicked*. His violation of rules is more an illness than a conscious choice to do wrong.[3]

The social sciences, meanwhile, pointed to the influence of complex learning processes, to conflicting subcultural influences, and to conditions of class and ethnicity as sources of nonconformity, rather than a deliberate misuse of free will. The result was a tendency to view the offender as a deprived or handicapped person whose major deficiencies were to be found in his mental or emotional make-up. Treatment rather than punishment was called for, professionalism and specialization rather than a generalized response.

The treatment orientation that was introduced resulted in two striking changes in legal and correctional decision making: (1) a *deferral* of correctional decisions from the time of sentencing, and (2) a *division* of responsibilities among more persons for making those decisions about the offender.[4] Prior to the second revolution, a criminal's fate was almost always decided once his guilt was established. The court was expected to impose sentence as defined by statute. If imprisonment was used, the legal system not only specified an exact duration for the penalty but even designated the institution to be used and the program to be followed, such as solitary confinement or hard labor.

With the introduction of the second revolution, however, all of this began to change. Statutes were introduced which permitted the court to defer sentencing decisions until the offender could be studied and recommendations made to the judge. Probation officers, psychiatric consultants, and others became advisers to the court. Decision responsibility was divided. Furthermore, it was divided not only among people close to the court, but throughout the whole correctional process. The indeterminate sentence was also introduced, so that classification processes and decision making within correctional systems were the means by which an offender's fate was decided.

In many systems, specialized treatment programs were added and housed in diversified correctional institutions. Maximum, medium, and minimum security prisons were established; forestry camps, farms, or small cottage programs were designed. Hypothetically, these were expected to respond to classes of offenders, rather than to classes of crimes: juveniles, addicts, sex offenders, habitual criminals. Specialized treatment also made use of professional counseling, psychotherapy, and medical care, as well as the more conventional academic and vocational training.

The result was such specialized roles for correctional people as administration, care and feeding, control, casework, education, therapy, vocational training. Planning was separated from operations, and treatment separated from custody. Even after incarceration, the use of parole further deferred the sentencing decision formerly exercised by the court and lodged it, instead, in parole boards and parole officers. Thus, at least in theory, the response of corrections during the second revolution concentrated much more upon the individual than upon his crime, more upon divided and deferred decision making than upon legal prescription and court action.

The shift of large masses of people from rural to urban environments contributed also to the increases in professionalization and specialization. As the informal controls and functions of the rural family and neighborhood diminished, such complex formal systems as police, court, welfare, juvenile court, probation, and parole were given the responsibility of responding formally to the commission of crime. In the larger cities these formal systems became complex bureaucracies and the people who manned them became the formal agents of social control.

Yet, despite these developments, there has been a disturbing accumulation of negative evidence relative to the efficacy of the second revolution. Current practices are undoubtedly more humane than earlier forms of punishment, but delinquency and recidivism seem to have continued at a high rate, and the few studies of individualized treatment that are available present discouraging results.

On one hand, there is some indication that, through specialization, the occupational and educational skills of offenders are being increased and that, within correctional programs, attitudes are being changed. But somehow, these changes are not translated to the community where the offender's adjustment is submitted to the ultimate test. Programs do not seem to address adequately what seem to be some of his most important problems, those having to do with his interaction with, and reintegration into, the law-abiding community.

There is a long list of difficult, unanswered questions: Is individualized and specialized treatment the answer? Do our efforts result in a correctional approach which constitutes a coherent system throughout? Are specialized functions related logically to each other and to the factors which lead to crime? Are the criminals with whom we deal a representative population or only the tip of a "criminal iceberg," which remains largely unstudied and untouched? In our concern with individual offenders, are we not missing other variables which may be crucial in determining the success or failure of correctional programs?

Current trends seem, even if indirectly, to be in response to such questions. It is Schrag's opinion, therefore, that we are in the early stages of a third major correctional revolution,[5] one whose philosophy is characterized by two main features. The first suggests that society, itself, is badly in need of change. As Schrag puts it:

> It is generally recognized that various kinds of unconventional behavior are sometimes richly rewarded. Wealth, power and prestige are frequently highly regarded irrespective of the means by which they are achieved. Political corruption and white-collar crime are often viewed as unavoidable nuisances. But there is also increasing evidence of public demand for control in these areas. New attention is

being devoted to the tendency for some respected and influential persons to be favorably disposed toward illegitimate activities if they provide sufficient material benefits and good prospects for escaping detection or censure. These are some of the previously neglected aspects of crime and correction that are attracting the systematic attention of correctional experts.

The second feature of the rising philosophy places more emphasis on the compelling pressures that are exerted upon the offender by persons living in his community, by the social groups to which he belongs, by our overall culture, and, within it, a host of dissonant subcultures. It is the cultural and subcultural matrix from which the offender comes that prescribes his goals and his standards of conduct. And it is this matrix which will heavily influence whether he will become a success or a failure, a criminal or a law-abiding citizen.

Delinquency and crime, and reactions to them, are social products and are socially defined. Society, not individuals, defines rules, labels those who break rules, and prescribes ways for reacting to the labeled person. There are times when the societal process of defining, labeling, and reacting is problematic, times when it is far more influential in determining who shall enter the correctional process and what its outcome will be than techniques designed solely to change offenders.[6]

The labeling process is often a means of isolating offenders from, rather than integrating them in, effective participation in such major societal institutions as schools, businesses, unions, churches, and political organizations. These institutions are the major access to a successful, nondelinquent career. Those who are in power in them are the gatekeepers of society and, if offenders and correctional programs are isolated from them, then the personal wishes and characteristics of offenders will have only marginal bearing on whether correctional programs succeed or fail.

This is not to deny individual differences, nor the importance of inculcating individual responsibility, but it does make clear that correctional techniques are terribly near-sighted which fail to take into account the offender's social and cultural milieu. Successful adjustment on his part will require some kind of personal reformation, but it will also require conditions within the community which will encourage his reintegration into nondelinquent activities and institutions. Fundamentally, this is a community function. Reintegration may succeed or fail depending upon the community's labeling and reacting processes. If they are such as to permit the offender to discard the label of criminal and to adopt another label, the integration process will be aided. But, if they insist on holding the former offender at arm's length, then any desire on his part for reintegration may be of little consequence. Until the labeling and reacting processes are changed he will remain, by definition, an offender, an outsider.

It is at this point that the third revolution and the interests of this paper are juxtaposed. Both are concerned with contemporary efforts to deal with reintegration as well as reformation. The paper will analyze correctional efforts which are concerned with establishing alternatives to incarceration and relating correctional efforts more closely to the community. The analysis will be limited to programs for the accused or adjudicated offender and not devoted to the broad field of prevention. This is an arbitrary choice, because sound preventative programs are the best alternative to incarceration. But recruitment to criminal and delinquent ranks will inevitably continue and, for that reason, the concern will be with means for preventing recidivism rather than preventing crime, with the known offender rather than the pre-delinquent.

The list of alternatives to incarceration is growing and includes pretrial release, probation, programs in which offenders live at home but are required to report daily to a correctional program, small residential group centers, halfway houses, and, finally, a variety of advisory councils and committees by which private citizens are enlisted to participate in the reintegration of the offender.

Such programs will be discussed in detail, but it is important first to summarize the implications of the historical review presented above. It includes emergent issues which should be made explicit and considered in any third correctional revolution. Community programs are the current fad, and if some of the mistakes of earlier revolutions are to be avoided, we should now benefit from these mistakes.

IMPLICATIONS OF CORRECTIONAL HISTORY

Our historical review has indicated, as Glaser suggests, that man's historical approach to criminals can be conveniently summarized as a succession of three R's: Revenge, Restraint, and Reformation. Revenge was the primary response prior to the first revolution in the eighteenth and nineteenth centuries. It was replaced during that revolution by an emphasis upon restraint. When the second revolution occurred in the late nineteenth and early twentieth centuries, reformation became an important objective. Attention was focused upon the mental and emotional make-up of the offender, and efforts were made to alter these as the primary sources of difficulty. Finally, we may be on the verge of yet another revolution in which a fourth concept will be added to Glaser's list of R's: Reintegration.[7]

Students of corrections, like those of mental health, feel that a singular focus upon reforming the offender is inadequate. Successful rehabilitation is a two-sided coin, including reformation on one side and reintegration on the other. Unless both are used, correctional programs will fail.

There are some who will argue that movement into a third revolution at this time is premature. For example, society itself is still very ambivalent about the offender. It has never really replaced all vestiges of revenge or restraint, simply supplemented them. Thus, while it is unwilling to kill or lock up all offenders permanently, it is also unwilling to give full support to the search for alternatives.

On the other hand, there are those who argue that the treatment philosophy of the second revolution has never really been implemented, that true diagnosis followed by individualized treatment has never been possible in correctional settings. If it were, better results would ensue. But this argument overlooks one very important program which, if uncorrected, will undoubtedly thwart efforts to make the treatment model work. The problem is the lack of knowledge and comprehensive correctional theory upon which to base clinical treatment models. They are in a primitive state. Consequently, as Gibbons has pointed out, more personnel, smaller caseloads, higher salaries, and better training can never solve the correctional problem until the conceptual deficiency is worked out. Until improvements are made in the theories which underlie treatment, changes in correctional structures, by themselves, will be unlikely to produce dramatic reductions in delinquency and criminality.[8] Instead, we will have more refined failure.

In a similar vein, Korn and McCorkle agree that our thinking is very muddy. The bleak facts are, they say, that just as the monstrous punishments of the eighteenth century failed to curtail crime, so, during the twentieth century, we have failed likewise to do so.[9] The reason, they say, is that we have equated humanitarianism with treatment and failed to recognize that the humane care of offenders is not necessarily the same thing as reducing crime, that our practices relative to reducing the problems are sadly lacking.

Perhaps it would be important, therefore, to try to focus more pointedly on just what our difficulties have been. The ones that stand out most clearly are our lack of knowledge and the unsystematic approaches we have taken to corrections. We have been guided, primarily, by what John C. Wright calls "intuitive opportunism," a kind of goal-oriented guessing, a strategy of activity.[10]

Instead of proceeding systematically to define and then to solve our correctional problems, we have made sweeping changes in correctional programs, without adequate theoretical definitions of the causes of crime or the development of logical strategies to deal with them.

The problem, however, is not inherent in some kind of human perversity. Society is far less sophisticated in the development of scientific procedures by which to deal with such human problems as crime than it is in the development of scientific methods to alter the technological elements of culture. The social sciences are just coming into their own. There is not only a profound lack of scientific knowledge about ways to develop better correctional methods, but a general disinclination to approach the search for that knowledge in a disciplined way. That is why a strategy of activity has prevailed. Correctional units—police, courts, rehabilitative programs—have seldom been considered on any total or comprehensive basis as constituting a single system. Theory has rarely been used. New practices such as casework, psychotherapy, remedial education, group counseling, have all been added piecemeal to existing systems and, instead of replacing older philosophies, have simply supplemented them. As a result, it is difficult to tell whether new practices contribute to, or only confuse, older objectives and practices.

The possibility has not been adequately considered that the impact of new techniques may be overwhelmed by negative influence, already existing in correctional systems, or the possibility that their introduction may produce negative effects upon procedures already present. Individual practices, which by themselves might have been helpful, often seem to generate conflict when joined irrationally with other practices. For example, the tendency for custody and treatment people to conflict with each other in correctional institutions often contributes to the cynicism, rather than the reformation, of inmates. Inmates are encouraged to concentrate upon means for exploiting the rift among staff members, rather than working with staff people to resolve common problems. What has been lacking in the past, therefore, is some consideration of correctional problems in organizational teams and the lack of adequate knowledge and theory-building by which to approach solutions in a more systematic way.

If the range of alternatives for solving the correctional problem were narrow, well organized, and familiar, then the best approach might be a strategy of activity. However, the range of possibilities for solving it is not narrow, but is broad, uncertain, and disorganized. Our state of knowledge is primitive. Consequently, a strategy of activity has not only failed to approach correctional problems systematically but has also failed to provide means either for avoiding repetitive errors or for pinpointing reasons for success, should success occur. Whatever progress has been made has been halting and uneven: the organizational patterns which have developed have been the product of a wandering kind of social evolution which is inefficient at best.

Perhaps a more promising strategy would be a strategy of search, one which would commit resources and set target dates which are more consonant with the difficult problems involved. The search for solutions will involve decades or generations and require a philosophy which recognizes that solutions cannot be stated in advance but must be pursued. No one knows with certainty just what the most promising programs will be. That is why careful study should accompany efforts to find better solutions.

A strategy of search would hope to impose the rigors of scientific investigation in a way that is analogous to contemporary efforts to conquer space. The efforts of theoreticians, scientists, and engineers are united in a common effort. It is recognized that solutions will cost millions of dollars and extend over decades. The strategy is such that new programs not only produce a cumulative record, useful in preventing repetitive errors, but also in organizing a plan of attack. Those who are involved have some shared idea of where they are going and where they have been.[11] Corrections could benefit from such a strategy, for it would give corrections people the advantage of being able to learn from failure, to benefit from adversity as well as success, so that their progress might be less random.

If the third revolution in corrections is to be more successful than the revolutions of the past, greater attention will have to be devoted to the theoretical and scientific problems inherent in the revolution. The problem is not just an abstract one for the theoreticians but is a fundamental issue confronting both state and federal governments. Rarely do public agencies, particularly on the state level, devote money to developmental research and quality control in the way that private enterprise does in its attempts to develop a more efficient technology. Yet, organizational and human problems are probably more complicated than technological problems and require a greater, not a lesser, expenditure of funds. Both local and national governments lack centralized information systems by which to evaluate their correctional efforts or to accumulate knowledge about such various organizations as police, judicial, and correctional, which contribute to the correctional endeavor. Literally, there is no repository by which one could study recidivism or correctional effectiveness on a national level.

Similarly, very little theoretically based, experimental research is being conducted within public correctional systems. Governmental organizations need not conduct such research as an exclusive endeavor, but they could certainly do more to bring action and research people together. Correctional innovation requires not only interdisciplinary collaboration but legislative, bureaucratic, and financial legitimation. It is significant that, while private enterprise may devote as much as 50 percent of its budget to research and development, states which are hailed as leaders in the correctional field devote less than 1 percent of their budgets to research. This picture obviously must be altered if correctional programs are to be made more effective.

THE CORRECTIONAL PROCESS

When methods of dealing with offenders are considered, there is a tendency to think primarily of imprisonment and what happens after the establishment of guilt in a court. But this is a very limited view of a vast correctional system in which police, courts, and correctional personnel play key roles. The correctional process actually begins with the first contact between the alleged offender and the police, and may not end until it culminates eventually in parole. Between these two poles are a host of decision points and correctional alternatives: whether to arrest; whether to place on probation, to fine, or to imprison; where to imprison, for how long, and under what conditions; when to parole, when to terminate parole.

These key points in the correctional process have rarely, if ever, been analyzed in total, because decisions at each of them are made by specialists in vastly different organizations, including police, district attorneys, various judges and referees, probation officers, jail and institutional personnel, and parole officers. The only people who experience all of them are the offenders who are inserted into the process and go through it. Yet, a better understanding of the total process is necessary if the key points are to be identified at which alternatives to incarceration might be implemented.

For purposes of this analysis, the total correctional process will be divided into three parts:

The pre-trial period. The pre-trial period is a port-of-entry into the correctional system. It is a crucial period because there is increasing evidence that the mere insertion of a person into the system—especially through detention or jail while waiting adjudication of guilt or innocence—may increase, rather than lessen, the likelihood that he will remain in the system and be a continuing problem to the state. The major concern in this period is whether the person should be incarcerated while awaiting disposition of his case or whether he should be released to one of a number of alternatives.

Important questions are: What are the consequences of detention? What are the virtues or dangers in taking other courses of action? What kinds of modification in the correctional process might be considered relative to pre-trial confinement?

The post-trial period. If the offender is found guilty, judges and correctional personnel are confronted with a basic choice of whether to imprison him or to choose among a variety of other alternatives. Ordinarily, probation or a fine may be used for the juvenile, the first offender, and the person who commits a nonserious crime. But what if there is serious concern over the use of fines or probation for some offenders? What other alternatives, other than incarceration, are available? What are the implications of these alternatives? What modifications in the correctional system might be needed if they are to be used?

The choices that are made here are no less important than those made in the pre-trial period. The post-trial period is a second port-of-entry, one which leads either into a supervised, yet continuing participation in ordinary community life, or into a complex time of incarceration in which the process of labeling by society or the process of labeling one's self by the individual is solidified. If the choice is incarceration, then, more than ever, the status of "criminal," "lawbreaker," "outsider," is likely to be assigned to the offender. These are not inconsequential definitions but are likely to leave an imprint that will be lifelong. That is why the choice of alternatives during this period is crucial.

The post-incarceration period. Assuming that all correctional decisions have led to incarceration for the offender, there is still the possibility that the period of incarceration might be shortened or supplemented by other alternatives. In addition to traditional parole, there might be other ways to deal with the offender so that his return to the community will be aided or speeded up. What are these alternatives? What is the rationale for using them, their possible strengths and weaknesses? What modification would have to be made in correctional systems to accommodate them? Theoretically, they are of crucial importance because incarceration enhances the problem of reintegration. The adjustment of the individual to his incarceration is not the same as that which is needed as he returns to the community. He is not the same person who left it; his imprisonment doubtless makes him a different person, one who possesses problems which he did not possess before he was imprisoned, especially if his confinement was for an extended period in a maximum security setting. Instead of being passive and obedient, as was expected of him in prison, he is expected on his return to the community to be self-sufficient and responsible; instead of having the smallest of decisions made for him, he now has to make career choices of the greatest magnitude. That is why considerable attention has been devoted to a search for post-incarceration facilities which will aid in the re-entry problem.

INTERDEPENDENCE OF CORRECTIONAL DECISIONS

A vital point in considering new correctional alternatives is the interdependence of the various choices that might be made. Whatever changes are made in one of the three major parts of the correctional process will influence all other periods. It is impossible to change police, judicial, or correctional practices at one point without organizational consequences at other points. For example, a decision during the pre- or post-trial periods to incarcerate fewer offenders very likely will mean that those who are eventually incarcerated may be the least promising of all offenders, and thus make more difficult the task of dealing with them. If this is the case, the impact on both prisons and parole will be noticeable. Parole failure rates will probably increase. If one is not conscious, therefore, of such a possibility he may misinterpret this rise in failure rates and blame it on the decreased efficiency of prison personnel and parole officers, when, in fact, the decreased efficiency is due to decisions made earlier in the process. Thus, the organizational consequences of decision making should always be kept in mind, even though the decisions are made by specialized groups, each of which may not be aware of its impact on others.

NOTES

1. For a broader development of issues, see Clarence Schrag, "Contemporary-Correction: An Analytical Model," preliminary draft of paper prepared for the President's Commission on Law Enforcement and the Administration of Justice, mimeographed, February 1966.
2. Daniel Glaser, "The Prospect for Corrections," paper prepared for the Arden House Conference on Manpower Needs in Corrections, mimeographed, 1964.
3. Jackson Toby, "Is Punishment Necessary?" *Journal of Criminal Law, Criminology and Police Science* 55 (September 1964): 332–37.
4. Glaser, op. cit., pp. 2–3.
5. Schrag, op. cit., p. 12.
6. For a summary of the subject, see Howard S. Becker, *Outsiders* (New York: Free Press, 1963), Chapter 1.
7. Glaser, op. cit.
8. Don C. Gibbons, *Changing the Lawbreaker* (Englewood Cliffs, N.J.: Prentice-Hall, 1965), pp. 14–16.
9. Lloyd W. McCorkle and Richard Korn, "Resocialization Within Walls," *Annals of the American Academy of Political Science*, CCXCIII (May 1954), pp. 94–5.
10. John C. Wright, "Curiosity and Opportunism," *Trans-Action* II (January-February 1965): 38–40.
11. Ibid., pp. 38–9.

chapter eight
A QUIET REVOLUTION: PROBATION SUBSIDY

Robert L. Smith

Not all revolutions are dramatic, involving radical upheaval and violent destruction. Some revolutions "do their thing" quietly, bringing about significant changes without a great deal of conspicuous attention.

A quiet revolution of significant proportions began in the California correctional system in 1966 with the introduction of a *special probation supervision subsidy*. It has begun to change the nature of corrections by quietly modifying the profile of the *entire* correctional system.

HISTORICAL PERSPECTIVE

County probation is the backbone of corrections in California. Introduced in 1903, it has grown immensely in size, professional competence, and importance. After World War II, the rapid expansion and unplanned growth of probation prevented probation from fulfilling its promise as one of the greatest social inventions of the twentieth century. The riddle facing California was how to help probation achieve its promise, to maintain the integrity and autonomy of local probation services, and to reduce the rate of commitments to state institutions, while reducing the costs to the taxpayers for a rapidly expanding service.

The 1964 Probation Study generated fifteen major recommendations for improvements in the state's correctional system. One of these was a proposal designed to improve probation supervision services and reduce commitments to the state. The first step in implementing this plan was

From *Delinquency Prevention Reporter* (May 1971), pp. 3–7. Reprinted by permission.

taken on March 22, 1965, with the introduction of Senate Bill 822, which became a new declaration of social policy in the probation field. This was the beginning of California's "quiet revolution."

Senate Bill 822, which subsequently became Sections 1820 through 1827 of the Welfare and Institutions Code, clearly recognized probation as the most viable alternative to a massive program of incarceration. Senate Bill 822 supported probation by encouraging its use as an alternative to incarceration. *The incentive was financial aid to those counties that voluntarily participated in the program and reduced commitments below a calculated level.*

California's Probation Subsidy was founded on three basic assumptions: (1) probation is the least costly correctional service available; (2) probation is as effective, if not more effective, than most institutional forms of correctional care; (3) grants of probation could be increased without substantially increasing the number of crimes committed by probationers. There is considerable evidence accumulating to suggest that these assumptions were correct. There is no question that one of the objectives of the program is being achieved—reduced commitments to state institutions.

WHY A SUBSIDY BASED ON PERFORMANCE?

Probation in principle had been accepted in California since 1903, but it had been county-based, county-operated, and county-financed. Prior to 1965, token support was offered by the state in the form of consultation, training, and limited subsidies for juvenile camps and ranches. The state had not, however, declared a social policy that accepted or acknowledged publicly that state correctional workloads are directly affected by the decision-making actions of the local courts and county probation departments to commit to the state or treat locally.

Studies carried out in 1948, 1957, 1961, and 1964 all concluded that the use of probation could be expanded safely and substantial numbers of persons diverted from the state correctional system, if the state were willing to offer some financial incentive to county probation for increasing the number of probation grants. In turn, each study had proposed to enrich probation services by improving the quality of protection offered the citizen and the quality of service offered the convicted offender. Each report was submitted to the proper authority, but no action resulted. Everyone believed in probation, but not enough to finance a level of service that might make a difference.

The 1964 Probation Study established that at least 25 percent of the new admissions coming into the Department of Corrections and the Department of the Youth Authority could be handled safely and effectively in the community with good probation supervision Services. There was every evidence that the courts and probation departments could and would increase the use of probation if given the opportunity.

Historically, one of the main problems facing probation was its inability to provide meaningful supervision. This was recognized by the courts, by law enforcement agencies, by probationers, and by probation officers themselves. Probation caseloads were excessive, in most instances. Probation officers were denied the opportunity to provide good surveillance and even less individualized care and help to probationers. The median caseload in 1964 was over 200 cases. Juvenile probation officers carried more than 80 cases. The problem then was to find a means whereby probation departments could provide an improved level of service, and the state, through offsetting costs, could support the enriched level of probation service in a way that would help control rising correctional costs and taxes.

Since state funds, like county funds, are not limitless, monies diverted to counties from the state had to come from savings made at the state level. The state had a real and vested interest in probation, but it could not commit funds blindly to the support of any or all probation services without some principle or criterion for performance. California elected to use as its measure of performance *reduced commitments to state institutions*. Reduced commitments produced state savings that could be diverted to support probation. In doing so, it forced counties to consider carefully the financial consequences to their own programs whenever making commitments to the state, a consideration that was frequently overlooked at the local level. Financial reward was to be based on reduced commitments and the delivery of a service.

Performance spoke to fiscal responsibility and reasonableness for both the state and county. It is a hard standard. In recognizing that institutional costs under any circumstances are much higher than excellent probation services, the adoption of probation supervision susidy based on performance permitted California to reverse a trend of institutionalizing offenders, rather than treating them in the community.

HOW SUBSIDY WORKS

Counties wishing to participate in California's Special Probation Supervision program submit a proposal to the Director of the Department of the Youth Authority by July 1 of each year, conforming to published standards established by the department. Counties operating approved programs and reducing their commitments from a previously established base rate (level of performance) are paid per case for the percentage reduction they achieve in commitments to state correctional institutions. The payment by the state is sufficient to provide enriched services for not only the one new admission the county does not commit, but several eligible cases already under local probation supervision. Experience during the first four years of operation shows that the county can offer improved services to three or five probations for every new uncommitted case held at the county level. Dependent children are the only cases excluded from special supervision, since it is the department's belief that these cases are more appropriately handled outside of the justice system.

The benchmark by which a county is measured is its average past commitment performance (for both adults and youths) over a five-year period beginning in 1959 and continuing through 1963, or the two years 1962-63, whichever was higher. This average commitment rate per 100,000 population becomes the "base experience rate." It is the permanent reference against which improvements, or reductions in commitments, are measured. The standard used to measure improved performance is particularly relevant, since it measures improved performance of the county's own commitment performance over a period of time, and in relation to its population. A county competes against its own past practice.

Under this plan, the state pays a county "X amount of dollars" based on the percentage that it reduces each year's commitments of adults and youths from its past base experience rate. For example, if on the basis of a county's population and base experience rate the state would expect the county to commit 100 people to state correctional facilities but, in fact, the county sends only 90 people, then a 10 percent reduction in the commitment rate has been achieved. The 10 uncommitted cases represent well over $40,000 savings to the state. The county can be reimbursed the portion of the money which it saved the state on these cases, up to a maximum of $40,000 (payments per case range from a low of $2080 to a maximum of $4000). A county is reimbursed only for actual expenditures made in providing specialized supervision services to probationers in a manner consistent with their *approved* proposal. The actual amount of reimbursement for a given percentage reduction will vary from county to county, since the base experience rates vary.

The fiscal soundness of the program is based on a very simple principle derived from business—*performance*, not promise, counts. It is performance by the county, and not promise or good intention by the county, that permits the state to reimburse any services which are provided more effectively and at less cost by county probation departments. Services are first rendered by the county and then paid for by the state.

The 1965 legislature intended that subsidy would increase the protection afforded citizens, encourage the more even administration of justice and the rehabilitation of offenders, and, thereby, reduce the necessity for commitments to state correctional institutions. As the following information demonstrates, probation has done very well in fulfilling these legislative expectations.

FOUR YEARS OF ACCOMPLISHMENT

California's Probation Subsidy began operations in July 1, 1966, with thirty-one counties involved. In 1970-71, there are forty-five counties participating, representing well over 97 percent of the total state population. Proposed programs are in excess of $14 million.

Probably the most marked change to be noted since probation subsidy began occurred in the types of sentences imposed by the superior courts. Sentences to prison and the Department of the Youth Authority have been substantially reduced, while there has been a corresponding increase in the proportion placed on probation. For example, in 1965, 23.3 percent of convicted superior court defendants were sent to state prison. In 1969, this figure had dropped to 9.8 percent. In the three years from 1966 through 1969, the active superior court probation caseload increased by 53 percent, whereas for the prior three-year period (1963-1966) the rise was only 17 percent.

About 51 percent of the superior court defendants in 1965 received probation. By 1968, probation sentences accounted for 62 percent of the superior court dispositions. In 1969, they accounted for 66 percent of the superior court dispositions.

Since 1966, 625 deputy probation officers provide special supervision to over 17,000 probationers. In addition to the new case-carrying probation staff, there are 107 aides, 113 supervisors, and 312 clerical workers employed under the program. Support staff includes 17 administrators, 17 trainers, 10 researchers, 70 specialists, and 45 miscellaneous employees. The result is better protection for the general public and better supervision for a substantial number of probationers than ever before.

Since July 1, 1966, 10,806 people who might otherwise have come into the state correctional system have been diverted from it and cared for at the local level. Construction of institutional beds to accommodate this number (at $20,000 per new bed) would cost approximately $216 million. In fact, this program has cost the taxpayers of the State of California only 27.7 million dollars to actually reimburse counties for providing special supervision, even though the counties actually earned 43.4 million dollars. The net difference in unused earnings amounts to 15.6 million for the taxpayer.

Reduced commitments occurred at both the adult and juvenile level. In 1966-67, 67 percent of the reduced commitments occurred at the adult level. In 1967-68, 51 percent were adults; 1968-69, 67 percent; and 1969-70, 50 percent.

There has been a general decrease in commitments to institutions in California and throughout the United States. The decrease in California is particularly marked in subsidy counties, with the decrease being roughly twice as great for those counties participating in the subsidy program as for those not in the program. The decline in Youth Authority population has been a precipitous decline since 1965, with an acceleration of the decrease each year.

Although critics point to the general decline in institutionalization of commitments throughout the United States, only California is in the process of closing down institutions and phasing out operating units— and only California has two new, unopened institutions. These concrete realities speak most eloquently to the program's success.

In 1966-67, the average decrease in rate of commitments by participating counties was 16.1 percent, while the median decrease was 36.7 percent. In 1969-70, the average decrease in rate was 29.7 percent and the median decrease was 38.8 percent. The goal set for the program in 1964 called for an ultimate decrease in commitment rates amounting to 25 percent. Projections made regarding the decrease in rate assumed that it would take five years to achieve the 25 percent reduction goal. In fact, that state goal was achieved in the second year of operation.

RESPONSE TO CRITICS

California's probation subsidy has gone a long way toward achieving the objectives laid down by the legislature, but it has not stopped crime. It was not supposed to, at least not in itself. A long-range benefit of subsidy may ultimately be the reduction of crime and delinquency, but subsidy itself cannot be held responsible for the increase or decrease in the many statistics that are labeled "crime rate." This is particularly true when the laws that determine these statistics change and are interpreted differently in different parts of our state.

Probation subsidy has not shifted state institutional costs to city and county jails or farms. The per capita rate for incarceration is less today than it was in 1965 prior to probation subsidy. The fact that the county jails are overcrowded has nothing to do with probation subsidy, but it has a great deal to do with the fact that we hold in California upwards of 50 percent of all unsentenced prisoners. Nor has subsidy increased the use of county camps for juveniles; the per capita use of bed space has actually gone down, and today there are more empty beds in county juvenile camps and detention halls than ever before in history.

SOME DISAPPOINTMENTS

In spite of success far beyond expectation, there have been some disappointments. The payment table containing the subsidy legislation has not been adjusted annually as was originally intended. Inflationary costs over a four-year period have eaten into the earnings of the probation departments, forcing them to reduce their level of special effort under the program. In a few cases, money, and not program development, has become the focus.

In many ways, probation departments have not made as effective use of training as might have been hoped, nor have they come to grips with the principle of classification, which matches offenders' needs to staff services. There has been too little research, too little use of volunteer and case aides, and too much copying of someone else's ideas regardless of the appropriateness.

Programs for adults have lagged behind some of the more creative programs advanced for juveniles. There has not been the development of halfway houses or day care centers for adults or juveniles that was expected. Most important, there has not been an enrichment of county jail services by probation departments working in concert with county sheriffs.

SUMMING UP

California's subsidy has performed amazingly well for a new piece of legislation and has, in fact, had an impact far beyond the simple reduction of commitments in state institutions. Although not as much as would have been hoped, the subsidy program has enabled probation departments to invest thousands of new dollars in training for their staff. They have been able to develop their own staff skills in providing clinical services that previously were not obtainable. Now special techniques, such as transactional analysis, operant conditioning, conjoint counseling, insight counseling, and group counseling are treatment modes frequently found in special supervision programs throughout the state.

Probably one of the major accomplishments is related to developing a higher standard of performance and ability to do critical self-evaluation. Probation has become introspective. Departments are beginning to ask if they really know what they are trying to do, with whom, and why. A willingness to question traditional methods and practices has emerged and is infecting departmental status outside of special supervision programs.

In addition to increased skills and treatment approaches and insight into need for changing, probation officers are beginning to demand that they be located in the area where their clients reside. They are also accepting of the fact that their work is not something that one can do between the working hours of 8 and 5, and they are making themselves available to clients after hours.

Organizationally, many changes are occurring. Departments are becoming sensitive to the need for good supervisory and management practices, and are implementing special supervision programs. Because of the uniqueness of the special supervision units, departments, are becoming extremely conscious of the need for good communication about goals, objectives, policies, and procedures. Organizations are becoming more flexible in responding to the needs of subordinates within the organization, as well as client needs.

Special supervision programs serve about one-tenth of the total state probation load. To insure the effective utilization of limited manpower, state standards call for probation departments to articulate a classification scheme that is directed at matching client needs with departmental resources. The departments are finding it more and more useful to reserve their special supervision units for intense care to those cases requiring it. Classification is beginning to emerge as one of the primary mechanisms by which the impact of probation subsidy is magnified.

The program has worked extremely well, but it is not perfect. Changes need to be made in relation to annual adjustments in the payment rates, in the kind of features which permits earning money one year and spending it in the two following years, as well as making a special adjustment to accommodate four counties with unusually low base rates. With these modifications, the present program will continue to contribute to the "Quiet Revolution" begun in California in 1965. We may well have advanced a principle that, in spite of misunderstandings and adjustment problems, is worthwhile because it does change practices, does maximize services to offenders, does reduce the cost of incarceration at the state level, and does provide a meaningful service to those who are placed under probation supervision. Quiet or not, these changes are of revolutionary proportion.

part three:
POST-INSTITUTIONAL COMMUNITY-BASED PROGRAMS

The term "halfway" implies the movement of the offender into the community after a certain period. Reverend James explores the history of the halfway house movement. He goes on to review the selection of prisoners for such programs, using the following categories: (1) probationer; (2) pre-release status while still in prison; (3) parolee; and, (4) those discharged without parole obligations. Richard Rachin reflects upon the utility of the halfway house as a substitute for incarceration, where there is no question of security or public safety. He discusses the difficulties involved in setting up houses for juvenile offenders. The strategic role of the community in carrying out rehabilitation is continued by Reuben Margolin. Support for the offender commences while he is still in prison. Upon release citizen involvement is necessary if reentry is to be successful. Frank Miller focuses on the fragmented criminal justice system. He assesses the potential of community corrections while cautioning against ill-considered use of the halfway house. Naturally, some offenders are unsuited for the community program. Miller identifies the prisoner most likely to profit from these post-institutional measures. Candidates for the halfway house should be chosen with care. Challenging programs are endangered when the selection process is haphazard. Bernard Kirby, in his contribution, provides us with a study of one county halfway house. This analysis of one community-based program concerns the application of criminological theory to an ongoing agency program. The Robert Trojanowicz article deals specifically with a halfway house for juvenile offenders. A number of operational problems having to do with this program are considered: the treatment versus custody dilemma, facilitating communication between staff and the program participants, and staff training for the purpose of implementing the purpose and goals of the halfway house.

chapter nine
THE HALFWAY HOUSE MOVEMENT

The Reverend J. T. L. James

Confusion and at times controversy exists about the meaning and legitimate use of the term "halfway house." The name has been applied to facilities as diverse as alpine refuges and English pubs; it is used for residential facilities for persons with a wide range of needs—alcoholics, drug addicts, unwed mothers, former mental patients, probationers, and ex-convicts. As the term "halfway house" has been publicly accepted for so many types of establishments, it is pointless to try to limit it to facilities in the correctional field, let alone in the specific area of after-care, and petty to argue (as some have done) that the latter type are the only true halfway houses. Some, indeed, feel that the term has been so abused that at least one house for ex-inmates refuses to call itself a halfway house.

While acknowledging the legitimacy of the wide use of the term, this article is concerned only with halfway houses in the field of corrections for many categories of offenders—probationers, inmates on gradual release programs, parolees, and men released at the expiration of their sentence.

Objective studies in articles and books by competent professional persons are as yet rather scarce but are beginning to appear. The possibility of research by social scientists is now being recognized as the passage of time makes available adequate data for scientific analysis. Still, the very concept of the halfway house needs clarification in the minds of the interested public. The significance of some of its component elements needs to be spelled out rather than being discovered by those involved only after perhaps bitter practical experience.

This paper, therefore, attempts to set forth some factors in the halfway house movement for consideration. It is based on the limited professional literature, promotional articles and press releases, annual reports, and personal experience and observation of halfway houses in Canada, the United States, and England.

HISTORY

Christians of the first century were exhorted to "practise hospitality one to another without grudging." This norm was institutionalized early by the Church. St. Benedict, who systematized monasticism in Italy in the early sixth century, included the following in chapter 53 of his Rule: Let every guest be received as Christ.

In the middle of the same century, another monk began to apply the same principle specifically to ex-prisoners. St. Leonard founded a monastery near Limoges in France, into which he took convicts whose release he had obtained by using his influence with Clovis, King of the Franks. Leonard has ever since been venerated as the patron saint of prisoners and has been the historic inspiration for many modern-day Christians who have revived his method of after-care.

Down to the present day, monasteries have constituted one sort of halfway house. While they are not common in North America, England provides several fine examples of religious communities which receive ex-convicts for short or long periods of residence. Transitional between monasteries and more conventional halfway houses are the numerous instances of clergy who take into their homes persons needing residential assistance. Their spontaneous and unstructured work has sometimes inspired the foundation of more formally run halfway houses.

Deriving his impetus from his experience as chaplain at Chicago's Cook County Jail, the Reverend James G. Jones, Jr., an Episcopal priest, founded the first contemporary halfway house in the United States in 1954, dedicating it to St. Leonard. Not long afterwards in St. Louis, Missouri, the Reverend Charles Dismas Clark, a Jesuit whose work has gained worldwide fame from the movie "The Hoodlum Priest," founded a similar house under the patronage of St. Dismas, the penitent thief of the first Good Friday.

Some of Canada's first halfway houses likewise have their origins in the Church. In 1954 the Anglican Houses Association of the Diocese of Toronto established Beverley Lodge, now operated by the Church Army, for youths on probation and from training schools and reformatories. Since 1961 the United Church of Canada has supported a board which now operates two halfway houses. In 1962 All Saints Anglican Church in Windsor founded St. Leonard's House, modeled closely after the Chicago prototype by its director, the Reverend T. N. Libby, the parish's assistant curate.

The proliferation of halfway houses had gained such momentum by 1964 that some of the leaders of the movement organized the International Halfway House Association, which now represents over fifty houses in Canada and the United States of America.

The senior halfway house in the British Isles is Norman House, which since 1954 has served as the prototype for a number of other foundations. Since 1959 the Langley House Trust, formed by an association named "Christian Teamwork," has operated a growing chain of houses provided by civic and religious organizations in a number of cities. So numerous are halfway houses of various types in the United Kingdom that the Voluntary Hostels Conference has been established, with an office in London to assist social welfare workers in utilizing the facilities available in hundreds of hostels, some specializing in ex-prisoners. Prison after-care projects are listed and briefly described in a directory published annually by the National Association for the Care and Resettlement of Offenders (NACRO), successor to the National Association of Discharged Prisoners Aid Societies (NADPAS). Not including Salvation Army, Church Army and other general hostels, in 1966 it listed fifty-six active or projected residential facilities, all primarily established for the rehabilitation of ex-prisoners.

A second point of origin of the modern halfway house is found in prison systems themselves. As early as the 1850s Sir Walter Crofton's "Irish System" included a transitional experience for parolees. After a term in maximum security, certain inmates were permitted to work outside the institution, returning to an "intermediate institution" at night. In the third stage they were given a "ticket of leave," the precursor of the modern parole. Only in very recent years have a few prison systems reintroduced the vital second stage of a halfway facility in their release programs.

Shortly after Robert F. Kennedy took office as Attorney-General of the United States in 1961, he "hit on the idea of the half-way house."[1] By the end of 1961 three "Pre-Release Guidance Centers" had been established as pilot projects, to test this method of rehabilitation for young men from federal youth institutions during the final months of their sentence.

Much less publicized than the halfway houses for those being released from civil prisons are the similar methods of the United States Defense Department. Military prisoners are transferred from a federal or military penal institution to a retraining center and from there are returned to active duty. Thus, although the procedure aims at reassimilating men into the military service, it makes use of the same principle of gradual transition.

Western nations are not the only ones to have adopted the halfway house concept into their correctional systems. Both Egypt and India are reported to use such facilities extensively for juveniles; "a kind of decompression chamber which gradually prepares him for the pressure of normal life."[2]

TYPES OF HALFWAY HOUSES

In the corrections field, halfway houses exist for four statuses of residents with criminal convicton: probationers (with or without previous institutional experience), men still under custodial sentence, parolees, and men released at expiry of sentence.

Probation hostels, as they are often called, have been used in many jurisdictions as an alternative means of housing those who, because of unsatisfactory domestic conditions, would otherwise have been deemed unsuitable for probation and so committed to a penal institution. Some in the halfway house field have objected to calling such hostels "halfway houses," pointing out that their residents are "halfway *in*" rather than "halfway *out*" of prison. This may reflect a cynical view of the success of probation as a method of treatment, but it does point to a valid contrast which is also illustrated in the refusal of most halfway houses to mix ex-inmates and probationers who have not had institutional experience. In some jurisdictions where the application of probation is not limited to first convictions, admission to a halfway house can make it possible for the court to grant a further chance to a man with a previous record, especially when the current conviction is on a less serious charge than earlier ones.

Halfway houses for men still in custody fall into the category of "pre-release hostel" or "pre-release guidance center." Such facilities may be in a special wing of the prison, in a separate building on the grounds, or outside in the community. Although usually operated by personnel of the prison service, the United States Federal Bureau of Prisons does utilize both community facilities and nongovernment staff for some of its pre-release guidance centers. A strong point in favor of such operations is that they make possible continuity of treatment, which is generally preferable to the discontinuity that results when a man passes from the prison to a private agency. A possible drawback, of course, is that the ex-inmate is well aware that the halfway house is part of the institutional system and so may retain negative attitudes in this stage of his treatment.

A number of halfway houses have been founded specifically to assist convicts who, in many jurisdictions, must have both a home and job before being released on parole. Some halfway houses are recognized by paroling authorities as meeting this requirement. One question any house which takes parolees must decide is whether it is better to assume official supervision (where regulations of the system permit) or insist that the parole officer be someone not involved directly with the house operation, in order to avoid role conflict. The length of a man's parole may also create problems for the house. Must the house keep a parolee for the full duration of his parole? Must a man with a short parole leave when it terminates?

Men who remain in a prison until the completion of their sentence are often in the greatest need of the services of a halfway house. They may have decided that they can make it on their own and so not have asked for help until after release. They may not want supervision and so not have applied for parole. They may have been refused parole, as poor risks. The halfway house that will accept men on the basis of their perceived need may make the difference between success and failure for such ex-inmates. In jurisdictions where compulsory after-care does exist, the halfway house provides a particularly intensive and supportive form of assistance.

SPONSORSHIP

An examination of the organization and structure of modern halfway houses shows three types of sponsor: religious, government, and community.

Religious. The deep involvement of the Church in rehabilitation work is obvious both in the distant past and in the present revival of interest in this sometimes neglected facet of corrections. Dioceses, parishes, religious societies, and individual church members have founded many after-care projects, and of course many persons are involved from Christian motivation in works not specifically sponsored by religious organizations. It must be emphasized that religious sponsorship of a rehabilitation project rarely implies that it caters only to men of the sponsoring denomination, and seldom are those being assisted required to participate in even the simplest religious observances as the price of being helped. Most conspicuously active in rehabilitation work are the Salvation Army, in many countries, and the Anglican Church Army, principally in England. Their hostels shelter the needy of every sort, many of whom are ex-prisoners, some hostels offering specialized assistance to these men specifically.

Government. Government-sponsored residential facilities are most commonly provided only for the benefit of men from the given prison system or specific institution. Pre-release facilities are sometimes contained in a wing of the prison, in a separate hostel building on the grounds, or in a separate parole camp. They are usually staffed by institutional personnel. Once men are released from the penal system, the government is no longer directly responsible for them, and so their after-care becomes the responsibility of other governmental departments or agencies or of society at large.

Community. The establishment of residential programs is a natural extension of the work of after-care societies which are primarily involved in outpatient casework. Other civic organizations whose basic concern is not with offenders have become involved in the halfway house movement, either operating houses themselves or providing physical facilities to be operated by an organization specializing in rehabilitation work of this sort.

The lines distinguishing types of sponsoring bodies cannot be sharply drawn. The divisions between religious groups frequently fade in the face of a common concern; in the halfway house movement are some of the finest examples of ecumenical cooperation. Community organizations inevitably involve people consciously putting their faith to work. Some government-sponsored projects are operated by nongovernmental personnel, and most penal systems are happy to make use of private halfway houses.

SUPPORT

In this practical area again, churches, organizations, industry, business, labor, and government frequently all contribute to many projects which might appear to have narrowly defined sponsorship. Any organization or group contemplating the establishment of a halfway house must count the cost and the available means of meeting it. The cost is high. Apart from capital costs, operating budgets of several Canadian and United States houses accommodating between twelve and twenty-one men range from a low of $16,500 to a high of $85,000 per year. Many sources must be tapped to raise such sums.

Publicity releases often claim that it is much less expensive to rehabilitate a man than to keep him in prison. On a net per capita per diem cost basis, this is not always true. Institutional costs are variously quoted at from $4.50 to $8 per man per day. But the per capita per diem cost of operating some Canadian and United States halfway houses runs as high as $7, although by contrast the financial reports of some English houses indicate a daily cost per man of less than $3. The "low cost of rehabilitating an ex-convict" can be claimed only when such men spend the shortest possible time in the halfway house. The ultimate question is in determining the optimum time any given individual should spend there to ensure his successful rehabilitation.

Of particular significance to the basic philosophy of the halfway house movement is the question of the guests' financial responsibility to the house. Rarely are men not required to pay anything to the house. On the principle that learning to assume responsibility in society involves supporting oneself, most houses charge guests at a rate commensurate with the cost of comparable boarding facilities in the community—usually $2 to $3 per day. Apart from those which demand payment weekly in advance, most houses find the application of their own rules about paying a very difficult operational problem area. How far can men be allowed to "use" a house without harming themselves, their follow-guests, and the house itself? When receipts from guests are correlated with numbers in residence, reports from some houses show that a minority of guests actually pay their way, leaving hundreds of dollars of unpaid board annually.

Revenue from guests' fees ranges from a low of 7 percent to a high of 62 percent of total receipts, according to financial reports studied.

Policy with regard to requiring guests to work in the house also varies widely. Some apply the term "guest" literally; others are entirely resident-operated. Between the extremes, many houses require unemployed guests to work for their keep in the house; others use a rota system for domestic chores, and others pay guests for work done. Most operate with a combination of hired or volunteer outside help and compulsory or voluntary guest assistance.

As the amount of assistance given *by* the guests varies, so does the amount of assistance given *to* them. Here again the rehabilitational philosophy of the management is revealed. Although some houses provide clothing, cash loans, cigarettes, shaving tackle, and sundries, most believe that it is basic to a man's rehabilitation to achieve self-support and self-reliance in the smallest matters first. As the motto of one house puts it: "A hand up, not a handout."

Support, therefore, is both an external and an internal problem. Strong and generous support from outside can encourage dependence in an already over-dependent ex-inmate. Yet the costs of halfway house operation are so great that guests' contributions alone cannot meet the budget. The maintenance of a sensible and responsible balance is a challenging task to operators.

TREATMENT

The role of the halfway house in the treatment of the offender is a very basic question which has as yet not been examined in depth. Yet the therapeutic orientation of each house can be determined and should be clearly stated. Much of the rivalry and invidious comparison between houses is based on their differences in treatment philosophy. Some operators see their work as a continuation of the treatment begun in the institution; they may describe their houses as "community residential treatment centers." Others repudiate the concept of "treatment" in a clinical sense, contending that the inmate has been subjected to professional treatment before in various forms and it has proven ineffective. Thus they offer simply (in the best sense of the word) as natural and home-like an environment as possible. Both types of house could be termed "therapeutic communities," one involving professionally trained persons in that community, the other comprising only persons occupying the role and status of family members.

The resocialization of the ex-inmate is the common goal of all halfway houses, however diverse their methods and different the qualifications of their personnel. The needs of released men are sufficiently complex that no method of approach should be overlooked or denigrated, but even the most competent literature produced reflects that rivalry in areas of social concern that seems to exist between "amateur" and "professional," between "religious" and "secular," between "government" and "private":

> Here and there in metropolitan areas of the United States, "shelters" operated by private agencies have been set up for ex-prisoners, but as often as not they have deteriorated into mere meeting places for ex-convicts, points of criminal contagion. The shelter itself provided food and a bed, and not much more.[3]
>
> Through the years, private organizations and individuals in the United States have attempted to establish boarding homes for released prisoners. For the most part, however, these were inadequately staffed, provided little more than room and board, and were not coordinated with the correctional system. Usually they were operated much in the manner of missions; indeed some were under the auspices of religious groups.[4]

Yet the following description of the purpose of a government-sponsored, professionally operated community residential treatment center equally well describes the primary goals of "inadequately staffed" religious-sponsored "shelters":

> We wanted to develop a center where in addition to the basic needs of food and a room the released inmate would be helped to find a job, where he would be given the support and guidance to enable him to live with his emotional problems, and where he might make the transition from institutional to community life less abruptly, less like slamming into a brick wall. We wanted a center which would be his sponsor in the "free world," introducing him to community life gradually and withdrawing when the procedure was completed.[5]

England's pioneer, the founder of Norman House, has written in defense of the nonprofessional approach:

> We who live and work there are not social surgeons who diagnose the illness and prescribe the remedy . . . Norman House is not a lodging house or a hostel, but a family group of some fifteen people, most of whom have been in prison more than once. While they are being helped with the more mundane, yet essential taks of resettlement, there is for them no feeling of isolation and detachment, and no opportunity of escaping from people, a factor which looms large in the history of many homeless offenders. They are now members of a family . . . In this climate relationships develop and deepen.[6]

What is needed in the halfway house movement are not arguments about the superiority or inferiority of different approaches, but investigations into the types of persons best helped by the various methods of treatment available. At the same time, houses can be classified with respect to their treatment orientation. The most readily discernible characteristic is in the area of staffing. Some are operated completely by nonprofessionals; others by nonprofessionals but with professional personnel assisting or advising; others by highly trained specialists.

Houses which have no professional workers are in a few instances completely managed internally by ex-inmate employees under the direction of an outside sponsoring body. More commonly, the internal operation is in the hands of house managers or house parents who are not themselves ex-inmates. They are selected not only for their qualifications for housekeeping but for their maturity and natural ability to establish relationships, particularly with disturbed persons. Some houses have found that older couples to whom the men can relate as to foster parents are best; other houses employ younger couples with children; still others find older single persons preferable. And frequently theology, psychology, social work, or other students assist in some capacity in houses.

Many such houses are assisted by part-time volunteers or paid professionals—social workers, psychologists, psychiatrists, counselors, etc. These workers concentrate on the more deep-seated problems of the guests, leaving the household management to others.

Professionally oriented houses are those sponsored or supported by governments or foundations, able to finance the employment of professionally qualified staff. A danger in this approach is that such houses may develop an institutional atmosphere, if the relationship between those involved is too coldly clinical or the connection with the sponsoring penal academic or psychological institution too obtrusive. A decided advantage of the professionally run house is that it offers greater opportunities for scientific study; for example, one house analyzes its group counseling program scientifically, each of the hundreds of remarks which made up group counseling sessions being classified by speaker and recipient for analysis by computer.

ADMISSION

Age. Apart from houses catering specifically for juveniles, most houses have defined age limits, based sometimes on the ability of staff members to relate to a particular age group, sometimes on theoretical considerations such as the belief that most convicts are psychopaths who may be expected to mature after age twenty-five. Few houses find it satisfactory to mix men of widely differing ages.

Criminal sophistication. The danger of "contamination" in halfway houses is often cited. Certain houses accept only "first offenders," meaning men who have had only one institutional sentence. Others are for recidivists. Others prefer men with a particular type of criminal history. Some limit their facilities to men who have served long sentences. A few houses specialize in the more difficult treatment problems—sex offenders, narcotics addicts, or drinking alcoholics; most exclude these types of cases.

Place of origin. In order to get civic support, some houses have had to make a commitment to take only men whose homes were originally in the community, who thus are more readily acknowledged as its responsibility. This raises another theoretical question of whether an ex-convict is more readily rehabilitated in his home town or in a community where he is less well known.

Application. Houses which are closely integrated with an institutional system are at an advantage in receiving only men individually selected as suitable for this additional care and treatment. In some instances, preparation for life in the halfway house is part of their institutional program in the final weeks of prison.

Most houses, however, are privately operated and draw men from numerous institutions. Admission is usually sought by direct application, with or without recommendation from institutional chaplains, rehabilitation officers, or other officials. Selection may be made by the house director or by a committee.

Some houses feel it highly desirable to establish personal contact with prospective guests well before their release date. By visits and letters a relationship is established between the man and those with whom he will be living. He is thus relieved of much of the anxiety that normally is experienced before release, commonly called "gate fever." In addition, such prior contact enables the house staff to prepare to meet his specific needs. Volunteer "out-mates" are sometimes used in this phase of the work, initiating a supportive relationship which may be continued even after the guest has left the halfway house.

Readmission. Most houses encourage former guests to consider the house as "home" even after they have established themselves independently. Not all houses are prepared to take a man back, but some encourage ex-residents to return if they are in danger of lapsing into trouble, or if, because of unemployment or other changed circumstances, they are no longer able to support themselves and need temporary accommodation. Some houses go one step further and welcome back—or at least entertain the application of—former guests who have subsequently been recalled or reconvicted. In spite of his recidivism, the desire of a guest to try again may be considered a measure of success for the house.

Success. "Success rates" claimed by halfway houses need to be carefully examined before being accepted at face value. Some list as failures only those who have been recalled or been reconvicted while resident in the house. It is often difficult to find out what has happened to former guests, and even more difficult to assess the responsibility of the halfway house for their success or failure. As with the "cost of rehabilitation," there is room for a clearer definition of the term "success" and for scientific study so that the value of the halfway house in the correctional process may be more objectively evaluated.

LENGTH OF STAY

How long any man remains in a halfway house is determined by a combination of factors—his perceived need, the house's ability to help him achieve independence, and his willingness to cooperate. It is implicit in the very term "halfway" that men are expected to move on, leaving room for others, as they themselves become self-reliant. For some this takes a long time, but the halfway house has not fulfilled its purpose if it does not help the guest overcome his institutionalized dependency. Men who are forced to leave prematurely or who leave on their own accord but not according to plan, are in a sense failures.

The term "guest" is often applied to men residing in halfway houses, indicating that they are only there for a limited time. Others call the men "residents," emphasizing the fact that they are welcome to stay as long as they wish. How long a man stays is usually determined by policy, though policy is often determined by experience. In terms of policy, houses may be classified as short-term, medium-term, and long-term.

Short-term. Short-term residential accommodation for ex-inmates is commonly provided by what are usually called "hostels." Providing dormitory accommodation, meals, and sometimes employment assistance and counseling, hostels seldom cater to ex-prisoners exclusively. For some released men, hostels provide enough assistance to make a new start. Hostels generally do not provide so much that the over-dependent are anxious to remain, as they may be in a more supportive halfway house. After-care societies frequently make use of hostel accommodation for their clients, while counseling them on an out-patient basis.

Medium-term. Most halfway houses anticipate that a guest will remain for a period of at least six weeks. Most North American houses recommend a stay of three to four months and will perhaps keep a man longer if necessary. But statistics reveal that, apart from the few who stay only days, most guests remain only a few weeks, until they have secured a steady job and received enough pay to enable them to rent other accommodations.

Houses generally like to plan with a man how long he will remain, if they offer casework assistance.

The English houses are mostly medium-term but show less tendency to have a policy about maximum stay. A man may remain as long as he feels the need to. Too hasty a departure may lead to unanticipated problems; the longer a man remains, the more the house can achieve and the more stable he is likely to be when he does move out on his own.

Long-term. It must be acknowledged that many ex-inmates, especially older ones, are so institutionalized and inadequate that completely independent living is a remote if not unattainable goal. Several halfway houses which operate with a medium-term policy have recognized the need of many men for long-term residential care and so have sponsored the formation of other residential facilities which have been dubbed "three-quarter-way houses."

Three examples of distinctive types of long-term facility may be noted. Norman House in London sponsors "The Second House," which is essentially a boarding house for former residents who need a less controlled, but still supportive, environment. For four years St. Leonard's House, Chicago, operated St. Leonard's Farm in Michigan, to assist some who needed a long-term resocialization process before returning to an urban environment. St. Martin of Tours in London has acquired properties adjacent to the hostel for rental to former guests. The need for more facilities of these and other types cannot be overestimated. It has often been suggested by enlightened penologists that many older recidivists should not be repeatedly imprisoned for offenses deliberately committed for the sake of achieving the security of the institution. Open residential facilities could better provide the support they need.

CONCLUSION

The new-but-old halfway house concept has survived the growing pains of its rebirth in the contemporary world of corrections. Its critics have become less vocal; its promoters less extravagant in their claims. Governments are coming to recognize the value of the halfway house and both to support those privately established and to incorporate this type of facility into their correctional system.

The movement gains momentum and the horizon expands. Houses spread in chains, organize in associations, diversify their operations. Outpatient services, wives' groups, legal aid schemes, associates, alumni, employment bureaus, service businesses—these and many others are the ancillary facilities developed by some halfway houses.

This study has not treated these recent forms of outreach to the ex-offender, his family, and society, nor has it even covered many important factors in the establishment and operation of houses themselves, such as location, types of buildings, their facilities, the controversial question of the desirability of publicity or anonymity.

From descriptive studies, those concerned with this topic must soon move on to analytical studies to validate scientifically the seemingly verified hypothesis that the halfway house is playing a vital role in the rehabilitation of offenders. Then, and only then, will the foresight and faith of the pioneers be confirmed for history to record to their credit.

NOTES

1. Kennedy, Robert F. "Halfway Houses Pay Off," *Crime and Delinquency*, vol. 10, no. 1.
2. Tunley, Raoul. *Kids, Crime and Chaos*. (New York: Dell Books, 1962), p. 20.
3. Kennedy, op. cit.
4. Nice, Richard W. "Halfway House After-Care for the Released Offender," *Crime and Delinquency*, vol. x, no. 1.
5. Kennedy, op. cit.
6. Turner, Merfyn. *Safe Lodging*. (London: Hutchinson & Co., 1961), p. 9.

BIBLIOGRAPHY

Promotional literature, press and popular journal articles, annual reports on the following projects:

United States of America, and Canada
Alexandrine House, Detroit, Michigan
Beverley Lodge, Toronto, Ontario
Brooke House, Boston, Massachusetts
Crofton House, San Diego, California
St. Dismas House, St. Louis, Missouri
Elizabeth Fry Center, Los Angeles, California
Harold King Farm, Keswick, Ontario
Helping Hand Halfway House, Cleveland, Ohio
Hope Hall, Minneapolis, Minnesota
St. Leonard's House, Windsor, Ontario
St. Leonard's House, Chicago, Illinois
St. Leonard's Farm, Three Rivers, Michigan
Peninsula Halfway House, San Mateo, California
Pre-Release Guidance Center, Chicago, Illinois
Robert Bruce House, Newark, New Jersey
308 West Residence, Wilmington, Delaware

England
Blackfriars Settlement, London
St. Dismas Society, Southampton
Golborne Rehabilitation Centre, London

Langley House Trust, Winchester
St. Luke's House, London
St. Martin of Tours, London
Norman House, London
Pilsdon Community, Bridport
Recidivists Anonymous, London
The Second House, London
Simon Community Trust, London

Books and professional journal articles:
Breslin, Maurice A. and Crosswhite, Robert G. "Residential After-Care," *Federal Probation*, XXVII, 1 (March 1963).
James, J. T. L. *Rehabilitation in Britain*. Toronto; D.C.S.S. 1964.
Kennedy, Robert F. "Halfway Houses Pay Off," *Crime and Delinquency*, X, 1 (January 1964).
Miller, Derek. *Growth to Freedom*. London: Tavistock, 1964.
Nice, Richard W. "Halfway House After-Care for the Released Offender." *Crime and Delinquency*, X, 1 (January 1964).
Phillips, B. *Adopted Derelicts*. Toronto: Harlequin, 1957.
Tunley, R. *Kids, Crime and Chaos*. New York: Dell, 1962.
Turner, M. *Safe Lodging*. London: Hutchinson, 1961.
Wallich-Clifford, A. *One Man's Answer*. London: Golborne, 1962.
Directory of Prison After-Care Projects. London: NADPAS, 1966.

chapter ten
SO YOU WANT TO OPEN A HALFWAY HOUSE

Richard L. Rachin

The *halfway house* is intended to meet a need for client services between highly supervised, well structured, institutional programs and relatively free community living. In its popular function, the halfway house has been a kind of decompression chamber through which institutional releases are helped to avoid the social-psychological bends of a too rapid reinvolvement in the "real world." Although increasing numbers of halfway houses include treatment components, many are still limited to providing bed and board, assistance in finding employment, and help in locating more permanent shelter.

The need for short-circuiting unnecessary institutional commitment has led to the development of the "halfway-in" house. Utilized primarily at this time for youth, treatment considerations and responsibility-oriented, reality-bound programming have been the hallmarks of these facilities. In addition to its traditional function, then, the halfway house can provide a means for diverting people from the institutional mill which, as so many have pointed out, has more often harmed than helped. As we are coming to learn, the need for removing anyone from community living should be confined to persons of legitimate danger to themselves—and how often this has been abused—or others. There are no other sensible reasons for doing this. The halfway-in utilization of the program for delinquents has catalyzed a movement away from the stark, antiseptic, emotionally uninvolved, and spiritually suffused programs which traditionally operate under the halfway house rubric. The small therapeutic community has replaced the way station, much to the advantage of people involved. This

From *Federal Probation*, vol. 36, no. 1 (March, 1972), pp. 30–37. Reprinted by permission.

article discusses the utilization of the halfway house for delinquent youths. The principles, however, are generally applicable to other groups whose need for this type of program are no less apparent.

THE HALFWAY HOUSE: WHAT, WHO, HOW

At one end of the residential correctional spectrum, the training school best meets the requirements of relatively large and seriously problem-ridden populations. The institution is designed ideally to be self-contained and largely self-sufficient in its day-to-day operations. Highly structured programming and security considerations are most appropriately met in this setting. The group foster home, at the other extreme, best accommodates children whose remaining in the community is jeopardized primarily by their own poor home situations. Provided with parent surrogates in warm, supportive, home-like settings, children with these needs require little or no planned treatment services.

The halfway house is a versatile program providing meaningful placement alternatives for youths with needs between these extremes. Its utilization can safely hasten release from institutions. It offers practical and realistic opportunities for testing out one's ability to deal responsibly and in a socially acceptable manner with the stresses of the "real world." It improves significantly upon traditional institutional assessments of readiness for parole or unsupervised discharge, which frequently bear little relationship to the realities of conventional community living. Youths failing on probation or with needs beyond that of foster or group homes can be placed in a halfway house and helped, while still remaining in their own communities. The halfway house can also assist parolees whose behavior indicates the need for closer or more intensive treatment services than they can receive under ordinary parole supervision. In some cases, revocations or recommitments can be made more suitably to a halfway house than to the institution from which a youth was paroled. In effect, its utilization is appropriate for a variety of needs within a broad middle-range of the correctional spectrum.

Youths, and not referral sources, should be considered in selecting program residents. It should make no difference whether one is "halfway-in" or "halfway-out" of an institution. Although offense data alone are a poor index of suitability for this type program, heavy emphasis is still placed here both by the public and correctional administrators. The same undue stress seems to have been laid on clinical impressions of personality difficulties. For some, diagnostic impressions have too frequently become self-fulfilling prophecies. With many youths, it has become interesting to speculate which came first, the disorder or the diagnostic impression. More dependable are selection procedures which minimize the past and focus on strengths, motivation, capacity for change, and more productive living.

Halfway house candidates should be mature enough and have the capacity for participation in confrontative, probing, and anxiety-provoking examination of their day-to-day behavior. Equally important, they must express some interest in doing this. It is unimportant how sincere a youth may be in professing his concern about examining the utility of his behavior. Candidates, however, must convey some uneasiness about their lives and indicate at least a willingness to consider the possibility of doing things differently. They should be able to acknowledge an ability to cope responsibly with daily, unsupervised, community living. It should not matter whether they were successful in doing this previously.

The importance of the peer group in influencing and directing behavior should not be neglected. For a treatment-oriented halfway house to operate effectively, residents must be able to concede that others with whom they live can understand their problems and empathize with their feelings, even though they might not agree with their explanations about these feelings.

Much can be gained by house membership which is representative of the "real world" in which residents are usually involved. People must learn to deal with life as they knew it and to which, realistically, they must be expected to return. Homogeneous groupings which therapeutically detour offenders from such "real life" exposures are, at best, apprenticeships from which most offenders must be expected to graduate. Variables such as socioeconomic class, race, clinical impressions of emotional disturbance, offense, and intellectual (nonmentally defective) capacity offer no serious obstacles to effective group participation, interaction, and the development of cohesive group cultures.

Age, however, cannot be discounted in designing group programs for adolescents. A variance of more than two or three years should be avoided in selecting youths for a halfway house. Program expectations, the kinds of responsibilities placed on residents, and peer pressure toward exacting norm-adhering behavior require a degree of maturity and impulse control which youths less than sixteen years of age do not usually possess. Emotional maturity is a more important consideration, however, than chronological age.

Youths whose behavior appears, both to themselves and others, to be beyond their ability to control, or who genuinely seem unconcerned about responsible decision making *at the time when interviewed for the halfway house,* should not be admitted. By the same token, the unreliability and questionable validity of diagnoses and conventional personality measures warrant consideration of applicants otherwise ordinarily screened on the basis of their past records alone. While a youth who evinces a *current* inability to control his behavior might make a poor program candidate, nevertheless his concern about this behavior and what has been happening to his life may be more important considerations.

Rather than establishing exclusionary criteria, a more realistic and productive approach would be to admit youths who possess certain positive characteristics, regardless of other considerations. These attributes should include: (1) a feeling of uneasiness, unhappiness, or discontent with oneself or his life and some concern about doing something to change it; (2) recognition and acceptance that one does or can control what happens to him, even though the past may have indicated he was unable to do much about it; (3) a willingness to examine things about himself with others, even though it may make him angry, unhappy, or embarrassed to do so; (4) a belief that other residents, and the program itself, will benefit from his participation.

A preplacement "peertake" meeting (one's peers take part in selecting youths for the program) is helpful in clearly and forcefully conveying the "program-means-something-to-us" and "we-make-decisions" nature of the group norms. Residence should be limited to young people who both choose to be involved and are found acceptable by youths in the program. In addition, the newcomer should be required to make his own decision whether he can accept the responsibilities which participation entails.

There are few delinquents who will not opt for what they perceive to be the more desirable of two alternatives placed before them. This does not mean that at the time he makes his decision, a youth should be expected realistically to choose between changing his behavior and remaining a delinquent; rather, in return for being in the community, under near-conventional living circumstances, a candidate must at least verbalize his acceptance of group (program) norms, values, and expectations. Of course, many youths will be doing little more than choosing between what they define as something which they want little part of (the halfway house) and something else which they want even less (the training school). Certainly, the more sophisticated youths should be expected to opt for admittance not as a willing challenge to some ingrown delinquent attitudes and values, but rather as a conforming game-playing exercise at which many are quite experienced and adept.

Changes in behavior do not usually occur unless some doubt is perceived about the efficacy of one's present conduct in satisfying his needs and some alternative is identified with which the person can experiment.

It is not important, therefore, that a candidate be truthful in discussing his "wanting," but rather his "willingness" to take a "good hard honest look at himself" and the utility of his behavior. To be accepted into the program, however, should be understood clearly by the newcomer to mean that he will be held to the terms of a "contractual arrangement" to which he must first agree. Stated succinctly, the following must be carefully stressed:

1. Residents will be accepted only after they fully understand what the program involves, what will be expected of them, and providing that their participation is approved by youth and staff with whom they will live. No one can be sent against his will. Everyone makes his own decision to come.
2. A youth cannot "stay the same" and remain in the program. Everyone must be expected to be doing more with himself tomorrow than he did today, and less tomorrow than he will do the day after.
3. Not doing anything "wrong" (irresponsibility) should not be considered an indication of progress and may more properly be interpreted to mean just the opposite. What a person does "right" (responsibly) is what counts.
4. "Good" or "bad" behavior has no meaning. Only responsible kinds of behavior have any value (utility). Everything a youth does or does not do he will be held accountable for from the day he enters the program. Self-defeating, escapist, or excuse-ridden antics should be viewed to be as deviant (irresponsible) as the more customarily recognized overt, antisocial actions.
5. The halfway house is neither a prison nor a sanctuary. Residents should neither be able to "do time," nor avoid doing the most with the time available to them to complete treatment. Residence should be indeterminate, with the actual length of stay being a decision in which a youth himself, his peers, and staff should participate. No one should be permitted to remain beyond a maximum length of residence (which can vary from program to program) and there should be no fixed minimum period of time required or permitted.

We have conceptualized our halfway house model as a residential treatment alternative for youths whose problems and needs, while beyond that of other community programs, are short of their requiring institutionalization. Our therapeutic community includes as the core of its program, intensive (daily, hour-and-one-half) responsibility-oriented, reality-bound, group treatment meetings in which the focus is on the "here and now" and the primary change agents are one's fellow program residents.

The self-help treatment model is believed to offer advantages over more traditional treatment approaches in working with young people. Youths are much more responsive to the encouragement and pressure of their peers (with whom they can identify) to change their attitudes and behavior than they are to the ministrations of adult professionals. An atmosphere of trust and concern is required, and the emotional involvement of residents and staff far exceeds that customarily expected or found in traditional correctional programs. It is the intensity of everyone's (staff and residents) involvement that distinguishes our treatment model from most others.

The voluntary nature of program participation must be emphasized. Admittance should not be automatic, and alternatives to acceptance must be clearly spelled out. It must be stressed with the newcomer that he does not *have* to be in the program but rather has to *want* to be in the program.

Residence of approximately four to six months may be anticipated in order to accomplish treatment goals. Candidates should clearly understand that residents must believe themselves to be capable of "solving their problems" within this period of time. Program expectations should be made explicit. Progress must be expected each day. The longer a youth is in the program, the less need there should be for his remaining in the program. Responsibilities can and should increase with the length of residence. It should be emphasized that there are no privileges but only added responsibilities, which are expected to accrue as one remains involved in treatment. Indeed, the longer a youth is in the program, the more demanding and difficult should his participation become. The expectations which staff have for residents—what they believe them to be capable of accomplishing, and the time in which they feel they can do this—can either enhance or inhibit goal directed behavior.

SIZE CONSIDERATIONS

The size of the program should be limited. An optimum population may range from twenty to twenty-five youths. Several factors are considered in determining this number:

1. *Per capita cost which, of course, changes as a variable population numerator is placed over a fairly stable fixed-cost denominator.* Approximately the same costs will be incurred for certain expenses (staff, utilities, communications, office equipment, building repairs, etc., give or take a range of about eighteen to twenty-five residents).
2. *Developing and retaining the advantages of small group interaction.* While face-to-face relationships are essential, the number of residents could vary depending on staff skills, architectural considerations, programming content, location, and other site considerations. Nevertheless, it appears that thirty is about the maximum number beyond which the attributes of close peer group interaction become jeopardized. Below twenty, cost considerations become a problem.

3. *Not overwhelming a community with large numbers of new residents.* Community acceptance, which we will discuss later, must be carefully considered and courted. It is not realistic to ignore the very real, if not too legitimate, fears and anxieties which people have when confronted with a halfway house opening in their neighborhood. While there is no simple relationship between program size and the crescendo of community concern, it is wise to assume that the more "threatening" the type of population—that is, the greater its number, the more visible the facility, and the more "problem-ridden" its residents—the more anxious and less tolerant is a community's reaction likely to appear.
4. *Given the many important and different considerations involved in selecting appropriate sites for a halfway house, there is an inverse relationship between the size of the population and the available number of desirable sites.* Site location committees frequently must choose second, third, and even less desirable alternatives, not because of the unavailability of facilities within the preferred area but because considerations of importance to the local community often have been neglected, if not ignored. A well-planned and meaningfully organized community relations campaign looms large as the most important consideration in planning halfway houses (or other community programs).

Insufficient funding may require changes from an optimum size. At times, this may mean that larger (more than twenty-five), or smaller (less than twenty) residents must be considered. The advantages of face-to-face interaction, however, must always be balanced against budgetary concerns.

SITE SELECTION

Site selection is extremely important. As much time as possible should be set aside for this purpose. The time allotted can vary depending on the nature of the program, the particular area being considered, whether the structure is to be built or leased, and the actual construction or renovation time contemplated. Six months should be a minimum and a year ideal. Plans must be drawn, contracts let, and changes made. An unhurried pace permits careful and important planning.

Community leaders should be contacted early and informed of an agency's plans. This is particularly true when programs are designed for offender groups. To do otherwise is to omit gaining and risk alienating the support of people and agencies whose acceptance and involvement is essential. It makes little sense, and it is unlikely that efforts to confront a community with a *fait accompli* will succeed. This simply polarizes community resistance and hinders understanding and cooperation.

Site selection requires planning and care. There are few, if any, ideal locations. Both the advantages and disadvantages of a site should be carefully evaluated and weighed against each other. Once a target area is chosen, it is helpful to consider the following:

Brokers familiar with the area can be engaged.

If the agency has a field staff in the prospective target area, its assistance should be enlisted.

Community leaders are well informed about available real estate. Their help in site selection is invaluable. In addition, their involvement makes it more likely that the program will gain recognition as a cooperative, community-agency venture to which all can more easily become committed. The expense in time and cost of site location efforts may be lowered appreciably by the cooperation and assistance of community leaders.

Public agencies in particular should seek out and contact other governmental agencies in the target area for a discussion and appraisal of the "do's" and "don'ts." Local social agency directors are usually privy to the kinds of information which indigenous leaders may be reluctant to furnish or find it difficult to be objective about. Directors of these agencies are important, therefore, to call upon for an assessment of the community pulse and the likely reactions of local leaders.

Agency staff who are residents in the target area can also provide important leads and information. These people should not be overlooked for other reasons—they can be of assistance, or on the other hand, they may make it difficult to establish positive community relations.

Selecting a site within the target area requires careful attention to several matters:

The neighborhood chosen must be zoned properly. It is important to have a statement in writing from the zoning board that the use intended for the property is not to conflict with local zoning regulations.

Public transportation must be accessible and within walking distance of the facility. Residents should be able to travel (to work, school, clinics, recreation, etc.) during most times and days of the week. If possible, locations which offer access to alternative means of public travel are preferable. The office vehicle should not be required to transport residents for any reasons other than emergency trips or group outings.

Residents should be able to come and go and mix in with the neighborhood as much as possible. Program participants must feel relatively comfortable and safe in the area selected. A racially, culturally, and economically diverse community offers advantages to mixed populations.

The architecture should be planned to blend in with that existing in the area selected. For example, a 25-bed multi-story, ultra-modern building would not be suitably located on a block of modest single family residences.

Signs, flag staffs, or other official-looking designations should be avoided. The facility will be no stranger to block residents who can, when necessary, quickly direct visitors to the building.

Offender groups are not readily received in quiet residential communities. Commercial-residential areas or locations adjoining light industrial sections are preferred. Areas in transition also provide good sites in which to locate. The community, however, should not be disorganized or deteriorating, but could be one where this process has stabilized or been reversed.

Commercial services (barber, shoe repair, snack shops, cleaners, etc.) should be within walking distance of the facility.

COMMUNITY RELATIONS

The halfway house should be designed to make maximum use of local resources, including educational, religious, vocational, recreational, and medical services.

Community programs have both an opportunity and obligation to tap in on the skills, counsel, and support of volunteers, local citizen groups, and service organizations. Local colleges are usually willing to develop mutually beneficial relationships.

As community-based programs, halfway houses must be community integrated and involved, and responsive to the concerns, fears, and anxieties of their neighbors. Halfway houses which fail to establish close and effective community relations may expect, at best, suspicion and frequent misunderstandings of their program. Open hostility is equally as likely an occurrence. It is unwise and mistaken to regard the community as a necessary evil into which the facility has been thrust. There are only advantages to be gained from open, regular, and responsive community relations.

Certainly, a careful assessment should be made of a community's probable reaction to a proposed halfway house. There are very few desirable areas to locate where much deliberate and time-consuming planning need not be spent in developing pre-program community relations. Some people and organizations will be antagonistic. Others may be equally as opposed but less open about it. People will be resistive; probably most will be suspicious and uncertain about whether the halfway house will not depreciate property values, result in a crime wave, or simply be a burden on already existing community services.

It is always helpful in the planning stages to meet *individually* with community leaders to discuss the program and their reaction to it. They must be permitted and encouraged to air their questions and misgivings. It is not likely that those who favor the proposal will acknowledge this at large community meetings. The numbers opposed initially are not nearly as important as determining who the opposition is, its following, and motivation.

Community leaders approached individually may be expected to react favorably in most cases. Their position as community leaders, however, must be considered and recognized as a factor which makes it difficult to gain their open support. Realistically, the problem of enlisting community support lies in assuaging the anxieties of the least-informed but potentially most vocal community groups. Community leaders often are placed in the difficult position of reconciling their professional judgments with their roles as the representative voice of their communities. Planning a halfway house requires recognizing the difficult position in which community leaders are placed when their support and assistance are solicited.

Communication is an ongoing and two-way process. It is extremely important to appoint staff early to assume responsibility for building and maintaining positive community relations. Enlisting community support requires recruiting indigenous spokesmen of whom and with whom citizen groups will be much less suspicious and more likely to cooperate. Early consideration should be given to organizing local leaders into a community relations committee. Their involvement serves quickly to establish a positive agency image. The committee's importance later on as a buffer between the program and community should not be ignored. Its value is inestimable in times of crises. A community relations committee can be employed for fund-raising, obtaining special services, and other important purposes. In a nutshell, forming this committee is probably the single most important task facing new program administrators.

Programs that are successful in establishing effective working relationships with local agency and citizen groups have carefully planned and systematically organized their efforts to enlist community support. It pays dividends to meet at least once monthly (once every two weeks before the program opens) with the community relations committee whose advice and assistance should be sought regularly. It must be made clear in the beginning, however, that this is not a policy-setting board.

A helpful sequence for establishing sound community relations is as follows:

> Meet individually with local leaders of government; planning boards; private and public social, health, and welfare agencies; fraternal, church, and neighborhood improvement groups. Local police support is essential. If school-age populations are involved, school authorities should be contacted. This list is not inclusive and is only suggestive of the many important groups to contact.

> A steering committee of local leaders should be formed. It is helpful to have this group meet regularly to permit recognition and assurance of its mutual interest and support for the program.

> The program should be explained honestly. It is inadvisable and mistaken to not discuss the program in all its ramifications—this means difficulties and problems expected, as well as benefits and advantages.

> The assistance of neighborhood leaders, whose support has been enlisted previously, will do much to temper community antagonism and help avoid negative opposition forces from polarizing.

> Regularly scheduled meetings should be held both during the planning stages and after the program opens. It is helpful to think of annual or semi-annual community meetings (open houses) to which all who are interested may come to visit, meet staff, and learn of the progress, problems, and needs of the halfway house.

Administrators should realize that there is a relationship between what is "put into the community" and what one expects to "get out of it." The halfway house should not only be able to utilize community resources, but it also should provide some reciprocal measure of service to the community. It is good practice to encourage various community organizations to hold their regularly scheduled meetings occasionally in the facility. The dining room or lounge may be large enough to lend itself for this purpose. Neighborhood block associations, civic improvement clubs, and fraternal organizations are examples of the many groups which could be scheduled periodically. The advantages to this type of community-center involvement far outweigh any inconvenience.

Given a sensitive and community-responsive staff, a halfway house can help strengthen the fabric of community organization and relations. The community should be encouraged to look upon the halfway house as intimately and meaningfully involved in neighborhood affairs—regardless of whether the facility is directly affected by particular issues or not.

It is a mistake for community programs not to be concerned about day-to-day neighborhood problems and activities. Communities will not accept halfway houses and offer their support until and unless the agency and its staff can convince local people of their concern and interest in neighborhood affairs. For this reason, it behooves administrators of community programs to avoid isolating themselves or even giving this appearance to their neighbors. It is also unrealistic to expect residents to benefit from halfway house programs in which the administration itself avoids rather than confronts the realities and responsibilities of community involvement.

SPACE REQUIREMENTS

Two youths to a bedroom is a desirable number. Although some raise questions about sexual problems where two youths share a room, experience would likely demonstrate that staff anxieties and expectations are a more important consideration. When space or economy reasons do not permit two to a room, as many as four youths in a single room could be accommodated.

The rooms can be small, but should allow enough space for furniture and lounging. It is important that each room have its own window. When more than two youths occupy a room, bunk beds are fine space conservers. Two youths can share a single dresser and one large table (in addition to having space available in some other part of the building) for school work, letter writing, etc. A single closet or clothing bar can be shared to hang garments.

Steel furniture is a much more practical investment both in terms of its durability and cost. Durable plastic chairs, table tops, etc., are also worth consideration.

Sleeping two to a room, twelve double and three single rooms would be ideal for twenty-five youths. The two additional single rooms should be available for emergencies (unexpected visitors, unanticipated admittances, and postponed releases). The single rooms would be multi-purpose quarters. Youths for whom some program crisis, illness, or other reason made it important for them to sleep alone, could have this space available. In addition, three larger, single sleeping rooms should be reserved for staff, trainees, and guests. Each of these rooms should also have its own toilet and shower.

When the sleeping rooms are above the first floor, brick or masonry construction should be preferred. Horizontal construction offers many advantages over vertical designs. The building should permit quick and easy egress in case of fire, especially from sleeping areas. At least three exits from any part of the building should be available.

Space should be provided for adequate storage of household supplies, clothing, recreation equipment, etc. These rooms should have adequate ventilation and be located in places where access and purpose is considered. Space should also be set aside for combustibles which meets with the approval of the local fire department. It is important to invite the fire marshal to inspect the (plans) building, and make periodic recommendations. Local fire regulations should be complied with and fire drills held regularly.

Both the dining room and kitchen should be situated in areas that can be closed at times other than when meals are being served. The kitchen should be large enough for a commercial freezer, refrigerator, and stove, as well as offer adequate working space for the cook and helpers. If a building is being constructed, some of the larger pieces of equipment should be delivered before the door-bucks and partitions are installed. Large equipment should not be ordered until all pertinent dimensions are known.

Conference rooms are intended primarily for the daily group treatment meetings, which form the core of our halfway house model. Their use, however, should be multi-purpose (staff meeting rooms, classrooms, and quiet study areas). A location should be chosen which is away from the noise and hub of building activities. The offices must also afford some privacy and quiet, but should be easily and readily identifiable to visitors and permit visual control of the main entrance.

There are many advantages to having a resident superintendent. It is not likely, however, that such a job requirement will interest qualified applicants unless salaries are made attractive and modern, pleasant, living accommodations are provided. If residence is required, it should be made available without cost.

Approximately 9,000 square feet is suggested for a 25-bed halfway house. Construction costs vary but can range from $20 to $30 a square foot in the types of communities discussed. Facilities can also be leased. Per capita operating costs for the halfway house model discussed are about $11.15 per day. Properly planned, halfway houses can still be built for less than half the cost and operated at about two-thirds the amount per bed of traditional institutional programs. Large investments in buildings, time-consuming architectural planning, and relatively long construction periods can be avoided by leasing, which also makes it possible to open these programs with comparative ease.

WHERE DO WE GO FROM HERE?

Cost considerations alone should make it necessary to explore alternatives to institutionalizing people. Studied in the light of any fair appraisal of the benefits derived from traditional correctional systems, our weary dependence on institutions would likely evaporate. The bulk of our offender populations (adult and juvenile) do not belong in institutions. An increasing number of legislators and correctional administrators have become aware of this and appear committed to see changes brought about. Our prisons and conventional juvenile institutional programs are as much an anachronism as a social cancer. One of these days we may understand that our horror and fear of crime and criminals are by no means unrelated to our ignorance and apathy as to their causes and our "medicine man" approach to their cure. Unwittingly, criminal behavior has been nurtured and exacerbated by the public's ignorance about the consequences of traditional correctional practices. In this regard, poorly located, punitively designed, and primitively programmed institutions, in which far too many offenders spend time, are monuments to our ignorance.

We are not discovering anything new. As Hans Mattick pointed out, in a volume which should be required reading for anyone apprehensive about the failings of our correctional system, some of the same points were made over a century ago.[1] Mattick reminds us that "The thirty-seven principles enunciated at that time (1870) by the foremost prison administrators in this country touched upon every significant phase of imprisonment and many of the recommendations made still remain to be implemented by most of the prisons existing today."[2] Not too much has happened since Mattick wrote this. There are exceptions, however, where dramatic progress, no matter how long overdue, is being made. The move toward community programs and more socially and psychologically productive living seems to be catching hold.

While institutions have become much more humane in treating offenders, vested interests which many have in jobs, contracts, and payrolls, remain as the most obvious and difficult problems with which reformers must struggle. When the needs of offenders, as well as the public, are placed above parochial interests and concerns, the use of community programs should increase significantly. Until this happens, halfway houses will remain a sorely needed, under-utilized, albeit readily available correctional "Best Buy."[3]

NOTES

1. Hans Mattick, "Foreword: A Discussion of the Issue," *The Future of Imprisonment in a Free Society*, vol. 2. (Chicago: St. Leonard's House, 1965), p. 8.
2. Ibid.
3. Space requirements for halfway houses and budgetary information may be obtained by writing to the author at 311 South Calhoun Street, Tallahassee, Florida 32304.

chapter eleven
POST-INSTITUTIONAL REHABILITATION OF THE PENAL OFFENDER: A COMMUNITY EFFORT

Reuben J. Margolin

Perhaps the greatest area of neglect in the field of rehabilitation is concern for the penal offender. Rehabilitation programs within most penal institutions are either very poor or nonexistent. A recent U.S. Department of Labor publication reveals the massive extent of this neglect:

> Although more than 100,000 persons leave Federal and State prisons each year, few of them receive the kind of training, while in prison, which would enable them to compete successfully for jobs. An even larger number of releasees, many of them teenaged youths, leave correctional institutions in cities and towns where modern training programs are, for the most part, not available. Most penologists emphasize that the purposes of imprisonment should be rehabilitation rather than punishment and that training and education are important instruments for rehabilitation. Our society, however, has not provided the facilities and personnel needed to develop the work skills of prisoners.[1]

The community has not granted top priority to the rehabilitation of the penal offender. Instead, the tendency has been to blot the problem out of our collective memory. Rehabilitation workers, those best trained to handle the problems of deviance and disability, also tend to avoid working with the penal offender. However, the reality and the pressures of our times are forcing society to become concerned not only with the prevention

From *Federal Probation*, XXXI, 1 (1967), pp. 46–50. Reprinted by permission.

of crime but also with the task of transforming the offender into a responsible citizen. The rehabilitation of the penal offender is a joint effort involving the offender, the professional worker, and the community. Unless the community accepts its responsibility and indeed plays a strategic role, successful rehabilitation of the offender will be jeopardized.

There is no need to cite the dramatic and increasing crime statistics, nor is it necessary to elaborate upon the daily consequences to the average citizen. The high recidivism rate of the offender is well known. These facts are too familiar to all of us. It is the pressing nature of these circumstances, combined with the trend of the times as reflected in the philosophy of the Great Society, which now makes the rehabilitation of the penal offender crucial.

A MODEL FOR REHABILITATION

The predominance of a custodial orientation among penal officials poses a major obstacle to the development of rehabilitation programs. Even those favorably disposed toward rehabilitation are sometimes overwhelmed by the enormity of the task. Yet, is there a better alternative? The majority of offenders, and this includes lifers, will eventually be discharged from prison. Without rehabilitation it is better than chance that the dischargee will leave the institution with his criminal behavior patterns more deeply entrenched. In addition, he will more than likely be shunned like the plague by respectable society; and as a result, the stage is set for the reenactment of criminal behavior, only this time with more bitterness and frustration. It is virtually impossible to correct these antisocial patterns without rehabilitation, because a substantial number of the offenders are socially and mentally sick.

The psychiatric model for rehabilitation is one from which we can learn a great deal, borrow, and build upon. Great strides have been made in the successful rehabilitation of the psychiatric patient. Today we accept the idea that the rehabilitated mental patient can return to employment and to family living. However, this crowning achievement was not attained without a struggle. Resistances came from within the psychiatric profession as well as from the community. On the other hand, there were dedicated professionals and nonprofessionals who relentlessly pursued the rehabilitation goal and demonstrated what could be done.

In many respects the problem of rehabilitating the penal offender is similar to that of rehabilitating the psychiatric patient. In both situations unpredictable behavior patterns constitute a central problem. One of the major tasks, then, is to encourage more stable behavior; otherwise, it would be difficult to establish realistic goals for the individual. Both situations require the establishment of a rehabilitation plan which would include measures to satisfy psychodynamic needs as well as job objectives. Thus the rehabilitation plan embraces necessary physical restorative treatment, guidance, testing, counseling, pre-vocational exploration, work conditioning, job training, placement, and follow-up.

GOALS OF REHABILITATION

Undoubtedly the most important element in the rehabilitation of either the psychiatric patient or penal offender is the matter of trust. Those who work with these clients must have a firm conviction that basically all human beings have a deep-seated drive toward health and normalcy. We must provide every opportunity for a trusting relationship, for without it rehabilitation cannot succeed. Penal offenders must change from an antisocial to a socially acceptable identity with all that such an identity implies—work, family living, social and civic participation. To help the penal offender establish a new identity is probably the major mission of rehabilitation.

Although there are similarities, the rehabilitation of the penal offender is more difficult than that of the psychiatric patient. Society needs scapegoats, something to feel moral about, and successful rehabilitation may choke off a convenient avenue for expressing moral indignation. This feeling of righteousness may be a reflection of the need to project our own larcenous impulses upon someone else.

Some questions may be raised about the great risk involved in rehabilitating offenders. Failure rates may be high for a number of reasons, but the major cause is that few institutions have adequately developed comprehensive rehabilitation programs. The trend toward the increasing use of work-release programs is an important step in the right direction. Through this procedure prisoners are released during the day to work on jobs in nearby communities and return to prison at night for confinement. Although the work-release plan is not new, having begun with Wisconsin's Huber Law of 1913, it is gaining increasing significance today because of its integral relationship to the total rehabilitation process. Work-release programs are now in operation in the Federal Bureau of Prisons (Prisoner Rehabilitation Act of 1965) and at least half of our fifty states.[2]

Similarly, the Manpower Development and Training Program being conducted in cooperation with the U.S. Department of Labor at the District of Columbia's Lorton Youth Center holds great promise.[3] If creative rehabilitation is unavailable, the offender will find it difficult to function effectively in the community. The failures may cause consternation and public outcry and even a demand to return to the safety of the custodial institution. But let us never forget the community is being insulted every day by aggravated incidents of crime, often by recidivists who in almost all cases were untreated in the prison.

It is axiomatic that if the offender is to be successfully returned to employment in the community, rehabilitation measures must begin in the penal institution. Furthermore, it must continue for a long period after discharge. To begin a rehabilitation program after the offender leaves prison generally will not work. The moment he enters prison, hope should be communicated through the potential of rehabilitation. Each individual should receive a thorough assessment to determine what he needs to meet in a socially acceptable way the demands of daily living in the community. A careful schedule of therapy and activity should be planned for each individual. This may include individual psychotherapy, group therapy, recreation, education, pre-vocational exploration, specific job training, and vocational counseling. All of these activities must be related to a central rehabilitation goal; otherwise, these activities become fragmented and meaningless.

THE COMMUNITY PLAYS A STRATEGIC ROLE AS A THERAPEUTIC PARTNER

When the offender is ready to leave the institution, the employer in industry must be taken in as a therapeutic partner.[4] The employer must be made cognizant of the ex-offender's special problems. We must recognize that all our hard work within the institution can go down the drain if we do not have both ample job opportunities and understanding employers. The offender, incidentally, should be thoroughly prepared for the stress, strain, and frustrations involved in job hunting. Role playing is the best medium through which this preparation can be accomplished.

Some people may feel that cracking employer resistance may be too overwhelming and thankless a task. I cannot agree with this point of view. Employers will hire discharged penal offenders, if a proper case for the job prospect is presented and if evidence can be provided that adequate rehabilitation treatment was received within the institution.

The author's experience of placing over 700 mental patients on jobs in industry is a substantiation of this hypothesis. A number of these patients had been confined in both mental hospitals and penal institutions. Four individuals, particularly, stand out as examples of successful rehabilitation as a result of a joint therapeutic partnership between industry and the hospital. Since their discharge from the military service, they had spent most of their lifetime alternating between prison and mental hospitals, depending upon the circumstances under which they were apprehended. One was a confidence man with a flair for fleecing; another was a car thief who delighted in banging up the cars after they were stolen; a third, an ex-professional boxer, was arrested thirty-five times for assault and battery while under the influence of liquor; and a fourth was convicted with a history of rape. Among them they represented over sixty years of confinement. All four, after a thorough rehabilitation program in which the employer was directly involved, were placed on jobs in the community. They are still working after a seven-year period and have remained out of trouble, also.

Just as the employer has been successfully involved as a therapeutic partner, other community agents can play a similar constructive role. The horizons of the penal offender would be greatly expanded if institutions and agencies such as civic clubs, churches, unions, fraternal organizations, and educational, recreational, and governmental agencies were to band together to provide the supportive framework for the offender to take his rightful place in society. Psychiatric rehabilitation has been primarily successful because community support has been mobilized in this way.

Here are a few examples of how community elements can be utilized as therapeutic partners. The Chambers of Commerce and other organizations with industrial affiliations can be a fertile medium for developing employer involvement in the rehabilitation of the penal offender. The author found that by developing a cooperative relationship with a local Chamber of Commerce, serious obstacles to employment opportunities were eliminated. The approach was simple. Each month the executive director would invite five employers to a luncheon meeting with a rehabilitation representative from a psychiatric hospital. A single case was presented and discussed in detail. Job placement assistance for this particular patient was asked for, either through their own firms or employment leads elsewhere. These monthly meetings achieved the goal of selective job placement without too much difficulty. An identical format was employed in working with volunteer organizations that sent their members to volunteer their services in the hospital.

Churches can perform a more vital function than they now assume. For example, clergymen can reintroduce the offender into the mainstream of living, through church suppers and other church-related programs. Unfortunately, some clergymen adopt a moralistic and even condemnatory outlook, which has the effect of driving the offender away from the church.

Big Brothers can be a strong stabilizing force with offenders. This is especially true of those in their teens and twenties. The emotional deprivation experienced by these individuals through rejection in quite pronounced and traumatic. Acceptance by societal representatives is essential. Because the ability to accept a person regardless of one's dubious past is so vital, Big Brothers must be carefully selected for qualities of understanding, empathy, and firmness. The last is important because individuals treading on uncertain grounds will always test their benefactors.

Unions can play a central role in breaking down employment barriers, if they can be encouraged to accept a rehabilitation philosophy.

With offenders who have retained their union membership, no difficulty is generally encountered with eliciting union cooperation for participation in the rehabilitation process. Major blocks occur when entrance into an apprenticeship program or union membership is sought for the first time. In the author's experience, pressure must be exerted at the local level in order to remove prejudicial and discriminatory practices. In some cases he was very successful, but in others he met a wall of resistance. Nevertheless, the fact that some unions did accept the challenge is indicative of the need to relentlessly pursue the goal of engaging unions as therapeutic partners.

In a similar vein, schools and universities must open their doors to offenders with academic potential. Admission criteria must be made more flexible because many of these individuals suffer from erratic school performance. Scholarship and other financial assistance must be readily available. Counseling through university services should be offered, when necessary prior to entrance and during matriculation. In one university, for example, where a scholarship was given to a penal offender, five counseling sessions were necessary to prepare this individual for admission. This person had a need to express his fears and anxieties about going back to school after many years, to deprecate himself for past sins, and to receive assurance that he would receive acceptance and support in the academic environment. If schools and universities can be magnanimous in this way, undoubtedly much productive talent would be salvaged.

Government agencies can be very helpful in the rehabilitation process. One of the most important developments in recent years is the growing interest in state rehabilitation agencies in rehabilitating the penal offender. Cooperative agreements between state vocational rehabilitation agencies and the state corrections department have paved the way for more comprehensive programs in penal institutions. At the federal level, the Vocational Rehabilitation Administration has provided grants for research and demonstration as well as for short-term training institutes. Through one of its grants it established the Joint Commission of Correctional Manpower and Training, which plans to make extended studies in this area and to offer recommendations for solving some of the persistent problems.

A community effort must also include wide participation from community citizens. All other areas dim in significance if citizen participation is neglected. Many a successful rehabilitation within a penal institution has been undone because of vindictive attitudes in the community, legal restrictions, and just plain misunderstanding. The correctional field needs to embark on a project similar to the mental health and mental retardation planning programs which are helping to bring about so many needed changes in these two fields. A correctional planning program would recruit citizen task forces to tackle such problems as helping the offender get a job when bonding companies will not provide bond, removing impediments in our states which prohibit convicted persons from obtaining employment in trades in which they are skilled, and removing from many of our states the criminal registration ordinances which demean the offender beyond reason and make it difficult or impossible for rehabilitation to follow to a successful conclusion. The rehabilitation process is stymied unless an aroused citizenry exerts the necessary pressure upon lawmakers, our trade associations, and others who continue archaic inhibitory practices.

Follow-up is essential if rehabilitation is to be successful. This process should not be too difficult to carry out, because a structure already exists in the parole system. Follow-up procedures should be carried out for a minimum period of a year, and longer if necessary. Actually, the services of the parole officer or whoever does the follow-up should be available whenever the ex-offender seeks help. There should be two major phases to the follow-up, namely, periodic regular follow-up and crisis intervention. Periodic regular follow-ups are necessary to evaluate the individual's progress and to assist him in building a firm foundation for community living. Crisis intervention is necessary because stresses and strains do mount up; and with the fragile egos of so many of the ex-offenders, they may find it difficult or even impossible to cope with critical situations without some assistance. Follow-up, if skillfully employed, represents a wise investment of the professional's time.

SUMMARY AND CONCLUSIONS

In summary, rehabilitation, if it is to be effective, must begin the moment an offender enters the penal institution. A favorable emotional atmosphere should be established in which the cultural expectation is that the offender has a chance of succeeding in rehabilitation. In this respect, we must develop a trust in the inmate's ability to respond to rehabilitation measures. A complete evaluation must be given to determine which psychodynamic needs and vocational goals can be met and through what rehabilitation activities. The rehabilitation program must be continued in the community, buttressed by periodic regular follow-up and crisis intervention. Employers and other community resources must be involved as therapeutic partners. If this combination of steps is pursued, the chances are good that the ex-offender can secure employment. However, we must not delude ourselves that employment opportunities can be obtained without faith in the offender and without the dedication and commitment to the idea that rehabilitation must be initiated without delay and is a crucial factor in each case. In the final analysis, extensive citizen involvement will provide the pillars of support for successful rehabilitation.

NOTES

1. U.S. Department of Labor, Manpower Administration, *Manpower Research*, Bulletin No. 8, April 1966.
2. Stanley E. Grupp, "Work Release and the Misdemeanant," *Federal Probation* (June 1965), pp. 6–12.
3. Thomas R. Sard, "A Chance on the Outside," *American Education* (April 1966), pp. 29–32.
4. The concept of the employer as a therapeutic partner has been described by the author in a number of articles, of which the following are representative: "The Former Mental Patient, An Untapped Labor Source," *Personnel, Journal of the American Management Association* (January 1961); "How an Employer Can Help Mental Patients," *Rehabilitation Record* (May–June 1964); "Ex-Mental Patient Succeeds: A Tribute to His Employer," *Rehabilitation Record* (March–April 1966).

chapter twelve
THE REINTEGRATION OF THE OFFENDER INTO THE COMMUNITY: SOME HOPES AND SOME FEARS

Frank P. Miller

The reintegration of the offender is a recurring challenge. At times we delude ourselves that we have the final answers, but in each succeeding generation—indeed, in each succeeding decade—crime shows up in new forms, and in each cycle the public needs to learn new lessons and to relearn old lessons.

The problem of the offender, like the poor, seems to be forever with us and perhaps for the same reasons. We have continuing dramatic examples of the offender's reaction to society and society's reaction to the offender. We have no cause for complacency.

Down through the years society has been concerned to defend itself from the criminal and, at the same time, to ensure proper treatment for the criminal. This concern has been expressed in demands upon the authorities "that something be done." Society is not always sure what should be done, but certainly something should be done! Some sections of the public have been concerned that the criminal has not been treated well enough and that not enough is done to assist him in his reintegration into society. Others have felt that he has been treated too well. From time to time, society's concern has found expression through Royal commissions and special committees. These commissions and committees have presented thoughtful and stimulating reports. Governments have, bit by bit, seen to it that their recommendations should be given effect (not always as quickly and as fully as some would like).

Reprinted from the *Canadian Journal of Corrections*, vol. 12, no. 4 (1970), pp. 466–81, published by the Canadian Criminology and Corrections Association, 55 Parkdale Avenue, Ottawa.

We are awaiting the publication of the latest of a long list. Some of my listeners will have worked as consultants with the Canadian Committee on Corrections headed by The Honorable Mr. Justice Roger Quimet. We are all anxious to learn the recommendations of that committee. I thought it might be useful to take a little "look back." I think this because I believe that progress is something relative. Anticipation of progress is only possible in an overview that is retrospective.

In 1938 the encyclopaedic Archambault Report was published. It was not the first report by any means—nor the last. Some reports since the Archambault Report have been the Report of the Saskatchewan Penal Commission in 1946, the report of a commission to inquire into the state and management of the jails in British Columbia in 1950, the report of the commission on the jail system in New Brunswick in 1951, and the Report of the Select Committee of the Legislative Assembly in the Province of Ontario in 1954. Finally, in 1956, the Report of the Committee headed by Mr. Justice J. Fauteux of the Supreme Court of Canada was published.

More recently a commission in the Province of Quebec headed by Batonnier Yves Prevost, Q.C., has published its first volume. This report, entitled "Crime, Justice and Society," sets out fundamental principles of a new social action program.

Here is a quotation from one particular Royal commission that you may find interesting:

> The vast number of human beings annually committed to prison in every civilized country and the reflection that there they may receive first lessons in crime or be led into the path of right—that after a brief space they are to be thrown back on their old habits more deeply versed than ever before in the mysteries of crime, or be returned to society with new feelings, industrious habits and good resolutions for the future—must ever render the management of penal institutions a study of deep importance for the statesman.

If you have been trying to identify the report from which that quotation was taken and you have gone only so far back as the Archambault Commission, you are just ninety-nine years too late. You could go back to the 1921 Report of the Committee to Advise upon a Revision of the Penitentiary Regulations, and find something of the same type there, or go beyond that to the Report of the Royal Commission on Penitentiaries in 1914. But for the precise words that I have just given, you would have to go to the Report of the Commissioners Appointed to Enquire into and Report upon the Conduct, Economy, Discipline and Management of the Provincial Penitentiary at Kingston in 1849.

My point is this (if I need to labor it at all): that wherever able and humane men have been called upon to examine closely the problem of the treatment society does accord and the treatment society should accord its offenders, these able and humane men always come up with somewhat similar conclusions. There is a remarkable insistence upon certain basic principles.

I do not mean that they had all the answers in 1849 and that we simply have wasted some 120 years, nor do I mean that we have all the answers today or that we are limited to the answers of 1849. I am speaking in a relative sense.

By making allowances for changing language and changing cultures, I can fairly say that all the Royal commissions have found common ground in a few basic principles. They soon discover that punishment at its best is not enough and at its worst defeats its own end. Report after report challenges the assumption that custodial punishment alone deters the criminal.

Having taken this step, they next decide that criminals cannot be thrown together in one group and then treated en masse with any hope that they will, in the end, result in being any better than when they first appeared before court. Whatever the language at their time, they always propose some sort of individualized treatment or classification. As a logical corollary to that conclusion, the commissioners are bound to much stress on productive work and, wherever possible, meaningful vocation training.

With few exceptions Royal commissions have acknowledged the importance of having a well paid, qualified, and properly motivated staff. Then they recognize that, even if the best is done by way of treatment during the period of detention, something must be done on a follow-up basis after prison. The Commissioners of 1849 had this to say:

> It must be confessed that the success of any system of prison discipline will be strongly affected by the treatment which the convict receives on his discharge from confinement. A convict may leave his cell penitent and determined to reform, but if he is met with harshness and refused employment, then his good resolutions treated with scorn, despair will soon overtake him, poverty and of course the circumstances will too often drive him back to the heart of crime.

Now having themselves found out so much, these able and humane commissioners easily recognize that the public as a whole has little understanding of the problem. And so every Royal commissioner proposes that something be done in this respect. The commissioners of 1849 said:

> Governments can do little to avert this snare [i.e., his rejection by society] from the path of the reformed criminal. The forces of public opinion will alone effectually remove the evil.

In 1938, the Archambault Commission recommended:

> The interests of the public should be enlisted in an organized manner, having regard to the vital importance of the prevention of

crime. Social agencies and churches and schools and cooperation of the home should be organized to this end.

The Fauteux Committee recommended:

> A serious effort should be made by all Governments concerned, whether Federal, Provincial or Municipal, to acquaint the public with the purpose of a sound system of corrections and the benefits to be derived from it.

What will the Quimet Report say?

The more recent reports in a more sophisticated age lay emphasis on two needs not so well recognized by their predecessors. Both the Archambault Commission and the Fauteux Committee recognized the need for integration—an integrated approach to the problem of the offender and the need for scientific examination of the problem.

The Prevost Commission only this year stated:

> The commission has become overwhelmingly aware of the fact that Quebec's traditional methods of punishment have provided unsatisfactory and even deplorable results. Individuals have been unnecessarily and systematically marked for life by short sentences of imprisonment without any real need for such action. Society has almost entirely neglected helping guilty persons to reintegrate themselves to a normal milieu. At the level of expenditures probationary measures and rehabilitation services have never merited more than token sums of money.

In the Parole Service, understandably if not always justifiably, we have felt that we were leaders in facing up to the real problems of reintegration of the offender into the community. I bow deeply in the direction of the after-care agencies and the probation services in that connection. Sometimes we have felt that the public has recognized our problem and the measure of success that we have achieved. Sometimes, though, it has been loud and clear (and sadly so) that the public does not feel this way about us. However, during the last three or four years we have been getting what is usually referred to as a "good press." Not always do our friends in the press get all the facts and figures as precisely as we would like them to, but generally speaking, they do a quite reasonable job.

I recently came across an editorial that I would like to read to you:

Our Parole System

If there is any faith to be put in figures, our parole system in dealing with criminals has proved its value during the eleven years it has been in operation. According to the head of the Parole organization, of the 3,072 prisoners released from penitentiaries on parole during that period, 2,000 have justified their right to freedom by living the lives of self respecting and industrious citizens, 999 are still reporting to the authorities, and only 62 have found their way back to the courts through the lure of their old habits and activities.

When only a fraction of 2 percent of the men whom we are forced to school in our penitentiaries can be classed tentatively as confirmed criminals, there are two legitimate deductions: first, the opportunities are not closed to the man who has made a slip but is desirous of living down the memory of it; and second, our system of bringing this about is one which, while still protecting society against the irreducible minimum of criminals, makes the way easy for the man who honestly means to lead a better life. The Parole Head's statement that Canada today can boast of a smaller percentage of criminals who persist in their crimes than any other country in the world is one which we have good reason to be proud.

I said "I recently came across that editorial"—I did not say it was a "recent editorial." I shall now confess to you that I made one slight change in reading that editorial to you: I referred to "Parole Head." The editorial actually refers to "The Dominion Parole Officer Archibald." The editorial appeared in the *Montreal Daily Star* on Saturday, January 14, 1911.

More than fifty-seven years ago, apparently, we were satisfied with our parole system.

What happened in the interim? There was perhaps an intoxication of victory. Paroles continued, but in the 1920s the system was not achieving the same success, and editorials changed their tone. Finally, a massive attack on the system was made by a concerned section of the public and there was a reorganization. The mood changed so considerably that a later head of the parole organization in the late 1920s was able to report with some pride to his Deputy Minister that he had succeeded over a two-year period in reducing considerably the number of paroles that had been granted.

Now that is enough looking backward. My purpose has been to challenge two kinds of complacency: (1) We have a good enough system now; and (2) All we need to do is adopt "this new system."

We have known so much for so long, why haven't we done a better job?

I am a humble student of Toynbee and find myself often using his concepts to answer many social questions. It seems to me that we have been creative in the past under the stimulus of *"new ground," "blows," "pressures,"* and *"penalizations"* —to use Toynbee's terms. There has been a "nemesis for our creativity" because of our "idolization of self—institution —and technique." We have been easily intoxicated with victory.

Having had somewhat the same experience as Preston Sharp, General Secretary of the American Correctional Association, I can easily agree with him in his warning last fall to a seminar in Regina:

> This period of innovation is in some ways reminiscent of the early 1930s when classification was introduced—the principle and philosophy was excellent, but the implementation fell far short.

Some of the past fast failure—in fact, in my opinion a great deal of the past failure—has been due to the fragmentation and lack of coordination in the whole judicio-correctional process. We are moving into a period of innovation and creativity—a period of change that is more significant than anything I have seen in my own twenty-three years of activity in Canadian corrections. That is what has inspired our Congress theme and set the context for our discussion today: "New Resources and Perspectives."

What do we mean by reintegration of the offender into the community? What is our aim? Why do some become reintegrated and others not?

Several years ago I was discussing the subject with one of my co-workers. I posed the question as to what made the difference. My friend replied that of the many rehabilitated men that he had known, there was this one common characteristic in their situations: Each had managed to get a stake in the "square-john community" that he could not profitably abandon by a return to crime. I have never found a better answer. It sounds like a truism, but we seem to forget that is what we are mainly striving for. It simply has to be worthwhile for a criminal to stop being a criminal. There has to be some satisfaction.

This stake in the community can have different forms. With some people, in fact with many, this has amounted to nothing more than a good job. With others, it has been a new and deeper relationship with friends and relatives. With still others, it has been a self-realization in service to the community or in creative achievements.

These people made some efforts in the direction of the square-john community and by chance (or by choice on the part of some far-seeing people in the community) they were reinforced positively in their efforts and so they went on until finally they were no longer criminals.

HALFWAY HOUSES

I make genuflection in the direction of the halfway houses and community release centers. There is no need for me in this paper to extol the virtues of the halfway houses or talk about the need of some phasing from the regime of prison to the full freedom of community life. This has been well done by people who are more knowledgeable and more expert in this area than I am.

I think the main contribution I can make today in this area is to throw out some cautions. Whatever may be the need, let us not so idolize the institution that we forget its purpose.

We should remember that some associations of criminals and ex-criminals, and those who want to become ex-criminals, may not always lead to an emphasis of noncriminal behaviour. A halfway house on the one hand may be simply a continuation of some of the undesirable features of the so-called prison subculture. A halfway house may, in other words, serve to preserve criminal values rather than be a stepping stone to noncriminal values.

It may foster a continuing dependence. Let us keep the halfway houses for those who can most benefit from the type of support it offers.

DAY PAROLE

We have been making considerable use of day parole in recent years, both in cooperation with the penitentiaries and with some provincial institutions. This is not really a brand-new thing. More than forty years ago, the Ontario extra-mural permit system operated a work release program on a huge scale. It fell into disuse, but a revitalization of the concept took place in the early fifties when the former Remission Service of the Department of Justice introduced what is called "gradual release." This is a procedure designed to assist particularly the long-term prisoner in his, or her, progressive adjustment to community life. Under this method the inmate to be released is allowed to leave the prison daily, and sometimes overnight, during a period extending from one week to as much as three months just prior to final release on parole or the expiration of sentence.

At its minimum, gradual release usually includes shopping trips, opening bank accounts, registration at the Canada Manpower office, attendance at church, visiting private homes, some recreational activities, movies, athletic events. In some cases local employers provide temporary full-time employment over periods of a few weeks. Here the inmate leaves the institution each morning on his own recognizance to do his day's work. In some instances prisoners are permitted to go out each day on their own to look for permanent employment.

The current use of day parole has reached the point where last year, 1968, the National Parole Board granted 259 day paroles; and in the first four months of this year, 128 day paroles were granted.

Day parole may be seen to offer continuity of institutional treatment that enables a partial move into the community. Generally, there are three types:

    1. *Mid-sentence day parole* will enable release for employment, attendance at educational institution, or other activities that

have rehabilitative content. These may include, for example, daily release of female inmates to attend to the needs of their family and home.
2. *Pre-release day parole* will provide for a socialization experience which may include employment, etc., prior to release on expiry of sentence.
3. *Gradual release* will provide a socialization experience prior to release on full ordinary parole, which will have already been granted either absolutely or in principle.

Section 26 of the Penitentiary Act has provided for temporary absences not to exceed fifteen days. These temporary absences are granted frequently for home visits on both compassionate and rehabilitative grounds, but do aid in the resocialization. The Commissioner of Penitentiaries has reported that approximately 1,000 such temporary absences were granted last year.

The new Omnibus Bill amendments to the Parole Act and the Prison and Reformatories Act has made provision for the temporary absence to be given to provincial authorities and has particularly defined day parole and given it a legal status that we have not enjoyed up to this time.

THE CHRONIC PETTY OFFENDER

I want to talk now about the reintegration of a type of offender who offers very little prospect of successful reintegration by our usual standards. I may be bold to suggest that we admit that he cannot be reintegrated into society in such a way that he will no longer require our help. I refer to what is usually termed the "chronic petty offender."

We all know the pattern: failure to hold a job—drinking—petty offense—arrest—conviction—short sentence—institution identification with the administration of the institution—relatively productive and useful time within the prison—sentence comes to an end—discharge—job for a short period of time or even the job bypassed—more drinking—another petty offense, and so it goes on.

Why not recognize from the start that many of these people are simply not able to cope in our complex society! Why impose a moral obligation upon them to take care of themselves! They simply cannot do it!

The tragedy of it is that they require so very little support. If we could identify them as being mentally retarded, we would have no moral problem in offering our continued support in a sheltered situation. Why then can we not support on a continuous basis those who are *socially* retarded!

It's not as if this would cost us more money. Horrors no! We are willing in our moral smugness to pay thousands of dollars for their continuing arrest, conviction, and incarceration in an expensive penal institution, and destroy their dignity into the bargain!

Some of them are living a life of some dignity already, in sheltered situations. This has been notably supplied by the Salvation Army in their rehabilitation centers. I know men who have gone in and out of prisons for many years, who today hold up their heads as contributing members of society in a Salvation Shelter Workshop with the support of an institutional head, who have the freedom to walk down the street—to visit with friends—to go to a movie—to say, "I am doing my part to the best I can."

I am not talking about halfway houses. I am talking about a permanent sheltered base for men who would otherwise be consistently in and out of prison. I acknowledge the contribution that the Salvation Army has made in this area, and I challenge the churches in Canada to follow their example and develop new methods. I challenge the after-care societies to see whether they might find a new field of activity here.

EMPLOYMENT

The question of employment for the ex-offender is, of course, crucial. It is a two-fold problem. There is the problem of discrimination against the offender by employer and potential fellow employee and there is the problem of the ex-offender's ability to meet the employer's needs.

In this changing society, it is quite evident that, while there are increasing opportunities for skilled workers, especially in new fields, there are decreasing opportunities for semi-skilled workers and a rapidly decreasing opportunity for unskilled workers. Moreover, large groups of people are leaving our educational institutions yearly, to offer aggressive competition to the ex-offender leaving the penal institution.

The vocational training programs or the lack of vocational training programs in penal institutions in this country have been the subject of sharp criticism. As one bureaucrat, I can only offer sympathy to my fellow bureaucrats in the institutional field who have striven to provide a suitable new vocational training program only to find that by the time it was implemented, it was out of date.

However, much is happening in this area. The very excellent cooperation of industry in the Montreal area in providing a training program for computer programmers has reached a point of producing results. We in the parole side have done our part to facilitate the exploitation of the training of new job opportunities both by way of day parole and regular parole.

The study undertaken by the Canadian Corrections Association with respect to the vocational training program in the Canadian Penitentiaries has moved to a point where an experimental project is being introduced at the new Warkworth Institution. This project is a joint effort of the

Canadian Penitentiary Service, Canada Manpower, and the National Parole Service.

There is still discrimination against ex-offenders. We are ever reminded of this in the continuing flow of applications for pardons that we receive. However, the change in the twenty-three years of my own personal involvement in corrections work is tremendous. I take the opportunity to pay tribute to both the humanitarian and good business sense of many small business proprietors and many large corporations who have established policies of non-discrimination against ex-offenders.

It is sometimes surprising the extent to which an employer will meet the challenge when it is put to him. I recall a case that I dealt with while I was a Penitentiary Classification Officer about eighteen years ago. I was working with a young man in the prison who had been there fourteen years on a life sentence; he was hopeful for parole, but he had nowhere to go and nobody to help him. He had some ideas of settling in a particular city in which I was acquainted. I decided—not easily—to approach a friend of mine in that city to give assistance in securing employment in the trade that the young man had learned in prison.

My friend's reply was that he would give him a job in his own firm and keep him, so long as he had work for him and for so long as the man did a competent job. He told me later that he had never been asked before to do anything like this and he had never thought of it before. He said to me,

> I didn't want to say yes, I could see a great deal of difficulty for me. I could see many reasons why I should say no, but the inescapable question in my mind was: *If I say no, who will say yes?*

Only this last year, we had the experience of one of our field officers in approaching an employer who was unaware that his employee was in prison. We had a proposal for day parole for this offender. The employer had assumed that the employee was ill. When we approached him with fear and trembling about the status of his employee who was now in prison, we were delighted with his response to the challenge and his willingness to make arrangements to have this employee continue on a day parole basis to the completion of his short sentence.

The Public Service Commission of Canada, as a matter of policy for many years, has not refused to hire a job applicant otherwise suitable on the grounds that he had been convicted of an offense. It has now gone so far as to eliminate from its application form any question in respect to this matter.

NEW PROGRAMS

I should like to single out for comment two types of program that are receiving some attention at this time.

The first is the "All-Around Attack Program." That is the best name I can give it. It is the converse of the "All-Around Defense" concept we were taught in the Army. To avoid confusion I have used the word "attack" rather than "offense." (Such are the problems of communication!)

This is the kind of thing developed by Harold B. Bradley (California) and others. They describe it as a "Model Treatment Program." It represents a synthesis or a syncretism (if you'll pardon the theological analogy) of many treatment approaches. Bradley says, in commenting on past performance, "But instead of trying to devise new programs we merely tampered with old ones." He and his colleagues have developed a new model which is institution-based, but the institution is in the community:

> The operating units are to be located physically and sociologically in the communities which supply the program's consumers.
>
> Each program unit is a community correctional center which combines, in one location and within one organization design, the present functions of correctional institutions, halfway houses, district parole offices, and work furlough units.

And beyond that the citizens can use the facility for social programs of a delinquency prevention nature.

Such a blurring of traditionally separated programs simply forces us to abandon the idolization of our own institution and techniques. As I see it, the treatment emphasis is by a reinforcement technique to teach the client "to make decisions and live with the outcome of their decisions." In other words, "you pays your money and takes your choice," and that's what life is all about.

The second type of program I wish to mention is the "Challenge-Response" program. This is typical in the Boulder Bay Program in British Columbia. The Detention Centre program in the United Kingdom is another example. Here the idea is to take a noninstitutionalized young offender—present him with a strong physical and social challenge, help him reach a high point of achievement, and then quickly place him back in the community. The National Parole Board, I may say, is working closely with the British Columbia Board of Parole and the Corrections Branch to enable the quick return to the community of the successful Boulder Bay students.

Both of these programs present a tremendous challenge to our procedural methods and divisions of jurisdiction. How can the parole authority, for example, play a useful role in these programs? From my position of vested interest, I suggest that a separate authority could best take responsibility for major changes in status. But the system must be flexible. There may be a place for delegation in the future—delegation within prescribed criteria subject to the control of a post audit.

THE NEW CAREERS CONCEPT

I now come to the question of the use of ex-offenders as case aides in the correctional process. (I might mention an excellent booklet on the subject put out by the Joint Commission on Correctional Manpower and Training. It is entitled "Offenders as a Correctional Manpower Resource.")

Offenders and ex-offenders are, and have been, an important manpower resource. We reject the exploitive use of the offender as simply a cheap source of labor. There are at least three ways in which the offender and ex-offender can be integrated into the correctional process as an agent.

First, he can become a volunteer helper. This is a challenge, particularly to the after-care agencies. There has been some contribution from the ex-offender but much less than we would expect. One or two old friends I see at annual meetings; sometimes I hear about help given to a new parolee from a former parolee. I am not sure that my impressions reveal the full story. Nevertheless, it seems to me there is much to do.

The second group of ex-offenders who can help is that group of people who have the potentiality for a full professional career. There are a very few full-time professional workers in the corrections field who are ex-offenders. I feel that there could be more. I am sure that there are others who have the ability and the desire, but who believe that the obstacles to success are too great. They believe they would never be accepted. We must all accept this challenge to identify and encourage the potential professional worker and finally accept him on our staff.

Finally, we come to what has been called the "New Careers" concept. Here is the greatest potential source of manpower. The offender becomes involved in the change process, first as the object of change and then as an agent of change. The logical final step is to use the ex-offender as a full-time employee. Personnel policies of job classification, educational standards, pay levels, and security of information must all undergo a great change to accommodate the recruitment of ex-offenders in this capacity. I think it is not beyond us.

chapter thirteen
CROFTON HOUSE: AN EXPERIMENT WITH A COUNTY HALFWAY HOUSE

Bernard C. Kirby

This account is offered as a preliminary report on the experience of one county correctional system with a small experimental treatment facility. Follow-up of its graduates is still in progress, and analysis of the group interaction is still progressing. However, the agency opened its doors in October 1964, and it is time for us to tell others facing the same problems how our solution is working out thus far.

The San Diego County Department of Honor Camps in 1963 was caring for some 450 male offenders, transferred from the county jail to the five rural camps. Most were misdemeanants, but about a third were felons given probation on condition of serving jail time. The camp programs were oriented to treatment, and new inmates were carefully assigned to the particular camps most likely to be suited to them.

The director and assistant director, James C. Reed, Jr., and Samuel D. Mock, were convinced that it was not necessary for public safety or desirable for treatment purposes that all of their men remain in rural custody. On the contrary, the direction in which they saw corrections moving was toward the community, with full involvement in it. Accordingly, they decided to establish a new agency in the city of San Diego where inmates would be employed at regular jobs, supporting themselves and their families, and engaging in an imaginative program of group counseling and guided group pressures. The consent of the judges to permit these committed men to walk the streets would have to be obtained. Selecting men for the new agency would initially be quite restrictive, with the expectation that

From *Federal Probation* 33 (1969): pp. 53-58; reprinted by permission. Investigation was supported by Public Health Service Research Grant No. MH01320, from the National Institute of Mental Health.

with experience a larger proportion of the camp intake might be found suitable for it.

The proposed agency, to be known as Crofton House, differed in significant ways from the usual halfway house. First, the entire period of incarceration was to be served there, except for a brief period in the jail prior to transfer to the camp system and then a short time in the camp's classification center for testing and assignment. This contrasts with many halfway houses, to which the inmate goes only after he has completed all or most of his sentence in regular custody. Second, Crofton House was a project of a county. Traditionally, in this country county correction has been by far the most backward of all levels, with jail populations commonly being treated with unenlightenment at best, and careless brutality at worst. It seemed especially desirable to experiment with better ways of handling this most depressed and forgotten group of inmates. Third, Crofton House was planned from its inception to be a demonstration, with its results to be rigorously appraised by an outside staff of professional research men. This is now being accomplished with funds from the National Institute of Mental Health, which also subsidized operating costs for a trial period.

THEORETICAL BASIS

Certain theoretical propositions regarding delinquent behavior and its redirection underlay the new agency, derived from such sources as E. H. Sutherland, George Herbert Mead, Richard A. Cloward, LaMar T. Empey, and Donald R. Cressey. These propositions may be summarized as follows:

1. Criminal behavior, like all behavior, is learned, especially in interaction with significant others.
2. People are likely to behave in the ways that they think other people expect them to behave. The men, then, at Crofton House should see themselves as ordinary people, living up to their neighbors' expectations. In this way the community will not only support them but will itself profit by knowing them as "whole persons," the occupants of many roles in addition to that of a convicted offender.
3. Offenders need to experience first-hand a comfortable, conforming, accepting atmosphere, so they may find out whether this kind of relationship to society is satisfying them. After all, there are legitimate opportunity systems as well as illegitimate ones.
4. Offenders have often experienced too little goodwill and friendliness and too much rejection, so they have learned to distrust, to wage preventive cold war in self-protection.

5. Inmates of institutions are likely to be torn between prosocial and antisocial loyalties. In these conflicts and anxieties there is opportunity for prosocial redirection.
6. Institutional inmates develop various techniques to handle such anxieties as well as to mitigate the objective hardships of incarceration. These techniques are likely to include the "contract," a tacit agreement with staff that they will not rock the boat so long as staff does not demand any painful reappraisal of themselves. Disruption of this contract is essential for movement to occur, and it may well be inconsistent with an orderly, peaceful agency. Such disruption may then be a major task of staff and residents.

CROFTON HOUSE OPENS ITS DOORS

These plans came to fruition in early June 1964, when federal funds became available. Lease agreements were signed, property remodeled, and the initial climate-setting residents selected and trained. On October 4, 1964, Crofton House opened its doors. Physically it is a once-fine old home built by a well-known merchant at the turn of the century. There is a separate cottage in the rear as well as a service yard and spacious side grassed area, with shade and picnic furniture. The neighborhood is working class and lower middle class, racially mixed, with many old homes and a sprinkling of newer ones, single or multiple. It is near a freeway, not far from downtown San Diego with its employment, recreation, and social agencies.

Living at Crofton House is "family style." Furnishings are durable and comfortable rather than elegant. The men eat around the big dining-room table, although few of them are likely to be around for lunch. As in most homes, the television set tends to be the center of attention during free time. The men go in and out the front door freely, but to go off the premises requires signing out, indicating destination and time of return. This may be going to work, seeking work, going to school, shopping, or approved recreation (the last always in a group).

THE MEN AT CROFTON HOUSE

The selection of men for Crofton House has been somewhat more critical than anticipated. During the experimental period a new honor camp resident has to meet the following criteria:

1. A resident of southern California (to facilitate follow-up).
2. Not a habitual or professional criminal, as measured by a minimum score of 45 on the California Base Expectancy scale.

3. Not a drug addict or peddler; this need not exclude a marijuana user.
4. Not a chronic alcoholic, though he may be a problem drinker.
5. Not a violently assaultive offender.
6. Not an active homosexual.
7. Normal intelligence—Beta score at least 90.
8. Minimum sentence of six months.

Approximately 10 percent of the honor camp intake met these criteria. This meant that with the eligibles divided into control and experimental groups, there were seldom enough persons to fill the house to its capacity of twenty men. This was the source of some disappointment, assuaged by our expectation that with the end of the experimental period—May 31, 1967,—the eligibles would be more than ample. (As indicated below, this did not turn out to be so.)

A typical Crofton House man is likely to be young, median age 24; to have had repeated serious offenses against the vehicle codes, such as drunk driving or driving without a license, or be guilty of failing to provide for his family; to be Caucasian; to be just short of a high school diploma, very likely with the help of some GED credits; to have a CBE score of about 50 and a Beta score of about 110; and to be single, although almost as many are married or divorced. He is likely to have a sentence of either six or twelve months and he will probably spend four or five months at Crofton before he leaves.

THE PROGRAM

In a sense, the program consists of everything that happens at Crofton House. It certainly includes regular employment, which some of the men have never or rarely had and which is for most of us a training and disciplinary measure itself. From this they pay board and room. It also includes the one-to-one services given the man by the staff (the supervisor has his master's degree in social work) and by other social agencies. And above all, it includes group counseling sessions, from three to five evenings a week, usually for two or three hours.

The scene is the big living room of Crofton House, the time is 7:30; the men have eaten, the TV has been turned off. With few exceptions, all the men as well as the supervisor and his wife are present. The analyst from Research has set up the tape recorder and sits inconspicuously with clip board and pencil.

What happens? It certainly is not unique. One would be reminded of Albert Elias and Highfields or Essexfields; or of LaMar Empey and Pine Hills or Silverlake; or possibly of Charles Dederick and Synanon. The emphasis is on open expression of feeling, "pulling off the covers" when a resident evades or distorts, obliging a resident to face his problems head-on. There is anger and resentment, laughter, kidding, and occasional expressions of deep concern and even affection.

The main business of an evening usually has to do with a single resident. It generally commences with the person giving personal background material pertaining to the parental family, military experience, and perhaps his marriage. His involvement with the law is sure to be thoroughly canvassed, from juvenile misbehavior to his present offense. At subsequent sessions his progress at Crofton House will be discussed, his relations with the other men, and his participation in the program. The last area includes his employment or efforts to get it, his house duties (cleaning, painting, kitchen, etc.), and his involvement in group counseling sessions. Attendance at these group sessions is required, unless excused by the men; likewise, participation is expected, both in reference to his own problems and in the helping of others with theirs.

Despite the norm of openness and candor there are deviations, of course. Men do evade and avoid; they do "contract," tacitly agreeing not to do anything that will embarrass anyone, in return for like protection from the others; they have occasionally concealed knowledge of misbehavior, such as drinking, marijuana usage, or unauthorized outside visiting during working hours. Nevertheless, the standard is clear: Each man is his brother's keeper. To bring another's misbehavior to the group's attention is not defined as "ratting," but as a service to the offender and as essential to the survival of the agency. With the responsibility for each other's conduct there also goes power; the men are expected to decide in group sessions if a member is not living up to his responsibility and, if so, to take appropriate action—the most severe being to recommend his return to the Honor Camps' classification center for reassignment to a regular camp or, rarely, to jail.

We have thought of Crofton House as intimately related to the community in order that the men might develop favorable perceptions of themselves as ordinary conforming citizens and neighbors. In various ways staff and men worked toward this goal. There were Easter-egg hunts on the big lawn for the neighborhood children, Hallowe'en and Christmas parties, open house for the entire community to visit, and even a wedding at the house. Perhaps as a result of these efforts, the neighbors who at first found Crofton House quite threatening have come to accept it with calmness, if not enthusiasm. Nevertheless, there has not developed the kind of over-the-back-fence neighborliness for which we had hoped. The larger community of business, law enforcement, social agencies, press, radio, and television from the beginning has been supportive.

Incidentally, in an effort to assuage fears of householders near us we conducted a careful survey of property values within four blocks. We found that in the eighteen months after the establishment of Crofton House values were not affected in the slightest, one way or the other, judging from actual sale prices. We also obtained data from the police department concerning crimes committed on our beat. There appeared to have been a slight but probably not significant reduction.

EVALUATION

Formal evaluation of Crofton House consists of the comparison of the post-release behavior of the eighty-eight Crofton House experimental subjects with that of the eighty-five control subjects who were assigned to the regular rural camps, each group being chosen in a random fashion from a common population of eligibles. The experience being evaluated occurred during the experimental period of twenty-eight months between February 1, 1965, and May 31, 1967, following a pilot period of four months. This was also the time during which the federal grant subsidized the operation of Crofton House and during which research staff observed intensively the activities of the agency, especially the interaction in the group counseling sessions.

The investigation of the men's post-release behavior included (1) the public records of law enforcement agencies, and (2) independent judgments of behavior based upon field investigations. These were made at three points in time: three months, nine months, and eighteen months after release. At these times research staff, with the permission of the subject—and only with his permission—interviewed, in addition to the subject himself, his wife or girl friend, relatives or neighbors, and perhaps his employer. Certain social agencies also were very helpful.

The 18-month follow-ups are not yet complete, but on the basis of data now available it seems likely that there will be no significant difference between the post-release behavior of the experimental subjects and that of the camp controls. This is true whether one considers only the official public records or the more extensive field inquiries.

This somewhat disappointing finding should in the clear light of hindsight not surprise us. The same administrative agency operated both programs; "leakage" from one to the other was not only inevitable but was good administration. Similar group counseling prevailed in the camps and at Crofton. Camp staff functioned as weekend and vacation relief at Crofton. It is probably naïve to expect any presently known short-term experience to influence markedly a style of life learned over twenty or thirty years. Furthermore, we do not know but we suspect that in follow-up the control subjects were less candid in self-disclosure of forbidden behavior than the Crofton House experimental subjects, who are much better known to the research staff. As a matter of fact, there was a very wide range of candor and responsiveness in both groups.

Several more general but tentative statements may also be made based on our follow-ups.

The nature of the offense has little to do with post-release behavior, except that felons are somewhat more likely to succeed than misdemeanants, probably because only the more promising felons go to jail (as a condition of probation) rather than to state prison.

Scores on the California Base Expectancy Scale do not predict post-release behavior of our subjects, probably because the CBE was used as a selective device and hence the range of subjects on the CBE is narrow, with scores usually over 45.

Race has only a slight bearing on success, with whites tending toward success somewhat more than nonwhites.

Older men are more likely to succeed than the younger ones.

We are also learning something about group interaction, although here, too, our data analysis is far from complete. We have prepared sociometric analyses of each group session, charting each "bit" of interaction separately by its originator and its target (a thousand or more interactions per session). After experimenting with Robert Bales' well-known analytic instrument, we developed our own classification scheme, the Norton Interaction Matrix, which permits us to code each bit by kind and degree of affect, and by referent.

Perhaps the most interesting finding is simply that despite many differences among other categories, there is none between interacting patterns of men later classified as a success and those classified as a failure, neither with respect to the affect level and direction nor with respect to referent—that is, the subject matter of their words. On the other hand there were fairly pronounced differences among subjects classified, for example, by socioeconomic status. In this instance, men of higher status were significantly freer in expressing affect, both negative and positive, than were those of lower status. Classified by offense, those whose crimes were against the self, as drug or alcohol related, were notably more inclined to talk about themselves in the group or about the group itself. Also, they tended to be less free in expressing affect.

The younger men's interaction tended to focus on the self and important other, and the older men on group members and the group, with little difference in affect. There appeared a curious inconsistency between response patterns of men classified first by Beta scores and then by level of education, with the less intelligent and the more highly educated showing similar patterns of both affect and referent.

Finally, the fifteen Negro subjects among the eighty-eight differed in that their responses dealt only slightly with their selves or important others, and they originated notably more negative interaction as well as receiving somewhat more.

Further analysis is now under way, holding certain factors constant while examining the influence of others.

The single overall table showing the distribution of all interaction, all 88 subjects, and all sessions (nearly 400 of them) is revealing. It is particularly notable that less than 1 percent coded positive affect, either slight or deep, and 7 percent coded negative affect, either slight or deep. The simply neutral or intellectual agreement or disagreement comes to 84 percent, with a residual of 8 percent. Almost 45 percent have as their subject matter content "group members" and 29 percent the speaker's self. Only 4 percent are coded "irrelevant," although a portion of the 12 percent non-person-oriented "topic" may also represent evasion of the therapeutic task assignment.

We have also used the Berzon Facilitative Behavior Scale to estimate the effectiveness of group sessions, the mean of these ratings being computed for each session. There appeared a clear tendency for groups at which fewer persons were present (from eight to thirteen) to be less therapeutically helpful than the larger groups (from seventeen to twenty-two). There was also a relationship between effectiveness and the degree to which the group focused its attention on a single target member rather than diffusing attention among several or many persons. The single-focus sessions were judged as more therapeutically facilitative.

The effectiveness of Crofton House may be estimated more roughly, and yet perhaps more realistically, by comparing the post-release behavior of the Crofton House and control subjects with that of men confined in the county jail who are not transferred to the camp system. Our problem here is that there is no way of insuring the strict comparability of the two groups. However, the trusties in the county jail tended to be similar to the Crofton House eligibles. From the trusties who were in jail during our experimental period, we therefore selected seventy-three whose characteristics matched quite closely those of our eligibles with respect to age, offense, intelligence, and California Base Expectancy scores. These men were compared with Crofton House men and controls, using in each case official law-enforcement records only, disregarding material acquired from field interviews. On the basis of slightly incomplete evidence, the proportion of the trusties who are failing is substantially larger than that of the Crofton men and the camp controls; the difference is clearly statistically significant and probably actually significant. This is, of course, to be expected, in view of the primarily custodial function of the jail and the treatment orientation of the honor camps.

It is interesting to note two changes about to be inaugurated by the administration of the honor camp system. Employment of Crofton House men will no longer be "free," that is, the men finding whatever employment they can or perhaps continuing their pre-offense employment,' at regular wages. Instead, Crofton House men will all be employed on some public project, going to work as a group, working side by side during the day. Their wages will be that of the camp inmate, about 50 cents a day, with no charge for board and room. At about the same time a new and larger in-town facility will be opened in a leased motel, carrying on the present work-furlough program of Crofton House. There some sixty or seventy-five men will live, working at regular employment at regular wages, and paying board and room to the county.

These changes obviously reflect the administration's belief in the constructive influence of employment in general. They believe, however, that treatment purposes are better effected by a common work experience where the men cannot escape from each other, rather than by the fragmented employment which occurs as men go off to separated jobs. Hence, the new Crofton House policy.

Control at Crofton House will be somewhat tighter than at present. However, this will be more than matched by less restrictive intake. In San Diego and California, as elsewhere, there is a steady tendency for persons to be placed on probation who at one time would have been jailed, and for men to be in jail or minimum custody camps who formerly would have been in closer custody in state institutions. On top of this, an explosive increase in narcotics and marijuana offenses has occurred in this border city of San Diego. In this situation Crofton House will accept men who during the experimental period were not considered suitable, including narcotics offenders who are so often considered untreatable. The house will then be filled to capacity, as it is not now, by men currently deemed eligible.[1]

Crofton House should be seen, then, in a larger context of time and place. It is, first of all, representative of a trend in corrections toward less restriction. This may be related to the pervasive influence of Carl Rogers and the other humanistic psychologists who currently dominate the field of psychotherapy. Closely associated with this is the long-time secular trend toward more humanitarian care of offenders. This is at least consistent with, if not an expression of, the somewhat newer school of thought sometimes titled "behavioral modification." Whatever prosocial effect segregation and deprivation may have as negative reinforcers is diminished almost to the vanishing point by the uncertain and delayed nature of this response to misbehavior. The more positive reinforcement of kinder and gentler treatment is at least defensible.[2]

Crofton House is also to be seen as a reaction to the intolerable expense of segregation. Even a medium-security penal institution will cost some $10,000 a bed. One may house a family of five persons in La Jolla for less than the cost of housing them in custody. Likewise, one should surely expect more than we receive from a regime which, apart from capital costs, involves continuing expenditures equal to those required for a Harvard education. The withdrawal of productive citizens from the economy, the interruption of their all-too-unstable careers, and the consequent dependence of their families on public assistance can be justified only by clear and positive long-term results. Crofton House does not solve this problem, but it may be seen as a short step in that direction. For these modest reasons we who have been associated with Crofton House hope that other communities will extend the basic principle of treatment-within-the-community to more extended populations of jail and camp inmates, the less promising as well as the more promising. This combined with other adventuresome and innovative treatment methods, may move local corrections from the eighteenth clear into the twentieth century.

NOTES

1. In January 1969 the County Board of Supervisors voted to establish facilities for women offenders within the honor camp system. They pointed to the experience of Crofton House as a successful precedent and, in an unusual step, recognized as crucial the treatment aspects of the program, rather than the usual considerations of security and degree of penalty. The new program for women will be carried out in part as an adjunct to one of the present camps, and in part as a new in-town agency, similar to Crofton House.

2. Defenders of the status quo can find no support in the record of even as imaginative a correctional system as the San Diego County Honor Camps. Crofton House eligibles were, in general, those likely to least affront the community (though that does not ipso facto imply that they also were those most open to rehabilitation). Yet eighteen months after release, or even nine months for some, not more than half could still be classed as a "success," that is, a "law-abiding, responsible citizen[s], with no crime against [them] beyond minor traffic violations; drinking controlled . . . self-supporting . . ."; except the proportion of successes would be about two-thirds if only official information were counted. Another portion of the subjects are "partial successes," with "minor exceptions to the above standards," and somewhat more than a third are classed as "failures . . . being guilty of more serious crimes ranging from repeatedly driving on a suspended license to grand larceny."

chapter fourteen

INHERENT TREATMENT CHARACTERISTICS IN A HALFWAY HOUSE FOR DELINQUENT BOYS

Robert C. Trojanowicz

Halfway houses, as supportive services between the institution and independent community life, made their first appearance in this country not for delinquents, but for mental patients. Halfway houses for delinquents are very recent. "There are increasing indications, however, that the appropriateness of this type of facility in a treatment program for delinquents is beginning to be recognized."[1]

HALFWAY HOUSES IN MICHIGAN

The idea for a halfway house program in Michigan began early in 1964, when there was considerable newspaper publicity regarding the need for additional bed space for delinquent children within the institutional program. One solution to the crowding at the state's Boys Training School was to provide living in the community for certain wards within the school who were ready to leave but had no place to go. Thus, the halfway house concept in Michigan originated.

The first house opened in Detroit on July 1, 1964. The second and third houses were opened at Flint and Kalamazoo in August of the same year. The fourth house, the only one for girls, was opened a month later in Detroit. No additional houses were opened until May 1965, when the house at Lansing was opened, followed in June by the third house in

From *Federal Probation*, vol. 35, no. 1 (1971), pp. 18–26; reprinted by permission. Prepared with the assistance of George W. Logan, Michigan State University.

Detroit. Shortly after two additional houses were established, one in Muskegon and a second house at Flint.

Halfway houses in Michigan are operated by the Department of Social Services and are an integral part of the total after-care program for wards released from the Boys Training School. They are utilized for those children who do not need the stringent controls of an institution yet need limits and supervision while moving back into the community to face its responsibilities and pressures.

Halfway houses appear to be of the greatest benefit to children who show an interest in the halfway house program and exhibit a willingness to utilize its resources, who are able to accept some limits, who are able to adjust to a group living situation, who for many reasons cannot go home, and who need more personalized living than can be achieved in an institution setting.

PINE LODGE HALFWAY HOUSE

This article will deal specifically with an innovative program at the Pine Lodge halfway house in Lansing, Michigan. The reason for selecting Pine Lodge House is because Mr. George Logan and I directed the program at different periods in time.

Pine Lodge halfway house is located in a residential area close to shopping, recreational, educational, and employment facilities. It is a large two-story, six-bedroom home, with a full basement which serves as an ample recreation area.

Like the other halfway houses in the state, Pine Lodge serves a maximum of twelve boys and is programmed to provide a school and work experience in the community. It accepts boys between thirteen and nineteen. The average stay in the program is approximately seven and one-half months.

As with the other halfway houses, Pine Lodge is staffed by a caseworker, who is the director, and five child-care workers (one who serves as a cook) who work on an 8-hour shift. All staff personnel are administratively responsible to the caseworker. He, in turn, is supervised by the supervisor of social services in the respective county and receives assistance from John E. Miller, director of group homes for the State of Michigan.

The child-care worker must pass a state civil service test, have a high school diploma, and be of high moral character and in good physical health. The caseworker must have at least a bachelor's degree and preferably a master's degree in social work.

Staff members who like children and have the ability to tolerate and understand aggressive behavior are the most successful. They must be mature, responsible, positive identification models and be able to work with other staff members. They must be understanding and flexible in their thinking, yet firm and consistent in using their authority.

A person who is negatively motivated can disrupt the program. Such an employee tends to satisfy his own needs and accomplish his own ends without regard for the boys, the staff, or the program. Other traits to guard against are extremes in permissiveness or discipline, a lack of commitment and dedication to the program, and a general inability to effectively communicate with the boys, the staff, and the community.

Although the halfway houses of the state are administratively a unit of the State Department of Social Services, there is flexibility to develop new techniques and methods of treatment in each house.

Pine Lodge Prior to Its Innovative Approach

All of the child-care staff at Pine Lodge had prior institutional experience and were well acquainted with the problems of working with social deviants. Moreover, the staff was aware of the friction that exists many times between the "treatment" staff (caseworkers) and the "custody" staff (child-careworkers).

The following policies, procedures and practices characterized Pine Lodge prior to its new approach in dealing with its residents:

1. The child-care staff considered their function as mainly custodial.
2. Custody terminology was used, e.g., "maximum security," etc.
3. Their concern was largely with behavior, generally as it affected the security of the house and the community.
4. The boys considered the child-care staff only as "guards."
5. The boys manipulated the caseworker and the child-care staff against one another.
6. The entries in the daily log were sterile; they reported mainly security aspects of the program and rarely gave an account of social interaction. Seldom did one of the staff members give an opinion as to the possible etiology of the boys' behavior.
7. Staff meetings were exemplified by discussing almost exclusively house management aspects of the program.
8. There was a hierarchy among the child-care staff, with the "head child-care worker" being the recipient of most of the manipulation by the boys in the absence of the caseworker.
9. There was much subversion in the program. For example, a particular staff member might tell a boy, "I agree with you and not the caseworker and the rest of the staff on this particular grievance, but I do not have any decision-making power." This had implications both from the standpoint of the

particular staff member not being cohesively identified with the entire staff and the program and also from the standpoint that the particular supervisor felt impotent in regard to his influence in the decision-making process.
10. Because of lack of identification with the program, the staff was comprised of small subgroups.
11. The "train of thought" among the staff was that a "tougher security line" should be taken.

Discussion of the Problems

The treatment-custody dilemma. The major problem at Pine Lodge was a communication breakdown between the child-care staff and the caseworker, namely, a symptom of the age-old treatment-custody dilemma. This phenomenon had been observed, to varying degrees, in a number of institutional settings in Michigan. Reviewing the literature in this area, it was readily observed that this problem was by far not peculiar to institutions in Michigan but is generally a universal phenomenon.

Briefly, the above-mentioned dichotomy exists because institutional staffs have historically been segregated by function and by training. On the one hand, there is typically the treatment staff whose function it is to "treat" (however this is interpreted). These personnel usually have extensive formal training. Also implied in the treatment-custody dilemma (either directly or indirectly) is the fact that the treatment staff usually holds most of the decision-making power in the institution. The custody individual is typified by his role as the "watch dog" and "inhibitor" of privileges, while the treatment person is the "giver of privileges." The animosity that can arise in a situation like this can readily be seen. This concept not only affects the relationship between the custody and treatment personnel but also has implications for the treatment of the clientele. The dilemma affords a "natural" and opportune situation for the clientele to manipulate the staff against one another, which can only have a negative effect on the total administration of the treatment program.

Appropriate questions to be asked in relation to this dilemma are: Is the treatment-custody dilemma inevitable? Will it always exist, because of the division of labor by function and training? What can an administrator do to alleviate this problem?

These and additional questions will be discussed later.

The type of clientele. Another problem that exists is the type of clientele served at Pine Lodge and generally in correctional institutions. Persons adjudicated as social deviants do not usually voluntarily seek treatment for their problems. Unlike neurotics and psychotics who are plagued by anxiety and distress, most social deviants are usually not aware of their problems. They usually are very manipulative. Because of their psychological make-up and learned social behavior they can be effective "con men." Being manipulative and "slick" is many times an integral and desired part of their value system. Manipulation is more than merely a prized and desired asset, it is a tool with which most social deviants "ply their trade." Hence, they have an extraordinary ability to manipulate people and, as can readily be inferred, the treatment-custody dilemma "plays right into" this pathological process and perpetuates it.

Furthermore, the social deviant throughout his life process has not had positive identification models who could transmit the values of the larger society. The result is that there is many times a social and moral void in his conscience structure. Hence the attitude, "Take what you can get," and, "It's only wrong or immoral if you get caught."

If, then, the social deviant is different from the neurotic or psychotic, should the techniques for treatment be different as well as the personnel performing the treatment?

Helping a human being. Another factor that can have implications for a treatment program is that these boys are not "commodities" that are being produced and serviced in correctional settings, but rather are human beings. Human beings have the innate ability to affect other human beings in many and varied ways. An assembly-line worker receives instructions and orders from his supervisor and then he performs, for example, his task of riveting the right front fender of a new automobile. The fender does not respond in a manner that can cause an emotional reaction in the worker. However, this is not the case when the worker (child-care staff member) is dealing with a human being (social deviant). The worker may get his instructions from his supervisor, but a second element is involved; namely, the worker not only performs an action but the object on which he performs the action is capable of producing a reaction in the worker. Thus, a reciprocal emotional connotation evolves. The social deviant accentuates this emotional reaction in others, many times because of his aggressiveness and antisocial attitude. Often he exhibits behavior which is boisterous, aggressive, and "cocky," in an attempt to disguise his feelings of worthlessness, fear, and insecurity. In effect, he actively attempts to antagonize society so that he will be rejected, thus reinforcing his own self-concept that he is worthless and a social outcast. The social deviant has been hurt emotionally and hence does not usually want to take the chance of being hurt again. The dynamics of rejecting before being rejected is a defense against "getting close" to people.

The questions to be asked are: How can positive communication be facilitated between the staff and the boys? What effect does an emotionally charged situation have on both the boys and the staff? What techniques can be utilized to keep negative reinforcement and reactions at a minimum?

Personnel. Persons attracted to the correctional field can also present certain problems. This does not mean that all persons attracted to this field are negatively motivated. It is readily recognized that people satisfy their emotional needs in a variety of ways. In most instances, social deviants are vulnerable to displaced hostility and negative reinforcement from persons working in correctional settings. It is possible that some persons are attracted to this field so as to over-assert their authority.

Conversely, there is the person who masks his intense hostility by being over-permissive and over-solicitous even to the point where he encourages the social deviant to "act out." If the staff member also has a problem accepting authority, he can receive vicarious satisfactions when the social deviant acts out against society and specifically against the correctional administration.

Some questions to be asked at this point are: How do delinquents affect persons who are negatively motivated and attracted to the correctional field and, in turn, how does this affect the treatment-custody dilemma? Do some staff members prefer and even perpetuate the treatment-custody dilemma? What are the ways in which staff members can be utilized most effectively?

The treatment concept. Another problem in correctional administration is the defining of the word "treatment." Many times, "treatment" personnel are not clear as to what is meant by the concept and what it entails. Treatment usually varies with the "treater" and the situation. Can "treatment" personnel expect custody personnel to understand and accept the treatment concept if, in fact, it is not clearly defined and changes like a chameleon depending on the circumstances? Does treatment mean being extremely permissive? Is treatment dependent on the treater's ability to use superfluous psychological jargon? Is it necessary that treatment be practiced in a clinical setting?

Isn't the definition of treatment really a definition of the particular organization's purpose and goals? Isn't it possible to transform theoretical concepts into manageable and practical terms for the "line staff"? The area of training also can present problems for the administrator. The training concept has implications for the treatment goals. If the goals and purposes of the organization are clearly defined and the treatment methods delineated, techniques for training will be a logical sequel.

Just as training will have to fit the organization, so will the trainer have to be acquainted with the problems peculiar to that organization. What are the implications and attributes of an effective training program? Also, should the trainer (treatment person) stay removed from the "firing line" so as not to taint his "humanitarian image"?

The community. The relationship to the community can also pose certain problems. A direct correlation between the amount of aggression exhibited in Pine Lodge and negative behavior in the community was observed. Those boys who would verbalize and rebel in the house had less of a tendency to displace their aggression onto the community. Therefore, our general philosophy was that we would rather have the boys "act out" in the house because we could deal with the problem "on the spot," and hence there would be less of a tendency for them to displace their aggression onto the community. This did not mean that the boys were free to "express themselves" in any manner they desired. They could not, for example, destroy the furniture, but they could express verbal anger and discontent to the staff.

Concomitant with this philosophy, of course, is the implication that the major emphasis was not on regimentation. Hence, on various occasions boys would rebel by not making their beds and doing their chores, etc. Pine Lodge, however, usually never looked any worse than if a "normal" group of teenagers were living in it.

It was interesting to note that even though the visitors to Pine Lodge appeared to accept our philosophy of "controls but not regimentation," they many times, nevertheless, expected to see a "shiny institution." The staff was in a dilemma. On the one hand they were attempting to operate according to the philosophy of the program, and on the other hand they were being evaluated according to criteria with which the philosophy did not adhere. What effect could this paradox have on the operation of the program? How could this situation be alleviated?

SOLUTIONS TO THE PROBLEMS: DEVELOPING A NEW SYSTEM

It was believed the staff should not have to be so stringently dichotomized into treatment and custody. It was also believed the same person could serve as both the "giver" and the "taker," the "controller" and the "liberator." In effect, with adequate staff selection and training, one person could make the decision as to the proper treatment technique that should be utilized at any given time.

Employing staff members who will perform what some people would consider a dual function (treatment and custody) implies certain alterations in the classical correctional concept; namely, the decentralization of authority from the caseworker (administrator) to the "line staff."

It was felt that if the new concept of decentralization of authority, which involves decision making by the entire staff, was introduced into the Pine Lodge program, the child-care staff would see their role more favorably and would feel a part of and identified with the total treatment program. Hopefully, this would specifically result in better communication between the caseworker and the staff, and would generally result in a more effective treatment program.

Also assumed was that each staff member would be given authority commensurate with his responsibility. Even though the major decisions would be made by the entire staff at the weekly staff meeting, there would still be day-to-day decisions that needed to be made. These day-to-day decisions would be made by the particular staff member who was on duty. His decision would never be reversed by the caseworker, and if a difference of opinion arose, the problem would be discussed either privately or at the staff meeting.

In addition, the entire staff was kept informed and involved in every phase of both the house operation and the particular boy's status in terms of past, present, and future diagnosis, treatment, and planning.

Finally, because the boys had also witnessed the treatment-custody dilemma prior to their coming to the halfway house, it was felt important that some tangible administrative responsibility be given to each staff member to reinforce the concept that the entire staff was involved in decision making and also to increase the status of the child-care staff in the eyes of the boys. Hence, each staff member was given a major administrative responsibility. For example, one staff member was responsible for all monetary transactions in the house, while another staff member was responsible for programming all house activities.

Administrative structure. Under the old system the head child-care worker did most of the actual staff direction, but the caseworker made most of the decisions. The decisions were categorized into treatment decisions (made by the caseworker) and house management decisions (made by the child-care staff). This was a very hazy line, however, and conceivably the caseworker could (and sometimes did) reverse a decision made by the child-care staff, using the rationale that it was a treatment decision. For example, if a boy were involved in a drinking escapade within Pine Lodge and the child-care staff restricted him to the house, the caseworker could reverse the decision on treatment grounds and allow the boy to go on a home visit, because "the boy's drinking was the result of an excessive amount of pent-up frustration and anxiety." It can readily be seen what effect this can have on the morale and motivation of the child-care staff and the treatment of the boy. The staff could undoubtedly feel impotent and the boy would be able to utilize the situation for manipulative purposes.

Under the new organizational system the caseworker is the director and is responsible for supervising the staff, providing casework for the boys, and administering the total program. However, in addition to the organization revision, the total structure of the house is considered the major therapeutic agent. This means that house management activities and house controls are considered as much a part of the treatment program as are direct casework services.

Differences in treatment. It was mentioned earlier that the treatment techniques in correctional settings need to be different because the boys are different. Also, treatment with the boy in the halfway house is a 24-hour-a-day job. In a clinical situation a boy may relate to the therapist that he was involved in a "beer blast" at home. The therapist will discuss the situation with him and try to determine the etiology of the problem and what psychological dynamics are present. In a halfway house, the staff does not have the luxury of merely discussing the problem. In addition to being concerned with the psychological dynamics of the boy, the staff also has to be concerned with controlling him. Obviously, the boys cannot be allowed to have a "beer blast," let alone on state property.

When the treatment is viewed from this philosophy, it is not feasible nor desirable that the house be divided into treatment areas and house management areas. Hence, decision making cannot be dichotomized into decisions that are made by the caseworker and decisions that are made by the child-care staff. The entire staff has to be involved in all of the decisions.

This, however, does not necessarily mean that there is no differentiation of duties according to the staff members' position, as determined by their civil service classification. There is still a hierarchy of varying responsibilities, the head child-care worker having more responsibility and so on. The responsibility, however, relates to objective administrative functions such as making out the staff payroll and being responsible for calling repairmen, etc., and not to decisions concerning the boys. Hence, the caseworker or the head child-care worker are not the only staff members who give boys permission, for example, to go outside of the house on "free time."

The more pronounced the hierarchial structure, the more the boys will have the opportunity to manipulate the "boss" against the "staff" and the more they will manipulate. A flattened hierarchial structure, with equal decision-making power for all, eliminates much of this manipulation and thus interrupts one of the boys' major pathological processes.

Even though the treatment objectives and purposes should be specifically delineated and defined, the techniques for attaining these specifically defined goals should be kept flexible, to encourage the staff to utilize their own initiative and personal assets. It also is believed that this facilitates decision making, because the staff member does not necessarily have to be concerned about using the "right" technique.

There are, however, specific guidelines under certain circumstances. For example, if a boy is placed on restriction by the entire staff, a staff member cannot make the decision on his shift to allow the boy to go out on "free time." This, however, refers more to the concept of consistency in decision making than it does to flexibility in the particular technique utilized.

Another point also needs clarification. Even though each staff member has the authority to make decisions that arise on his shift, he can always call another staff member for advice (usually the caseworker). Initially the staff followed this practice, but when they became confident and comfortable with their decision-making ability, consultation via the telephone decreased.

It is also emphasized to the staff that treatment does not necessarily mean a clinical setting and the use of psychological jargon. Treatment can be taking a boy shopping for clothes, giving him advice on dating, or helping him with his homework. Treatment can take place over a pool table or at the dinner table. In other words, treatment is considered anything that relates to the boy's total life process.

The treater: facilitating communication. It was mentioned previously that people are attracted to work in the correctional field for many reasons—psychological, educational, monetary, etc. It was also pointed out that since the social deviant is clinically different from the neurotic or psychotic, it follows that the "treater" does not need the same clinical experience. It was proposed that the clinical difference between the social deviant and the neurotic or psychotic is that the social deviant lacks an adequate conscience structure as a result of inadequate identification models. Hence, the major treatment device should not be the use of clinical jargon and knowledge to alleviate guilt and anxiety—because, in fact, the boy has a minimal amount of both—but should be able to provide him with a positive identification model. Positive identification models can be found in every walk of life. We did not look for persons with a particular educational background. In fact (according to our definition and requirements) formal education is not a prerequisite to being an effective "therapist." In addition to being a positive identification model, it is mandatory that the person be mature and understand his own personal dynamics. This will enable him to transmit to the boy that he is genuinely concerned. If a staff member's actions toward a boy are inappropriate, it is important to determine whether he is displacing negative feelings from other persons or situations onto the boy. Hence, the need to be constantly introspective.

It was observed that certain boys were attracted to, confided in, and communicated with certain staff members. This natural attraction is encouraged because, as was mentioned before, a relationship with a positive identification model is the most important way in which the boy modifies his socially deviant behavior. A positive relationship with a particular staff member is very beneficial because it not only accelerates the treatment process, but it also affords the boy a positive identification model whom he can emulate and please via socially acceptable behavior. In effect, the "natural" channels of communication are utilized and perpetuated. The caseworker still provides supervision to the particular staff member, but the actual casework is performed by the staff member the boy trusts and has chosen as his friend. The caseworker's supervision mainly involves interpreting the meaning of various behaviors and helping the staff member understand what dynamics are present and operating in the boy.

Hence, because a particular type of formal education or a particular type of personality is not required to work in Pine Lodge, the staff is composed of a variety of personality types.

As mentioned previously, a person's positive personality characteristics are utilized to the program's best advantage. For example, an athletic staff member is used in programming athletic events for the boys. In many cases, this means altering the organization to fit the employee. Altering the organization to fit the employee is done by choice, as in the above-mentioned case, but it is also done by necessity. Some staff members also have negative personality characteristics, but these can also be utilized to the program's advantage. For example, there may be a staff member who has difficulty exerting even minimal controls for fear that he will lose his "nice guy" image. This person can be put on a shift that has the greatest amount of flexibility in regard to controls. He can also be used effectively to perform duties that involve being "nice" to the boys. Conversely, a staff member who is excessively controlling can be utilized effectively in another phase of the program where, for example, the setting of the controls and limits is beneficial to the program.

The boys have reached adolescence with many of the same likes, dislikes, and pressures as normal adolescents, but with far fewer social, intellectual, and occupational skills. They have experienced but little success in life. The staff attempts to intervene in their life process and acquaint them with positive life experiences.

Staff members are encouraged to react spontaneously. If they are angry at something a particular boy has done, it is better to express the anger than to suppress it, displace it, and have it come out in a subtle, punitive, passive-aggressive manner that the boy can neither accept nor understand.

Because the boys are extremely impulsive, hedonistic, and unable to tolerate much frustration, they need constant support and encouragement to stay on their jobs, in school, and to refrain from acting-out behavior.

The staff is always willing to give a boy a ride to and from work, advance money from the house fund until he receives his first paycheck, and allow him much freedom in purchasing, with his pay, such items as record players, guitars, bicycles, and radios.

This action not only supports the boy while he is experiencing the first few frustrating days on the job, but it also helps to satisfy his need for immediate gratification and illustrates to him that through employment, it is possible to acquire pleasurable items legally.

It is not naïvely assumed that a boy who has already utilized almost every state and local service available will suddenly succeed in the community because of some deep psychological insight into the nature of his behavior. If he refrains, for example, from shoplifting, it is probably due more to the fact that he has money in his pocket earned from a job to purchase the items, rather than any insight into the nature of his "oedipal problem."

The approach with the boys is direct, always emphasizing the reality of the situation. We do not attempt to delve into the unconscious, mainly because of the type of boy, with his impulsivity and need for immediate gratification. Time is also a factor.

If, for example, a boy has the "urge" to steal a car, we emphasize the reality of the situation rather than the boy's "unconscious conflict." Stealing the car is the important event. We have neither the time nor the boy's desire to introspectively look at the unconscious conflict. We have to deal with the present event and its consequences, because otherwise, unlike the neurotic who has an anxiety attack, the boy will act out in the community and be in conflict with the law.[2]

The structure of Pine Lodge is constantly utilized in the treatment of the boys. There are not many rules, but the ones that exist are enforced consistently and firmly.

The boys also have the opportunity to go on home visits. This assists them in experiencing home and community pressures in a less intensified manner. It gives them the opportunity to test out new skills and attitudes and then return to the halfway house to share their experience with staff members. The staff not only supports them in their responsible home behavior, but also assists them in seeking and implementing alternative socially acceptable solutions to problems.

Training. Utilizing the personal assets of the staff also has implications for staff training. Even though staff training is usually geared to impart certain general principles and techniques for the entire staff, training also has to be geared to individual needs and abilities. Some staff members have innate, intuitive, and empathic qualities that assist them in relating positively to the boys and reacting appropriately to emotion-laden situations. Others don't have these innate personal assets and, in effect, have to be "conditioned" to act in a certain manner even though they don't "feel like it." Of course, it isn't merely a matter of either having the qualities or not having them. It should be viewed on more of a continuum with some individuals having both more innate assets and a better ability to be introspective. Training can accentuate a person's positive traits and provide him with new skills.

One of the trainer's major responsibilities is to transform abstract theoretical concepts into practical terms, so they can be more readily accepted and utilized by the staff. Working with delinquent boys can be very frustrating, and many times the staff need something tangible to look at in terms of what they have accomplished. The trainer is much more effective if he points out to the staff that a particular boy has improved a great deal because he is staying in school or on the job regularly for the first time in his life, rather than saying the boy has increased "frustration tolerance" and "impulse control."

The trainer also has to be realistic and able to empathize with the staff. The caseworker covers at least one shift a week, so as to have an opportunity to observe what takes place "on the firing line." After having experienced various situations it is easier to be more tolerant and less judgmental of a staff member who may have reacted angrily in a particular situation. To say the least, it affords the trainer new insights into the dynamics of human behavior and interaction.

In relation to the caseworker covering a shift, many persons have the faulty idea that the "treatment person" should not become involved in the areas of disciplining and controlling. If the thesis concerning the staff (including the caseworker) acting as parental substitutes is extended, in how many families is one parent the "good guy" and giver and the other parent the "bad guy" and disciplinarian? Hence, the same parent can perform both functions effectively and the child readily accepts and wants this. Why, then, can't parental substitutes perform the same dual function? It realistically illustrates to the boys that adults play many roles and perform many functions, some pleasing and some displeasing.

Learning the system. It was mentioned that after the boys are in residence for a few weeks, they begin to "learn the system." Although every organization has a system, we attempt to keep some aspects of our system unpredictable, because many times the boys spend much of their time trying to "beat the system" and a minimal portion of their time trying to positively increase their social and personal functioning. The structure of the house with its consistent enforcement of the rules is an asset, but a system that is completely predictable can eliminate all anxiety and place a premium on conformity and "playing the game" to attain a release.

It is important to point out that the organization and the organization's system have to be constantly evaluated in terms of the implications the system might have for the program.

In the case of Pine Lodge, the system is unlike that of an institution which many times places a premium on conformity and regimentation. However, the boys learn quickly what is emphasized—namely, expression in the house rather than in the community—and some of them begin "playing the game" in regard to our system. In other words, they express themselves in the house so as to elicit the response, "Well, at least you must be improving because you are able to express yourself directly (in lieu of displacement) in the house." However, this same boy may also be "expressing" himself in the community. In effect, much of his energy may be expended in playing "our game." Thus the need for constant organizational evaluation.

Relation to the community. In the first part of the chapter it was mentioned that there were many community visitors. This in itself was not a problem. The problem arose when the visitors transmitted to the staff surprise and disappointment that there was not more uniformity and regimentation.

Quite naturally, the staff wanted to operate within the philosophy of the program, but they were also concerned that the visitors would interpret the "lived in" look as being a symptom of poor functioning.

Even though much of the negative communication from the visitors could be interrupted, the problem took care of itself. As the staff identified more with the treatment program and was committed to the philosophy of the program, they were less concerned with negative comments and were more enthusiastic about the program and the special techniques we utilized in the treatment of the boys. This increased enthusiasm and "esprit de corps" made a positive impact on the visitors, with the resultant effect of fewer negative comments about the lack of uniformity and regimentation.

EVALUATION

From June 1965 to June 1969, eighty boys were accepted at Pine Lodge. Eleven boys were returned directly to the Boys Training School after a short stay, twelve were residents at the time of the evaluation, and the remaining fifty-seven were released to the community.

Of the fifty-seven boys released from Pine Lodge to their home communities after an average stay of seven and one-half months, eleven (19.3 percent) were released to independent living arrangements, three (5.3 percent) enlisted in the Armed Forces, twenty-seven (47.4 percent) were released home, and sixteen (28 percent) went to live with relatives or at a foster home.

Eleven of the fifty-seven (19.3 percent) had contact with law enforcement officials necessitating a return to the Boys Training School or some other form of incarceration (an adult institution, jail, etc.). The remaining forty-six boys (80.7 percent) did not become involved in future negative behavior in the community. Some of the boys have been released for up to three and one-half years. All of the boys, as mentioned earlier, have been released at least one year.

Although some of the boys may not have gained any additional insight into the etiology of their behavior, they have experienced some success and gratification in the areas of employment, education, and recreation. Most have been able to delay immediate gratification and tolerate unpleasant situations even though the temptation to become involved in deviant behavior is ever present.

SOME GUIDING PRINCIPLES

1. The most important aspect of the program is to have a competent staff dedicated to the philosophy that delinquents are persons worth helping.
2. The entire staff should be actively involved in the treatment process.
3. There should be a sound administrative structure with clear lines of communication.
4. There should be a minimum of rules and regulations but a firm and consistent enforcement of the rules.
5. There should be a refined selection process for accepting boys to the program. It is important to be alert to each boy's individual needs as well as the group interaction and the problems that can result from either overplacement or underplacement.
6. There should be adequate programming with good working relationships with various agencies such as the police and the schools.

CONCLUSION

Halfway houses are no panacea for the treatment of the delinquent. They cannot serve all children, in particular those who need a good institutional treatment program, with more stringent controls and at least partial separation from community pressures. However, the halfway house does introduce a new resource which seems to be a better answer for certain children.[3]

NOTES

1. Kenneth S. Carpenter, "Halfway Houses for Delinquent Youth," *Children* (Washington, D.C.: Children's Bureau, Welfare Administration, U.S. Department of Health, Education and Welfare, November–December 1963), pp. 224–29.
2. William Glasser, *Reality Therapy* (New York: Harper and Row, 1965).
3. Martin Gula, *Agency Operated Group Homes* (Washington, D.C.: Children's Bureau, Welfare Administration, Department of HEW, 1964).

part four:
EDUCATION AND EMPLOYMENT PROGRAMS

Community-based corrections recognizes that the offender without education or work skills is at a disadvantage. The NewGate Project, initially under the direction of the National Council on Crime and Delinquency, operates in a number of states. This program tries to ease the transition from prison to campus life for prisoners who are motivated and capable of college study. Clyde Sullivan shows the importance of vocational skills for the released offender. He sketches the historical impact of the work ethic and speaks of the conflict this necessitates in the ex-prisoner. George Pownall, in his selection, reviews post-prison employment problems and their relation to offense patterns. He is concerned, also, with the plight of the older felon trying to enter the labor market. Whether for old or young, the vocational training of prisons is depicted in relation to labor market needs. Elmer Johnson looks searchingly at work-release programs to find out if goals and practice are consistent. He feels that these programs can be successful if innovative thinking accompanies them. In the final selection, Lawrence Root researches the criteria for participation in work-release programs. He warns against hasty judgment of programs that fail.

chapter fifteen

NEWGATE: NEW HOPE THROUGH EDUCATION

National Council on Crime and Delinquency

> It is unreasonable to treat a man as an animal or automaton while he is serving his sentence, and then, at the finish of it, appeal to him as a human being to win his rightful place in society.
>
> —Winston Churchill

NewGate, it has often been said, is a "concept." Theoretically, perhaps. But to many men and women, it is also real, functioning programs working to motivate and aid offenders in their efforts to alter their lives. It offers post-secondary education, counseling, and follow-up services —options open to offenders only within the past decade.

Prisons originally were intended simply to isolate and punish, and if rehabilitation followed at all it was attributed to either or both. Not until almost the nineteenth century was even the most rudimentary form of education officially introduced into a U.S. prison. In 1798, the first prison school was established, but then only to provide the "three R's" as leisure-time occupation for inmates. Although a few institutions followed with similar programs, real change would not come for almost a century.

The starting point for this change was the American Prison Association's endorsement, in 1870, of academic learning as one step in the path to reform. But again, sixty years would pass before the importance of education as an essential element in modern correctional treatment would be fully recognized.

Reprinted, with permission of the National Council on Crime and Delinquency, from *NewGate: New Hope Through Education* (1972).

A confluence of events occurred in the America of the 1930s that ushered in, along with the other great changes of the period, a change in approach to corrections. Not only had prison industries broken down, but new attitudes were developing with respect to education and offenders, fueled by the recommendations of sociologists, economists, and psychologists. Many offenders at the time had little or no formal education, and educational programs in the prisons proliferated. Across the nation, programs were established offering education through high school, including business courses and vocational training. For the most part, however, higher education was available only through correspondence—if at all.

During the next two decades high school programs flourished. Inmates were proving highly responsive and educable, and several received college degrees through correspondence. The first tentative experiments in counseling were attempted. Between 1962 and 1967, a smattering of pilot programs was initiated to test the feasibility of introducing college-level instruction into correctional institutions. The results were encouraging.

One such program, the Upward Bound Oregon Prison Project, established in 1967, sought to combine the best features of other programs with several innovations of its own. For the first time, inmates of a maximum-security prison were given the opportunity for higher education and counseling both in and out of the institution and additional follow-up support services in the post-release period. An evaluation of the program one year later stressed its potential worth, and in 1968, funded by the Office of Economic Opportunity, the Oregon program became *Project NewGate*.

Interest in the program grew rapidly. By 1971 additional NewGates had been federally funded in Colorado, Kentucky, Minnesota, New Mexico, and Pennsylvania. While academic offerings and counseling methods varied among the programs, all the NewGates offered essentially the same services.

Programs similar to NewGate were established in several other states and are still operating effectively. However, NewGate remains the only *national* post-secondary education program in the country. Its unity of purpose results in frequent exchange, coordination, and communication between program administrators and correctional and government personnel. Further, NewGate locates itself physically inside the institution with its own full-time staff, and operates as a residence program rather than an extension program. Its value, therefore, in terms of its working relationships with institution personnel, as well as with the students, is inestimable. Equally important are the benefits that may accrue to the institution by virtue of the professional status of NewGate personnel and their access to outside agencies and resources.

In the past, an inordinate proportion of offenders have come from economically and educationally deprived backgrounds. Now, however, just as the nation's population has changed, so, too, has its prison population. Inmates are generally younger, more perceptive, and better educated than ever before; the number of prison inmates capable of doing college-level work is presently estimated at 20 to 25 percent.

NewGate concerns itself with inmates who possess the *capacity* to do college work, and not merely with those who possess the credentials. This, plus the offender's desire to change his patterns of behavior, is the major consideration for acceptance into the program. As a result, the NewGate student body, insofar as possible, reflects the make-up of the total inmate population.

College preparatory courses enable students to enter the NewGate program who would otherwise have been ineligible. Others, often with feelings of inferiority or unworthiness, find their self-concepts changing along with their accomplishments, as good grades appear and their enjoyment of learning grows.

Courses offered within the institution are designed to effect a smooth transition to college work after release; credits accumulated in freshman and sophomore courses may be easily transferred to the outside program. The NewGate student is required to maintain a grade-point average acceptable to the college in which he is enrolled. Tutoring services often help to reverse a temporary setback.

However, since NewGate's main goal is rehabilitation or reintegration of the offender, no amount of education alone can insure this result. Only when his education includes knowledge of himself and the root causes of his difficulties can effective change be expected. To this end NewGate offers counseling programs geared to the needs of the individual. Intensive personal counseling and/or group counseling are provided to students both inside the institution and outside in the post-release phase.

Several NewGates are able to provide an education release housing facility for students on study release. Unquestionably, such a facility helps to minimize the problems of transition from the institution to the outside. Where such facilities are not available, NewGate personnel aid the released and paroled student in a variety of ways. They help him to find suitable housing, select educational programs, and prepare the necessary forms for financial assistance or admission to a college or university. When necessary, all NewGates offer some measure of gradually diminishing financial aid to students continuing their education outside the institution.

Follow-up services are a crucial part of the total NewGate offering. The adjustment problems of an offender emerging from confinement are at once numerous and unique, and although counseling or therapy may have reduced them somewhat, many areas of his daily activity will remain difficult. The NewGate student continues to have access to NewGate staff and counselors. Program personnel work also with parole officers, vocational rehabilitation agencies, community service organizations, colleges and universities, veterans' organizations, and similar agencies. Every effort is made through this liaison to ease reentry for the NewGate student. Even after graduation the ex-offender may utilize NewGate's services, for the program's commitment to its students includes job counseling and assistance in securing employment.

NewGate programs have been in existence for varying periods of time. For this reason, measures of success are proportionate to the total number of students who have completed the program. However, NewGate students are highly motivated and hence their achievement level is greater and their drop-out rate, both in the institution and in the outside community, is significantly lower than that of regular on-campus students. Moreover, their recidivism rate, compared with national recidivism figures, is dramatically lower—it is estimated at 15 to 20 percent.

NewGate students have won art and poetry competitions, scholarships, and awards. They have received certification in business and technical fields, A.A. degrees, and B.A. or B.S. degrees. More than 50 percent of the latter have continued their education with graduate studies. NewGate graduates have been able to enter professions previously inaccessible to them, and the effects of their achievements on public opinion and correctional education are enormous.

But what of the future for NewGate? The original programs were funded by the Office of Economic Opportunity as pilot projects. Now, having proved their viability and efficacy, they are moving from the research and development phase into the fully operational phase of their state or federal programs. Funding sources, too, are in the process of change.

In anticipation of this exigency, the NewGate Resource Center was established late in 1971 under the aegis of the National Council on Crime and Delinquency (NCCD) in Paramus, New Jersey. The center's function is threefold: (1) the collection, analysis, and dissemination of statistical and other data and reports on NewGate and similar programs throughout the country; (2) the development of studies, manuals, and descriptive documents to inform and aid persons, institutions, and agencies interested in supporting or establishing programs like NewGate; and (3) on-site technical consultation and assistance, including the evaluation of existing programs, analysis of the needs of the institution in planning new programs, and direction and advice in the preparation of grant proposals. The NewGate Resource Center also offers help in identifying and developing potential funding sources.

NCCD's field staff in twenty-two state and regional offices across the country also disseminate information on NewGate in their respective areas, keep the NewGate Resource Center abreast of developments regarding educational programs in the states they serve, facilitate or convene meetings with correctional and educational personnel for NewGate planning sessions, and assist the NewGate Resource Center in supplying technical consultation upon request to states within their geographic areas.

Although the prognosis for NewGate is encouraging, funding remains the chief problem. Nonetheless, the growth of the NewGate concept is evident. By July 1972, another NewGate program had been established, approximately five states had written and/or submitted proposals, eight were in the process of doing so, and eighteen more had begun exploratory or preliminary work in the planning of programs that would incorporate the components of NewGate.

The NewGate experience has taught us a great deal. It has also reinforced something we have long suspected—that it is not enough to eject a man from a correctional institution with nothing more than a few dollars, a suit of clothes, or even a degree. For unless something has happened to change him, the likelihood is that he will be back.

More than 2 million people are put into some type of confinement each year. At any given time, the number actually incarcerated is in excess of 300,000. Over 95 percent of all those who serve a sentence will ultimately be released, and the national figures on recidivism range from an optimistic 40 percent to 80 percent. Further, the estimated annual cost of crime in America is over 5 billion dollars. Economists, however, supply a far different figure: when the costs of incarceration, the justice system, juvenile crime, organized crime, white collar crime, the destruction of property, and welfare to families of inmates are totaled, the sum is a gargantuan 60 billion dollars. And unless realistic solutions are applied to these grave problems, the price in hopelessness, disillusionment, despair, and rebellion may well exceed 60 billion.

NewGate is but one answer to these problems. Like any other endeavor, it cannot claim total success. But certainly it has changed the direction of the lives of many offenders. A "concept," yes. However, to the men and women who have worked within the program or observed it at first-hand, NewGate is growth, struggle, and hope.

chapter sixteen
CHANGES IN CORRECTIONS: SHOW OR SUBSTANCE?

Clyde E. Sullivan

In the past two decades, correction has experienced a renewed emphasis upon the relationship between work and socialization in the management and treatment of legal offenders. Much of the impetus for this trend has come from a growing awareness that crime and delinquency are as symptomatic of the failure, deficiency, and intransigence of the community as of the failure, deficiency, and intransigence of individual offenders.

Thus, the President's Commission on Law Enforcement and Administration of Justice criticized such failures on the part of the community ". . . as depriving offenders of contact with the institutions that are basically responsible for assuring the development of law-abiding conduct . . ." and concluded that: "The task of corrections, therefore, includes building or rebuilding solid ties between the offender and the community, integrating or reintegrating the offender into community life. . . . This requires not only effort directed toward changing the individual offender, which has been almost the exclusive focus of rehabilitation, but also mobilization and change of the community and its institutions."

Increasing numbers of correctional programs and personnel have been devoted to developing resources and services to reduce the social isolation of incarcerated offenders, facilitating social reintegration of released offenders, and giving offenders new, realistic, but noncriminal access to the world of work and to the opportunity structures of a society that tends to equate capacity for self-management with having a legitimate job and money in one's pocket. Many of these correctional efforts have received support from public agencies concerned with the reduction of

From *Manpower*, vol. 3, no. 1 (1971), pp. 2–7. Reprinted by permission.

hard-core unemployment, such as the U.S. Department of Labor and the Office of Economic Opportunity. And with the expansion of community-based correctional programs such as work-release and community residential centers, support also has come from the private sector—business, industry, and organized labor.

The philosophy and theory motivating many of these new programs obviously are intended as a direct challenge of traditional beliefs about offenders. In evaluating these programs, then, it is fair to ask whether the goals of challenge and change really are being achieved. Are the foundations of entrenched belief systems being challenged, or only the superstructures? Is part of a system being replaced, or all of it? Are traditional intervention premises being discarded, or only traditional practices? Obviously, such elements are intertwined, but modernizing an operation does not necessarily mean that its purposes are being changed or that it will produce better results. A modernized operation may only appear more relevant because it is dressed in new clothes and does not look old-fashioned.

Substituting modern for obsolete equipment in a prison industry, for example, may not help the inmate in any significant way. Indeed, if this is the only change made, it may both worsen his present state and increase his sense of alienation from society. Given the shortage of work in the prison setting, one of the unfortunate byproducts of more efficient equipment in a prison industry can be increased idleness. Further, even if an inmate has experience with modern equipment, this does not insure that he will be accepted in a similar job outside. Membership in a union may be a more critical barrier than lack of experience with up-to-date equipment.

Such observations are not intended to cast a shadow of cynicism across reports of new programs, nor do they imply support for maintaining archaic systems and obsolete equipment in prisons as alternatives to idleness and its evils. The point is that innovation can be subverted or absorbed in a prevailing pattern of operation without really changing the main effects of the operation. We must be able to recognize when this is happening and when it is not.

Today's prison system itself is a prime example of an innovation gone awry. The prison is a product of the social and moral reforms of the eighteenth and nineteenth centuries, proposed as a humane and rational approach for dealing with offenders without resorting to the brutality of ancient punishment patterns. But in a brief period of time it became an institutionalized substitute for the system of banishment which had been part of the criminal sanctions of earlier societies. And now not only was the offender banished from the community, but so were his keepers and the institution to which he was sent. This, of course, had a tremendous impact upon work and other activities inside the prison.

Work as punishment considerably antedates imprisonment as punishment. In Roman times public offenders often were sentenced to work at demeaning and arduous tasks beneath the dignity of citizens. Similarly, in seafaring cultures offenders were sentenced to serve in the galleys. Chaining and restrictions of liberty were simply practical measures to make sure that the sentence was completed and the work done. One essential feature of such sentences was that the convict was not paid. He received the minimum amount of food, clothing, and care required to maintain his potential economic value.

The reforms which began in the latter part of the eighteenth century did not challenge basic attitudes and conceptions about the role of work in a prison setting. In fact, one modern criminologist has suggested that "the convict condemned to hard labor was the galley slave on land, removed from the sea more because of progress in navigation than for any reason connected with progress in penology."

DIGNITY OF WORK STRESSED

Since most free men avoided painful, degrading work, it was assumed that such work might have a "repressive" effect and help to bring an offender to a "penitential" frame of mind. Work thus became a stressful, humiliating intensification of the sentence. The ultimate expression of this point of view came somewhat later as prisons in the United States were barred legally from engaging in industry that would bring them into competition with production of the free labor market. Prisoners were still required to work, but now at hard, monotonous, useless tasks, such as moving rocks from one side of an enclosure to another.

It does not seem accidental that this repressive synthesis of work and punishment for prisoners arose simultaneously with an opposite insistence outside the prison on the dignity of work, the rights of the individual to the products of his labor, and labor as the basis for the right to private property. It was during this period that John Locke argued that "every man has a property in his own person. The labor of his body, and the work of his hands . . . are properly his." Whatever a man was able to take from nature, from the common domain, by his own labor, rightfully became his property.

Similarly, Adam Smith declared that "the property which every man has in his own labor, as it is the original foundation of all other property, so it is the most sacred and inviolable." Still later Marx proposed public ownership of the means of production to protect the property rights of labor.

Gradually, the conception of a relationship between productive work and the right to participate in political life became part of the basis for defining work and its values differently for prison inmates than for free men. This linking of productive work to political rights also has been used to justify social vindictiveness toward those who have violated property rights of others. If work was conceived as a democratic right inseparable from the rights of citizenship, a convicted thief might be held to have lost both his citizenship and his right to work because he had violated the property rights of others and had not supported himself by the honest labor of his own hands.

In recent years there has been increasing dissatisfaction with the idea that work should be used as punishment, but laws still exist which allow men to be sentenced to "separate and solitary confinement at hard labor." And although most prison administrators do not follow the letter of the law, there still is more than an echo of the older, harsh practices in most prisons and jails in the United States.

The problems with which we are struggling arise, in part, because society has mixed and conflicting feelings about work. Moreover, the conflict is not a simple one. It is more than a question of different work and different opportunities for law-breakers versus law-abiders. This is only part of the larger problem of cultural and subcultural contradictions and conflicting definitions arising from differences between ethnic groups, social classes, sexes, and age levels. The perspective provided by the U.S. Department of Labor in viewing the offender labor force as part of a composite problem of hard-core and minority unemployment is probably one of the most significant factors contributing to current changes of attitude in corrections and in society about the rights of prisoners to work.

PUBLIC IDENTITY ALTERED

Contradictory interpretations and definitions of work have a particularly unfortunate impact on offenders, because work and occupation are used judgmentally in our industrial society and have a profound effect on self-confidence, personal identity, and personal freedom. To be free of the threat that social agencies can intervene and take over his life, the ex-offender must convince probation and parole officers, judges, employers, and society that he can establish an effective transactional relationship with society, negotiating legitimately for enough money to meet his needs, to pay his bills, and to care for others who may be dependent upon him.

Consider the situation of a typical offender—a poor, badly educated, culturally deprived young adult—who has been arrested and charged with having committed a crime. Carefully, and quite formally, he is moved through a series of public ceremonies in which he is prosecuted, defined as guilty, sentenced, and confined. One almost unavoidable outcome of this sequence is destruction of the individual's public identity and substitution of a new identity of "convict" or "criminal." This new identity may be reinforced and given further definition as the result of incarceration.

Ultimately, the individual may come to deal with himself and with others as if the definitions applied to him were totally valid. His public and personal identities become fused. The inmate also may develop a self-protective posture which rejects those who reject him and reinforces an identification with a criminal culture. Such identifications and the social expectancies generated by them act as barriers to subsequent successful adjustment in the community.

Supposedly a released offender has "paid" for his crime with a certain number of days and nights in his life. Ostensibly, he is restored to society with a "clean slate." Anyone who knows the basic dynamics of human relationships should be suspicious of such clichés.

Discharge from jail or prison, whether it is probation, parole, or even outright release, usually is nothing more than "letting-go"—a loosening of social control. It is more of a legal reinsertion into society than social restoration or reintegration. Ordinarily, there is no intention of restoring the offender to his previous state. Instead, most prison and probation and parole agencies are organized to serve the expectancies, fears, and needs of people outside the correctional system rather than those who are inside, either as inmates or staff workers.

Nor have adequate status-restoring ceremonies been developed to offset the impact of invidious definitions and expectancies generated by public "exposure," conviction, and incarceration. Until recently it was only a rare and powerful person who could tolerate public knowledge of his prison record. Some new manpower programs for prisoners have recognized this problem and have developed bridging mechanisms and human supports, such as ex-offenders working as job coaches and counselors, to help manage the transition.

Few released offenders are equipped to compete successfully in today's labor market. Their previous employment record is spotty—a history of short-term jobs interspersed with frequent periods of unemployment. Most of their work has been low skilled and low paid, and competition for even these jobs is increasing. Technological advances, changes in the occupational structure, and fluctuations in the economy also reduce the relative number of these jobs. In addition, educational and training requirements are increasing for many entry-level jobs. This is particularly critical for many jail and prison inmates, since they tend to leave school at an early age and are more poorly educated than the general population.

The ex-offender also is handicapped in searching for work because referrals from family and friends are a major source of job-getting in our economy. But the family and friends of ex-offenders are not likely to be a very helpful resource. For the most part, they also come from marginal, impoverished, and culturally deprived sectors of our communities and are struggling with many of the same problems and handicaps as the offender.

Delinquent and criminal populations often are accused of not being motivated to work. It is often suggested that willing men always can find some kind of work and that ex-offenders should use it as a stepping-stone to better jobs. Such stereotyping ignores the fact that many of the low-paid, mediocre jobs that always seem to be available are dead ends rather than stepping-stones to better employment. Further, unless an individual has sufficient resources or social support to take the risks involved in attempting to move up, he can become dependent on a mediocre job and permanently fixed in its limitations.

JOB CRUCIAL TO PAROLE

Another difficulty is that parole rules often require offenders to have jobs before they can be considered for release, although good jobs rarely are negotiated from inside prison. Nevertheless, steady work habits while on parole are viewed as evidence of reformation. No leeway is allowed for job exploration. Periods of unemployment are questioned sharply, even though brief lapses into unemployment are considered natural for ordinary young adults entering the labor market.

It is true there is a correlation between steady employment and lowered recidivism. But unless parole rules relating to employment are applied with good judgment and perspective, there is danger that both parolee and parole officer will be preoccupied with superficial evidence (e.g., pay stubs) that the parolee has been working every day rather than with the quality of work and its career potential.

"Steadiness" can be misleading in its apparent promise for reducing recidivism. It may postpone but probably will not prevent further delinquency. While a small, steady income may ease some pressures, and regular work attendance may reduce the free time in which delinquency might occur, there is evidence that these do not offset the influence of other, more potent factors.

Low prestige, low-paid, temporary jobs tend to fix disadvantaged youth in a milieu where they are exposed to excessive criminal behavior and environmental stresses, which in turn contribute to further delinquency. Finally, steady employment in a marginal occupation may tend to confirm an offender's view that there is no future in legitimate work and impel him back to crime.

WORK MUST HAVE MEANING

It has become increasingly clear that programs to rehabilitate offenders must be linked as closely as possible to society and culture outside prison. The required diversity of opportunity, controls, rewards, resources, experiences, and definitions cannot be generated in an institution isolated from society. These are reasons why transitional facilities, such as work-release and community residential centers, are regarded so hopefully. The flexibility required to shop for better opportunities and to risk the stress of social mobility can be provided in a well-designed transitional facility that has proper legal and administrative support.

Attention should be focused on programs which begin working with individual offenders on the transitional process early in the correctional cycle and follow through until they have been fully reintegrated into the community. (Such programs also may serve persons who are moving from the community into the institution.) To increase the likelihood that offenders will receive appropriate recognition and support for socially acceptable behavior, the best transitional programs try to influence the way society rewards or punishes the ex-offender by enlisting support from other social agencies and employers. These programs also offer successful role models and counsel offenders who have been released on how to adjust and be accepted in their actual work situation.

If society is serious about social reintegration of ex-offenders, transitional management programs and facilities must have the capacity to establish and reinforce the rights of prisoners and ex-inmates to work. This requires that prisoners know that work or work training in prison has as much meaning and value for society as work training in a transitional facility or in the free community.

Further, the right of society to punish and restrict an offender's freedom may limit the range of work available but should not deprive him of the right to work. Competition between the work of prisoners and that of free men should not be judged strictly as an economic matter but approached as a fundamental problem of respect for human rights. Finally, the idea that it is appropriate to relate work in prison to punishment rather than to general patterns and values of work in the world at large should be abandoned.

Correction agencies are only one segment of community health and welfare services and as such have limited authority and resources. They cannot be effective if other social agencies do not cooperate and develop a network of human services and programs which reach offenders and ex-offenders. There has been an unfortunate tendency for corrections to try to develop its own full array of services because it has been isolated from existing community resources. This has resulted in makeshift duplication and needless competition.

Genuine reintegration of the ex-offender requires that he have access to community resources on the same basis as any other citizen and that he be taught how to avail himself of his rights when he needs help. This means corrections must join the family of community social agencies and accept its discipline. To establish effective ties with other organizations, corrections agencies and projects must be willing to modify authoritarian ways and submit to genuinely collaborative relationships.

It is of prime importance that correctional workers who manage the transition of ex-offenders into the world of work know who the gate-keepers to jobs really are and the means of access through their gates. For some jobs, access is controlled exclusively by employers; in others, it is possible only through unions or trade associations. Training must be designed to meet the requirements of these gatekeepers.

TRADE COUNCILS HELPFUL

Such knowledge, which is not now generally available in corrections, requires regular contact with people who are in touch with technological and occupational developments and shifts in hiring practices. A prime source of such information can be the state employment service and its local offices. Trade advisory councils, like those developed by the California Department of Corrections, are another source of information and generally provide a good channel of communication to business and industry.

Fortunately, private business has been increasingly involved in correctional problems in recent years. A series of case studies published by the National Association of Manufacturers describes ways in which training resources, techniques, and pilot programs have been initiated and managed by industry and have effectively met the employment problems of ex-offenders.

But much more is needed than such efforts. Even when ex-prisoners are placed in high-quality, good-paying jobs, they may become ambivalent about their new work roles and identifications, feel threatened by the emotional and social demands generated by the flow of work, and return to family and friendship patterns which reinforce older self-concepts and hinder development of new perceptions and adjustments.

Managing the transition of the ex-offender is essentially a problem of stimulating and supporting upward mobility from an outcaste status. The correctional worker involved in this task must have access to the ex-offender's family, friends, employers, and teachers and to the police, the courts, and health and welfare services personnel in the community. In these relationships the correctional worker will have to function as interpreter and coordinator. It is not likely or necessary that he can

Comparison of Occupational Experience

	%	
Professional and technical workers	2.2	10.4
Managers and owners, incl. farm	4.3	16.3
Clerical and sales	7.1	14.2
Craftsmen, foremen	17.6	20.6
Operatives	25.2	21.2
Service workers, incl. household	11.5	6.4
Laborers (except mine) incl. farm laborers and foremen	31.9	10.8

Inmate prior work experience ■
General labor force ■

Comparison of Educational Levels

Years of School Completed	%	
COLLEGE 4 years or more	1.1	8.4
1 to 3 years	4.2	9.4
HIGH SCHOOL 4 years	12.4	27.5
1 to 3 years	27.6	20.7
ELEMENTARY 5 to 8 years	40.3	28
None to 4 years	14.4	6

Federal and State Felony Inmates and General Population

Inmate population ■
General population ■

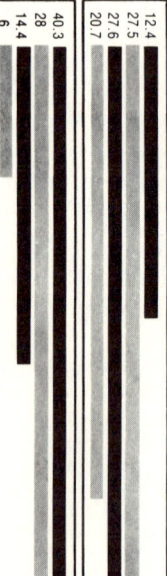

[1] All data are for males only, since the correctional institution population is 95 percent male. data for males were used to eliminate the effects of substantial differences between male and female occupational employment patterns.

Source: Manpower Administration, based on Census data.

control what happens, but together he and the ex-offender should be able to assemble a variety of constructive choices.

It may be that we are standing on the edge of a major breakthrough in corrections. The presence of such factors as the Joint Commission on Correctional Manpower and Training; the correctional research and offender training projects supported by the U.S. Department of Labor and of Health, Education, and Welfare; and increased funding for the Law Enforcement Assistance Administration offer hope that the future can be bright.

But tradition's weight is heavy. Centuries-old beliefs and fears remain deeply rooted in society, and corrections itself is strongly committed to the perpetuation of older patterns of operation because of outmoded administrative and personnel practices and massive capital investments in antiquated buildings.

Moreover, corrections is being asked to totally reverse its direction and this is difficult. Rather than seeking increasingly sure ways of "holding" offenders, corrections now must find improved ways of "letting-go." And modern trends and information indicate that, instead of trying to establish greater managerial control by adding to existing patterns of deprivation, we should increase opportunities and rewards even when offenders do not demonstrate that they deserve them, but only that they need them.

Unless there is a basic commitment to the different philosophy, policies, strategy, and tactics required for community-based programs of corrections—with reintegration of the offender as the goal—it is unlikely that any widespread practical changes will come about. As in the past, new stimuli will be assimilated in such a way as to minimize dislocation of the existing system; and American corrections will continue its ponderous preparation to enter the twentieth century while the rest of American society prepares to enter the twenty-first.

chapter 17
EMPLOYMENT PROBLEMS OF RELEASED PRISONERS

George A. Pownall

Are employment problems a major factor in recidivism? Many corrections experts think so. Certainly a released convict must have adequate employment if he is to achieve a socially integrated life style that will keep him from returning to prison. But while theories and assumptions about the job problems of released prisoners have been plentiful, facts were in short supply. Information has been limited to state or regional data coming primarily from the California correctional system. Now, through a study completed for the U.S. Department of Labor's Manpower Administration, more substantial national data are available.

Many of the problems revealed by this study are being attacked by a variety of federal and local programs to remove barriers to employment for ex-offenders. But we still need major changes in vocational training for prisoners, expansion of community treatment centers and work release programs, better job counseling and job placement services, and more liberal hiring policies.

The study *Employment Problems of Released Prisoners* was based on three separate surveys. The first was an analysis of the official records of a 10 percent sample (945) of all released male federal prisoners under parole and mandatory release supervision on June 30, 1964 (see Chart 1).

The second survey was based on a review of official records of, and interviews with, all federal releasees under supervision as of October 31, 1965, in Baltimore and Philadelphia, a total of 169 persons. In the last survey all federal prisoners released between October 1, 1965, and March 31,

From *Manpower* (January, 1971), pp. 26-31. Reprinted by permission.

1966, under the jurisdiction of the Baltimore and Philadelphia probation offices—a total of 51—were interviewed upon release and once a month for three months thereafter.

All three surveys revealed that unemployment was very high among released federal prisoners. The first survey showed that nationally they had an unemployment rate of 17 percent, more than three times the U.S. rate for males in June 1964. The unemployment rate for released male prisoners in Baltimore and Philadelphia was four to five times greater than for the male civilian labor force in those two cities.

Furthermore, former offenders had a much higher rate of part-time employment and were relegated generally to low-paying unskilled jobs. Like their "civilian" counterparts, former offenders having the most difficulty in the job market were the poorly educated, the unmarried, the very young, older men, and blacks.

JOBLESS RATES COMPARED

The study showed a 15 percent unemployment rate for white released prisoners, compared to a 22 percent rate for other releasees. Male unemployment nationally at that time was less than 5 percent for whites and less than 10 percent for all others.

Only 8.5 percent of married releasees were unemployed. The rate for single men was twice as high and for all others—mostly divorced—the rate was almost 24 percent.

Ex-offenders under twenty years of age had an unemployment rate of 36 percent. The rate for those fifty-five and over was 23. It sank to 18 percent for those 20 to 24 and 45 to 54; to 16 for those 25 to 34; and to less than 9 for those 35 to 44.

One out of every five released prisoners with a ninth-grade education or less was unemployed. For those who finished the tenth or eleventh grades, the rate was one in seven and for high school graduates one in ten. Education meant more for whites than blacks, however. Some 81 percent of whites with ninth-grade educations or less had jobs, compared to 93 percent of high school graduates. Among blacks there was hardly any difference; the employment rate for high school graduates was 79 percent compared to 77 percent for those who completed the ninth grade or less.

The median monthly income for those who had jobs was $256. For those with full-time jobs it was $280. One-fourth of the full-time workers earned $200 a month or less. The overwhelming majority worked at blue collar jobs. Nearly 40 percent were in jobs classified as unskilled labor and another 23 percent were service workers or operatives.

The most difficult time for ex-offenders is the first six months after release, and this was decidedly true for employment. The survey showed significantly higher unemployment rates for men out of prison less than six months.

The number of incarcerations and the offenses for which a man was convicted also affected his employment prospects. A criminal record is an obstacle to any job-seeker, but it is harder on minorities. Of those surveyed who had no prior commitment or only one, whites had much lower rates of unemployment than all others. With two or more commitments, there was little difference.

Stealing and drugs seem to go with inability to find and hold a job. Narcotics law violators and men committed for burglary, larceny, possession of stolen goods, and interstate transportation of stolen vehicles had higher rates of unemployment and lower rates of full-time employment than those guilty of other offenses. (These men usually had high recidivism rates as well.)

Work experience is important for ex-offenders, as it is for others in the work force. Those who had never held a job had an unemployment rate twice as high as those who had held a job lasting two years or more. The gap was even wider for full-time employment. Only half of those without experience had full-time work compared to three-fourths whose longest prior job lasted two years or more.

EMPLOYMENT HELP LACKING

Other significant facts turned up by the survey were:

> The offender's work assignment in prison was not significantly related to his employment status at the time of survey, with one exception: those who worked at skilled maintenance jobs in prison had low rates of post-release unemployment. A more significant factor was the evaluation of the offender's work performance in prison. Those with excellent ratings had the lowest unemployment rate.
>
> The majority of men leaving prison did not have prearranged jobs (see Chart 2). Most of those who did were parolees; having a job traditionally has been a requirement for parole. Most prearranged jobs were obtained through the help of the prisoner's family, friends, and former employers (see Chart 3). Correctional institutions, probation-parole officers, and state employment agencies provided minimal assistance.
>
> Released prisoners found unstable employment. The median stay on the first job was four months; on the longest job held it was eight months.

Over half of the ex-offenders had one or more periods of unemployment. They required a median of twenty-nine days to find their first job.

Unemployment was a major factor contributing to new violations of the law by former prisoners.

Inadequate supervision by the corrections systems contributed to failure by ex-offenders to find and hold jobs. Union discrimination and inability to be bonded also were handicaps.

There was evidence that some ex-offenders do not work, even when they have acquired a skill and received placement assistance, because they live in a subculture which is nonsupportive. This subculture (families and peer groups) does not emphasize upward mobility or achievement, nor does it place much value on steady employment.

An area of real weakness in the correctional system was training. Prisons offered vocational training programs, but they were misnamed; most of them were training programs associated with institutional maintenance and were usually concentrated in institutions for youth. The negligible differences in employment rates between those who did and those who did not have vocational training demonstrated that these programs did not benefit released prisoners very much.

One hopeful finding was that prisoners who had a year or more of vocational training had a higher employment rate than those who did not. Unfortunately most prisoners were in such programs for less than one year.

Those trained in professional or technical skills were most likely to have successful post-release full-time employment, but only a very small percentage of inmates qualified for and received this type of training. Ex-offenders trained in processing occupations also did extremely well, but again, only a small percentage of inmates were involved. One-fourth of the prisoners who received training were trained in bench-work occupations, clerical-sales, farming, forestry, and fishing. They had the highest unemployment rate.

FEW USED PRISON TRAINING

Less than one-third of those who received training used it in their first post-release job. There was some indication that those trained in professional, technical, managerial, or clerical–sales work obtained and maintained employment in a related skilled position. But more than half of those releasees who allegedly received vocational training were employed in unskilled or semi-skilled jobs upon release. Only one-fifth of those with training in structural occupations, machine trades, and processing occupations (with their high demand level and, consequently, the greatest employment potential) were able to obtain employment in these fields.

Before discussing possible solutions of these problems, it should be noted that the raw data for this survey are now five years old or more. Since then, a number of government programs have brought to bear on the problems of the disadvantaged, including former offenders. Among these are the federally funded Job Opportunities in the Business Sector (JOBS) Program, New Careers, the Concentrated Employment Program (CEP), and the Work Incentive (WIN) Program. Generally, these programs seek out the hard-core unemployed and prepare them for jobs.

Further help has come from the U.S. Department of Labor's bonding program for ex-convicts. The Labor Department also specifies a majority of Manpower Development and Training Act (MDTA) enrollees be disadvantaged. And MDTA is now providing modern training for a limited number of inmates in prisons around the country—7,200 were enrolled through June 1970. Some state employment services, often through CEP, are stationing job placement specialists in penal institutions to aid men about to be released. And local, state, and federal government agencies have begun to relax their hiring requirements and practices to admit more ex-offenders.

The federal work-training programs are obviously having some impact. A rough estimate places the number of former offenders in the work or training in four major programs—MDTA classroom and on-the-job training, WIN, and CEP—at more than 10,000 on June 30, 1970. Others were enrolled in JOBS, Neighborhood Youth Corps, and similar programs.

REALISTIC WORKLOAD URGED

We have as yet no comprehensive evaluation of all these new efforts. But on the basis of what we do know about them, and what we know about the problems revealed by the study, it is possible to make concrete recommendations for improving services to offenders inside and outside prison.

First, vocational training for prisoners needs a major overhaul and redirection. The priority in prison should be to meet inmate training needs rather than to fulfill work requirements of the institution.

Prison industries should be structured so inmates learn useful skills and develop good work habits.

Basically, prisons should stimulate work experiences comparable to those found in outside industries. One way to accomplish this might be to locate prison industries outside the institution. More importantly, supervisors of inmates should be trained to encourage good working habits on the part of inmates. Also, each inmate should have a sufficient workload to keep him occupied the majority of the time, thereby facilitating good supervision and the development of good work habits.

BETTER FOLLOW-UP REQUIRED

Vocational training should be limited to occupations in which releasees can be trained effectively and which provide good employment opportunities upon release. The study revealed, for example, that instruction in drafting led to successful employment; yet this training was offered only on a limited basis and needed to be expanded. Institutions might work jointly with industry to establish more realistic training programs and to improve public relations with businessmen who could be a more fruitful source of jobs. Ideally, industry would recruit employees from correctional institutions much as they do now from colleges and high schools.

More pre-release community treatment centers should be established to give inmates additional opportunities for vocational and on-the-job training outside prison. These centers provide close supervision and gradual re-entry into the community, which is highly effective for many men preparing for release. Work-release programs should be expanded for younger offenders to permit them to study in vocational schools within the community. These schools have better equipment and more up-to-date programs than can be found in prisons.

We must guard against spending great sums of money training inmates and then leaving them to find jobs for themselves. More placement officers in institutions and more job counselors in the community are needed. Working together, these specialists can coordinate job placement programs among prisons, parole and probation authorities, and employers. Groups of specialists working together—they are called employability teams—already are being used to help participants in the CEP and WIN programs. All prisoners being released should receive intensive job placement and job coaching and a long follow-up period of counseling.

Improvement of these three services—training, counseling, and job placement—should help ease the difficulties former offenders encounter within the first six months after release and should help reduce the recidivism rate, which is highest during this period.

Because of the Labor Department bonding program, some private bonding companies are demonstrating more willingness to take a chance on former offenders. And some employers with group bonding programs have altered their practices to permit offenders to post their own personal bonds. Bonding is still a problem, but it is far less a barrier to jobs for ex-offenders than it was five years ago.

Other barriers, however, still remain. Occupations which require licensing—such as barber, beautician, practical nurse, insurance and real estate salesmen—often are closed to released prisoners by the qualifying requirements imposed by each state. A forthcoming study by the Educational Testing Service, Princeton, New Jersey, will provide detailed information on this problem. The lack of acceptance of released prisoners into various craft unions also has closed off opportunities to former offenders. Improved cooperation between the federal government and some national unions is beginning to alleviate this problem. However, on the local level, unions often have an autonomy which permits them to operate somewhat differently than national union policy indicates.

OLDER OFFENDERS NEGLECTED

An ironic problem is found in government employee policies. The federal government encourages private employers to hire ex-offenders but often will not hire them itself. There has been some breakdown in these exclusionary practices by some government agencies and, specifically, some correctional programs. And some states and cities have adopted more liberal hiring practices. Nevertheless, there is still a great need in most systems—local, state and federal—for evaluation of existing policies and practices to determine the steps necessary to provide work for ex-prisoners. A study of actual hiring practices of local governments in regard to ex-offenders is now being conducted by the Georgetown University Law Center, Washington, D.C.

The emphasis in most correctional training and placement programs often has been on youthful offenders. As an unfortunate consequence, older offenders experience a proportionately greater hardship in finding jobs than older persons in the civilian labor force. There is an obvious need for special programs emphasizing job placement and community-based treatment to aid older offenders.

Finally, we must recognize the implications of the fact that released prisoners who benefit most from training and placement are those who believe in the desirability of steady work, upward mobility, and achievement. Training and placement alone are not enough for prisoners who do not reflect these beliefs, and who may be influenced by negative attitudes of families and peer groups.

These men can be helped in two ways: by transferring them before discharge from prison to a pre-release community treatment center, where they can get specialized counseling and job placement; and by special counseling for their families. Including the inmate's family in the counseling process may give him the added support he will need to make a successful adjustment to the outside world. In some situations, of course, the best

Profile of Released Prisoners in National Sample

CHARACTERISTICS	NUMBER	PERCENT
TOTAL	945	100.0
COLOR		
White	721	76.3
Nonwhite	224	23.7
MODE OF RELEASE		
Parole	742	78.5
Mandatory release	203	21.5
AGE, JUNE 1964		
Under 20	55	5.8
20-24	292	30.9
25-34	317	33.5
35-44	166	17.6
45-54	75	7.9
55 and over	40	4.3
MEDIAN: 29.0		
MARITAL STATUS		
Single	513	54.3
Married	317	33.5
Other (divorced, widowed)	115	12.2
EDUCATION AT RELEASE		
9th grade or less	573	60.6
10th-11th grade	193	20.4
12th grade or more	179	18.9
MEDIAN: 9.0		

Chart 1

Job Arrangement Prior to Release

Chart 2

	TOTAL	Parole	Mandatory release
TOTAL SURVEYED	169	118	51
No job arranged	92	47	45
Job arranged	77	71	6
Secured and worked one week or more	62	57	5
Not secured	15	14	1

How First Postrelease Job Was Arranged

	First Job
TOTAL SURVEYED	162
Family, friends, former employer	92
Own efforts	36
Probation office or institutional personnel	9
All other sources	25

Chart 3

SOURCE: Employment Problems of Released Prisoners.

answer may be to transfer the released man to a different environment, away from the family or peer group whose influence is destructive.

Basic to all these recommendations is the need for continual record-keeping and evaluative research to keep these programs up-to-date and functioning effectively.

The failure to obtain and maintain suitable employment goes hand-in-hand with recidivism. All parolees who violated parole before interview in the study were either unemployed or had unstable employment experiences. If recidivism is to be meaningfully reduced, the released prisoner must be trained in terms of his ability, placed on the right job, and provided with the sustained support needed to keep it.

chapter eighteen

WORK-RELEASE: CONFLICTING GOALS WITHIN A PROMISING INNOVATION

Elmer H. Johnson

Work-release has been hailed by some correctional leaders as a breakthrough for penal reform:

> This is not just a work program, but a structured, planned, and well-coordinated effort to interrupt criminal careers and restore the inmate's faith in, and contact with, society.[1]

The warden of a county prison employing work release wrote:

> Our prison is not a human junk yard. We use the methods available to us to tackle some of each prisoner's problems, to assess the worth of the individual, and to prepare him for re-entry into society with a more positive attitude.[2]

Although the enthusiasm for this correctional strategy is not shared by all prison executives, we suggest in this paper that advocates of work-release find themselves in fundamental conflict once they confront the practicalities of implementation. These conflicts hold greater possibility of eroding the promise of the strategy than the open rejection by the

From *Canadian Journal of Corrections*, vol. 12, no. 1 (1970), pages 67–77; reprinted by permission. This paper is derived from research reported in Elmer H. Johnson, *Work Release – Factors in Selection and Results* (Carbondale, Illinois: Center for the Study of Crime, Delinquency, and Corrections, 1969) and was supported by the Division of Research and Demonstration Grants, Social Rehabilitation Services, U.S. Department of Health, Education and Welfare (Grant RD2425-G-67).

opponents. Because of the unprecedented interest of correctional systems of Canada and United States in work-release, an examination of the conflicts inherent in goals of work-release is especially useful at this time.

WHAT IS WORK-RELEASE?

In the work-release approach, an individual sentenced to prison is permitted to work for pay in the free community but spends his nonworking hours as an inmate in a correctional institution. His earnings are collected by the correctional authorities. After deductions for board and travel to and from his work place, the prisoner is given an allowance for his immediate personal needs. As directed by the court, funds are provided through a public welfare agency for support of his dependents. Any balance is paid the prisoner on his discharge on completion of sentence or parole.

Work-release is intermediate between probation and imprisonment, and between parole and imprisonment in another sense. Granting of work-release implies that the offender is a better prospect for rehabilitation than the other inmates. It is assumed the particular offender has sufficient motivation to provide for his dependents through work while under sentence. However, since he was sentenced to prison, there also is an implication that the offender requires firmer control during off-work hours than a probation officer can provide.

Work-release resembles parole in that the inmate usually has served a portion of his sentence and that he is released under supervision into the community. However, it differs from parole in that he continues to reside in and is subject to the control of the prison. Except for working hours, he assumes the status of a prisoner, although usually quartered apart from other kinds of prisoners.

For appropriate inmates, work-release has theoretical advantages over parole. Work-release permits a form of conditional release earlier in the sentence than parole usually provides. In this way correctional authorities have greater flexibility than parole statutes usually provide, for releasing the inmate at the moment in his prison career when he is best prepared psychologically. Work-release can test inmates for parole.

Authorization for work-release may be part of the court's sentencing procedure, or a part of the prison authorities' release procedure.[3] In the first instance the court's authority is of paramount importance. In the second instance, the correctional agency usually has exclusive authority. A third procedure is to authorize work-release sometime during the course of the sentence, most likely near the end of the sentence. In the third version the correctional agency may have sole authority or may share it with the sentencing court.

MAJOR GOALS SET FOR WORK-RELEASE

The several goals set for work-release are not necessarily consistent. In fact, the inherent assumptions of one goal may be diametrically opposed to those of another goal. Under the generalized praise for this "revolutionary" approach are the familiar contradictions which have hobbled corrections since the first prison was opened.

Alternative to total confinement. Reformers have been appalled at the debilitating effects of prison life on the initiative, self-respect, and value system of the prisoner as suggested by the comment of one work-release inmate:

> This is the best thing that ever happened to the prisoner. At least here I can walk a straight line, not those damned circles in the prison yard.

In 1873 the Wisconsin State Board of Charities and Reform declared:

> Here are scores and hundreds of men, some of them young and in vigorous health, who are compelled to spend from a few days to a year ... in absolute idleness, while the taxpayers of the various counties are supporting them. What a waste of labor! What an injury to the men themselves to keep them in a state of enforced idleness! What an unwise expenditure of public funds to support healthy, able-bodied men in such idleness![4]

The special pertinence of alternatives to imprisonment for America is indicated by imprisonment rates per 100,000 population for several countries: Norway, 44; United Kingdom, 59; Sweden, 63; Denmark, 73; Finland, 153; United States, 200; and Canada, 240.[5] The United States and Canada are amongst the most incarceration-oriented in the Western world. A large share of the inmates in the United States serve sentences too brief to permit any effective treatment program. In 1965 a third of the inmates in the United States were in misdemeanant institutions with a sentence usually of less than twelve months. Many served sentences of only thirty days. The "revolving door" jail is reflected in a study of five misdemeanant institutions in which half of the inmates had a prior commitment and a fifth had been committed ten or more times.[6] There is no reason to believe that, under these circumstances, incarceration has any perceptible positive effect on the bulk of the individuals contributing to the high rate of imprisonment.

Reshaping conceptions of the prisoner. Public attitudes toward inmates are colored by what has been called the "convict bogey."[7] The prisoner often is regarded as a totally evil and highly dangerous being. Work-release focuses attention on the rehabilitative purposes of prison confinement rather than the retributive purposes. The image is of a person sufficiently trustworthy to work along with free workers, sufficiently responsible to be willing to support his dependents, and sufficiently self-disciplined in work attitudes and habits to maintain employment.

Nevertheless, many of the objections against work-release expressed by correctional employees assume the prisoner is socially unworthy of the extra attention he receives. Some sheriffs have complained about the "extra work" entailed in checking inmates in and out of jail, especially when the work-release jobs require unorthodox working hours. The inmates must be searched as they come and go to prevent smuggling of contraband. The policy of search itself, incidentally, reflects the persistence of the "convict bogey." The work-release program also imposes tasks such as administration of an accounting system for inmate wages, storage and handling of civilian clothing in addition to inmate uniforms, and search for jobs for unemployed work-release candidates.[8]

These additional tasks tend to emphasize the individual qualities of the inmate, an emphasis which is the core of a genuine rehabilitation program. However, the emphasis undermines the standardized handling of inmates as a means of reducing employee workload. The conception of the prisoner as socially unworthy affords grounds for moving inmates about in blocks of unfeeling "things." Grupp cites opinions of sheriffs reflecting this attitude toward work-releasees:

> I believe staying in jail is more of a punishment than to be out during the day and use a jail as a sleeping place at night. I am against day parole to private employment. I feel a jail is not a hotel and why should a sheriff in smaller counties have to put in extra time, etc., putting prisoners in and out of jail. He could not be available at all times. They would have to be searched in and out of jail and sheriffs in smaller counties would not be able to get any sleep having to get up early after being out all night . . .
>
> Takes more help. We work too many hours now. . . . In my opinion it makes a farce out of punishment by jail sentence.[9]

The half-free status of work-releasees undermines the usual custodial definition of discipline as inmate submission to the keeper's authority. Discipline becomes more a matter of inmate self-control. The acceptance by staff of the second version is a matter of evolution of relationships between staff and inmate derived from the half-free status.[10]

The program of the Oregon Corrections Division experienced this process of accommodation. Initially, heavy reliance was placed on the inmate's self-discipline, but it was soon learned that a *system* of relationships would have to be created to put together the behavior of various classes of persons (inmates, correctional personnel, employers, and police). The corrections division reported:

> The Work-Release Section recognized that acceptable levels of discipline and conduct could not be maintained through authoritarian control alone. It was felt that best results would be derived from the self-discipline imposed by participation in regular employment and daily living with the limited controls of confinement. Therefore, most of the original rules for work release were concerned with operational procedures rather than conduct and behaviour. Enrollees were specifically instructed concerning the need for compliance with rules of the confinement facility. Controls within the community were established by the local law enforcement agencies.[11]

This initial policy was based on certain assumptions. Self-discipline of the inmate would be strengthened by the habits and rituals incidental to the regularity of employment as a form of social interaction. At the same time, the return to the place of confinement at night would remind the inmate that he was, after all, subject to the risk of withdrawal of work-release. Initially, it was assumed that the norms of two different roles (employee in work place and prisoner in prison) could be combined to create norms for an unprecedented role (work-release inmate) functioning in a new social situation (prisoner working in the free community for pay). Furthermore, it was assumed that persons unrelated to the program (employers and the local police) would be able to frame and impose rules without being a formal participant in the design and administration of a correctional strategy alien to the traditional interpretation of the presence of a prisoner in the free community. Because experience demonstrated these assumptions were in error, the Oregon program moved to a second phase of accommodation.

> Time and experience revealed a need for more formalized controls. Controls by some local authorities in certain cases proved quite permissive. Enrollees were quick to take advantage of such opportunities. Further experience indicated that many of the men did not respond well to the sudden change from the rigid control and discipline of the institution to the relative freedom of the community. Policies and guidelines were written and distributed to the authorities at the confinement facilities. These guidelines defined the areas where they might exercise their authority and reserved certain authority for the Work-Release Representative and the Work-Release Section. The local authorities responded fully to this policy with the

result of few program failures and an improved spirit of cooperation. The culmination of the efforts was a more equitable treatment of all enrollees under the same set of rules.[12]

In this second stage of accommodation, it is necessary to establish rather clear-cut rules for measuring inmate conduct and to provide a basis for the participation of correctional employee, employers, and police in a set of unprecedented social relationships. In this sense the prison system took the initiative in establishing the norms for a set of relationships in which the prison system had primary official responsibility.

Because the inmates and correctional employees were most familiar with the traditional prisoner role, prison administrators are likely to emphasize those aspects of work-release pertinent to norms imposed on the usual prisoner. Authoritarian control probably will be given particular emphasis at this transitional stage more than at later phases of program development to minimize adverse community reaction. Rules are easier to communicate when staff, police, and employers are oriented to their place and function with an unfamiliar social system. A key advantage of Oregon's change in procedures was that the necessity to create a new social system was recognized. Nevertheless, this retreat to a more authoritarian approach conflicts with the long-term objective of creating new conceptions of the prisoner.

Reducing financial burden on taxpayer. A prime argument advanced by its advocates is that the program requires the inmate to contribute from his pay some of the costs of maintaining him in prison. Furthermore, the prisoner is able to support at least partially his dependents who otherwise probably would require public assistance. Incidentally, the inmate may be placed in the unfamiliar position of paying income taxes, fines, and court costs.[13]

When a staff has been fully employed in custodial tasks, the introduction of work-release to reduce the tax burden frequently overlooks the additional costs involved in maintaining a staff sufficient for the additional tasks.

Olson concludes that the work-release is not as fiscally attractive as the more ardent work-release proponents claim.[14] He asserts that, at best, it partly defrays the cost of certain services, but the administrative costs cannot be predicted in a general way. Direct costs will accumulate proportionately with the degree of casework and the closeness of supervision. Direct costs include counseling services, selection procedures, interviewing, testing, record keeping, contacts with various persons in course of case investigation, field supervision of inmates, special housing, feeding at unusual hours, and similar matters. Indirect costs raise complicated questions: Does work-release increase costs of apprehending escapists? What is the effect of a high rate of inmate turnover on administrative costs?

How does the program ultimately affect recidivism? How many families of work-release inmates would receive public assistance if work-release did not exist?

Although costs can be estimated reliably only in terms of particular work-release programs, it is possible that work-release costs no more than other alternatives to the usual prison sentence. Then the central issue is whether the taxpayer is benefited by the social advantages of work-release and an ultimate reduction in the extent of crime.

Maintaining the labor force of the free community. The strategy prevents interruption of the prisoner's labor contribution to the economic system of the free community. When the prisoner is a skilled worker, this interruption can have adverse consequences for his employer. When the ultimate impact on the nation over a number of years is considered, the loss can be high.

Ideally, the inmate can resume his civilian job immediately after admission to prison. For a number of practical and administrative reasons, this degree of work continuity cannot be assured. Nevertheless, the period of interruption can be reduced. Work-release may add to his work experience. Then he is better prepared to re-enter the community's job market upon completion of his sentence. The "employment shock" is eased compared with the situation for the prisoner discharged after a period of total or partial idleness in prison. The usual releasee encounters difficulties in readjusting to such "tremendous trifles" as regular work hours, employer's expectations for punctuality and sustained effort, cooperation with work colleagues, and matters such as arrangements for travel to and from the work place.

Final phase of vocational training in institution. Ideally, work-release complements the educational and training programs of the correctional institution. It can be a valuable alternative to a work assignment within a prison industry. A wider range of opportunities becomes available for fitting the prison job to the motivations, career aspirations, and specialized work experience of the inmate. Work-release potentially can be a remarkably effective bridge between penal confinement and work in the free society. Employment in a regular job exposes the inmate to the work pace, working conditions, and social environment of work he will encounter after release from imprisonment.

But there are many problems. The use of work-release depends largely on the supply-demand relationships in the local labor market and the receptivity of employers, co-workers, and, in some cases, clients of the particular enterprise. Within a geographical area accessible from the prison, does the work-release program have access to the kinds and quality of jobs required for individualized fitting of inmate to job in terms appropriate for his vocational training program?

Stating the same issue in reverse, can the prison meet the needs of the local job market, while accomplishing purposes of rehabilitation? There must be a supply of skills available amongst prisoners to coincide in quality and specialization with the labor needs of the available job market. Because a great proportion of prisoners lack high work skills and reliable work habits, the supply of excellent job candidates is easy to exaggerate. Then the issue centers on the capacity of the prison to produce a greater supply through vocational and attitudinal training.

Once the few prisoners, who are qualified at admission for skilled jobs, are assigned to work-release, expansion of the program can proceed in two ways. First, and probably most likely, the assignment of inmates to low-paying unskilled jobs becomes increasingly characteristic, to the detriment of the ideal conditions stated initially. Second, the vocational and attitudinal training programs of the institution are geared with the work-release program in the long term to upgrade unskilled inmates for future job openings in the community adjacent to the prison. Then the immediate savings to the taxpayer are lost.

Period of transition from prison to community. Because of the half-free status of the inmate, work-release has been advocated as a bridge between life in prison and his life after release. At first glance, the work-releasee is the equivalent of an average employee in the work place. However, the incarceration dimension of his half-free status probably makes him something different in his responses to to the behavior of others and of the others' responses to him. His physical locale and the imposition of the role of orthodox prisoner varies for the work-releasee amongst the many work-release programs. With these variations come differences in the discrepancy between his role in community employment and his role as inmate in the prison setting. However, some degree of discrepancy is inevitable because of the differences in these aspects of the two social settings: the physical environment, types of recurrent situations, authority relationsips, and living routines.

When the discrepancy is marked, work-release offers the advantage as a period of transition. When the discrepancy is held to a minimum, work-release experiences can blunt the shock of release by focusing the inmate's attention on the realities he will have to face as an employee and breadwinner for his dependents. Through his work-release job, he gains earlier access to the community labor market. This early access may reduce post-release problems of finding employment. Through his work-release savings, he has a hedge against the problem of supporting himself and his dependents during job search. His work-release employment might enhance his qualifications as a job candidate.

Maintenance of family ties. When the prisoner can support his dependents, he has means of maintaining his status as head of his family. Elimination of the breadwinner role for the inmate strikes at the roots of his status as head of the family and as a man. By continuing to contribute to the support of his dependents, the work-releasee can maintain his status within the family and demonstrate his moral worthiness to occupy that status. In this sense, the stability of the family is safeguarded as an offshoot of the benefit of work-release in providing a period of transition from prison to the community.

Reformation of inmate attitudes and behavior. If the offender is to be moved toward attitudes consistent with law-abiding behavior, certain principles are particularly apt. *First,* the offender is to be convinced that a hostile environment is not solely responsible for his difficulties. Somehow he must be brought to the realization that his own motives and perceptions have influenced his experiments. *Second,* the frequency and intensity of his frustrating experiences should be lowered sufficiently to enable him to bring them within his capacity for control. *Third,* his attentions should be diverted away from futile efforts to change his environment drastically and toward the undertaking of changes within himself. This strategy involves the acceptance by the inmate of noncriminal associations and noncriminal value system in evaluating himself. *Fourth,* the inmate should be provided with experiences which will enable him to test his new modes of perceiving his environment and relating himself to the persons making up this environment.[15]

As a facet of the more generalized approach of community-based corrections, work release implies certain fundamental assumptions. Human beings tend to behave in accordance with their perceptions of how other persons regard them. The offender is more likely to behave as a criminal when he is convinced the community defines him as unreliable, violent, or larcenous. To initiate change in his attitudes and behavior, the offender must be offered evidence that the community does (or will) define him less adversely than he now believes. As evidence that he has been deemed worthy of trust and responsible behavior, work-release can initiate this process of revising self-conception.

A fundamental basis for effective participation in community life is the individual's access to the economic opportunity structure of the community. To the extent work-release provides a means of access, the inmate gains a starting point for reorganizing his personal goal-striving to be more in gear with the social order of the community. Work-release provides an organizational framework for therapeutic strategies, through improved communication between the offender and counselors, teachers, psychiatrists, and so on.

One element of the work-release strategy has particular pertinence. In contrast with the authoritarian character of strategies based on punishment, work-release requires that the inmate *volunteer* for (or at least be permitted to refuse) the privilege of salaried employment in the free community. The involuntary inmate would be less likely to exhibit the self-discipline essential to prevention of transgressions in the community. The voluntary element has been consciously promoted by the authorities of many states for the deliberate purpose of providing the inmate a greater degree of choice.

The work-release experience can generate an attitudinal climate wherein correctional employees are joined by employers and co-workers in demonstration of goodwill toward the offender. Potentially, the inmate can learn that his own constructive behavior will win a reciprocal constructive reaction. His earlier pessimism can be eroded as he learns that his changes in perspective *can* improve his situation. At the same time, he can constitute a one-man demonstration project for the citizens of the community that rehabilitation of offenders is possible and that arbitrary rejection of past criminals is inappropriate.

Lending new flexibility to court-prison interrelationships. As an alternative to the orthodox prison sentence, work-release provides a means for extending the jurisdiction of the court further into the period of imprisonment. Now in the United States the sentencing judge can recommend that the correctional institution provide certain treatment services or deal with the particular prisoner in a particularly stern manner. However, the actual implementation of such recommendations is determined by the prison or parole authorities. Work-release lends itself to providing greater flexibility in demarking the jurisdictional boundaries between the sentencing court and the correctional agency.[16] The conditions of the sentence could be altered later, to coincide more precisely with the results of more intensive testing of the qualities of the particular inmate and his demonstrated eligibility for conditional release into the community.

CONCLUSION

Because work-release must function within a total penal-correctional process, the results of its application depend on overall philosophy and goals of the correctional department within which it functions. The introduction of the idea of work-release, in and of itself, is not a substitute for the quality of personnel and other sources necessary to implement a program capable of transforming offenders into law-abiding citizens. The goals for a particular work-release program must be selected from more than the wide variety delineated above. Then the resources must be provided and the procedures developed to implement those goals. Otherwise, the conflict between several goals will doom the program that blindly tries to achieve all purposes at the same time.

NOTES

1. William C. Farrell, "U.S. Convicts Hail Outside Job Plan," *New York Times,* January 22, 1966, quoting Warden Frank Kenton, Federal Correctional Institution, Danbury, Connecticut.
2. John B. Case, "We Operate a Salvage Business—Not a Junk Yard!" *Federal Probation* 30 (September 1966): 30-31.
3. Stanley Grupp and Jacques Verin, "Work Release for Short-Term Offenders in France and the United States," *Canadian Journal of Corrections* 10 (July 1968): 490.
4. G. M. Parker and Paul H. Kusuda, quoted in *Private Employment for County Jail Inmates* (Madison: Wisconsin Department of Public Welfare, Division of Corrections, November 1957), p. 1.
5. John Hogarth, "Towards the Improvement of Sentencing in Canada," *Canadian Journal of Corrections* 9 (April 1967): 124.
6. President's Commission on Law Enforcement and Administration of Justice, *Task Force Report: Corrections* (Washington, D.C.: Government Printing Office, 1967), pp. 45, 74.
7. Harry Elmer Barnes and Negley K. Teeters, *New Horizons in Criminology* (3rd ed.; Englewood Cliffs, N.J.: Prentice-Hall, 1959), pp. 354-59.
8. Dean V. Babst, *Day Parole and Employment of County Jail Inmates* (Madison: Wisconsin Division of Corrections, February 1962), p. 10.
9. Stanley E. Grupp, "Work Release as Viewed by Illinois Sheriffs," *Police* (July-August 1965), pp. 22-23.
10. Elmer H. Johnson. For further amplification see "Work Release: A Study of Correctional Reform," *Crime and Delinquency* 13 (October 1967): 529.
11. *The Work Release Program: Progress Report, March 1966 Through March 1968* (Salem: Corrections Division, Oregon State Board of Control, April 1968), p. 4.
12. Ibid.
13. The Probation Department of Los Angeles County reports that the county program inaugurated in 1964 includes some 32 percent of inmate families, which would have been on public welfare rolls had the inmate served his sentence under usual custody. See "Work Furlough Program," *Information Series,* No. 10 (Los Angeles, Calif.: County of Los Angeles Probation Department, June 1968).
14. Bruce Olson, "Pay-as-You-Go Penology Program," *Tax Digest* 37 (California Taxpayers' Association, July 1960): 151-53.
15. Lloyd W. McCorkle and Richard R. Korn, "Resocialization Within Walls," *Annals of the American Academy of Political and Social Science,* 293 (May 1954): 96-97.
16. This point is made by Grupp and Verin, op. cit., pp. 491-92.

chapter nineteen

STATE WORK-RELEASE PROGRAMS: AN ANALYSIS OF OPERATIONAL POLICIES

Lawrence S. Root

If you were to visit a correctional institution in the United States in order to learn about its rehabilitative programs, you would probably find that one of the programs described with pride would be work-release. You would hear that work-release incorporates the concepts of vocational training, social responsibility, and governmental economy. Comparisons might be made with the community treatment trend in the field of mental health. Someone might mention the more subtle benefits of work-release; for example, breaking down of stigmas associated with incarceration and encouraging public interest in the problems of prisons and prisoners.

After hearing the possible goals of the program, it would be natural to ask a few questions about how the program is implemented to achieve them. Who is eligible to participate? When can they participate? Where do they live during this period? Answers to these questions might give an idea of the scope of the program, as well as the possibilities for comprehensive program development. Program directors are usually adept at writing attractive descriptions of programs—institutional procedures ensure that. In order to determine how work-release programs conform to their stated goals, I have attempted to examine policy in terms of the answers to the above three questions. This inductive approach is intended to identify the *operational policy* which determines the implementation of a program and, consequently, its feasible goals.

From *Federal Probation*, vol. 37, no. 4 (1973), pp. 52–58.

In January 1971 I sent a letter to each of the state correctional authorities requesting information about their work-release programs. Forty replies were received, including responses from the authorities in New York City and the District of Columbia. These replies were in a variety of forms: letters, memos, directives, standards, fiscal statements, magazine articles, forms, studies, and public information brochures. A comparative examination of these responses yielded answers to questions about operational policy.

WHO PARTICIPATES IN WORK-RELEASE PROGRAMS?

Work-release is intended to be a *rehabilitative* program and, as such, one would assume that those who participate would be chosen on the basis of rehabilitative criteria. In practice, however, institutional concerns determine eligibility. The following quotation from the policy statement of the Georgia correctional authority reflects the tension between institutional and treatment considerations.

> Work release is intended as a rehabilitative tool having many possible applications. However, there can be no compromise of essential safeguards, community acceptance, and careful supervision.

Fear of hostile community reaction leads too many state programs to restrict participation severely.

Of the twenty-four states which reported their program qualifications (Table 1), twenty stated that they excluded individuals whom they considered to have a high assaultive potential. The actual specification of this *assaultive potential* varied from the exclusion of those who are "violence prone" to the exclusion of only those who were actually *convicted* of a violent crime. The classification of "crime against the person" is found in some program restrictions; this classification includes crimes of violence, but also a variety of other crimes which do not actually involve violence.

Sexual offenses are the second most common reason for exclusion of individuals from work-release programs. Eighteen of the twenty-four states restrict sexual offenders from participation. Some exclude all those with any record of sexual offenses, while others specify that "careful consideration" of such offenders must be undertaken. In an institution, such an admonition of special care often has the same effect as a blanket exclusion.[1]

Occasionally the prohibitions delineate specific kinds of sexual offenses. Minnesota "ordinarily" excludes those who have been convicted of "serious" sexual offenses, while Michigan specifies "compulsive" sexual

Table 1
CRITERIA FOR EXCLUSION FROM WORK-RELEASE PROGRAMS BY OFFENSE OR BACKGROUND

	VIOLENCE	SEXUAL CRIMES	NARCOTICS SALE	NARCOTICS USE	NOTORIETY	ORGANIZED CRIME
California	X	X	X	—	—	—
Connecticut	X	X	X	X	X	X
Florida	—	X	X	—	—	X
Georgia	X	—	—	—	X	X
Illinois	X	X	X	X	X	X
Indiana	X	X	X	X	X	—
Louisiana	X	—	X	X	—	—
Massachusetts	X	X	—	—	—	—
Maryland	X	X	X	X	X	—
Michigan	X	X	X	—	—	X
Minnesota	X	X	X	X	—	—
Montana	X	—	—	—	X	—
Nebraska	X	—	—	—	X	X
New Jersey	X	X	X	—	X	X
New Mexico	X	—	—	—	—	X
New York	X	X	X	X	—	—
New York City	X	X	X	X	X	X
North Carolina	—	X	X	X	X	—
South Carolina	—	X	X	X	X	—
South Dakota	X	X	—	—	—	—
Texas	X	X	X	X	—	X
Virginia	—	X	X	X	—	—
Washington	X	—	—	—	X	—
Wisconsin	X	X	—	—	—	—
TOTALS	20	18	16	12	12	10

crimes. Eligibility criteria in California have evolved to the point that now only molesters of children are not permitted on work-release.[2]

Drug offenders are excluded in sixteen of the twenty-four states. In four of those sixteen, a distinction is made between users of illegal drugs and those convicted of the sale of drugs. In some cases, the institutional staff is instructed to examine a person's record to determine if drug addiction may have existed, even though he was not arrested for a drug offense.

Restrictions for those with a dependency on alcohol are often found along with the statements about drug dependency. South Carolina excludes those with either an alcohol or a drug problem, and Minnesota does not allow "impulsive" drinkers in its work-release program.

Twelve states exclude individuals whose offenses have been accompanied by "notoriety." The motivation is clearly seen in the Washington State program which excludes those "whose failure on a work or training release program might bring public disfavor." Institutions take on a life of their own, and fear of adverse public reaction is often more important in determining policy than is the actual purpose of the institution. This is most clearly seen in the notoriety exclusion, but it is just as true for the other restrictions mentioned. As we shall see, work-release programs usually operate in the final months of incarceration only. Does it protect the community to exclude those with a history of violence or sexual offenses, if these same individuals are to be released in a few months anyway? These exclusions are clearly a result of public relations pressures. The pressures are real and the institutional reactions are understandable, but these restrictions should be recognized as responses to institutional, not treatment, needs and, as such, detrimental to the scope and possible effects of the program.

Although the exclusion of those with a dependency on drugs or alcohol has similar institutional motives, it must be acknowledged that those with such dependencies have exhibited the highest failure rate on work-release pograms. But these individuals also are to be released in a few months, anyway, and the personal test which they experienced in their failure on work-release could prove valuable in clarifying adjustment problems to themselves.

These three types of restrictions on participation (violence potential, history of sexual offenses, and drug dependency) eliminate a large portion of those incarcerated. On the basis of present convictions, approximately one-third of those incarcerated are ineligible for most work-release programs. If one considers previous records and "personality factors," the proportion enlarges.

A further restriction which relates to institutional, not rehabilitative, concerns is the exclusion of escape risks. Some states specifically exclude those with histories of escape, while other states restrict participation to those who are eligible for minimum security status, thus implicitly excluding escape risks. Occasionally "escape risk" is more carefully defined. In Virginia, a person may not have more than two escapes on his record and a year must have elapsed since his last escape. These prohibitions against escape risks reflect both the monetary cost and the embarrassment occasioned by an escape. Consideration of escapes is one of the motives for the variety of restrictions based upon the length of the sentence remaining to be served.

In addition to the exclusions already discussed, one usually finds a catch-all category which can be employed with considerable latitude. Most often this category takes the form of a prohibition against those with a "serious emotional or personality defect." The wording ranges from labels which sound very specific (e.g., "simple schizophrenics") to the most general descriptions (e.g., "mentally and emotionally unsound"). Whatever the wording, such exclusions allow a great deal of discretionary application.

Occasionally, along with the restrictions based upon criminal records and personality traits, a geographic factor is added. An Idaho policy statement indicates that no community will "tolerate its becoming a dumping ground for offenders."[3] This assertion reflects the reality that state institutions incarcerate individuals from all parts of the state and a work-release program could result in a higher number of "criminals" working in the area of the prison than would be the case if the program did not exist. In view of this, prisoners who are from other parts of the state may tend to be excluded.

The exclusion of members of organized crime is based upon three considerations. First, a person involved in organized crime could easily continue criminal activities while in a work-release job. The supervision to which work releasees are subjected might not be sufficient to prevent organized criminal activities. Second, the participation of an individual with influence in organized crime could create a situation which would breed corruption within the institution. Third, a work-release program is not a rehabilitative program designed for such an offender. Incarceration for an individual whose criminal activities have been "rewarding" (i.e., both lucrative and lasting) is usually considered useful as a deterrent and the benefits of work-release are not appropriate to the furthering of this end. The first two considerations relate to institutional concerns; the third introduces a consideration of work-release as a specific rehabilitative program with its own set of goals. This is the first time that the answer to the question of eligibility has considered "need" for the program—a rehabilitative consideration.

Few of the regulations specify who *is* appropriate for the programs. The regulations only exclude, and the remaining people are the negatively defined group of those suited to and in need of work release. One of the few examples of an attempt to specify who is appropriate for work-release comes from Texas, which defines need in terms of financial obligations, adjustment problems, and training opportunities. One gets the impression that work-release is considered a generic benefit; that it is desirable for everyone in prison and, therefore, the only regulations needed are exclusions which protect the institution.

WHEN IS ONE ELIGIBLE?

Work-release is often assumed to be an *alternative* to traditional incarceration, but the rules of implementation for those convicted of felonies mitigate against that end. In the case of misdemeanants, the sentencing judge usually determines eligibility for work-release. The misdemeanant sentenced to one year or less can participate in a work-release program for his entire sentence, thus disrupting his community ties less than would be the case if he were undergoing traditional incarceration. In the case of the committed felon, however, the regulations limit his participation to the latter part of his sentence, thus restricting the program to a "transitional" role, rather than an alternative one.

The most common type of regulation determining when an inmate is eligible specifies a *maximum period of time remaining* until his expected release. Though the limits range from three months in the community work-release centers of Michigan to twenty-four months in Georgia, the most common maximum is six months. This form of time limitation serves to minimize escape risks, while ensuring that the individual will have spent some time in a more traditional institutional environment.

Another time-related restriction establishes a *proportion* of the individual's sentence which must be served before he is eligible for work-release. This form of restriction requires a period of traditional incarceration which is proportionate to the length of the individual's sentence, but it allows those with longer sentences to spend relatively long periods of time on work-release. For example, the legislation of North Carolina requires that one-quarter of a man's sentence must be served before he is eligible.[4] Oregon combines the two systems: Those with sentences of five years or less are eligible in their last year of incarceration, while for those sentenced to more than five years, the one-year maximum rule may be waived. Illinois, capturing the restrictive elements of both systems, has a maximum limit of one year *and* a statutory restriction specifying that a person must serve one-half of his minimum sentence before he is eligible.

It is obvious that work-release as it is currently structured for committed felons does not serve as an alternative to incarceration. And in most cases the participation is only authorized in the last six or twelve months before release.

Before leaving the subject of sentence considerations, it is necessary to note specific prohibitions for those serving life sentences. North Carolina excludes such individuals, though other states have made special provisions for their inclusion. The legislation of Vermont includes those with life sentences after they have served "at least five years." Hawaii excludes those with life sentences "without parole." In Oregon, a "lifer" is considered when within one year of the parole hearing where the granting of parole "appears probable." By and large, those with life sentences would be excluded for reasons of offense or personality factors.

In the case of a few states, notably Florida and Oregon, flexibility may be exercised in waiving time limits on eligibility when work-release is being used for educational purposes. This kind of flexibility is needed when trying to coordinate institutional regulations with community facilities. A lack of flexibility often can negate the opportunity for constructive use of community resources.

WHERE DO PARTICIPANTS LIVE?

This question is perhaps the most significant in determining the nature of a work-release program. Eligibility requirements, as we have seen, define program participants in terms of institutional priorities, not treatment priorities. The time considerations restrict participation to the latter part of one's sentence. Living arrangements determine what kind of employment education opportunities will be available and whether the work-release structure can be used to implement a constructive living environment. The housing of work-releasees living within the prisons presents several institutional problems. Many items which are normal and necessary outside of an institution are prohibited within one. Problems of contraband necessitate elaborate security precautions when the work-releasee enters and leaves the institution. Such procedures are time-consuming and annoying to all those involved. The work releasee finds that for eight hours a day he is treated as a normal human being, and then he returns to the institution to be treated as "just another inmate." His frustration is deepened by the fact that as a work-releasee he is paying for his room and board: He is paying for his imprisonment. Correctional officials, recognizing the work-releasee's half-free situation, generally try to isolate him from other inmates. New York City and the State of New York both mention that participants are to be housed in separate quarters within the institution. New York State goes on to specify that the housing should be "on an easily accessible gallery." This provision is an attempt to facilitate movements into and out of the institution and to reduce contacts with other inmates. It also provides the opportunity for the development of programs during nonworking hours which are designed to complement the work-release program itself. The isolation of participants also serves to lessen the pressure from other inmates to smuggle contraband items into the institution.

Correctional institutions are usually located in rural areas where there are not a variety of employment opportunities. Though most of the state authorities did not include information about the kinds of jobs that work-releasees had, those programs in rural areas are necessarily limited. The easiest way of establishing a work-release program within the structure of a traditional institution is to have all of the participants working in the same place. All fifteen work-releasees on the prison farm at Concord, Massachusetts, were working as attendants in a nearby school for retarded children when this study was undertaken. Those working at the Norfolk site were also employed as attendants in a nearby mental hospital. In the Concord area, "almost none of the men continued on the jobs after release."[5] This is in part because of a desire to return to their home areas, but also because the jobs were not desirable enough to merit relocation. From this example, it can be seen that when work-release programs are located within or around traditional institutions in rural areas, the employment and educational opportunities are few. When many work-releasees are employed together the situation threatens to take on an institutional character, and the job may become an "inmate job."

My own experience with a work-release program in an industrial area of New Jersey indicated that work-releasees were usually hired in the least desirable positions for the lowest wages. A state regulation prohibited more than five work-releasees from being employed together, and so the work-release program never took on the aspect of contracted prison labor. But because the men were only able to work for the six months prior to their release, there was little opportunity for learning skills. Those of the men who were already "skilled" were hired at what would be considered very low wages for the work. Often an employer would say that he would start a man at the minimum wage and raise it after the man's worth had been demonstrated. Raises were rarely commensurate with ability.

A study of the North Carolina work-release program[6] found that most employers of work-releasees considered their work to be as good or better than that of other workers. In an annual report from Indiana, employers indicated that work-releasees exhibit a lower absenteeism than other workers, alcohol is not a problem, and there is less garnishing of wages or other court actions which are inconvenient for the employer. These observations indicate that the employers are comparing work-releasees with a low-skill unstable work force, and so suggest the low level of employment experienced by work-releasees. In this context, the "vocational training" aspect of work-release does not seem particularly progressive.

Most state programs have the option of contracting with county and city jails for the housing of work-releasees from state institutions. Use of such facilities permits a person to work in the vicinity of his home. These arrangements enable a person to become acclimated to his community and to start working in a job where he might conceivably continue after release. But local jails are notorious for their inadequate facilities, usually lacking even the amenities of state institutions.

Community-based work-release centers offer another possible housing arrangement. Most often these are renovated buildings, specifically designated to house work-releasees. The legislation of Vermont authorizes housing for work-releasees which would segregate them "from more hardened criminals."[7] In April 1969 four "Community Correctional Centers" were opened to serve this purpose. In Texas, the Jester Unit houses work-releasees, allowing them "occasional outside activity trips to sports and religious events."[8] Community correctional centers in Hawaii are called "conditional release centers" and seem to allow a great deal of freedom for interaction with the community.

When a state has more than one such center, they are usually spread throughout the state and often are differentiated in their purpose. Pennsylvania and South Carolina have four and three centers, respectively, which are located in different sections of the state. In Illinois, those who are considered to have a great "need" for the program are placed at the Joliet Center. "Need" is defined in terms of developing vocational skills and fulfilling financial responsibilities to dependents. "At the Southern Illinois Center less emphasis is placed on need and more on the probability that the inmate can be changed by the program."[9]

Michigan, having opened its first center in 1963 in a joint venture with the Federal Bureau of Prisons, opened two centers in 1968 and nine more in 1969. These centers house both work-releasees and parolees. There is one center for women and one offering specialized technical and rehabilitative programs.

In Delaware, one center is in an urban area (Wilmington) while the other center is in the southern part of the state and emphasizes agricultural employment.

The answer to the question of "Where do work-releasees live?" determines the possibility of creative programming for the participants. If work-release is only intended to respond to the financial needs of the individual, his family, and the state, then the nature of the living arrangements is relatively unimportant. But if work-release is to play a role in a rehabilitative process, the employment itself should be only one dimension of the program. Most adults in prison have had work experience of at least six months; work-release must be more than just six months of unskilled employment. It should provide a proving ground for trying out those resolutions which most prisoners make while incarcerated. As a proving ground, failures are to be expected—if there are no failures then a program is not reaching those who need it. To be a proving ground, the program must allow for the exercising of personal responsibility. If every movement of the work-releasee is watched and monitored, does he ever have the opportunity to break the dependencies which have been built up in the institution? Creative programming means helping the individual to deal with his environment in a constructive way. Work-release should challenge the participant, and support his efforts to adjust to the pressures and temptations of the noninstitutional world.

The picture of the long-termer who sees the outside for the first time in twelve years because of the existence of a work-release program warms our hearts, but of what benefit is it to the participant? I believe that work-release has value if only to break down the isolation of the prisoners and the prison. It does get some (and often only a few) inmates out of the institution, and it brings some members of the community into an awareness that there is an "inside." The operational policies of most programs, however, exclude a large part of their populations for reasons that do not have any rehabilitative basis. Those who are included are usually only allowed to participate during the last part of their sentence. This rule restricts the program to the status of a *transitional* program and denies its use as an alternative to incarceration. Until the selection of participants is based upon the needs of the individuals, not the institution, work-release will be a "showcase program" with few long-term benefits.

The status of work-release programs is indicative of a more pervasive problem in corrections. Generally, four goals of institutionalization are recognized: deterrence, retribution, isolation, and rehabilitation. Deterrence represents society's threat of punishment *before* the commission of a crime. Retribution is its institutionalized revenge after the fact. Both of these goals call for an implicitly punitive policy of implementation in which the deprivation of physical and social stimuli, such as varied diet and recreational activity, is employed to enhance the already punitive nature of confinement itself.

Deterrence and retribution, as correctional goals, are based upon two related assumptions. The first is that man functions according to a "pleasure-pain" principle, with the resultant theory that the pain of imprisonment must be greater than the "pleasure" derived from the crime. The second assumption is that most crimes are committed after a rational deliberative process, in which consideration of the possible legal consequences is a major factor. Both of these assumptions are highly questionable. Any contact with the population of a correctional institution soon reveals that most crimes are *not* committed for pleasure, but rather out of real or perceived necessity. Furthermore, crimes of violence, which are dealt with most severely, are the least likely to be the result of a consideration of consequences.

Isolation of the offender, the third traditional goal of institutions, *does* protect the community, but only for a limited period of time. And, for the most part, the embittered man emerging from such isolation has even fewer loyalties than before to the law of that society which has so stigmatized him.

The fourth goal, rehabilitation, is perhaps the most elusive and difficult to define. In practical terms it is generally understood to mean the inducement of a change which results in a more productive, integrated member of society. This goal is in conflict with the other three and its presence in a correctional institution is historically an afterthought. It is generally treated as a frill which can be tolerated only as long as it does not interfere with the three traditional goals. This subordinate position of rehabilitation is seen clearly in the evaluations of government officials of correctional institutions. Such evaluations are usually based solely upon the criterion of efficiency in control of the population. It is true that this is partially a reflection of the fact that rehabilitation is difficult to judge operationally; but it remains clear that when there is a conflict between rehabilitative considerations and the demands of control the latter will predominate.

In work-release programs specifically, the conflict ultimately occurs between the goal of isolation and that of rehabilitation. If a work-releasee commits a crime, the public cries out against the breakdown in isolation, saying in effect that any attempt to rehabilitate an individual should not interfere with his continued separation from society. There is no recognition of the fact that had this individual *not* been on work-release he would eventually have been released on parole anyway—thoroughly alienated from the community and from the day-to-day routine of personal decision making and self-imposed life structure which the "outside" demands but which the "inside" tends to deny.

The potential of work-release is as an alternative for those who need closer supervision and support than possible under probation, but are not considered grave threats to the community. In order for this potential to be realized, correctional personnel must actively work to educate the public to the rationale underlying new approaches in corrections. Until such a positive effort is undertaken by those in the field, correctional innovations, such as work-release, will be subject to a poorly informed public reacting solely to those cases which have "failed."

NOTES

1. The following quotation, from a description of the Connecticut Department of Corrections brochure *Work Release: A New Lease on Life*, is a good example of inflexible flexibility: "Inmates who have unquestionably demonstrated their trustworthiness by a *long* record of stability may be considered for Work Release in some of the above cases, but this must be approved directly by the Commissioner."

2. According to Joe C. Crow, work furlough administrator, Parole and Community Services Division Department of Corrections, Sacramento, California, January 8, 1971. Evolution of the regulations may be occurring in many of the programs discussed in this chapter. In New Jersey, where I have had personal contact with the program, the restrictions against participation according to offense have relaxed considerably. At one point in 1971 there were fewer than twenty-two men in one correctional section of the Youth Reception and Correction Center, Yardville, who were eligible for work-release. In the fall of 1972, over 70 young men were actually on work-release. This increase in the size of the program was attributable to the easing of the restrictions according to offense and the innovative utilization of the flexibility by the staff.

3. Idaho, State Board of Corrections, "Policy and Procedure Statement: Furlough," File No. 570, June 1, 1969. In a policy statement from Georgia, much the same statement is made, with "haven" substituted for "dumping ground."

4. Allen Ashman, "Work Release in North Carolina," *Popular Government* 32 (June 1966).

5. Massachusetts Department of Correction, "Characteristics of Men Accepted and Rejected for Day Work at M.C.I. Concord," Document No. 5114 (May 1970).

6. W. D. Cooper, "Employers and Employees in the Work Release Program in North Carolina," *Crime and Delinquency*, vol. 16, no. 4 (October 1970), pp. 427–33.

7. Vermont, *Laws* (1968), Ch. 3, Title 28, Sec. 207.

8. Texas, Department of Corrections, "Work Furlough: Jester Unit."

9. Letter from Russell H. Levy, Research and Long-Range Planning, Illinois Department of Corrections, December 23, 1970.

part five:
JUVENILE OFFENDERS

This concluding section deals with community-based programs in juvenile delinquency prevention and control. Irving Spergel begins by providing a historical overview of community delinquency prevention programs. This is followed by two articles on the youth service bureau concept, a form of diversion, or alternative to the court system, strongly supported by the recommendations of the National Advisory Commission on Criminal Justice Standards and Goals. Elaine Duxbury, one of the outstanding advocates of the youth service bureau, wrote the paper included here for the National Advisory Commission. Margaret Rosenheim, in her offering, takes a somewhat skeptical view of the youth service bureau. Her statement is in response to the affirmative position of the President's Commission on Law Enforcement and Administration of Justice of 1967; it was then that the concept of a youth service bureau was first formulated. The next reading presents the views of the National Council of Juvenile Court Judges on diversion of the juvenile from the traditional court system. Finally, Vernon Fox delimits the role of volunteers in the juvenile court. Their introduction to corrections is a promising new experiment. He pinpoints the skills needed for active involvement in this helping activity. The future will be bright if the community and existing agencies in delinquency control provide a viable program for potential offenders.

chapter twenty

COMMUNITY-BASED DELINQUENCY-PREVENTION PROGRAMS: AN OVERVIEW

Irving A. Spergel

Recent years have witnessed the development of a social movement to deal with deviants in the context of the community. The movement, in its physical and social sense, has been from outlying or rural to urban areas; from large to small institutions; from custodial, corrective, rehabilitative, even therapeutic milieus to family arrangements or special facsimiles thereof; from isolation and stigma to more normal and equal involvement in the mainstream of community living. Service patterns for the aged, the mentally ill, the mentally retarded, children in need of protective care, drug addicts, public aid recipients, and others have been affected by the effort to involve deviants more fully in the control and development of their own destiny. The latest outcast to become the beneficiary of changing professional, public, and legislative thinking and morality is the delinquent. For example, Massachusetts has already implemented its recent decision to close correctional institutions for youth and deal with them in community facilities.[1]

The following is a discussion of selected policy and program issues that face or will face policy-makers and administrators in developing community-based programs. Interorganizational and political or interest-group constraints constitute the framework of the analysis. The discussion is organized into three major sections: policy and program rationales, past and present programs, and program effectiveness. However, the complex

From *Social Service Review*, XLVII (1973), pp. 16–31. Copyright 1973, The University of Chicago Press. Reprinted by permission of the journal and the author.

issues of the decision to close down residential institutions in the first instance will not be addressed.

POLICY AND PROGRAM RATIONALES

The problem of developing community-based institutions and programming for and with delinquents in the open community requires consideration of three types of questions: What is a community-based program, and who is a delinquent or pre-delinquent? What is the rationale of the program, or what is the connection between the program and the social or community problem to be solved? What are the objectives of the program, and how are they to be achieved?

Definition. The terms *community-based program* and *delinquent* or *delinquency* require some explanation and, ideally, agreed-upon definitions. In fact, the terms are used to identify variable elements and qualities. In fact, the terms are used to identify variable elements and qualities. Meanings are often implicit, and one man's community or delinquent is often not the same as another man's. For example, the term *community* may suggest a geographical area, a collection of people, an organization of local groups and institutions, or a desirable state of relationship between people and institutions. Discussions or debates on community problems may focus on one or more of the following related elements: power or negotiating capability; voluntary association, participation, self-determination, or community control; service-delivery systems; common or comprehensive interests; social change and/or its effects. The terms *neighborhood* and *community* may be used interchangeably.

Suggested for purposes of the present discussion is the following geographically oriented definition: A community is a collectivity of individuals and groups, often located within a specific geographic area, and variously organized and differentiated by sex, age, race, ethnicity, status, interest, need, and purpose. The area tends to be identified both locally and externally, not always sharply or consistently, on the basis of administrative, historical, physical, political, economic, social, and cultural considerations.

A greater problem arises in the definition of *community-based program*. For most administrators it probably refers to a program run on a decentralized basis, still governed by established agency interests, but more sensitive to the needs of individuals defined as delinquent; the program also involves local citizens in some way. It is important, however, to think of community-based programs in political as well as administrative terms. One must consider such questions as: For whom is the program primarily run? Who makes key policy decisions? What is the character of community participation in and identification with the program?

Organizations and agencies may differ further in certain distinctive ways. In somewhat oversimplistic and general terms, community programs for delinquents may vary along certain strategic dimensions of intervention, such as goals and locus of decision making. Organizations may be concerned with providing effective services, yet be status quo–oriented, with decisions made by professional workers, bureaucrats, and established group representatives. Organizations may also be concerned with limited forms of community development and protection, and still be status quo–oriented, but with decisions made by interests identified as highly local or indigenous. Other organizations may be change-oriented; that is, certain professional workers and reformers, even within the establishment, may run programs seeking institutional changes on behalf of a deprived or stigmatized population; however, local citizens may not be involved in key decisions. On the other hand, organizations and their programs may be run for, by, and with local community people, even by the disadvantaged or deviant sector or their direct representatives, to bring about institutional change.[2] In reality, of course, community-based programs are different blends of these orientations, which produce varying strategies of service provision, community development, advocacy, and conflict. At one extreme, community participation may indicate little or no policy and administrative involvement and, at the other, complete control and staffing of programs by local adults and/or offenders.[3]

The definition of *delinquency* is critical for the development of a community-based program. The term is just as variable and complex as community. In fact, it may be even more variable within a community than across the juvenile justice system. There appears to be no across-the-board operational definition of delinquents or pre-delinquents in community-based programs. It is not at all clear what a community program to prevent or to treat delinquents really is or should be.

Some agencies established specifically to deal with delinquents may seek to avoid isolating or stigmatizing certain youths by serving mainly nondelinquents. The process of working with youth in delinquency-control programs may nevertheless contribute to a negative labeling and delinquency-creating process. Several years ago, a public delinquency-prevention agency in a large city utilized its suddenly expanded budget to work with a variety of street-corner groups heretofore not served. A number of youths who did not participate in antisocial acts but hung out occasionally on street corners were identified, screened, and referred for service. In consequence, the police began to pay more attention to them. Several who ordinarily might have escaped agency and police attention were picked up for minor offenses; for example, breaking a window or unlawful assembly. The illustration is used not to suggest that community agencies should not ordinarily maintain open intake and include delinquents and nondelinquents, but to raise questions about program definition and attendant problems of purpose and client labeling.

The definition of the delinquency problem and, in part, the character of the program and its rationale are determined on the basis of organizational interests under market conditions. Organizations may be concerned primarily or only peripherally with services for delinquents. Programs may be derived largely as an effort to bolster the agency's capacity to achieve other purposes; for example, general services to community, institutional change, or community development. Delinquency-prevention or delinquency-control programs may come to be more an arena for general competition among institutional interests or service suppliers than a specific means to identify or solve a problem that derives primarily from individual youth and family needs and from the breakdown of basic urban structures and processes. Under these conditions, it is not hard to predict that community-based programs can ignore or aggravate rather than ameliorate or control delinquency problems. Delinquents or pre-delinquents, however defined, may become targets for community attention and agency services that contribute more to the growth and status of organizations than to the solution of problems of individual or collective delinquency.

Program rationale. While there may be some limit on definitions of the delinquency problem, there seems to be no limit on the number of rationales for programming; that is, for what to do about the problem. The logic of problem analysis somehow is never rigorous enough to provide a clear or an interrelated set of program objectives and solutions. Organizational and professional ideology and particularistic access to resources appear to determine the connection between the problem and the program. The market for solutions to the delinquency problem seems unlimited, particularly if agencies or community groups promise quick and dramatic results. While the problem of delinquency among youngsters under sixteen years old may be assessed as growing worse, either in the ghettos or in the suburbs, in relation to drug use, gang behavior, and runaways, the cures are unclear, multiple, and competing. Everybody gets into the act of explaining the problem and providing answers to it. The causes of delinquency include everything from family breakdown and inadequate ego development to a defective juvenile-justice system and the collective powerlessness of ghetto people. The solutions also vary, from long-term therapy to revolution and counter-revolution. The individual and the community as complex but interacting and interdependent entities seem not to exist. The delinquent, the gang, the agency, the community "power structure," and specific community conditions become targets for fragmented attack or change according to particular interest-group perspectives and remedies. Everyone wants a piece of the action. Nobody wants the whole thing, or is even concerned with it.

Often the rationales for service and program answers seem to precede the problems and the questions. The views about who the delinquent is and what to do with or about him, furthermore, do not originate generally in data derived from the delinquent or his situation. They reside largely in the minds, hearts, and pockets of community-concerned beholders, professional workers, and bureaucrats. Reality appears not to have a uniform or objective character. Indeed, diverse definitions and views would not be bad if they could simply bypass each other; but community interests interact and collide. Community conflict and controversy become cause and effect of the delinquency problem and of programs established to deal with it.

Program objectives and means. Once an agency or community group has selected its delinquent population or delinquency-generating condition and established its rationale and the general intent of its program, the problem of relation between goals and objectives, ends and means, arises. While the agency may set out in pursuit of stated objectives, very quickly and tenaciously it may settle down to pursuit of means or, in current parlance, the efficient service-delivery system. The system aspects, usually in terms of methods and procedures, may become dominant. Even when the system is open and flexible, even when explicit guidelines for the worker are not initially established, whatever it is that has to be done becomes in due course the end as well as the means. Agency operational problems and daily activities consume administrative energies. Organizational maintenance rather than goal achievement becomes the test of survival. The agency purpose seems to be to build a better mouse trap, but who gets trapped and what happens to the object of entrapment, manipulation, control, or change is unclear and perhaps of secondary importance.

Basic program decisions are usually not centrally made and are susceptible to many influences. Indeed, the separation between the internal and the external structure of a community-based program is difficult to make. Furthermore, environmental influences are not consistent or reinforcing; usually they are in a state of flux.

Organizations have conflicting approaches, norms, and practices in regard to delinquents. The impact of varied community forces on a given delinquency-control or treatment program is therefore not clearly predictable. For example, the police, the district attorney, and certain citizen groups are primarily concerned with control of delinquent behavior and protection of the community. Their objectives and practices are defined in official, legitimate, middle-class, and often traditional terms. The outreach or street-worker program may be concerned primarily with social and recreational development of the gang and its members; the counseling agency may be interested primarily in interpersonal, educational, or employment problems of the individual; the employer is concerned mainly with the extent to which the delinquent can contribute to certain objectives of production and profit; still other organizations, including churches, social agencies, and civil-rights and militant groups, are concerned with delinquents as a way to change the community or societal system so that institutions will work better and produce less delinquency and other types of social problems. Delinquents themselves may be organized into gangs, nonprofit associations, economic development corporations, or social-action groups. The various organizations represent, in a sense, different communities of interest. Each views and utilizes delinquents quite differently. Each not only tailors its program to meet the needs of delinquents, but also adapts to the needs of other interest groups in the immediate community. Furthermore, the organization must adapt to the larger societal system of influences, in which federal funding policies, public values, and technological change, as well as time itself, are important variables.

PAST AND PRESENT PROGRAMS

While considerable organizational and technical innovation has occurred in recent years, it is possible to question whether the basic nature of the problem of delinquency and the general community response to it have changed.

Historical perspective. The problems of delinquency and the response of community agencies and groups to these phenomena appear to have some historical continuity, if not indeed some cyclical characteristics. Some knowledge of history helps us to build on past experience in a clear and rational way, lest we find ourselves reinventing programs that have been tried and found wanting. The phenomena of urban gangs and community response to them will serve as examples. In Chicago there are striking similarities between the Ragen Colts of an earlier era and the Black P. Stone Nation of today. The Ragen Colts, organized in 1912 by Frank Ragen in the Back of the Yards area of Chicago, was reputed to be composed of 3,000 young toughs. The gang considered itself an athletic club. The gang and its members were involved in a long series of delinquent and criminal activities, which have been described as follows:

> Their headquarters at 5412 South Halsted Street was a reputed hangout for South Side gangsters. Thomas Shields, a beer runner wanted by the police, was killed in their clubhouse and a black man was executed there by two Colts.
>
> Fifty Colts broke up a speech by "anti-papist" crusader Eli Erickson in 1922 and sent him running from the Viking Temple. Later, trying to improve their image, they offered to help Illinois Governor J. C. Walton stamp out the Ku Klux Klan activity in 1923.
>
> Several Colts developed into distinguished citizens. One was Hugo Bezdek, head football coach at the University of Chicago. Many other

members did not, however. Danny Stanton, one of Al Capone's hottest gunmen, was in this category. He died on a saloon floor after a shootout.

Chicago police repeatedly tried to eliminate the Ragen Colts, but were hampered by a special injunction obtained from City Hall which barred them from the clubhouse. The Ragen Colts were not the only gang to receive protection from high officials, however. Many gangs had political patrons or protectors. Ward heelers and even aldermen sponsored the groups because gangs were useful in getting out the vote on election days. Gangs often did this through intimidation, bribery, or fraud.

The Ragen Colts finally disbanded in 1927 after a member was shot in an internal dispute. Their demise left a power vacuum on the South Side, which the Taylor Colts filled for a while. They were quickly eclipsed by the 42nd Street Gang, a group unmatched for sheer terror.[4]

The Blackstone Rangers and other Chicago gangs of the 1960s and early 1970s seem to possess similar characteristics and to elicit remarkably similar community responses, highlighted in the following brief description:

> The leaders of the Blackstone Rangers . . . (Bull) Hairston, then Jeff (Black Prince) Fort, gained control through their organizational abilities and personal charm. . . .
>
> The Rangers popped into the news in 1964 when 49 of the most battle-hardened members of Woodlawn's 12 fighting gangs marched thru the South Side carrying motorcycle chains. . . .
>
> In 1965 the Rangers reorganized with 1,500 members and a board of directors called the Main 21. . . .
>
> The Rangers [along with other gangs] soon expanded into city-wide coalitions, calling themselves nations.

Between 1968 and 1970, a total of 209 youth-gang killings was recorded by the police. What proportion could be attributed to the Rangers involvement is unknown. During this period the Black P. Stone Nation, formerly the Rangers, was the largest and most influential gang in Chicago. Violence was a means to profit:

> The violence that gangs used to become powerful, however, created problems in the neighborhoods. Small businessmen were finding it hard to exist. City agencies compiled a confidential report of extortion activities of youth gangs in 1970. . . .

> The Stones asked an auto dealer to supply them with several cars. The dealer couldn't afford to let the gang break his windows because of high insurance costs, so he arranged financing for the vehicles. When the payments stopped, he did not ask the Stones for money. . . .
>
> Black radio and T.V. personality Daddy-O-Daylie was threatened by the Cobra Stones. . . . He would not pay, denounced them as "black monsters" and hired a bodyguard. . . .
>
> Four teenagers introduced themselves as Stones, told a foreman on a Woodlawn construction site that he had to pay or be shot. A woman tavern owner left the state after a group of Stones told her the same. . . .
>
> The Black P. Stone organization has continually denied that extortion as well as drug peddling and gun running were ever sanctioned by the gang's leadership.[5]

Like the Ragen Colts, the Black P. Stone Nation had organized community support for some of its activities. While support did not come from City Hall, it came from certain aldermen and state and Congressional representatives. One of the leaders of the gang was a guest at a Washington reception for President Nixon's inauguration. The Stones got out the vote for several candidates for local and state elections. Two members ran and won office as members of an advisory council to a model-cities program in the Woodlawn community.

Major support for the Stones, however, came from local neighborhood organizations, including the Woodlawn Organization, a Presbyterian church, Operation Breadbasket, and the Office of Economic Opportunity. The Stones joined welfare-rights groups in a march on the state legislature. They assisted the police and won a commendation for their role in the prevention and control of riots, especially after the assassination of the Reverend Martin Luther King, Jr. They joined an association of black social-action organizations in demonstrations against building contractors and unions to obtain more opportunities for black and other minority groups.

In 1972 five of the organization's top leaders, including Jeff Fort, were sentenced to long terms in federal prison for fraud and conspiracy in relation to their conduct of a youth manpower program funded by the Office of Economic Opportunity. The organization still remains, however, the single largest and most powerful gang in Chicago.

In large cities the underlying social, economic, and political dynamics generating delinquency and associated phenomena may not have changed much in the past fifty or sixty years, or perhaps certain precipitating factors recur at various times. Even some of the current community-oriented approaches to dealing with the problem seem remarkably similar to those of an earlier period. In the 1930s the Chicago Area Project devised various community-based delinquency-control and delinquency-prevention programs. The key principle was organization of local community interest and leadership in behalf of the welfare and development of predelinquent and delinquent youghs. Saul Alinsky—originally a worker for the project—claimed that social agencies had been too building-centered, had depended primarily on professional and bureaucratic rationale and expertise, and had focused on individual rather than community problems and collective responsibilities. These grass-roots efforts emphasized the legitimate aspirations, norms, values, and skills of local people.

Many of today's so-called innovations are reverberations of approaches developed in these early projects. The Alinsky approach emphasized political style and conflict strategies and tactics. Adult leaders, some of whom were former prisoners, worked with street gangs. Counseling and jobs were stressed. The Back of the Yards Council opened an estimated thirty recreational centers and dozens of storefront clubs in the local area.[6] Teenagers operated these storefronts as self-governing recreational clubs. Other highly progressive or radical ideas were tried, with apparent success. Born describes the work of the Back of the Yard Council as follows:

> Children were given priority in all neighborhoods projects. Instead of sending them to juvenile court, the council formed its own court. It consisted of the deviant child's parents, [the director of the council], clergymen, a probation officer, and a policeman.
>
> The humiliation of appearing before the court was enough to straighten out most errant children. The community slowly came under tight control as a result of close cooperation between community leaders and residents in trying to properly raise the children. By the mid 1950s, the neighborhood juvenile crime rate there had dropped from the highest to one of the lowest in the city.[7]

Probably forces other than the community organization were also operating during this period. The population in the Back of the Yards area was stabilized; economic and social status of first- and second-generation white ethnics rose. Local community cohesion was intensifed as the surrounding area on the South Side witnessed a massive influx of black and brown residents to the expanding ghettos. The area-project idea in its community dimension did not "catch on" immediately outside of Chicago. At the present time, while a score of local community committees under the aegis of the Chicago Area Project still exist, it is questionable whether they have continued to be successful at either community organization or delinquency control. It is possible that the Chicago Area Project, now largely under state government auspices, has become too simplistic, routinized, and perhaps apolitical in dealing with urban problems more complex than those of an earlier period.

After World War II, social agencies appeared to take the leadership in various delinquency-prevention and delinquency-control efforts. Emphasis was no longer on community participation and control but on the provision of social services, usually under the aegis of large public and voluntary agencies. But change again occurred in the late 1950s and early 1960s. First, the Ford Foundation, through its Grey Areas Projects, sought to increase coordination of public agencies and schools and thereby to improve the quality of social development and educational opportunities for ghetto youth. A little later the President's Committee on Juvenile Delinquency and Youth Development, assuming a structural basis for delinquency, funded a number of large-city projects. These programs, under reform-minded leadership, were established within the framework of public and voluntary agencies. Based in part on the Cloward-Ohlin "opportunity" thesis,[8] a variety of "innovative" programs were created, particularly for education, training, job-development, and social action. However, many of these programs, in response to changing federal funding patterns, quickly shifted emphasis from delinquency to poverty, from the needs of delinquent youths to the needs of the mass of poor youths and their families in the ghettos. The Office of Economic Opportunity and the Department of Labor, aided by the civil rights movement, stimulated the change. The focus turned to institutional and political mechanisms in order to deal with a variety of interrelated civil rights, social, and economic problems. Opportunities could be created only as the existing structures of agency and local-government decision making were changed. Community participation and control efforts were initiated. Controversy about "maximum feasible participation" was precipitated.

In the late 1960s, the national polical pendulum swung back: control of delinquency-prevention programs devolved again upon city and public agencies and, to some extent, upon the state, particularly with the implementation of model-city and safe-street legislation. There was a return to more specific concern with delinquency and greater emphasis on services. Yet all these different approaches in various shapes, sizes, and intensities are present in urban communities today, but there is a great lack of clarity about their relationships. Interacting with the development of the above community approaches have been programs spawned through urban renewal, mental health, and educational and general social welfare legislation, as well as the impact of the ghetto riots of the mid-1960s.

Present programs. Community-based programs today seem increasingly directed to overlapping populations of delinquents and nondelinquents.

They seek various goals: to divert youth from the juvenile justice system; to provide a variety of social, economic, and cultural opportunities for youth; to improve the effectiveness and efficiency of direct-service programs; to avoid "bad labeling" of vulnerable youth; to diminish the distance between youth and adult generations; to deal with problems of racism, poverty, housing, employment, education, and social services; or to be concerned with youth involvement, participation, and control.[9] Perhaps two general program approaches have evolved: innovative service and institutional change. The service-oriented programs have included street work and new approaches to counseling and guidance—for example, guided group interaction and behavior modification; special education, training, tutoring; decentralized job referral, placement, development; "hot line" and crisis intervention in relation to drug use, suicide, pregnancy, and abortion; legal aid, medical services, and economic-development activities—through drop-in, multiservice, or more general community-center arrangements. [Not included for purposes of this discussion is community-based residential care, which includes group homes, foster homes, hostels, and open-shelter facilities for temporary emergencies, such as runaway centers.] These programs are operated under the auspices of youth-service and social agencies; benevolent or voluntary associations; church and businessmen's organizations; independent grass-roots and social- or economic-development organizations; schools; police departments, courts, or probation agencies; park departments; or housing projects. They may be in relatively small isolated units or in large complex structures. Professional and paraprofessional workers, citizen volunteers, youth, and adults may be involved at different levels and in varying policy-making and staffing arrangements.

In partial contrast to these service-dominated programs, it is possible to identify certain institutional-change approaches or even adversary approaches to programs. These programs emphasize change or more appropriate development of organizational policies and practices; mobilization of youth and/or adults for collective action; use of local advisory councils and policy-making groups; and various forms of political and parapolitical activity. These activities involve leadership development and training, planning, legal proceedings, mass education, protest, and street action. In the instances in which these institutional-change programs have operated outside established or traditional agencies and community organizations, they have tended to be more experimental, controversial, and militant. The guiding spirits and staff members of these efforts, whether they are well or poorly organized, include reform-minded professional workers, bureaucrats, citizen volunteers, youth, and even the clientele themselves.

Many of the more complex and relatively stable community-based programs seem able to incorporate both service and institutional-change approaches. Indeed, impressionistic evidence suggests that, whereas one program may emphasize a service approach and another a militant institutional-change approach, in due course a convergence takes place. The well-balanced and viable organization apparrently is required to pursue both types of objectives, often in some interactive manner. One writer has recently observed that these programs represent "a return to the political clubhouse style of help, with social workers instead of politicians dispensing the aid," but that they go "far beyond the clubhouse into the realm of the institutional ombudsman, functioning as the watchdogs of public agencies."[10]

PROGRAM EFFECTIVENESS

How effective have these community-based programs been? To what extent, for example, have particular programs diverted youth from the juvenile justice system? Firm and satisfactory answers still elude us. The failure to obtain clear answers may be due to various factors: defective program methods or delivery systems, insensitive evaluative instruments, or defective research designs. It is possible that delinquency is a function of general urban, industrial, class-stratification, or cultural process, as suggested above, and that no specific institutional changes or particular programmatic efforts will make much difference unless they are part of broad, large-scale structural efforts. Perhaps we also expect too much in light of our limited knowledge, limited expenditure of resources, and rapidly changing urban conditions. On the other hand, we have been reasonably successful in achieving certain modest and preliminary or intermediate objectives. Community-based "innovative" programs have proved to be effective mechanisms for reaching large numbers of adolescents, many of whom were not served in established agencies. For example, the visibility and accessibility of service centers for adolescents have been important in attracting teenagers. Such programs have been successful as first-aid stations in handling crisis situations. They have been useful mechanisms of training, job referral, and job development. They have provided opportunities for social, educational, cultural, and political development of street-oriented youth, but the relation of these varied results to delinquency prevention, reduction, or control remains obscure.[11] It is true that evaluations have been restricted almost exclusively to service programs. It is possible that current efforts at institutional change—for example, through diversion of delinquent youngsters from the juvenile system and avoidance of "bad labeling" processes at schools—will lead to positive and measurable results, but we cannot be sure yet.

We can identify the failures of community-based programs more readily than we can the successes. The reasons for the failures are becoming clearer. Some community-based programs may be nonprograms. They may accomplish little, or serve simply to aid in confining youth to certain ghettos, subcommunities, or public-housing sites. It is possible for a part of a community to be so encapsulated and isolated that it becomes for many purposes an institutionalized environment. A highly deprived, barricaded, and coercive community can be created as functionally equivalent to an institution. An unanticipated consequence of closing down correctional institutions could be dumping delinquents into and further barricading such communities.

It is also possible to develop programs of a group or counseling character that are "successful" within or even outside four walls, yet relatively isolated from significant aspects of the community surrounding them. A program may not be effectively interactive with the community. It may not serve to reintegrate youth into important role structures. For example, the use of group-interaction approaches and social or recreational activities per se in the open community with highly delinquent youth and with gangs has proven generally unproductive. Several recent gang studies have shown no positive relationship between reduction of delinquent behavior and street-gang work efforts.[12] Indeed, there may be a negative association between gang delinquency and intensive street work. Delinquency may increase as the worker spends more time with the gang and the gang becomes more cohesive. The problem of delinquency may not be amenable to planned worker intervention unless the gang structure is modified or even dissolved. This is not to denigrate street work or outreach efforts so long as the focus moves beyond counseling and group activities and toward integration of individual delinquents into legitimate community subsystems, such as education or employment.[13]

We have learned or should have learned by now that programs on behalf of youth, especially delinquent youth, will not succeed unless there is significant community support. If the police, established agencies, politicians, and active community groups do not want them, certain programs may be denied resources or may be attacked and made to fail.[14] Youth clientele cannot be served successfully under these circumstances. Viable working relationships, especially with police, schools, and employment resources, must be established. To ignore these subsystems or to attack them frontally may be a grievous error. In exceptional situations, of course, such attacks may be necessary if humanitarian and social-development objectives are to be achieved. If this route is selected or required, powerful allies should be available and the possibilities of success should be relatively high.

Institutional-change programs based largely on the organized or unorganized inputs of delinquents usually do not succeed. Despite wishes, fantasies, and propaganda to the contrary, the primary involvement of delinquents in social or political action is not tolerated by the community, and it usually results in strong counter-mobilization. The ingredients of failure include manipulation of community leaders and program personnel by gang leaders for delinquent or highly personalized purposes. Civil-rights militants and radical professional workers or bureaucrats interested in social causes and general community problem solving may be viewed by delinquents as exploiting, and in turn may be "conned" and exploited by delinquents. Programs that undersell or oversell the potential of youth leadership do not succeed. Youths, let alone delinquents, will not participate for long in activities that do not meet their interests or needs at a given stage of their development. Also programs for education, social action, economic development, and other goals may fail because youths lack organizational "know-how," motivation, or capacity, as well as adequate adult support, supervision, or consultation.

Perhaps the major cause of program failure is interorganizational and community conflict. Youth programs and problems, especially those concerned with delinquency, become public issues that are readily politicized. They become sources of agency and community-group development, prestige, power, and funding. In such instances, the key problem may not be youth-adult or intergenerational conflict but adult-adult or interorganizational conflict. Furthermore, the source of the conflict may lie only partially in issues of community participation and control, racism, unemployment, poor education, and inadequate social service systems. It may well be based mainly in defective national social policy and planning in regard to youth development. There appears to be no set of interrelated goals, objectives, and priorities for the social development of the youth of the nation. Each organization concerned with youth, including delinquents, operates essentially on a short-term, crisis, fragmented basis. The national commitment and policy to provide those opportunities and services required for each youth to achieve his social potential do not yet exist. Even the identification of needs of various categories of socially handicapped youth has not yet been achieved on a community or national basis. Particularistic organizational priorities and programs continue to be emphasized; they have produced a crazy-quilt patchwork of programs to deal with community and national problems of delinquency.

Ideally, community-based programs of delinquency prevention should be related to each other in a socially ordered and effective way. The freedom of community groups, agencies, and independent youth groups to deal with youth problems must be safeguarded, but it probably also should be functionally limited. The question of local organizational autonomy and funds to sustain it must be viewed within a larger framework of what makes sense on a community and national basis for the social development of youth. Issues of national policy and planning must be identified and must take precedence over local and idiosyncratic community interests, which in turn are more important than particularistic organizational interests. These levels are interacting, of course, but the overall goal- and standard-setting responsibility of the federal government has to be more fully developed.

While the economic interdependence of various sectors of American society have been recognized and national economic and fiscal policies gradually but firmly established, the social needs of youth, including delinquents, and the interdependence of various groups of society dealing with youth have not yet been adequately recognized and national goals and policies have not been formulated in regard to them. Technological development, the rapidity of social change, the complexity of human and social problems, and the limits on economic resources demand a more systematic approach to problem solving. It may be that a major break with the past is appropriate and required at this time. A new and rational approach to delinquency prevention and control would require as a first step that the federal government take a strong stand and establish general, coordinated criteria for youth development as a framework for community-based programming.

NOTES

1. "Programs and Policies of the Department of Youth Services," mimeographed (Boston: Massachusetts Department of Youth Services, 1972).
2. Robert Perlman and Arnold Gurin, *Community Organization and Social Planning* (New York: Council on Social Work Education and John Wiley & Sons, 1971). See also Irving A. Spergel, *Community Problem Solving: The Delinquency Example* (Chicago: University of Chicago Press, 1969).
3. Alan A. Altshuler, *Community Control* (New York: Pegasus, 1970). See also Sherry R. Arnstein, "A Ladder of Citizen Participation," *Journal of the American Institute of Planners* 35 (July 1969): 216–24.
4. Peter W. Born, *Street Gangs and Youth Unrest* (Chicago: Chicago Tribune Educational Service Department, 1971), p. 14.
5. Op. cit., pp. 18–19.
6. Op. cit., p. 15.
7. Op. cit., p. 15.
8. Richard A. Cloward and Lloyd E. Ohlin, *Delinquency and Opportunity* (New York: Free Press, 1960).
9. Robert J. Gemignani, "National Strategy for Youth Development and Delinquency Prevention" (Washington, D.C.: Youth Development and Delinquency Prevention Administration, Department of Health, Education and Welfare, 1971). See also *Delinquency Prevention Through Youth Development* (Washington, D.C.: Department of HEW, 1972).
10. Hettie Jones, "Neighborhood Service Centers," *Individual and Group Service in the Mobilization for Youth Experience*, ed. Harold H. Weissman (New York: Association Press, 1969), p. 49.
11. William C. Berleman, James R. Seaberg, and Thomas W. Steinburn, "The Delinquency Prevention Experiment of the Seattle Atlantic Street Center: A Final Evaluation," *Social Service Review* vol. 46, no. 3 (September 1972), pp. 323–46. See also Richard Block, "The Chicago Youth Development Project: An Evaluation Based on Arrests," (Master's

thesis, University of Chicago, 1967); LaMar T. Empey and Steven G. Lubeck, *The Silverlake Experiment* (Chicago: Aldine, 1971); Malcolm W. Klein, *Street Gangs and Street Workers* (Englewood Cliffs, N.J.: Prentice-Hall, 1971); Walter B. Miller, "The Impact of a 'Total Community' Community Delinquency Control Project," *Social Problems* 10 (Fall 1962): 181–91; and Irving A. Spergel, Castellano Turner, John Pleas, and Patricia Brown, *Youth Manpower: What Happened in Woodlawn* (Chicago: School of Social Service Administration, University of Chicago, 1969).

12. Op. cit. *supra*.

13. Irving Spergel, "Street Gang Work," *Encyclopedia of Social Work* 2, ed. Robert Morris, (New York: National Association of Social Workers, 1971), pp. 1486–94.

14. ———, "Community Action Research as a Political Process," *Community Organization: Studies in Constraint*, ed. Irving Spergel (Beverly Hills, Calif.: Sage Publications, 1972), pp. 231–62.

chapter twenty-one

YOUTH SERVICES BUREAUS

National Advisory Commission on Criminal Justice
Standards and Goals

YOUTH SERVICES BUREAUS: A MODEL FOR THE DELIVERY OF SOCIAL SERVICES

Neighborhood agencies providing community services for young people can be important elements in the prevention and reduction of crime and delinquency.

The agencies are identified in this report as youth service bureaus, and the Commission believes that they have provided some of the most successful examples of the effective deliveries of social services within the framework of a social service delivery system.

An effective service delivery system, in addition to upgrading the quality of life for its clients, can reduce the feelings of alienation many citizens have, increase the confidence of these citizens in public and private institutions, and foster citizen cooperation with these institutions.

In the past decade, there have been many attempts to develop a service delivery strategy to deal more effectively with such seemingly intractable social problems as poverty. There have been problems with this implementation strategy, as shown by the early experiences of the Community Action Program, under the sponsorship of the Office of Economic Opportunity, and of the Model Cities Program, under the sponsorship of the Department of Housing and Urban Development.

Youth Services Bureaus in large part were the result of a recommendation by the 1967 President's Commission on Law Enforcement and Administration of Justice, which urged communities to establish these bureaus to

From *Report on Community Crime Prevention,* National Advisory Commission on Criminal Justice Standards and Goals (Washington, D.C.: U.S. Government Printing Office, 1973), pp. 51–69.

serve both delinquent and nondelinquent youth referred by the police, juvenile courts, schools, and other sources. That commission envisioned these bureaus as central coordinating units for all community services for young people.

In its recent report, *The Challenge of Youth Services Bureaus,* the California Youth Authority stated that youth services bureaus serve as models for developing direct service to children and youth. The report indicated that these bureaus are a pioneer example of a service delivery component of a comprehensive youth services delivery system.

The commission goes even further and states that the standards set forth in this chapter could serve as standards for the delivery of services within the framework of a comprehensive social services delivery system.

The "essence" of any social service delivery system, according to the Commissioner of the Social and Rehabilitation Service Administration for the United States Department of Health, Education, and Welfare, is to marshal all resources in a coordinated way to bring the client to his best functioning level.[1]

Social services are made available to clients who have a need for such services, which include employment, job training, education, housing, medical care, psychiatric care, family counseling, or welfare. At present, these services for adults as well as for youth are fragmented. A family with multiple problems is often seen by several agencies at the same time. Often one agency does not know what another is doing, and it is not uncommon for agencies to be working at cross-purposes with one another.

The service delivery system would solve this problem by integrating the services available to the individual through a central intake unit, which analyzes the individual's needs and refers him to the appropriate agency. It is critical to the success of these programs that the clients are involved in the actual development and operation of the programs, both in an advisory role and as employees.

Many youth services bureaus have been effective in integrating and coordinating the services available to youth and have acted as the central intake unit for analyzing a juvenile's needs and referring him to or providing him with services. The utility of youth services bureaus as a model for all social delivery systems was highlighted by Sherwood Norman in his book, *The Youth Services Bureau, a Key to Delinquency Prevention:*

> The Bureau strengthens existing agencies by performing an enabling function rather than its attempting to fill gaps in service. It bridges the gap between available services of youth in need of them by referral and followup; it acts as an advocate of a child to see that he gets the services he needs. The Youth Services Bureau is not itself a service agency so much as an agency for organizing the delivery of services to children and their children and their families.

The integrated nature of the youth services bureau approach and the multiple functions of the bureau are portrayed graphically in the chart on pages 294-95. The chart shows that a youth can walk into the youth services bureau on his own or be referred by his family or a number of community agencies.

The chart also shows how the bureau itself utilizes a number of existing resources to help to develop a program appropriate to the individual youth. The program might involve direct assistance such as counseling, education, training, and health checks. It might involve activities in which the youth can become involved, such as social or issue-oriented activities. And, for youth with particular difficulties, it involves utilization of drug programs, hotlines and crisis centers, and other resources.

BACKGROUND

A strong impetus for establishing youth services bureaus came from the President's Commission on Law Enforcement and Administration of Justice in 1967. The commission's major specific recommendation for preventing delinquency called for the establishment of youth services bureaus throughout the country.

That commission recommended:

Communities should establish neighborhood youth serving agencies —youth service bureaus—located if possible in comprehensive neighborhood community centers and receiving juveniles (delinquent and nondelinquent) referred by the police, the juvenile court, parents, schools, and other sources.

Efforts, both private and public, should be intensified to . . . establish youth services bureaus to provide and coordinate programs for young people.

Police forces should make full use of the central diagnosing and coordinating services of the youth services bureaus.[2]

In elaborating on these recommendations, the President's Commission's Juvenile Delinquency Task Force indicated that long-term recommendations for youth services bureaus required the creation of new social institutions. However, the task force suggested that currently existing neighborhood centers could serve as the basis for the necessary institutions, even though they did not appear to be making a sufficient impact on delinquency control at that time. Nevertheless, the task force favored the expanded use of community agencies, ideally to be located in comprehensive community centers, for dealing with delinquents nonjudicially and close to where they live.

The task force suggested exploring the availability of federal funds, both for establishing the coordinating mechanisms basic to the youth services bureau's operations and for instituting programs needed in the community. A range of operational forms was mentioned as a possibility. Staffing advocated in that report focused on laymen, engaged as volunteers or paid staff, to augment the professional staff in the official justice system agencies.

The target population recommended for youth services bureau programs ideally was to be both delinquent and nondelinquent youth. While anticipating that some cases would normally originate with parents, schools, and other sources, the task force expected the bulk of referrals to come from police and juvenile court intake staff. "Police and court referrals should have special status in that the youth services bureau would be required to accept them all."[3]

The task force report continued, "The youth services bureau should also accept juveniles on probation or parole . . . It should accept 'walk-ins' and parental requests for voluntary service. It should respond to requests for aid from other organizations and individuals. But the compelling priority would be youth who have already demonstrated their inability to conform to minimal standards of behavior at home or in the community."[4] "Trouble-making" and "acting out" were two other terms the report used in describing the target population.

In conjunction with the key group of youth to be served ("trouble-making") and the primary referral sources proposed (police and court intake), it is critically important that the President's commission envisaged that referral to the bureau and acceptance of the bureau's service would be voluntary. Otherwise, the commission said, "The dangers and disadvantages of coercive power would merely be transferred from the juvenile court to it."[5]

The Need for Voluntary Participation

The proposed youth services bureau was to render service on request of parents or with their consent. Voluntary participation by the juvenile and his family in working out and following a plan of service or rehabilitation was to be fundamental to the bureau's success, since it was designed to offer help without coercion. Moreover, the task force report stated, "In accordance with its basic voluntary character, the youth services bureau should be required to comply with a parent's request that a case be referred to the juvenile court."[6]

Significantly, the task force proposed the youth services bureau as an alternative to the juvenile court, rather than a substitute for it. In other words, the youth services bureau proposed by the 1967 President's commission was to offer juveniles and their parents a choice between juvenile court and the youth services bureau and was not planned to take the place of the juvenile court completely.

While a broad range of services and certain mandatory functions were suggested for the youth services bureau, individually tailored work with trouble-making youths was proposed as a primary function. The task force recommended that the bureaus would have a mandatory responsibility to develop and monitor a plan for service for these youth.

In addition, the task force intended youth services bureaus to act as central coordinators of all community services for young people and to provide services, especially ones designed for less seriously delinquent juveniles, lacking in the community or neighborhood. Services were to be under the bureaus' direct control either through purchase or by voluntary agreement with other community organizations.'

Suggestions for service included group and individual counseling, placement in group and foster homes, work and recreational programs, employment counseling, and special remedial or vocational education.

Court Referral

Even though the task force stressed that acceptance of the youth services bureau's services would be voluntary, it nonetheless recommended that ". . . if the request to seek available help is ignored, the police or, in certain communities, another organized group may refer the case to court."[7] However, the task force suggested that the option of court referral should terminate when the juvenile or his family and the youth services bureau agree upon an appropriate disposition. "If a departure from the agreed-upon course of conduct should thereafter occur, it should be the community agency (the youth services bureau) that exercises the authority to refer to court."[8]

More specifically, the task force proposed, "It may be necessary to vest the youth services bureau with authority to refer to court within a brief time—not more than sixty and preferably not more than thirty days —those with whom it cannot deal effectively."[9] Paradoxically, the task force also stated that it is inappropriate to confer on youth services bureaus ". . . a power to order treatment or alter custody or impose sanctions for deviations from the suggested program."[10]

The Commission also envisaged some of the consequences that could result from instituting youth services bureaus and some of the choices to be considered in planning for them:

> The relationships among the parts of the criminal justice system and between the system and the community's other institutions, governmental and nongovernmental, are so intimate and intricate that a change anywhere may be felt everywhere. . . . A reform like organizing a youth services bureau to which the police and juvenile court, and parents and school officials as well, could refer young

Youth Services Bureau

REFERRAL SOURCES

- PUBLIC WELFARE DEPARTMENT
- POLICE
- COURT
- SCHOOL
- FAMILY
- CHURCH
- WALK-IN

↓

YOUTH SERVICES BUREAU

↓

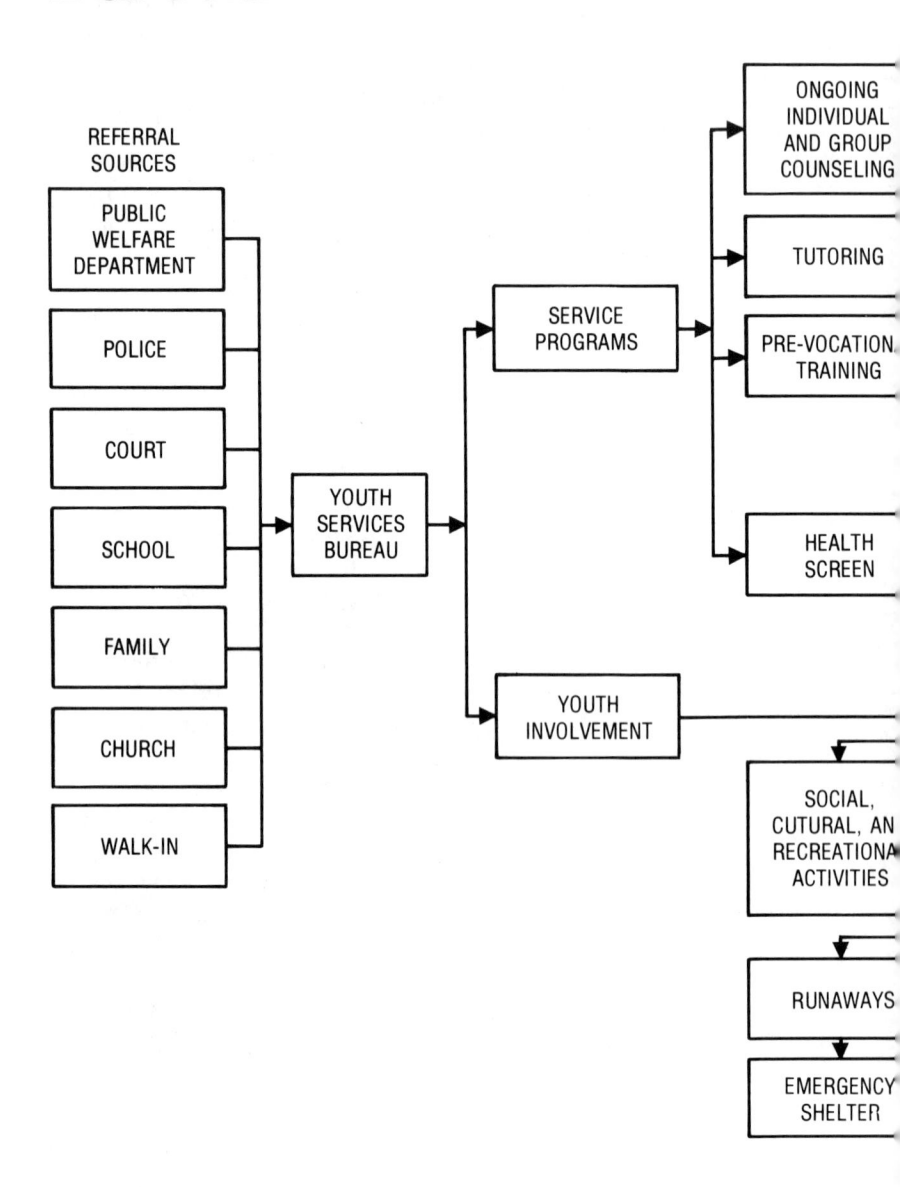

- **SERVICE PROGRAMS**
  - ONGOING INDIVIDUAL AND GROUP COUNSELING
  - TUTORING
  - PRE-VOCATION TRAINING
  - HEALTH SCREEN

- **YOUTH INVOLVEMENT**
  - SOCIAL, CUTURAL, AN RECREATIONA ACTIVITIES
  - RUNAWAYS
  - EMERGENCY SHELTER

Source: Derived from material developed by the Youth Development and Delinquency Prevention Administration, U.S. Department of Health, Education, and Welfare

YOUTH SERVICES SYSTEM

```
FAMILY COUNSELING ──► INDEPENDENT HOUSING LOCATED

INDIVIDUAL COUNSELING ──► UTILIZE INDIVIDUAL AS COUNSEL AIDE ──► PERMANENT VOLUNTEER

G.E.D. PREPARATION ──► AWARD OF G.E.D. ──► ADMITTANCE TO COLLEGE

VOCATIONAL TRAINING ──► JOB DEVELOPMENT AND PLACEMENT ──► JOB UPGRADING

TATTOO REMOVAL

PSYCHIATRIC AND PSYCHOLOGICAL TESTING

EYE CHECK
DENTAL CHECK

         ↓                              ↓
ISSUE-ORIENTED CONCERNS          DEVELOPMENTAL PROGRAM
e.g., ECOLOGY, AGING,            PLANNING OPERATION
DELINQUENCY, POVERTY, etc.       AND EVALUATION

         ↓                              ↓                    ↓
HOT LINE                         YOUTH TO                DRUG ABUSE
CRISIS CENTER                    YOUTH ADVOCACY              ↓
                                                         SCHOOL DRUG
                                                         INFORMATION
                                                         PROGRAM
```

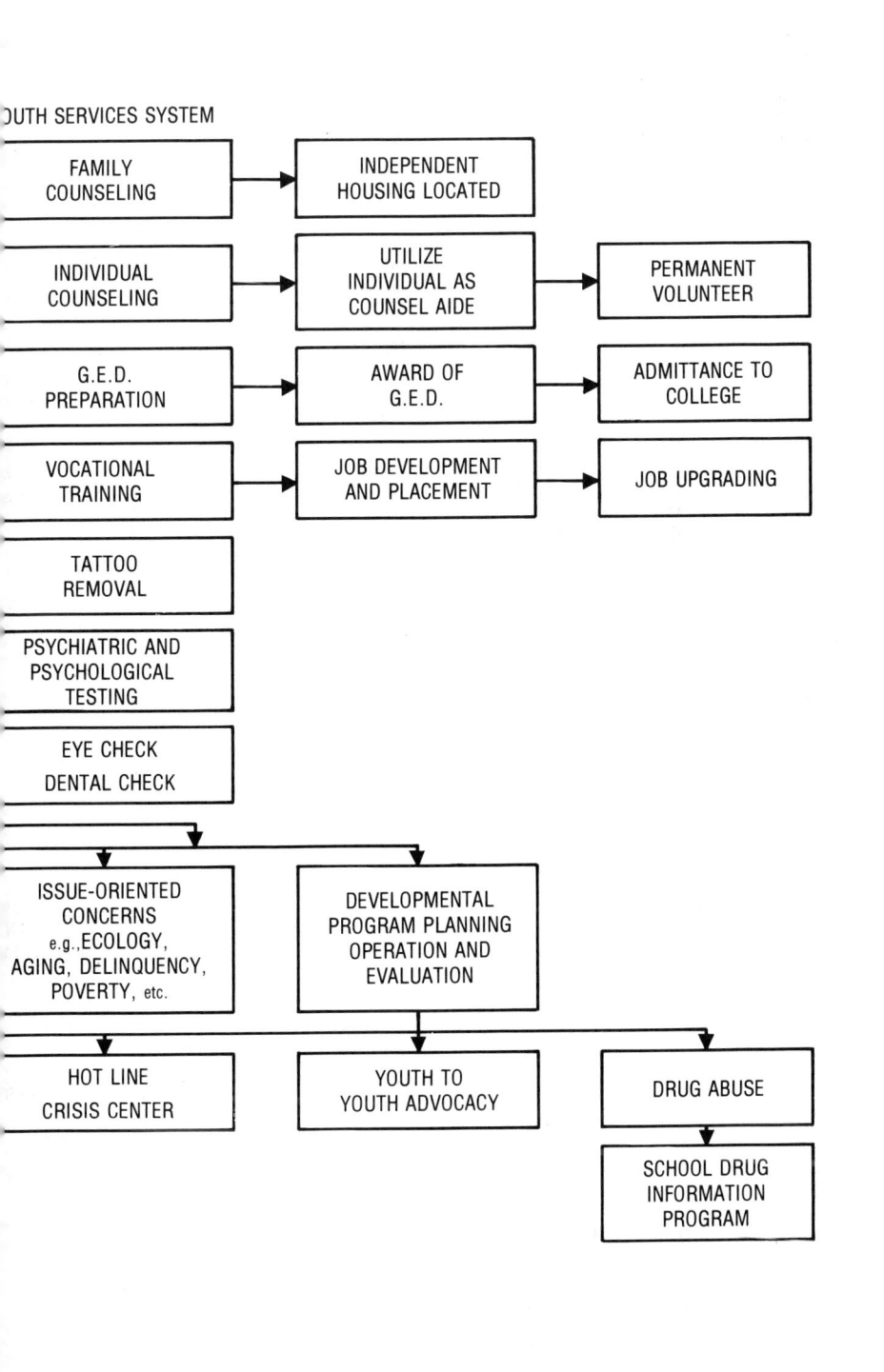

people will require an enormous amount of planning. Such a bureau will have to work closely with the community's other youth serving agencies. It will affect the caseloads of juvenile courts, probation services, and detention facilities. It will raise legal issues of protecting the rights of the young people referred to it. It could be attached to a local or state government in a variety of ways. It could offer many different kinds of service. It could be staffed by many different kinds of people. It could be financed in many different ways.[11]

Thus, with this brief description, the 1967 President's Commission recommended the youth services bureau as a major delinquency-prevention program. But what it recommended was an idea rather than a plan for action.

Three dimensions define the character of delinquency-prevention programs. These dimensions are: (1) the goals to which the people and groups within the program are committed; (2) the decision structure of who makes the important decisions and on what basis; and (3) the methods of intervention, or functions of the program.

The first two dimensions, goals and decision structure, determine the program's strategy.[12] Because the goals and functions were not explicitly detailed and because the 1967 commission suggested a wide range of operational forms, youth services bureaus have developed with a wide range of strategies. As one writer noted, there is ". . . no common agreement as to what a youth service bureau is, what services it should provide, or under whose auspices it should be operated.[13]

The experience of communities across the nation in operating youth services bureaus makes it plain that the original recommendations should be refined and some of the originally proposed description discarded.

YOUTH SERVICES BUREAUS TODAY

Since 1967, youth services bureaus have been established across the nation in large cities and small, in overcrowded inner city neighborhoods, middle income suburbs, and sprawling rural counties—joining the few pioneering youth services bureaus that had preceded the commission's recommendations.

A national census in 1972 identified 150 youth services bureaus currently in operation in many states and territories throughout the country.[14]

The task force in 1967 suggested exploring the feasibility of federal funding for establishing youth services bureaus. However, the national study in 1972 was able to identify less than $15 million annually in federal dollars supporting the youth services bureau movement. Clearly, the youth services bureau movement does not currently appear to be the nation's most popularly supported delinquency prevention effort.

The majority of federal funds granted to support youth services bureaus has come from the Law Enforcement Assistance Administration (LEAA) of the Department of Justice, with the Youth Development and Delinquency Prevention Administration (YDDPA) of the Department of Health, Education, and Welfare and Model Cities of the Department of Housing and Urban Development also contributing substantial amounts to their support. A sizable number of the LEAA-funded bureaus receive $50,000 or less in grant funds each year, while the YDDPA-funded projects, although fewer in number, more typically are funded for $75,000 or more per year in federal funds.[15]

The experiences of 150 communities in developing and operating youth services bureaus during the last five years, many of them partially financed by federal funds, form the basis for the standards suggested in this chapter.

GOALS FOR YOUTH SERVICES BUREAUS

The goals for youth services bureaus suggested by the President's Commission in 1967 were principally to provide and coordinate programs for young people. As bureaus have come increasingly into operation, these basic goals have been expanded. At the present time, youth services bureaus have at least five goals. These include: (1) diversion of juveniles from the justice system; (2) provision of services to youth; (3) coordination of both individual cases and programs for young people; (4) modification of systems of services for youth; and (5) involvement of youth in decision-making, and the development of individual responsibility.

The discussion that follows examines the rationale of each of these goals, presents some of the most effective decision making structures for each, and looks at some of the programs that are oriented toward attaining these goals.

Diversion

While the concept of diversion was discussed less often in 1967 than today, youth services bureaus were proposed in part as a response to the problems created by processing juveniles through the justice system. More and more frequently, questions were being raised whether justice-system processing was the most effective method for preventing further juvenile delinquency.

Each year, a vast number of young people enter the juvenile justice system for acts that are not crimes for adults: incorrigibility, truancy, running away, and even stubbornness. In addition, a substantial number of juveniles are processed by the justice system for minor offenses that are neither recurring nor a serious threat to the community.

Yet, because laws regarding juveniles' behavior are ambiguous and because opportunities for minor law infractions are numerous, the massive number of officially labeled delinquents represents only a portion of the young people who could potentially be defined as delinquents. "Given the broad mandate of the juvenile court, and the catch-all character of the statutes which define delinquency, there are virtually no nondelinquents. Juveniles have committed, and commit acts daily, which, if detected, could result in adjudication."[16]

Clearly, this catch-all character creates an uneven response to delinquency by the community, the police, and the courts—uneven in defining and reporting delinquency and also in apprehending, detaining, and referring the young person for further processing by the system. Ideally, this processing would be through a system of procedures by which illegal behavior by juveniles would be handled through stages of decision and action according to some deliberate plan. In reality, the processing technology is faulty.[17]

At each decision point, there is a selective reduction of young people who penetrate to the next stage of the juvenile justice system.[18] For example, estimates for 1970 indicate that almost 4 million juveniles had a police contact during that year; 2 million of these contacts resulted in arrests; and over 1 million of the arrests resulted in referral to the juvenile court.[19] Of the cases referred to juvenile court throughout the nation, nearly 500,000 were handled judicially.[20] Thus, roughly one out of eight police contacts resulted in a court appearance.

Although some of these cases were closed for lack of evidence, a large part of this reduction in cases is based on the over-referral for service. For example, many more young people are referred to court by police, parents, schools and others than could realistically be processed by the justice system at the present time.

The absence of clear-cut criteria for selective reduction from justice system processing encourages screening based on idiosyncratic choice. Currently, law enforcement and court personnel are tacitly encouraged ". . . to develop their own policy, for good or evil, and perhaps 'discover' policy by looking backward to determine what has been done."[21]

Diversion criteria. Studies have reported a variety of bases for decision making at each stage of juvenile justice-system processing. Decisions are heavily weighted by individual discretion and are often based on factors that may be irrelevant to preserving public safety in the community. For example, one study pointed to the youth's demeanor, style of dress, and ethnic group as factors used in making an arrest decision.[22]

Another study of police-juvenile interaction showed that decisions to arrest juveniles are greatly affected by the presence and preferences of a complainant, with arrests more frequent when the complainant is present and when he urges strong action.[23] Thus, police attitudes and the attitudes of community residents toward the youth are significant factors affecting whether he will be processed further by the justice system.

These examples are, in part, manifestations of the social and economic inequities in the present nonsystem of discretion in decision making in response to crime and delinquency. More specifically, "The power of a group determines its ability to keep its people out of trouble with the law, even in instances where they have actually violated it. . . . When a group's general capacities to influence are high, the official delinquency rates of its children and youth tend to be low."

The same writer also points out that competent communities have long been reducing official delinquency by meeting the problem by unofficial means, utilizing the community's—not an individual's—sustained, organized, recognized, and utilized power.[24] In this way, community conditions and organizational arrangements significantly contribute to and differentiate between who is or is not to be a delinquent.[25]

Other experts have cited individual economic power to buy services for one's child as another method of selective reduction from justice system processing.[26]

Thus, there is abundant evidence that the administration of juvenile justice is often unjust.

Juvenile court. Yet, when the first juvenile court was established nearly seventy-five years ago, it was an outgrowth of the movement at that time to advance the welfare of children—in education, protective services, and child labor laws. Its goals were similar to those proposed for youth services bureaus today. One goal was to provide individualized treatment and social services for children coming under the court's jurisdiction, instead of primarily dispensing punishment. Court proceedings were to be informal, nonadversary, and confidential.

Even though initial hopes for the juvenile court were high, history has demonstrated that for many young people juvenile court processing has magnified some of the problems it was created to resolve.

Individualized treatment and service have seldom become a reality for young people adjudicated by the juvenile court. High probation caseloads have allowed little time for adequate service.

One obvious solution might be to increase the capacity of the juvenile court's probation services to supervise more effectively large numbers of young people. However, the evidence indicates that the sanctions of the juvenile court should be imposed only as a last resort, after all diversionary alternatives have been thoroughly utilized.

Once a juvenile is identified as delinquent, labeling and differential handling allow him fewer opportunities for positive participation in the normal or more acceptable institutions of his community. There are many examples of how the stigma resulting from a delinquency record can produce multiplied handicaps: increased police surveillance, neighborhood isolation, lowered receptivity and tolerance by school officials, and rejection by prospective employers.[27]

Being labeled a delinquent further reduces the self-esteem of the juvenile selected for justice system processing and diminishes his stake in conforming to even minimal community expectations.

Furthermore, there is evidence that the more a juvenile is engulfed in the justice system, the greater are his chances of subsequent arrest.[28]

There are, therefore, many reasons for developing youth services bureaus with a diversionary objective, and with a focus on providing an alternative to the justice system for young people in trouble. Planners for youth services bureaus need to consider these flaws in the justice system as they attempt to create workable, effective alternatives to this system.

Two alternatives to justice system processing merit consideration: (1) some of the actions of children and parents now subject to definition as delinquency or unfitness should be considered as part of the inevitable, every-day problems of living and growing up; and (2) many of the problems considered as delinquency or pre-delinquency should be defined as family, educational, or welfare problems, and diverted away from the juvenile court into other community agencies, such as youth services bureaus. In this manner, ". . . problems will be absorbed informally into the community, or if they are deemed sufficiently serious, they will be funneled into some type of diversion institution, staffed and organized to cope with problems on their own terms rather than as antecedents to delinquency."[29]

Diversion—definition and strategies. With the problems inherent in juvenile justice system processing, diversion emerges as a strong need; a clear understanding of what is meant by diversion is important.

Diversion is defined in this discussion as the process whereby problems otherwise dealt with in a context of delinquency and official action will be defined and handled by other nonjustice system means.[30] Advocates of diversion propose that diversion should be the goal of pre-judicial processing, with a clearly defined policy and with decisions based on predetermined criteria.[31] In this analysis, the term diversion is limited to identified programs that have clearly stated objectives, that are selected as rational and visible alternatives to further processing into the justice system, and that are operational rather than theoretical.[32]

Strategies and programs other than youth services bureaus that have diversion as their goal could have a great impact on the role of the youth services bureau in the community. Therefore, an awareness of their implications is essential.

Political-legal methods represent one potential strategy for diversion. Many of the proposed changes for limiting the legal definition of delinquency focus on narrowing the jurisdiction of the juvenile court.

Among the proposed legal strategies for diversion, the most sweeping is to limit court jurisdiction to young people who have committed acts that would also be crimes if committed by adults. Another potential strategy is to create legal barriers that would make it difficult or costly to refer young people to court when their only offense is being beyond control, truant, or runaway.[33] This legislation could also spell out screening procedures that must be followed before a child is referred to court.[34]

Another approach to a legal strategy of diversion is to pass statutes requiring law enforcement and court intake ". . . to find that no alternatives to juvenile court dispositions are available for all law violations short of serious felonies or dangerous disturbances of public order, before making referrals to juvenile court or filing petitions."[35] Legislation either to create barriers to court or to mandate exploration of alternative resources for each case will require developing specific objective criteria for the types of youthful behavior and the situations for which the community and its alternative programs will assume increased responsibility.

The diversion programs discussed above are not currently operational throughout the nation and remain theoretical. One of the major objections to implementing these political-legal strategies at this time is the insufficiency of effective alternative resources to which young people can be diverted.

In the absence of political-legal strategies, administrative policy strategies with the goal of diversion have been implemented in some communities where youth services bureaus are operating. This points to a major role for youth services bureaus in the mid-1970s: to demonstrate with the aid of administrative policy strategies that diversion of substantial numbers of juveniles from the justice system is practical; that youth services bureaus can be effective vehicles through which diversion strategies can be implemented; and, therefore, that diversion should be firmly mandated by legislation.

Under-use. Where youth services bureaus are in operation, have police forces made full use of them? Have the bulk of referrals to youth services bureaus come from police and juvenile court intake staff, as the President's Commission on Law Enforcement and Administration of Justice anticipated?

Overall, the answer is no. In many communities with youth services bureaus, police seldom or never refer young people there. A nationwide sample of more than 400 cases from 28 youth services bureaus showed that only 13 percent of the referrals were from law enforcement, while 30 percent were referred by self, friends, or family, and 21 percent were referred by schools.[36] Findings from California's nine pilot bureaus reveal a slightly larger proportion of referrals from law enforcement (21 percent), with referrals from probation accounting for an additional 11 percent of the cases served.[37]

Therefore, it is clear that youth services bureaus have generally been under-used as a diversionary resource by law enforcement, and a greater proportion of young people than the commission anticipated have referred themselves to the bureaus, voluntarily seeking help for problems.

Nevertheless, where police have diverted significant numbers of young people to youth services bureaus, there has been a related impact on court intake. For example, in the nine pilot project areas in California, the most dramatic decreases in initial referrals to probation were in the project areas where law enforcement most frequently utilized the bureau as a referral resource. This research concluded that many of the youth referred to the bureaus by law enforcement might otherwise have been referred to probation.[38]

There are many reasons that police officers have not made greater use of the youth services bureaus. These reasons include negative attitudes of individual policemen toward diversion and the likelihood of juveniles' participation in a voluntary program, lack of support from the department's policy-makers, perceptions that the community is content with the existing dispositions, real and imagined legal restrictions, and, by no means least often, negative opinions held by policemen of the youth services bureau itself.

Many times law enforcement's opinions of the bureau are neutral. However, all too frequently police opinions of the local youth services bureau are unfavorable. In some instances, individual officers have negative attitudes toward the bureau's youthful staff members, who may themselves be participants in alternative life styles and may not fit the bureaucratic mold of traditional juvenile justice agencies. In a few communities, police officers feel the bureau is too permissive.

Some of the unfavorable attitudes of law enforcement toward the youth services bureaus are due to the basic areas of controversy regarding the role of youth services bureaus: Should all referrals be voluntary? Should the youth services bureaus be accountable to the police for the services they provide to each of their referrals? Should the bureaus provide police with information on offenses committed by their clients? Whose role is crisis intervention? Should the bureaus refer youth elsewhere who have been referred there by police? Should the bureaus refer youth for whom they cannot provide service back to the police?

In communities where these issues have not been resolved, relationships between the police and the youth services bureau have not been strong, and diversionary referrals have been few. Some communities, however, have developed mutual expectations regarding what the service will be and how it will be provided. The experiences of these communities are worth noting.

Earlier it was noted that the goals and decision structure of a delinquency prevention program determine the program's strategy. A youth services bureau committed to a goal of diversion cannot unilaterally implement an administrative policy diversion strategy—unless its decision structure includes people or groups who have the power to bring about changes in referral patterns of juvenile offenders. Another alternative is a decision structure that develops the power through community organization to bring about such changes.

Thus, justice agency policy makers should be included in planning for a youth services bureau that will place a high priority on rapidly bringing about diversion. In addition, widespread diversion will inevitably affect referral patterns between agencies of the juvenile justice system, making an impact on workloads and on the proportion of young people referred to court for serious offenses.

Relationship with criminal justice agencies. Although many recommend that a youth services bureau should not be operated by any agency of the juvenile justice system,[39] it appears that the bureaus most genuinely capable of diversion are those with a linkage to the juvenile justice system. The most successful bureaus maintain immediate communication but are not coopted by the justice system, its traditionally most powerful leaders, or its existing practices.

In a diversion oriented bureau, criteria should be developed jointly by justice agency policy makers and other youth services bureau planners for diverting young people to the bureau and for the bureau's acceptance of them for service.

Some of the criteria presently considered by juvenile justice agencies in diverting youth to youth services bureaus in California include: nonprobation status, first offense, age, minor offense that does not threaten public safety, residence in the project area, cooperative attitude of youth (or youth and parents) toward voluntary referral, and the need for additional services the bureaus can provide, as perceived by the referring agency.[40]

The planning process for a diversionary bureau was particularly successful in San Diego, California. Here the probation department hosted a meeting for administrators from seventeen agencies to discuss the need, concept, and possible services and direction of a youth services bureau. A smaller community team, with the police and probation departments providing the core leadership, developed the plans in more detail and periodically reported back to a larger group of administrators for approval.[41]

The Youth Services Project in San Antonio, Texas, provides an example of an administrative policy change by the police department that is bringing about diversion in that city. The police chief has ordered all officers to deliver juveniles picked up for such offenses as glue- or paint-sniffing, liquor violations, running away, ungovernability, disorderly conduct, truancy, or loitering, to one of three project neighborhood centers in the city.

Availability of bureau staff to respond immediately to a case being handled by the police also increases the likelihood that diversion will take place in San Antonio. The Youth Services Project places bilingual intake workers in the juvenile aid bureau of the police department at night and on weekends to guarantee immediate follow-up on a case. This often saves police a long drive to juvenile hall. As a positive gain to police for making a referral to the youth services bureau, this is a stimulant to implementing a diversion policy.[42]

Accessibility to law enforcement. Accessibility of the bureau's offices to law enforcement is another asset in encouraging diversion. Until recently, the Youth Services Bureau of Greensboro, Inc., in North Carolina was located across the street from the police department. Not only did this permit bureau staff daily to pick up paper referrals from the police department but it also increased understanding between the police department's juvenile officers and the bureau staff during the bureau's developmental stages.

Detaching law enforcement officers from the juvenile division to work full-time in the bureau is another method of increasing the confidence of the police department and thereby enhancing diversion. it should be noted that this method of staffing could defeat the confidential, noncoercive stance of the bureau if the role of these officers is not clearly defined in advance.

This system, however, has worked well in the youth services bureaus in San Diego and San Jose, California, where the officers working in the bureaus make no arrests, gain a better understanding of youth problems by counseling youth and their parents, and are rotated back to the police department after several months to provide broader police department exposure to the benefits of diverting youth to the bureau.

After the youth services bureau was established in 1971 in Dekalb, Illinois, each of the eighty-six youths arrested by the police department was referred to the youth services bureau; none was referred to the court system. Only twenty of the eighty-six again came to the attention of the police department. All again were referred to the youth services bureau. Court statistics for youth from Dekalb reflect this policy change.

In several communities, youth services bureau staff have participated in ride-along programs with police patrolmen, often for several evenings, in order to increase their sensitivity to the problems of law enforcement officers in working with juveniles and families.

In many communities where law enforcement has been closely involved with establishing the youth services bureau, the bureau has found it necessary to break down distrust among the young people it serves. Only after a period of providing services have some of the bureaus successfully developed a reputation of providing voluntary and confidential service.

Perhaps no topic presented in the report of the President's Commission on Law Enforcement and Administration of Justice on youth services bureaus has generated more controversy than the issue of noncoerciveness. While emphasizing that participation would be voluntary, the report also proposed that bureaus have the authority to refer to court within thirty to sixty days those youth with whom it cannot deal effectively.

Critics of this policy point out that this would merely be an extension of control over the youth by community institutions, without providing the legal safeguards that are currently emerging in the justice system itself. Other critics note that if agents of the diversion program impose the same sanctions for trouble as would persons in the law-enforcement setting, the program remains diversionary in name only.

Recent guidelines for youth services bureaus indicate that bureaus should accept referrals from all law enforcement agencies on the condition that the authoritative agency close its case upon bureau acceptances of referrals.

In addition, these guidelines note that the youth referred to a bureau should not be subject to court action unless he subsequently commits an offense warranting court referral by police or is the subject of neglect. To refer to court upon the young person's failure to cooperate ". . . would be a clear indication to him that the youth services bureau was not a voluntary agency but rather part of the justice system and therefore coercive."[43]

It appears that many youth services bureaus are providing probation supervision. In communities where probation services are particularly limited, court referrals ordering youth to participate in the bureaus may seem to be an expeditious alternative. The same is true of informal probation referrals to bureaus. But this action negates the role of bureaus as programs in which young people participate by choice.

PROVIDING SERVICES FOR YOUTH

Having considered earlier the problems attached to processing by the juvenile justice system, one may question whether delinquency prediction and early identification for prevention programs, perhaps through the schools, would be a preferable alternative.

Because the reasons and methods for selection for justice system processing are often arbitrary, there is no accurate method for predicting delinquency. Indeed, most prediction methods overpredict and include many children who never come to the attention of the justice system. In addition, early identification magnifies the negative labeling process, putting the young person in a pre-delinquent or delinquent-prone frame of reference from the community's point of view.

Channeling young people into traditional delinquency prevention programs, moreover, perpetuates the fallacy that what is wrong with a delinquent is caused solely by the youth or his family.[44]

One potential role for youth services bureaus, then, is to challenge this fallacy and to recognize that part of the problem may rest with an inappropriate response of the community and its institutions to the situation.

This inappropriate response includes problems of accessibility of existing community services to youth. Inconvenient locations, unrealistic hours, impersonal styles of delivery, and unresponsiveness to the needs of youth currently living in the area prevent youth in trouble from seeking the community's public and private services. In addition, some of the services systematically exclude troublemaking youth from participation.

"Social agencies generally resist working with hard-to-reach youth and are seldom equipped to do so. Furthermore, young people themselves resist seeking help unless they are assisted by a youth worker in whom they and their peers have confidence."[45]

Many of the services needed to respond to young people's problems are simply not available, particularly when the youth or his family do not have the financial means to pay for them.

An area of controversy in the youth services bureau movement is whether a bureau should develop and provide services itself or should function principally as an information and referral service, following up with individual advocacy or case coordination for the young people it refers.

The President's commission was unclear on this. While it recommended that bureaus should be established to provide services, perhaps in existing neighborhood centers, it also suggested that services should be purchased or obtained through voluntary agreement with other community organizations.

One set of standards for youth services bureaus states explicitly that bureaus should not provide service directly: "The bureau strengthens existing agencies by performing an enabling function rather than itself attempting to fill gaps in services."[46] It ". . . bridges the gap between available services and youth in need of them by referral and follow-up. It acts as an advocate of the child to see that he gets the service he needs." In short, "The youth service bureau is not itself a service agency so much as an agency for organizing the delivery of services to children and their families."[47]

Drawbacks

There are, however, many drawbacks to operating a youth services bureau primarily as an information and referral program. Among the handicaps in referring substantial numbers of youth to other services are: the expectations of the youth or his family when they are referred to the bureau, the expectations of the agency referring them to the bureau, the availability of other services for youth in the community, the bureau staff's knowledge of community resources, and the style of delivery of existing services in the community.[48]

In communities where the services exist in other agencies but are inadequate to meet youth needs, a prospective youth services bureau will be faced with the question of whether to set up competing programs. A negative answer to this question could serve as the point of departure for a bureau oriented toward system advocacy.

If a youth services bureau were to focus on providing service only to diverted youth referred by law enforcement and court intake personnel, it could develop the same stigma that is now attached to justice system processing if it became known in the community as a place for delinquents.

Instead, with a nonauthoritative approach, youth services bureaus can have unique contact with and provide assistance to youth in trouble whose activities (such as running away or drug problems) could shortly lead to official detection or apprehension. Young people with problems in their homes, schools, or communities can contact the bureau, enabling the bureau to provide help as it is requested—not merely when an official agency deems that it is necessary.[49]

An important consideration in accepting self-referrals to the youth services bureau is whether service should be provided without parental permission. Traditionally, parental permission has been required for participation in social services. In some instances, particularly for medical services or for shelter care, it has been legally mandatory unless court permission has been obtained.

Yet, there are many instances where a young person needs a service but either parental permission is refused or is not sought by the youth because of severe communication problems with his or her parents. Most frequently, the youth has then not been able to obtain the service.

There are two strong arguments for youth services bureaus to provide services without the necessity of parental permission: (1) many youth services bureaus increasingly are becoming advocates for the child or youth. When the best interests of the parent and of the youth are in conflict, bureaus must select the interests of one as a priority. Because the bureaus' focus is service for youth, the youth's interests should be their first choice; and (2) in an era of increasing youth responsibility, the choice to participate in a needed service should be increasingly theirs.

Most youth services bureaus have focused primarily on developing alternative services to fill existing gaps rather than on facilitating access to ongoing services in the community. As a result, they provide direct service to youth considerably more frequently than they refer youth to other agencies for service.

The fundamental strength of most bureaus has been in their provision of a variety of innovative services for youth—services that include counseling, tutoring, job referrals and other employment services, crisis intervention, crisis shelter care, and medical services. A basic element of these services is that they are generally provided at accessible locations and hours and in an appealing manner to their clients. Moreover, several of the bureaus that primarily provide direct service also provide referral services—follow-up, individual advocacy, and service brokerage.

Obtaining Self-Referrals

Although many youth services bureaus ostensibly have diversion as one of their primary objectives, their decision-making structure and the functions they perform have caused them to move away from criminal justice diversion as the primary source of clientele. Not the least of the reasons for this shift has been the inability to convince law enforcement and probation intake personnel of the value of diverting young people from the justice system to the bureaus.

Youth services bureaus seeking to assist youth with problems without the intervention of the justice system, the schools, or other agencies have developed a variety of methods to obtain self-referrals. In addition to community publicity, bureaus have made their services accessible to young people through their convenient locations and hours, by instituting hotlines and drop-in centers, and through the activities of outreach workers.

For youth services bureaus whose offices are the focal point of activities, accessibility has been increased by locating near a school or in a business and commercial area frequented by young people. In San Antonio, Texas, accessibility of its Youth Services Project is increased by locating each of its three centers in a ground-floor apartment of a housing project. In rural areas or other communities with widely dispersed populations, some bureaus (such as the Tri-County Youth Services Bureau in Hughesville, Maryland) have opened 1-day-a-week outreach centers in churches and other locations.

Accessibility of bureaus in other areas also have been improved by maintaining evening and weekend office hours.

In some communities, youth services bureaus have organized and operated hotlines—anonymous listener services. Examples of hotlines linked to youth services bureaus include those in Peru, Indiana; Palatine, Illinois; Shamokin, Pennsylvania; and El Paso, Texas. In these communities, volunteers staff telephones to aid young people who call in to discuss their problems and personal crises anonymously with a concerned, trained listener. In many instances, the telephone conversation is the only assistance needed. However, the volunteer listener refers the young person to the bureau or another resource if further help is necessary. In Palatine, Illinois, college students receive credit for volunteering to staff the hotline. Although it does not operate a hotline, the Hughesville, Maryland, bureau urges young people with problems to call collect, thus overcoming economic and transportation barriers to accessibility.

A more aggressive approach to initiating contact with young people is seen in the use of outreach or street workers. Many of the outreach workers go where groups of youth gather—in order to link individual youth to services, to divert the groups into constructive activities, or to attempt to prevent confrontations between young people and the police. Traditionally, outreach workers have worked with gangs in urban areas. But in many of the youth services bureaus located in suburban communities, outreach workers have instead attempted to involve unaffiliated and alienated youth in purposeful activities.

In Pacifica, California, high school and college age students are employed by the youth services bureau as outreach workers, with a few assigned to each of the young people's gathering places in this suburban town, including the beach. In Fairmont Heights, Maryland, the Roving Youth Leader program concentrates on an outreach approach. This program sends five part-time teams, each composed of a young adult male and a high school student, into the community to provide positive role models and to encourage idle youth to participate in the Roving Leader's recreation programs and community services.

Even though the methods by which the bureau encourages self-referrals, diversionary referrals, and other third party referrals may differ, the needs of the young people referred from these sources are often indistinguishable. Moreover, one of the basic purposes of youth services bureaus is to avoid labeling youth. Therefore, the services provided to each type of referral should be limited only by his needs.

Individually Tailored Services

Although it has been suggested that counseling should not be the primary service of youth services bureaus, it is, in fact, the nucleus of many bureaus. This does not appear unreasonable, for, in many of the communities, this service has not existed elsewhere. It also appears that many activities of the youth services bureaus are inadvertently obscured by the term counseling; individual services for youth also deal with the solution of many concrete problems, sometimes through individual advocacy with other institutions in the community.

In the Youth Services Bureau of Greensboro, Inc., (North Carolina) counseling of young people, many of them runaways, is a principal program. Accessibility is greatly magnified by the staff's willingness to respond immediately to youth in trouble—regardless of the day or hour. This program is unique in its ability to gain the confidence of youth in trouble while maintaining the respect of other agencies in the community. Confidentiality is so great that staff do not take any action without the young person's knowledge. Although the bureau must inform the police when it knows the location of a runaway, the police have agreed that the bureau can continue to work with the runaway and need not turn him or her in. When a young person is battered or abused, he is urged to make the decision for court referral and protection himself, and bureau staff counsel him on the ramifications of this procedure.

Family counseling is a frequently provided service in San Diego and Pacifica, California. This is in sharp contrast to the services in Greensboro, where the focus of the bureau's counseling is the youth himself and on developing his responsibilities. In Pacifica, the agreement is generally for five counseling sessions. Families in need of long term treatment are referred to other agencies.

Hughesville, Maryland, offers diagnosis and evaluation, and most referrals (often from schools) receive a variety of tests before counseling begins.

In El Paso, where court approval is required before any youth under 16 can drop out of school, the juvenile court requires youngsters to be counseled first by the youth services bureau. The bureau attempts to solve the underlying problems, such as employment, and then makes its recommendation to the court regarding leaving school.

A drop-in clinic frequented primarily by youths experiencing identity problems characterizes the Glastonbury, Connecticut, youth services bureau. Individual, family, and group counseling are the main services provided.

The program of the Kansas City, Missouri, Youth Intercept Project does not provide traditional casework services. Instead, it helps the child stay in school and helps his family provide support for that kind of success.

In the Bronx, New York, the Neighborhood Youth Diversion Program has developed a program based on the premise that indigenous workers who know the problems and who have minimal training in conciliation and arbitration techniques can help resolve interpersonal and interfamily problems without relying on the formal judicial system. In the forum, three indigenous workers trained for the project act as judges. The differences between a youth and his parents or guardian are mediated and aided by the youth's advocate, a caseworker. Positive plans for action to develop a better relationship between them are agreed upon, and a follow-up forum is scheduled for a week or two later.

In Los Angeles County, California, the Bassett Youth Service Bureau focused on strengthening the community's efforts to meet youth needs. It developed a free clinic in conjunction with other community groups, staffed primarily by volunteers. The clinic includes a counseling and drop-in center in addition to an outpatient medical clinic. Venereal disease, pregnancies, and drug problems are among the most frequently treated medical problems.

Individually tailored work provided by the bureau has occasionally been supplemented by purchased services. For example, the Tucson, Arizona, Youth Service Bureau supplements its range of services by contracting for services for its clients, including remedial reading.

Other methods used by youth services bureaus to link youth to services are referrals with systematic follow-up and case conferences, in order to insure continuity of service.

Coordination of services for individual youth is taking place through case conferences in Worcester, Massachusetts. Representatives for all agencies involved with the youth meet in an attempt to attain a complete view of the problem and to develop a comprehensive plan to meet the youth's needs. In some instances, the youth or the youth and his parent attend the case conference. In order to strengthen the youth's responsibility, he is encouraged to contribute to the decisions that will affect him. After the youth is referred to another agency, the Youth Resources Bureau systematically follows up, generally by telephone, to assure that services are being provided.

The Youth Services Bureau of Tarrant County (Fort Worth, Texas) emphasizes its role as a crisis intervention service by attempting to understand each client's problem and by making a referral to the most appropriate agency. In a one-year period, 65 percent of the clients were referred to other agencies.

The outreach program of the Omaha, Nebraska, YMCA Youth Service Bureau also emphasizes referral to other existing agencies for service.

Individual advocacy is another role some bureaus fulfill. The most notable example of this is the youth services bureau in Ponce, Puerto Rico —Youth and Community Alerted. Here, twelve young people were trained to act as advocates for youth who had come in contact with the police or the juvenile court, or were in danger of becoming delinquent. The cultural style of the people living in the Playa of Ponce was considered in developing the advocates' role. At times, these advocates are friendly mediators between a child and parents; at other times, they intervene in a court hearing. In Bridgeport, Connecticut, one staff member of the youth services bureau appears in juvenile court each day to "stand up" for young people for whom they feel they can provide service. And in Fairmont Heights, Maryland, Roving Youth Leaders staff act as a third party contact with school authorities and juveniles in instances where parents or guardians are unwilling to act.

Crisis Shelter Care

Meeting the needs for shelter has been a subgoal in several bureaus.

The Omaha YMCA Youth Service Bureau operates a group home, which is responsive to the runaway problem and emphasizes family reconciliation. Whether a youth stays is his choice, but parental permission is required.

The Youth Crisis Center, Inc., in Jackson, Mississippi, provides shelter and services for up to five days for a few youths at a time. Parents are not contacted unless the youth agrees. Professional volunteers, including medical and legal people, supplement the small staff.

In Scottsdale, Arizona, the youth services bureau is located in a four-bedroom home, with two of the bedrooms used as offices and two for youth if they need overnight accommodations. If the youth is under 18, parental consent is required.

The youth services bureau in Boise, Idaho, provides temporary shelter care in lieu of incarceration.

In Las Cruces, New Mexico, the Council for Youth operates a group home for boys, most of whom remain there for a few months. The council's outreach program provides aftercare.

Although its operation has since been taken over by another agency, the Yuba-Sutter Youth Service Bureau in California developed crisis homes where youth could stay for short periods of time. These were private homes volunteered for short-term care. Volunteer homes were paid a nominal sum per day for expenses.

Group Programs

Programs for groups of youth and parents are to be found in many of the youth services bureaus—or organized by the bureaus in several communities. These group programs include new approaches to youth-police relations, education, and parental education.

The El Paso Youth Services Bureau bridges gaps in understanding between youth and police by its youth patrol, youth-police dialogues, and youth-police recreation program. The youth patrol permits youth to spend four hours on patrol with a police officer during periods of high activity. The youth-police dialogues involve anti-authority youth and selected police officers in encounter sessions, under the supervision of psychiatrists. The youth-police recreation program pairs an off duty police officer with a selected youth, identified as a natural leader in his community, to establish communication with young people in a neighborhood and develop constructive programs in cooperation with the neighborhood's residents.

In California, informal group discussions take place in several of the bureaus, with the bureaus in San Diego, Bassett, and Pacifica holding them most regularly. Classes and activity groups have been organized by several California bureaus, either alone or with the cooperation of other agencies and organizations in the community. Subjects have included cooking, sewing, self-improvement, preparing for and finding a job, writing a newspaper column, various crafts, and photography. Volunteers and volunteered supplies have been essential to these classes.

In the Tri-County Youth Services Bureau in Hughesville, Maryland, staff are joined by correctional camp inmates in leading group counseling for boys who have been referred to the bureau. One evening a week the inmates are driven to the bureau to participate in the sessions.

The Youth Advocacy Program in South Bend, Indiana, contracts for a street academy, an alternative school program for junior high and high school youth who have dropped out of the regular schools. In Ann Arbor, Michigan, the Washtenaw Youth Service Bureau, funded through the school system, has set up an alternative school program.

In Kansas City, Missouri, the program instituted art classes in several schools, to which problem children are referred. A prominent local artist teaches these classes, including discussions of social problems that relate to the content of the art.

Coordinative programs with the schools have been part of the East San Jose, California, Youth Service Bureau's program. One example is a cross-age tutoring program organized by the bureau, where high school students are released from class to tutor elementary school students. Another example is a truancy program—jointly funded by the schools and the bureau—in which an attendance counselor conducts group counseling sessions during school hours for chronic truants. Assisted by volunteers, this program also makes daily telephone calls to the homes of absent pupils in an effort to help solve problems which may hinder their return to school.

In addition to operating alternative education programs, some bureaus have also created alternative recreation programs when they have found that existing programs are geared to younger age groups, offer activities that are no longer popular, or exclude troublesome youth from their programs. Nevertheless, a youth services bureau oriented solely or primarily to providing recreation, overlooks the more urgent needs of troubled youth.

Parental education classes have been provided to several hundred parents in the San Diego, California, area as a result of a program developed by the youth services bureau in coordination with other organizations. This bureau also published a booklet for parents on "Guidelines to Discipline."

San Angelo, Texas, conducts a parent training program in cooperation with several other agencies.

COORDINATION OF CASES AND PROGRAMS

One function proposed for youth services bureaus by the President's commission was, "To act as central coordinators of all community services for young people." Because coordination can refer to a multitude of activities in the social services field, a variety of interpretations of the commission's intent have been suggested and much confusion has resulted. One level of coordination is case coordination. Another is program coordination.

On an individual case level, services to youth and other groups have often been fragmented and duplicated. There often has been no concern for the consistency of approach and policies of various agencies or parts of agencies from the viewpoint of the client. Youth workers have more frequently been responsible only for the content of their endeavors rather than for both their content and consequences. One observer noted, "We have not yet established the principle that . . . an agency which has rendered incomplete or unsuccessful service has some obligation for assuring continuity of community concern when its own contact ends."[50]

Referrals and case conferences are two frequently cited examples of case coordination. Youth services bureaus providing examples of these techniques were discussed in the preceding section.

Consistency of approach and integration of services are reasons case conferences have been used traditionally in some communities. Many observers suggest that case conferences are most suitable for smaller communities.

Referrals are another method of case coordination. Often when referrals are made, they are made superficially and without expectation of success. This has been called "community self-deception,"[51] but it has been perpetuated because of the lack of continuity of responsibility between agencies.

Accountability to the agency making the referral can decrease this lack of continuity. However, accountability is more likely to be assured when the referring agency has some control over the desired service. Purchase of service is one way of assuring this. Another, depending more on personal relationships or power than on money, is individual advocacy.

In large agencies, referrals may be made to specialized personnel within the agency, thus reducing exchanges of similar resources with other organizations. This practice leads to duplication of services within a community.

To reduce such duplication and to fill gaps in services systematically, coordinated planning of programs is frequently suggested.

Program coordination is most likely to be effective when the following characteristics are present:

> If the agency's goals exceed its resources.
> If the participating agencies' resources complement each other.
> If the agency's needs are served or at least not jeopardized.
> If the agency is more oriented toward maintaining social stability than toward instituting social change.
> If an external authority has control over agency programs, such as by possessing economic or legal power.

Information gathering and distribution. One of the first steps toward coordinated program planning is information gathering and distribution. A thorough and systematic approach to this is seen in the Youth Services Bureau of Wake Forest University, in Winston-Salem, North Carolina. Rather than providing direct services to juveniles, the bureau had developed a comprehensive, community-wide approach to coordinated planning of youth opportunities. Both young people and agency representatives participated in the planning. To document the needs and problems of youth, the bureau conducted an inventory of youth services and programs. The inventory provided profiles of youth serving agencies in the county, information about youth problems in the community, and a list of recommendations for improving youth opportunities. Subsequently, the bureau worked with other agencies and organizations in the community to attempt to implement the recommendations.

Another example of information gathering and distribution is a directory of community services, compiled and printed by the Youth Services and Resource Bureau, Inc., of San Angelo, Texas.

Another effort to plan systematically and create change in existing institutions was conducted by the Youth Services Bureau of Wake Forest University. This effort included a study of attitudes and knowledge of drug abuse, a study of drug use, a participant-observation study among black youth on factors preventing their involvement in recreation and character development programs, and a survey to determine which recreation or youth opportunities programs low income white youth would like to see developed.

Another program focuses on systems change in the schools. In an attempt to bridge the gap between community resources and schools, the bureau coordinates a project team of agency and school personnel in order to create a more positive learning experience and to reduce truancy.

The Youth Development Service in Billings, Montana, provides consultant and technical assistance to a variety of other social service agencies in the area. Coordination efforts bring agencies together to agree on community priorities, to eliminate service duplication, and to redirect resources where current projects are inappropriate. Efforts include printing a newsletter, which is mailed to about 800 professionals in the community and identifies community agencies' social service activities, and coordinating volunteers who tutor in the high school, work in court, and serve as big brothers and sisters. It has also developed a training program for foster parents.

The Washtenaw Youth Service Bureau in Ann Arbor, Michigan, also provides a minimum of direct service to young people. The bureau emphasizes the initiation of programs for troubled young people who have not yet had contact with the justice system. It has published a youth services guide, which is updated every three months. It conducts demonstration projects, primarily in the schools, and attempts to develop skills and resources within the system. It also provides consultation on problems in youth services. This bureau has developed youth task forces who identify youth problems, make recommendations, and take appropriate action.

The Youth Advocacy Program in South Bend, Indiana, also attempts to influence youth serving agencies to develop innovative programs. Its methods are positive proposals and involvement. Field workers are assigned to five youth serving agencies—the recreation department, schools, a family and child agency, city government, and Model Cities—with the task of making them more responsive to youth needs.

A completely different type of coordination characterized the initial youth services bureau legislation and standards and guidelines in California. Seed money was to be used as an incentive for local public and private agencies to pool their delinquency prevention resources, with staff and supportive services to be contributed by participating agencies and organizations, as well as volunteers. In San Diego, this concept was implemented by detaching experienced personnel from probation, police, and social welfare work to the bureau on a full-time basis. Psychiatric consultation was also contributed on a part-time basis. Pooling of resources has permitted this bureau to offer a drug identification service to the community, serving as a dropoff for drug analysis.

There is often confusion about the roles of police and probation officers working in this bureau and others in California, particularly as some bureaus in other States masquerade as youth services bureaus while providing probationary surveillance. In the California concept, police and probation officers provide staff services in the bureaus because of their interpersonal skills in working with youth—not because of their ordained authority.

SYSTEMS MODIFICATION

A focus on interagency coordination may improve efficiency by reducing duplication and fragmentation of services, thereby benefiting the young recipients of services. However, interagency coordination may serve primarily to support the status quo of existing service. By itself, this administrative strategy may do little to change agency practices which may not be responsive to the current needs of young people in the community and may be contributing indirectly to crime and delinquency.

Some critics predict that the development of informal antidelinquency agencies, " . . . will increase the possibility of arbitrary official action and will tend to consolidate, rather than change, the practices of established institutions."[52]

Earlier in this chapter, it was pointed out that the power of a group determines its ability to keep people out of trouble with the law. A youth services bureau that places a high priority on interagency coordination would contribute little to the development of opportunities for indigenous adults and youth vulnerable to the justice system to share legitimately community responsibility for reducing crime and delinquency. Maintaining social control primarily through the efforts of professionals and specialists may merely extend government control, without encouraging the development of a responsible community of youth and adults concerned with the equitable administration of justice.

In short, interagency coordination would enhance social stability, while youth development and community involvement would foster social change.

The examples of program coordination in this chapter are, in fact, often as closely related to systems modification, focusing on social change, as to maintaining social stability. Moreover, there are some elements of both coordination and systems modification in most of these examples.

For example, the decision structures in the Youth Services Bureau in Winston-Salem, North Carolina, and the Youth Advocacy Program in South Bend, Indiana, both include recipients of the services. While this characteristic does not further interagency coordination by rapidly providing the program with power to coordinate resources, it nonetheless institutes the beginnings of a power base that could ultimately bring about changes in the system of social and judicial services.

This approach requires a sense of security that the bureaus will continue to exist beyond a single funding year. It also requires continually training, developing, and involving young people in decision-making. Only in this way will the youth services bureaus evolve to meet the needs of the middle and late 1970s, as today's youth themselves become recognized as established leaders of the adult community.

YOUTH DEVELOPMENT

Developing youth responsibility for delinquency prevention, modifying existing services, and providing alternative services are all closely interrelated, if one accepts the premises that the recipients of services have useful opinions and creative ideas about the services, and that increasing their input into the planning of services is valuable.

Several notable examples of youth development for delinquency prevention can be found in youth services bureaus.

In South Bend, Indiana, for example, the Youth Advocacy Program involves youth in planning and administering the program. This program attempts to increase the capacity of youth groups, particularly the Youth

Coalition, to make established community institutions more responsive to youth needs. Several task forces of the Youth Coalition study youth problems and make recommendations that are reviewed by an advisory committee, representing the youth serving institutions of the community. These recommendations become the basis for the field workers' task assignments.

NOTES

1. Committee on Appropriations, Hearings before the Subcommittee on the Departments of Labor and Health, Education and Welfare, and Related Agencies; House of Representatives, 91st Congress, Second Session (1970), p. 270.
2. The President's Commission on Law Enforcement and Administration of Justice, *Challenge of Crime in a Free Society* (1967).
3. The President's Commission on Law Enforcement and Administration of Justice, *Task Force Report: Juvenile Delinquency and Youth Crime* (1967).
4. Ibid.
5. President's Commission on Law Enforcement and Administration of Justice, *Challenge of Crime in a Free Society*.
6. President's Commission on Law Enforcement and Administration of Justice, *Task Force Report: Juvenile Delinquency and Youth Crime*.
7. Ibid.
8. President's Commission on Law Enforcement and Administration of Justice, *Challenge of Crime in a Free Society*.
9. President's Commission on Law Enforcement and Administration of Justice, *Task Force Report: Juvenile Delinquency and Youth Crime*.
10. Ibid.
11. President's Commission on Law Enforcement and Administration of Justice, *Challenge of Crime in a Free Society*.
12. Edwin M. Lemert, *Instead of Court: Diversion in Juvenile Justice*, National Institute of Mental Health, Center for Studies of Crime and Delinquency (1971). Irving A. Spergel, *Community Problem Solving: The Delinquency Example* (Chicago: University of Chicago Press, 1969).
13. Daniel Skoler, "Future Trends in Juvenile and Adult Community-Based Corrections," *Juvenile Court Judges Journal* vol. 21, no. 4 (Winter 1971).
14. William Underwood, *A National Study of Youth Service Bureaus*, (Washington, Youth Development and Delinquency Prevention Administration, U.S. Department of Health, Education and Welfare, December 1972).
15. Ibid.
16. LaMar T. Empey and Steven G. Lubeck, *Delinquency Prevention Strategies* (Washington, Youth Development and Delinquency Prevention Administration, U.S. Department of Health, Education and Welfare, 1970).
17. Robert D. Vinter, "Justice for the Juvenile, Myth or Reality?" (lecture presented at the University of Delaware under the auspices of the E. Paul du Pont Endowment for the Study of Crime, Delinquency and Corrections, Newark, Delaware, March 26, 1969).
18. Ibid.
19. Robert J. Gemignani, "Youth Services Systems," *Delinquency Prevention Reporter* (Youth Development and Delinquency Prevention Administration, U.S. Department of Health, Education and Welfare, July-August 1972).
20. *Juvenile Court Statistics 1970* (National Center for Social Statistics, U.S. Department of Health, Education and Welfare).

21. Ted Rubin, "*Law as an Agent of Delinquency Prevention*" (paper prepared for the Delinquency Prevention Strategy Conference, California Youth Authority and California Council on Criminal Justice, Santa Barbara, February 1970).
22. Irving Piliavin and Scott Briar, "Police Encounters with Juveniles," *American Journal of Sociology* (September 1964).
23. Donald Black and Albert Reiss, in Edwin M. Lemert, op. cit.
24. John M. Martin, *Toward a Political Definition of Delinquency Prevention*, (Washington, D.C.: Youth Development and Delinquency Prevention Administration, U.S. Department of Health, Education and Welfare, 1970).
25. Spergel, op. cit note 12.
26. Margaret K. Rosenheim, "Youth Service Bureaus: A Concept in Search of a Definition," *Juvenile Court Judges Journal*, vol. 20, no. 2 (1969), pp. 69–74.
27. Edwin M. Lemert, "The Juvenile Court: Quest and Realities," *Task Force Report: Juvenile Delinquency and Youth Crime*, President's Commission on Law Enforcement and Administration of Justice.
28. Op. cit.
29. Edwin M. Lemert, *Instead of Court: Diversion in Juvenile Justice*.
30. Ibid.
31. Eleanor Harlow, *Diversion from the Criminal Justice System* (Center for Studies of Crime and Delinquency, National Institute of Mental Health).
32. See "Diversion from the Juvenile and Criminal Justice Process" (Chapter 3), *Corrections Task Force Report*, National Commission on Criminal Justice Standards and Goals.
33. Lemert, op. cit.
34. J. A. Seymour, "Youth Services Bureau" (paper prepared as background material for a seminar on Youth Services Bureaus sponsored by the Center for the Study of Welfare Policy and the Center for Studies in Criminal Justice, University of Chicago, January 24–25, 1971).
35. Lemert, op. cit.
36. Underwood, *supra* note 14.
37. Elaine Duxbury, *Youth Service Bureaus in California: Progress Report No. 3* (Sacramento: State of California Department of the Youth Authority, January 1972).
38. Ibid.
39. Martin, *supra* note 24.
40. Duxbury, op. cit.
41. Joyce McBride Devore, "A Descriptive-Evaluative Study of the Youth Service Bureau" (Master's thesis, San Diego State College, June 1970).
42. Lemert, *supra* note 29.
43. Sherwood Norman, *The Youth Service Bureau: A Key to Delinquency Prevention*, (National Council on Crime and Delinquency, 1972).
44. Martin, op. cit.
45. Sherwood Norman, *The Youth Service Bureau: A Brief Description of Five Current Programs* (National Council on Crime and Delinquency, June 1970).
46. Ibid.
47. Norman, *The Youth Service Bureau: A Key to Delinquency Prevention* (National Council on Crime and Delinquency, June 1970).
48. Elaine Duxbury, *Youth Service Bureaus in California: A Progress Report* (Sacramento: State of California Department of the Youth Authority, January 1971).
49. Rosenheim, *supra* note 26.
50. Alfred J. Kahn, *Planning Community Services for Children in Trouble* (New York: Columbia University Press, 1963).
51. Ibid.
52. Anthony M. Platt, "Saving and Controlling Delinquent Youth: A Critique," *Issues in Criminology*, vol. V, no. 1 (Winter 1970) pp. 1–24.

chapter twenty-two

YOUTH SERVICE BUREAUS: A CONCEPT IN SEARCH OF DEFINITION

Margaret K. Rosenheim

Picture a mini-skirted girl of fifteen standing on the street corner of one of the city's shadier neighborhoods ogling the boys as they walk by. The hour is 11:30 or midnight. There is some indication the girl has been drinking. What is she: A police problem? A welfare problem? Solely her parents' problem? Who should inquire, who should act?

Picture also, if you will, a young boy of twelve. This time he has been apprehended by the manager of a five-and-dime with a pocket full of ballpoint pens and candy. The juvenile officer comes in and takes him back to the station. A check of his records reveals a history of truancy, shoplifting, theft of a motorcycle. Again I ask, what is he? A police problem, a welfare problem, only his parents' problem? Who should inquire? What ought to be done?

Or imagine a defiant thirteen-year-old boy with a long history of truancy and of disruptive school behavior on the days when he chooses to appear. His grade performance is poor, as you might expect. His reading level is well below the average for his age. He dislikes school, he hates his teachers. He keeps tough company. Again, whose problem is he? How should we respond? What do we want to do?

These examples—and they could be multiplied in kind and number many times over—illustrate the all-pervasive problem of the "juvenile

From *Juvenile Court Judges Journal*, vol. 20, no. 2 (Summer 1969), pp. 69–74; footnotes from vol. 20, no. 3 (Fall 1969), p. 128. Reprinted by permission. Adapted from an address delivered at a symposium on "New Concepts in Juvenile Court Services," sponsored by the League of Women Voters and the Oaklawn Foundation for Mental Health, Elkhart, Indiana, April 11, 1969.

nuisance." The "juvenile nuisance" is an international phenomenon.[1] He (or she) arises under legal systems reliant upon juvenile courts and also under those where child welfare boards are used. He is present in small hamlets, where informal means of control are widely relied upon, and he is also present in the big city, where informality more frequently gives way (at least we think it does) to reliance on the formal process of police and other types of control agents. The juvenile nuisance is neither a serious confirmed offender nor a severe threat to his own well-being. He is an irritant, whose failure to conform worries us because it may jeopardize the smooth future development of a law-abiding healthy adult. Just as the juvenile nuisance of an earlier day was the grist of the reformative drive to found juvenile courts, so the juvenile nuisance today is the subject of youth service bureaus.

One of the most widely discussed proposals of the President's Crime Commission is that of youth services bureaus.[2] Part of the excitement, I have no doubt, stems from the fact that it is among the few *new* suggestions in the commission's report—which is not to criticize the commission, for novelty was not one of its objectives. Its charge was to draft a plan for social change responsive to the most authoritative statements of the problem of crime in modern America. A major purpose was to focus public attention on a balanced assessment of the weaknesses of present law and procedure. One of its notable strengths was "its recognition that disturbing the perimeter of one subsystem influences the others, and that reform requires planning perceptive of these inter-relationships."[3]

This is another source of the interest generated by youth service bureaus. For the proposal is inextricably intertwined with the commission's desire to narrow juvenile court jurisdiction and divert the bulk of current business away from law enforcement and juvenile justice. The proposal indicates its supporters' recognition that manipulating juvenile court jurisdiction has consequences outside the formal system. It is not enough to say that the present handling of juvenile nuisances is ineffective, or arbitrary, or punitive, or unconstitutional. The existence of common patterns of response to juvenile nuisances worldwide is evidence of society's reluctance to permit too wide a scope for the folly of youth. Therefore, we must address ourselves not only to the question, what is wrong with today's methods, but equally to the further question, what should we substitute or what alternatives should be provided?

What, then, is the purpose of the proposal? How would youth services bureaus be organized and operated? What problems are foreseeable? To my way of thinking, the best way to describe the youth services bureaus is as a device for applying middle-class strategies of intervention to lower-class deviant youth.[4] Any experienced observer of the juvenile justice system feels in his bones that it has disproportionate impact on children from lower-class homes.[5] These children may be variously labeled as pre-delinquent, school refusers, or the like; their families may be labeled as disorganized, multi-problem, chronically dependent, etc. Underneath the labels, however, the records on the children and their families display not only a series of problematic encounters with official agencies but also economic marginality and instability. I think it is important that we face up to this fact and its consequences.

But neither officials nor authoritative publications have described the youth services bureaus in these terms—as a middle-class strategy. If we turn to the Crime Commission report and to the drafts of guidelines for YSBs being formulated by certain standard-setting agencies we find the purposes stated as follows:

1. Youth services bureaus are appropriate resources for petty offenders and troubled children, because their aid and services will avoid the stigma which flows from juvenile court contact, whether it involves informal treatment or action following formal adjudication.
2. The bureaus are advocated as more effective behavior-changing mechanisms. Unlike traditional children's agencies, the youth services bureaus are expected to be oriented to the needs and communication styles of aggressive, rebellious youth. Unlike the courts and police, they will eschew an authoritative didactic stance in favor of counseling and concrete assistance.[6]
3. Youth services bureaus are also advocated for their predicted impact on local communities. It is said that they can exploit community concern in delinquency prevention and stimulate volunteer assistance from the ranks of those who feel unwelcome as aides in a bureaucratic setting. Hope is expressed that local bureaus will provoke a greater sense of responsibility for problems thrown within community boundaries and lead area residents to take a more active role in working for playgrounds, tutorial centers, hostels, homemaking classes—a few items from the endless list of resources which might appropriately be brought to bear on juvenile nuisances.

Thus, the stated purposes of the bureau are threefold: avoiding stigma, relying on more appropriate change agencies, and energizing community involvement. Yet these three are, in my judgment, very much part of a middle-class approach to juvenile problems. Middle-class parents not only work to develop the social utilities of a Good Life (e.g., Boy Scouts, community centers with youth programs, good schools with strong supporting services) but they also invest their energies individually and vigorously to head off the risk of stigma[7] attaching to their own precious children, when and if their children run afoul of authority. They are sensitive and quick to react to unlawful behavior by officials. Middle-class parents are also aided by their ability to tap alternatives to official legal intervention into the lives of their children. Many of them are so positioned as to be able to "buy a little time" at camp, to enroll a youngster in a remedial reading class, to arrange a school transfer through cajolery (sometimes even threat!), to send a child out-of-town to military academy or to Aunt Jane's for a period, or, in the case of pregnant daughters, to arrange discreetly for abortion or adoption in a distant place. But these alternatives are unavailing to children of the poor, largely because the money needed to secure them is unavailable.[8]

Having said this, let me sketch the main contours of the youth services bureaus as envisioned by the President's Crime Commission. First of all, youth services bureaus are conceived as local units, preferably lodged in neighborhood services centers which offer a wide range of material and other resources to the total population of a deprived area.[9] The services bureaus themselves, however, are intended to serve children who are the rejects of most traditional agencies. The Crime Commission's strategy is to require acceptance by the bureaus of a certain group of referrals or seekers of its aid.[10]

How should the YSBs meet this challenge? The *General Report* and the *Juvenile Delinquency Task Force Report* of the Crime Commission offer some clues but few details. Local planners are thought to know best what particulars of organization and operations are realistically attainable. Recently, however, national bodies like the National Council on Crime and Delinquency and the Children's Bureau have directed their attention to formulating guidelines. Moreover, a few states and localities have proposed establishment of the bureaus on an experimental basis. From these materials we can discover how the general idea might be implemented and what issues it presents.[11]

It is clear that the Crime Commission conceived the YSB as a resource for "both delinquent and nondelinquent youths."[12] The target population, as indicated, would be what I term "juvenile nuisances." While some would presumably come to YSB attention at the insistence of schools or parents or upon their own initiative, police and juvenile court intake staff are expected to provide the bulk of client contacts. Those troublesome youths who are referred by court and police would have "special status in that the youth services bureau would be required to accept them all. . . . A mandate for service seems necessary to insure energetic efforts to control and redirect acting-out youth and to minimize the substantial risk that this group, denied service by traditional social agencies, would inevitably be shunted to a law enforcement agency."[13]

The aim is "individually tailored work" responsive to the needs of particular boys and girls, whether their needs be tutoring, supervised work experience, temporary residence in a hostel, individual counseling, or one of countless other requirements. The YSB is seen as a neighborhood resource, not as a tool of coercive rehabilitation. "The key to the Bureau's success would be voluntary participation by the juvenile and his family in working out and following a plan for service or rehabilitation."[14]

The concept of coercion has a troubled history in juvenile justice. Too often we have confused "helping" with enforcement of conformity, the rhetoric of treatment with the oppressive reality of punishment.[15] The painful fact remains, however, that certain forms of youthful nonconformity trigger vociferous neighborhood complaints. These pressures are borne most heavily by the police, though schools do not escape their force. Diversion of juveniles from the law enforcement-juvenile court systems would appear, therefore, to require a combination of remedies: regulation of police discretion coupled with provision of genuine alternative modes of action for the police. If service is the desired alternative for punitive action —or for inaction—then someone must provide it. The YSB is intended as the resource umbrella for youths, who, in today's market, do not command a "benefit response" from traditional service or control agencies.

Thus, while a bureau is compelled to accept certain clients, no one is required to use its services. Compared to customary referral relationships, compulsion is, so to speak, on the other foot. It is to be felt by the *agency*, this is an effort to overcome the understandable tendency of administrative agencies to serve the most tractable population first. Compulsion is not to be felt by parents and their child, at least not in any sense that is meaningful from a legal standpoint. It can be argued, of course, that referral to a youth services bureau by police or juvenile court intake workers is hardly classifiable as "voluntary" in the purest sense of the word. Unquestioning acceptance of referral by clients will probably result from a realistic appraisal of a YSB appointment as the lesser of two evils.[16]

Concern about the possibility of subtle over-reaching led the Crime Commission to specify certain limitations on YSB authority. Neither parent nor child must accept a YSB referral, nor the service plan which eventuates. Parent and child each has the option to request a juvenile court referral. I submit there will be a few cases, where the social danger of the youngster's situation is clear enough but where legally admissible evidence is lacking, in which child or parent (or counsel) would see an advantage to court referral, confident that the case would be dismissed.

Even greater protection against coercion lies in the requirements that the youth services bureaus operate under a time limitation both as to the decision whether to accept the case or refer to court, and as to the length of the service period. One draft of YSB guidelines, for example, provides for case acceptance within thirty days. Only client reluctance or jurisdictional grounds would suffice for YSB rejection of cases. The draft further provides that a written agreement be worked out between the child, parents, and agency. A limit of six months as a service period, with provision for extension, is recommended. "Where care outside the home is contemplated, the agreement should also set forth terms for support if appropriate. It should also protect the child and family from any arbitrary action on the part of the youth service bureau." It adds the salient comment: "Such an agreement would help focus both parties on the resolution of the problem within a particular time limit."[17]

In keeping with the voluntary character of YSB help, coercive sanctions would not lie within its power. Insofar as possible the youngster would be protected against stigma attaching to service. (Parenthetically, I may say that one of the troubling questions is whether knowledge that a YSB had served a youngster will result in attachment of a stigma comparable to that which flows from juvenile court contact today!)

In short, the youth services bureau cannot order child or parent to do anything. Its only power is referral to court within a predetermined time period. Its only authority derives from funds and expertise, which enable it to offer benefits to the child and his family. Its knowledge of the youngster ought to be protected; the information it acquires in the course of service to youth ought to be treated as confidential.

Now, then, what should be the content of the bureau program? First of all, it must be stressed that youth services bureaus cannot contribute to juvenile nuisance-control unless they command greater resources for service to acting-out child and youth than are customarily available. It is troubling, for example, to see material—from a standard setting agency, in one case, and a state which has already funded four YSB proposals—which reads as if the magic ingredient is coordination. While the term may possess a rhetorical advantage, a not unimportant consideration, I submit that the youth service bureau concept is conceived of not only too narrowly but quite falsely, if justified as a "delivery system." In one state the chief administrator of the bureau is called a Youth Services Coordinator. This implies that services to nonconformist youth are available, that only the delivery system is creaky. But clearly the inadequacy of current services cuts deeper than this. In fact, services to this age and condition of mankind are *not* available, at least not in a volume commensurate with the needs of juvenile nuisances for help.

If we believe in diverting petty trouble-makers and endangered youngsters from the juvenile court, and if we endorse a strategy for bringing middle-class approaches to bear on the problems of low-income juveniles, then the youth services bureau should be required to allocate resources to a group of youngsters who are given short shrift by a wide range of official agencies—educational, welfare, child guidance, and even the special manpower agencies of recent date.[18] Relatively few people choose to work with the rebellious girl whose presence in the home creates a scene every evening as she walks in the door. Relatively few want to work with the youngster whose behavior in school is persistently disruptive, partly perhaps because of the school's failing to offer him a basic literacy foundation. People with talent to reach the disturbed, aggressive, rebellious youngsters are necessary—but hard to find. Indeed, at present, juvenile nuisances are handled with greater frequency (and possibly even with more sympathy) by police officials than by others. Yet we have said that law enforcement contacts should be discouraged because of the threat of punitive action and the risks of stigma inherent in police and court records. The realization that this is a difficult and unattractive group, on the whole, prompted the Crime Commission to recommend YSBs be required to accept referrals from certain sources.[19]

According to all the schemes so far proposed, YSBs must accept youngsters referred by the police.[20] Court and school referrals get high priority. YSBs are also encouraged to accept walk-ins and referrals by parents and others. YSBs could perform a valuable function for adjudicated youngsters on probation or under court supervision or home on trial by way of parole but, it has been suggested, this is not the crucial group.

It is also intended that an accountability mechanism be built in. The youth services bureau must report back on its decision to the referral source and, if the youngster is deemed unsuitable for service, it must state why. If the case is accepted, the bureau should also report its plan of action (and possibly provide regular reports thereafter to the referral agent).

The funding formula would take note of the difficulty of serving a population which is less tractable and older compared to the clients of traditional child welfare and family agencies. The Crime Commission says on this point: "Through application of differential formulas or earmarked grants, funding of the bureaus should take into account the special difficulty of serving this youth group and provide financial resources adequate to its responsibility . . . The financial and legal leverage provided under this proposal is intended to insure intervention in cases (of youth who have already demonstrated inability to conform to minimal standards of behavior)."[21]

This blueprint stimulates hard questions. What precisely ought the bureau to do? What resources will it require and where will it find them? From what administrative base will it derive authority? It is probably not surprising that the Crime Commission report is not helpful on this matter. A report of this character could scarcely be specific about patterns of administrative sponsorship and authorization, regardless of the importance of these issues. The Crime Commission clearly preferred to create a youth services bureau as an integral part of a comprehensive center providing social utilities and services to a local community. Moreover, its recommendations implicitly relate to urban areas. This attests principally to the urgency of the crime problem in cities; it does not imply that the usefulness of the concept to rural areas would be any less. But it is fair to say that the organizational issues are compounded if one strives to propound a framework to cover both urban and rural versions of YSBs. In urban areas one can readily see how to lodge such bureaus in comprehensive service centers. It is harder to picture the role and mechanics of a comprehensive center in a rural community. Is the case for a one-stop service-and-remediation center as compelling in rural as in urban areas? Similar questions are important. They undoubtedly are vexing in regions like Elkhart County, now establishing a YSB and confronting such issues as: Where shall it be located? For what population should it be defined? From what organizational auspices should it derive? What geographical area should it serve?

For myself, I confess to being content at present to contemplate a range of organizational solutions.[22] The principal criterion, to me, is what agency will try to do the job. Who demonstrates the zeal to forego established ways of doing things in an effort to respond to the juvenile nuisance problem? Once this question is resolved, it becomes obvious that the key issue is *power*. How can youth services bureau bring about tailor-made plans of service for each youngster accepted for help? Power flows chiefly from money. But the guidelines tend to emphasize the *coordinating* function. They also talk the *referral* language of social-agency bureaucratise.

Certainly, referrals will be necessary. No youth services bureau can, nor should any try to, provide all the remedial aids a youth population might require. The kinds of problems conceivably attracted to its doorstep are various. It is likely that YSBs will deal with runaways, drug abuse, school-based rebellious conduct, petty theft, and the like. These various problems call for varied response. To be an effective alternative to court referral for runaways, for example, the youth service bureau must offer parent and child, by voluntary agreement, the prospect of refuge—not jail, not detention, but perhaps a hostel—while the family argument cools off. To be of effective help to the disruptive school pupil, the youth services bureau may well have to support new forms of attack on the three R's, to take aggressive measures against the damage of earlier indifference and ineptitude. In any case, a youth services bureau would be misconceived, in my judgment, if thought of primarily as a counseling establishment. On the contrary, it ought to be a first-aid station, a place where patching-up occurs, where immediate crisis aid is freely given, where one can find a broker of benefits for youth. This is a vision of a YSB functioning as that effective advocate and protector which an enlightened parent (or an adult friend or paid custodian) so often successfully becomes for middle-class children.

Underlying the organizational issues, with their ramifications of political control, professional tone, tax basis, and the like is another issue. If YSBs are defined in response to age and a nuisance level of nonconformity, how will they fit in with broad preventive strategies which have already assumed defined character? If recreational agencies are hostile to juvenile nuisances, should the bureau set up competing enterprises? If tutorial programs in a local school are more suited to the dull and tractable than to the provocative restless boy, who should cope with him? If repeated encounters by the YSB with girl runaways reveal a weakness in local family counseling services, should the bureau mount a similar service effort?

These are relevant questions, but hard to answer in the absence of a convincing model of social services. They go to the heart of a perplexing question: Precisely what are social services? Existing pronouncements on both the form and content of services are deficient. Yet one hope stands out: that YSBs, if generously funded, can stimulate, persuade, create, freely pick among possible strategies—in order to enhance the life situations of the youths who come to them.

How might a youth services bureau piece together such different strands of aid as individual youngsters need? The vocational rehabilitation model offers an example. Ideally, the bureau should have sufficient free funds to tailor plans for individual children through purchase from agencies, public or private, or even on the open market. It should be able to buy a few hours of tutoring, make arrangements for accommodation in a private home or, under a long-term contract with a children's agency, buy group home services, arrange with the local manpower agency a special program (or a special emphasis in existing programs) to reach the less disciplined, more inflammable youngsters who strain themselves in the work-a-day world. But YSBs must be able to sweeten these bargains not merely with the rhetoric of charity or common purpose but also with the clink of cash on the countertop.

At the most optimistic, youth services bureaus represent the possibility that society will accept responsibility for offering juvenile nuisances constructive opportunities and help as *they* call for it (not solely as *we* deem it necessary). Yet we must ask, will the youth service bureaus experience the fate of juvenile courts? Looking at the current proposal from a historical perspective, is there not the danger that enthusiasts for the bureaus may experience the same disillusionment, may fall into the same trap of mistaking rhetoric for reality, as was true of our forebears who urged establishment of juvenile courts?[23] This is a live possibility. We must try to guard against it by continuing evaluation of program. Such an injunction is a call for research.

Evaluation must be built into each unit's operation, complemented by independent efforts from outside—from funding agencies and independent investigators. It would also be desirable to establish experimental types of youth service bureaus. There is much to commend one state's approach to select the four from counties presenting different problems and types of bureau proposals.

In conclusion, my judgment is that the youth services bureau concept promises a rosier future. It offers a means to closer collaboration, to reduce the level of serious delinquency (perhaps), and to give professionals the gratification of success which often escape those who work with more seriously deviant or disturbed youth or adults. It can rescue the child from unnecessary stigmatization. It can institutionalize a community's helping hand. It can do all these things, and undoubtedly even more. This is its promise. But it will be judged by its performance. That is up to all citizens to determine.

NOTES

1. The concept, "juvenile nuisance," derives from the author's work in Britain and Scandinavia during 1967–68 under a Ford Foundation Travel-Study Award.
2. See *The Challenge of Crime in a Free Society*, 82–83 (1967), hereinafter cited as *General Report*, and *Task Force Report on Juvenile Delinquency and Youth Crime*, 19–21 (1967), hereinafter cited as *JD Task Force*.
3. Norval Morris, "Random Reflections on 'The Challenge of Crime in a Free Society,'" *Law and Society Review* 2 (February, 1968): 279.
4. An important question not dealt with in this article is whether immoral conduct, not criminal per se, should be the target of organized response, either in the juvenile justice system or in an administrative system of services. For present purposes, I shall assume both the legitimacy and reality of social pressures to respond in organized fashion to amorphous deviancy among juveniles and deal only with the technical problems associated with that response.
5. However, it should be noted that not all data point unequivocally in the direction of lower-class bias.
6. "A primary function . . . would be individually tailored work with troublemaking youths. The work might include group and individual counseling, placement in foster homes, work and recreational programs, employment counseling, and special education (remedial, vocational)." *General Report*, p. 83.
7. The stigma risk is currently a fashionable argument against juvenile court process. Anthony Platt has called to my attention an article casting doubt on whether *youths themselves* experience a feeling of stigma. See communication by David B. Harris, "On Differential Stigmatization for Predelinquents," *Social Problems* 15 (Spring, 1968): 507–508. I would also not deny that benefits may be realized from formality of process, the dangers of stigmatization notwithstanding. Insofar as a stigmatized reputation among officials will influence subsequent official processing of nuisance behavior, however, I would argue that efforts to reduce the number of stigmatizing records which police, court staff, and school personnel maintain *and* share with one another are well-directed. To succeed in this endeavor requires, in my judgment, provision of concrete alternative responses to the nuisance behavior. Thus, the YSB!
8. In an unpublished paper Anthony Platt has compared the YSB proposal in spirit and probable effect to the rescue mission of the child-savers who founded the courts. (Platt, "Saving and Controlling Delinquent Youth: A Critique," Ms., April, 1969.) From this I infer he might object to the middle-class orientation of YSBs, the very virtue I am stressing. My belief, stated over-simply, is that most families, including those of lower-class status, share the desire to produce conforming behavior in their children. For poor families to accomplish this end dictates opening to the lower class much the same range of options which the middle class now enjoys. This does not necessarily mean that one who advocates this strategy would endorse the "middle-class approach" to child-rearing unqualifiedly or should relax in efforts

to improve the quality of education, recreation, nurture, and discipline for all children. Cf. Edgar Z. Friedenburg, *The Vanishing Adolescent* (1959).

9. *General Report*, p. 83. Also see Michael S. March, "The Neighborhood Center Concept," *Public Welfare* 26 (April, 1968): 97–111.

10. *JD Task Force*, p. 20.

11. I am grateful to the Children's Bureau and the National Council on Crime and Delinquency for sharing their drafts of youth services bureau guidelines with me. I am also indebted to Allen Breed, Melvin Philbrick, and Richard P. Lindsay for supplying me with information on YSB proposals in California, Colorado and Utah, respectively.

12. *JD Task Force*, p. 20.

13. Ibid.

14. Ibid.

15. See generally Anthony Platt, *The Child Savers* (1969).

16. See Joel F. Handler and Margaret K. Rosenheim, "Privacy in Welfare: Public Assistance and Juvenile Justice," *Law and Contemporary Problems* 31 (Spring, 1966): 377–412.

17. Children's Bureau, *Guides for Demonstration Projects for Youth Services Bureau* (April, 1969), p. 8. Statement in process.

18. Cf. comments on OEO and related agencies in *JD Task Force*, p. 20.

19. Given inadequate understanding of official agency patterns of response and of the etiology of delinquency, it is probably more satisfactory to describe the nuisance group by reference to sources of referrals than precise characteristics of the youngsters in question.

20. The Children's Bureau *Guides* outline several methods of limiting referrals, the assumption being that referrals will otherwise almost immediately inundate the infant YSB and inhibit its extending the thoughtful response to individual cases which is its raison d'être. See *Guides*, p. 6.

21. *JD Task Force*, p. 21.

22. There are arguments pro and con creating a new, independent agency or lodging the YSB in an existing organization. These are stated in the Children's Bureau *Guides*, pp. 3–5, and in NCCD, *The Youth Services Bureau: An Introduction with Preliminary Guidelines for a Youth Resources Agency*, pp. 10–19 (material in preparation; n. d.). It is perhaps noteworthy that in each instance the material on administration and structure is the longest single section in the draft!

23. See Platt, op cit. *supra* note 7.

chapter twenty-three
RESOLUTIONS OF THE NATIONAL COUNCIL OF JUVENILE COURT JUDGES

The following resolutions were among those passed at the regular membership meeting during the 35th annual conference of the National Council of Juvenile Court Judges, July 13, 1972, in Milwaukee, Wisconsin.

Statutory Diversion

WHEREAS, it has been suggested that by statute children who commit acts such as incorrigibility and truancy, should not be subject to the jurisdiction of the juvenile courts, and

WHEREAS, it has been further suggested that such children be diverted from the juvenile court system into social agencies and/or youth service bureaus, and

WHEREAS, the removal of certain of such children from the court system may be desirable but in other cases may deprive those children of fundamental constitutional rights, and

WHEREAS, the inherent power of the juvenile court is often an effective means of dealing with the problems of incorrigibility and truant children and their families,

NOW, THEREFORE BE IT RESOLVED, that the National Council of Juvenile Court Judges is opposed to the statutory diversion of such children from the juvenile court system.

BE IT FURTHER RESOLVED, that the National Council of Juvenile Court Judges pledges its support to the development and maintenance of community based facilities for the treatment, rehabilitation and control of such children in cases where such children and their parents are willing to utilize such facilities voluntarily.

From *Juvenile Justice* 23 (November, 1972): 44. Reprinted by permission.

Resolution unanimously adopted.

Juvenile Case Indexing

BE IT RESOLVED, that the West Publishing Company and other legal publishing organizations consider indexing juvenile cases under the heading "Juvenile Court" in order that the law might be more readily researched.

Resolution unanimously adopted.

chapter twenty-four

A HANDBOOK FOR VOLUNTEERS IN JUVENILE COURT

Vernon Fox

PART I: THE PHILOSOPHY OF VOLUNTEERS

Throughout history, private individuals and groups have provided service to people in need, whether medical, economic, or social need. The Good Samaritan symbolized this activity on an individual basis, and early religious organizations took the lead in organized group activity to help others. The first asylum for wandering children was established by a Catholic organization in 1648 after the abbeys and monasteries had served them for centuries. Pope Clement XI established the Hospice di San Michele in Rome in 1703 to serve children with social problems now called delinquency, and it still serves the same purpose. Houses of Refuge began on a private basis in Danzig in 1824 and in New York City in 1825. The first state services for delinquent children were provided in New York and Massachusetts in 1847, when state training schools were established. A Society for the Prevention of Cruelty to Children was organized in Philadelphia in 1874, a half-century after the organization of the Society for the Prevention of Cruelty to Animals. Judicial services to juveniles were established in 1899, when Judge Ben Lindsay presided over a children's court connected with the school system in Denver, Colorado, effective April 1, and the Illinois legislature enabled the first juvenile court as it is now known to be established in Chicago in Cook County effective July 1, 1899. In the meantime, juveniles were being served by private citizens and organizations and informally in the existing adult courts.

Today, the activity of private citizens and organizations fills many gaps left by governmental services. The United Fund movement has organized

From *Juvenile Justice* 23 (February, 1973): 5–31. Reprinted by permission.

many charities. There are many other charities outside the United Fund movement, such as the Easter Seal Drive, the March of Dimes, the Heart Fund, and many others. Many private schools for delinquent children are supported by private donations, such as Father Flanagan's Boys' School in Nebraska, Starr Commonwealth for Boys in Michigan, Berkshire Farms in New York, and many others. The tradition of giving funds, goods, and services has been basic not only to Americans and Englishmen, but in all societies.

The volunteer is as old as society itself. The recent focus on juvenile courts by volunteers is a reflection of governmental authority beginning to share responsibility with the community after relaxing its traditional defensiveness and apprehension concerning "outsiders" over whom the judge has no control. The advantages of extended service and wider knowledge of the court's functions, problems, and needs have outweighed the "risks" involved. Consequently, the number of volunteer programs in juvenile courts has grown in America from three to four in 1961 to 2,000 in 1972. The organization, objectives, and concerns of the PTA make that group a natural for volunteer services to the juvenile court.

Different Approaches

There is a wide variety of approaches, agencies, and programs in the United States aimed at assisting juveniles. Some are fairly strong and adequate, while others fail to meet the minimum standards of humane treatment.[1] In 1965, for example, there were 7,706 persons employed in community-based juvenile court, while the estimated need was 15,800 persons[2] to handle an average daily juvenile population in the community of 285,431.[3] In 1968 there were approximately 900,000 cases of delinquency involving about 774,000 children.[4] In addition, there were 554,000 traffic cases[5] and 141,000 dependency and neglect cases referred to juvenile court.[6] In addition, more than 500,000 runaways and other missing children are reported each year.[7]

It is obvious that even the number of personnel needed as estimated by the President's Commission on Law Enforcement and Administration of Justice is very minimal and does not approach a capacity for handling the problem. In fact, that estimated number would only handle the more efficient processing of cases administratively through the judicial system in terms of writing pre-hearing social histories, handling complaints, and other routine matters. It would still not permit adequate time for counseling or casework with children in trouble and their families. The average caseload for a worker in a child guidance clinic is twelve to fifteen children with problems—and these children have not run afoul of the legal authority of society.

The estimated needs call for only one worker for every 150 children who come to the attention of the juvenile court, based on simple computations; this does not include the large number of children who cause problems in school and to police and other law enforcement agencies who are not referred to the juvenile court. Consequently, even the estimated need appears to be unrealistically conservative. While it appears to be paradoxical that a serious manpower shortage accompanies social concerns about "over-populations" and "superfluous people," the shortage is really in the number of people committed to solving the problems of children in trouble. The shortage is in the number of people who "care."

Solving the Problem

Volunteers and private groups have always been a major factor in working with social problems, including juveniles. Volunteers and lay visitors were prominent in England and America in jails, prisons, and juvenile work. It was John Augustus, the shoemaker and volunteer, who established probation as early as 1843. It was the Quakers who organized in 1787 and established the first penitentiary in Philadelphia in 1790.

Volunteers have come from many sectors of society. Volunteers in the juvenile court have come from: (1) friends and acquaintances of staff or volunteers, (2) women, (3) middle class people, (4) churches and religious groups, (5) service organizations and volunteer bureaus, (6) well-educated people, and (7) "people-contacts" occupations and professions, such as attorneys, teachers, insurance men, personnel and sales people, and others who contact the public.[8] Volunteers in a misdemeanor program have been recruited from the following sources:[9]

Friends and relatives of volunteers 27%
Newspapers, magazines, or pamphlets 23%
Clubs, business groups, and organizations,
    including churches 22%
The organization needing the volunteer (The courts) 28%

The three primary reasons for volunteering have been:[10]

Personal humanitarian goals 78%
Personal interest in corrections 36%
Personal sense of community responsibility 27%

A president of the National Congress of Parents and Teachers has indicated that the PTA should be an excellent source of volunteers for the courts, because of the children they serve. Mrs. Lillie Herndon says:

> For PTAs to participate in the Volunteers in the Court Program is an opportunity to administer to children and youth who need rehabilitation, compensatory services, and special guidance in setting

values. It gives to many PTA members the privilege of working on a one-to-one basis with children and youth and the parents, or if one does not feel suited to this goal there are so many other services that can be rendered. Even if financial resources of a PTA are limited, this program is ideally suited to our organization because of the wealth of human resources.

I believe there are professional and lay members of the PTA who will gladly give their valuable time to this program, when it is adequately interpreted to them and they are made aware of the needs of the children and youth in their own community. A long-established role of the PTA is to make the needs of the community known to its membership and to the general public. Volunteers in the Courts offers PTA a real challenge for action where it counts the most—in touching the life of a child and helping nurture him into an able responsibly acting adult.[11]

Coordinated Effort

The development of a normal personality and a well-socialized personality is a long process.[12] The most important social units in the development of any personality are: (1) the family; (2) the gang or peer group; (3) the school, in a slight way; and (4) the church, in an almost negligible way. The influence of the church is dependent upon the family.

The family is the most important factor, the gang or peer group being a close second on the average, with the school having a tendency toward influence but not being significant. In some families, the family function is much more important than any other factor, while the gang or peer group becomes more important than the family in other settings. The family is most important by a close margin on the average, but family breakdown, neglect, or default results in the gang or peer group being more supportive, with delinquency, need for supervision, or dependency being most frequent results.

When the child is old enough and ego is strong enough to withstand conflict, he goes to school. At school, he tests the values in the defense or adaptive mechanisms he has learned, changes some, modifies some, tends to discard others, and learns to get along. He learns about sex roles and other social definitions.

As the child approaches puberty, the father becomes more and more important. In Western civilization and in most societies, the father is the cultural symbol of authority. It is the father's function to integrate the child and his value system into the power structure of the community. Whether he knows it or not, the father provides the symbol of masculinity as defined in this culture.

The mother, then, is most important during the preschool period, while the father is most important around puberty. Both are important, of course, to develop a normal personality. The emotional snags occur when either the mother function and/or the father function is not adequately carried out within the family. Problems of various types occur as a result.

The father is most important in the field of delinquency. Comparisons of delinquents and nondelinquents on the basis of the presence or absence of the mother show differences, but they are not statistically significant. Comparisons of delinquents and nondelinquents on the basis of the presence or absence of the father, however, have been shown to be significant.[13]

While there is no such thing as a criminal or delinquent personality, there are maladjusted personalities who find conformity more difficult than others. Some of the types of maladjustment originate in the family patterns. The family frequently determines the direction of maladjustment.[14]

Many aggressive delinquents come from homes in which they have been always rejected. Many socialized delinquents, who are those who never get into trouble alone but are sufficiently dependent that they go wherever the gang goes in order to be accepted, come from homes in which they were originally loved and given attention but, subsequently, were replaced by other parental interests such as a new baby, divorce, or other significant event. Some self-indulgent offenders come from over-protective families.

The social environment in which the child grows also influences the direction of personality development. This social environment includes the gang, the peer group, the school, the church, recreation, and other social and cultural factors. In a small town or in a rural area, where everybody knows everybody else, the expected social norms are relatively simple and clear. Right and wrong are well defined. A child can grow in this rural setting with full confidence in the social expectations and can internalize society's value system easily and almost automatically. When his emotional maturity, ego-strength, his "social gyroscope" is stabilized, he can venture forth in early adulthood with confidence and assurance. On the other hand, a person raised in the urban ghetto or the inner city is immersed in a confusion of value systems that tend to result in a "survival-of-the-fittest" life style. He learns to deal with people "at arm's length" and may see a man coming down the street either as a threat or as an opportunity. Consequently, the social environment influences personality development. As mentioned previously, the social environment through the gang or peer group generally has greater influence than an ineffective family.

Delinquency is not an isolated phenomenon. It emerges as a symptom of pathology in society and it becomes a concern of the total community.

Like any other symptom, the cause of the pathology does not go away by treating the symptom alone. Rather, the need is for broad and coordinated community effort.

PART II: WHAT VOLUNTEERS CAN DO

Volunteers can recapitulate the family functions that have been missed. A substitute father is most important for the growing child. A substitute mother can help provide the emotional concern and reinforce accepted values. Growing personalities deprived of significant adults frequently accept substitutes, such as the high school football coach, the shop teacher, or another person who represents the cultural definition of masculinity or, in the case of women, femininity. One of the primary functions of a volunteer is to provide the growing child with a meaningful relationship with an adult on whom he can depend. So few children in trouble have had that experience.

For some children in trouble, the volunteer can be more effective than a professional in that the child may see the professional as "copping out" or "selling out" to the establishment, since that is where his livelihood is. A volunteer does not have that materialistic vested interest in the establishment, at least not in the juvenile court. His interest is in the intrinsic reward that comes from helping people. This has an impact on many juveniles who have grown cynical and resentful about the power structure.

Volunteers can function in many areas and can provide many services. Some coordinators of volunteers have indicated that they could use in some way anybody who volunteered. If a potential volunteer has personality or other deficiencies that might render him ineffective with children in trouble, then he can be used in clerical work and other services where he does not come into contact with the young people. Others do not use those persons who might be damaging or ineffective for anything, but eliminate them completely. The volunteers who come into contact with children in trouble need to be screened, trained, and supervised, although supervising a volunteer can be delicate and should probably be in the form of assistance or counseling the volunteer in his working with children in trouble.

There is considerable variance in opinion as to how volunteers can successfully be used in the juvenile court. There is also considerable variation in opinion as to whether all persons can be used at something, or whether the selection of volunteers must be limited only to those people who can work with other people. During the four meetings of the Judicial Concern for Children in Trouble project in Boston, Jackson, San Francisco, and Chicago, several functions of volunteers were mentioned. Not all persons agreed with all the suggested functions. In order to obtain some idea as to the realistic spread of opinion as to what volunteers can do in the juvenile court, letters were mailed to 107 persons experienced in volunteer work to determine how experienced people viewed this question. All fifty states and Puerto Rico were represented, with established volunteer programs receiving inquiries. While there were only thirty-two responses, they were predominantly from established volunteer programs, with no responses coming from states without programs. Consequently, the evaluations of what volunteers can do in the juvenile court appear to be reasonably valid and reliable.

The single contribution agreed upon by all programs was the relationship between the young person in trouble and an adequate adult. Consequently, the most important function of the volunteer has to be:

1. Providing a child in trouble with a meaningful one-to-one relationship with an adult he can trust.
2. Private tutoring in school subjects to help the child learn academic and vocational skills away from the school setting, thereby allowing him to keep up in subjects he might be failing and to avoid school phobia that leads to dropping out of school.
3. Providing experience at the constructive use of leisure time; taking the child to ball games, fishing trips, and other acceptable recreational pursuits to replace his habitual leisure-time pursuits that seem to bring him close to trouble.
4. Providing the child an image of normalcy in society in a meaningful way, including participation in socially accepted groups, such as organized athletic and other competition in leagues or with other long-term experiences, Boy Scouts, and similar experiences with "establishment" groups that can be gratifying to him.
5. Obtaining volunteers from indigenous groups where the child in trouble lives can be of assistance in counseling delinquents, drug users, bitter children from minority groups, or any other indigenous group. Crisis rap sessions, bad trip counseling, and similar activities can help avoid more serious crises.
6. Implementing various programs in detention homes and other facilities for children in trouble.
7. Retired professionals can assist other working professionals and can work alone in volunteer services. These retired professionals in social work, psychology, psychiatry, dentistry, medicine, law, and other professions can work as general volunteers, or, probably better, serve the court or volunteer program in their specialties in service to the children and/or in training the volunteers.

8. Volunteers can maintain constructive liaison with the newspapers, radio, television, and other news media to interpret the available services, needs, problems, and objectives of the court to the public and to the political leadership.

There were other functions generally thought to be governmental services that could be rendered by volunteers, but which were questioned by some people responsible for volunteer programs in the juvenile court. Some wanted functions eliminated that others called essential. Functions accepted by most people were:

9. Responding constructively to the child's negative questions as to "What's your angle? What are you getting out of this? Getting your kicks?" To promote socially accepted approaches to constructive association, communication, and counseling without monetary reward as a normal form of social interaction. Help the child view the volunteer as not on the payroll of the establishment, but with wholesome and sincere concern for the child in trouble.
10. Accepting the child in the family so he can get a "new look" at men, women, and others in a normal family relationship. This keeps him from stereotyping all people in the image of his own father, mother, or other persons who might not fit society's role definitions or what the normal expectations are.
11. Provide the child with an improved self-concept by teaching him to be competent in some field, such as chess or auto mechanics, or by giving him a new look at authority or an adult that is supportive and friendly.
12. Provide leadership for parent group sessions. This was considered to be a "must" by some.
13. Provide leadership for group sessions for the children in trouble.
14. Help reduce the paranoid, picked-on feeling that emerges in some minority racial and ethnic groups. Social distance like this can be reduced or accepted by identification with pride, to reduce or counteract the negative connotations associated with social distance.
15. Canvas the job market and serve as an employment coordinator. Getting jobs for children in trouble. This was considered to be a "must" by some.
16. Provide free charm school lessons for girls to learn the social graces and improve self-concept. Provide free beauty parlor and hairdo services.
17. Interpreting needs and problems to the public and to political leaders who can help provide resources for the court. This was

considered to be classified information by some who thought volunteers should not be involved in this function.

Some of the functions suggested for volunteers in the four regional meetings, but which were rejected by two or three respondents as inappropriate for volunteers although they had enough support to warrant inclusion in the listing of functions as possible, depending upon local opinion and practice, were as follows:

18. Counseling after a trusting relationship has been developed, in order to enhance insight in the child.
19. Serve as a confidant who will not "squeal" or "rat" on the child in trouble, so he can develop the capacity to relate to others through trust, which provides the child with an alternative from the survival-of-the-fittest milieu to which he has become accustomed.
20. Front for the child in trouble as an advocate in court, school, and elsewhere, to provide the child with a new look at authority that is supporting and accepting, rather than aggressive and hostile.
21. Promote acceptance of his father by the child, since the father-function is most important in delinquency situations that involve conflict with authority. Further, the volunteer may have become a threat to the father, a situation that must be made easier by bringing the father into a meaningful and acceptable relationship in some way.
22. Obtaining volunteer professional services, such as those involving an optometrist, dentist, physician, psychiatrist, psychologist, social worker, nurse, or other professional person. While three respondents said that this should be outside the function of the volunteer, three also wrote special comments that it was most important.
23. Expose the child in trouble to establishment institutions in an accepting way, such as museums, art galleries, the church, and other places where he will make cultural contacts in an accepting manner. There is considerable neglect of this exposure to many children in trouble, sometimes leading to outright hostility toward agencies and institutions representing "the establishment."
24. Provide secretarial, receptionist, and clerical assistance in the office of the juvenile court, detention home, and other agencies concerned with children in trouble.
25. Provide constructive means of relieving tensions, such as boxing, swimming, debating, and other means of constructive competition.

26. Hold formal classes in volunteer education, whether academic, vocational, self-improvement, motivational, social problems, or other classes.
27. Assist the child in emotional maturation so he can learn to postpone immediate gratification for future reward.
28. Writing grant requests and participating in fund drives.

Realistically, a volunteer can do many jobs in addition to these mentioned at the conferences and accepted, some with reservations, by the respondents to the above inquiry designed to identify acceptable roles for volunteers. One recent excellent publication lists no less than 192 separate jobs that have been assigned to volunteers.[15]

The following is a list of volunteer services provided at the Lane County, Oregon, Juvenile Department:[16]

1. Recreation and instruction (detention): grooming, woodworking, sewing, cooking and baking, arts and crafts, sports and games.
2. Special activities and entertainment (detention): variety shows and musical entertainment, dance and party arrangement, programs for holidays and special occasions.
3. Education (detention): Skipworth Library Board, field placements from the University of Oregon, special interest speakers.
4. Religious (detention): voluntary religious services through the "Minister of the Month" (provided by the local ministerial association).
5. Annual projects: Christmas Project and Open House.
6. Counseling assistance: transportation, clothing, dental aid, special resources (furniture, groceries, temporary housing, etc.), case aides, big brothers, caseload assistants.
7. Clerical assistance: typing, filing, phone, gathering statistics, running errands.
8. Administrative assistance (volunteer program): recruiting, screening, training, evaluating, assigning, supervising public relations, Speaker's Bureau, coordination and consultation with other agencies and their volunteer services.
9. Miscellaneous assistance (general community involvement): donations of gifts, money, or equipment.
10. Advisory (Juvenile Department Advisory Council): a lay advisory council established by law to study and make recommendations
    a. for juvenile court operation,
    b. for community programs and services to prevent and correct juvenile delinquency, and
    c. to stimulate community interest in the problems of youth.

It becomes obvious that volunteers in the juvenile court can be used in many ways. Whether the use of the volunteer is restricted to a one-to-one relationship with the child or he does other things is dependent upon local conditions and opinions of the court. In however way he is used, the volunteer can expand and improve the function and effectiveness of the court by working with children in trouble, or, in some cases, working for the court without contacting children. The experiences and views of many capable and competent juvenile court judges, court administrators, and volunteer coordinators cover a broad spectrum that leaves room for a variety of contributions by volunteers in the juvenile court.

Philosophy of Volunteers

Participation by volunteers from the community in juvenile counseling and probation services on a one-to-one basis has significantly increased socialization and decreased repeating of delinquent behavior, according to the faculty and participants in these four conferences on Judicial Concern for Children in Trouble. Reduced delinquency was associated with reduced hostility and an increased anxiety or concern, sometimes called social motivation, for an identification in society. Frequent contacts by the volunteer with his caseload of one young person can produce the interpersonal confrontations, identity crises, and their socially acceptable resolutions, so that more problems can be worked out through interpersonal interaction and less through acting-out behavior that gets the child in trouble.

Involvement is basic to the volunteer program. This involvement brings the schools, law enforcement agencies, and the citizenry together to help solve the common problem of children in trouble. This involvement results in positive relationships with all sectors of the community. This better understanding can be the base for coordinating community effort to help children and control delinquency.

Nonauthoritarian approaches by volunteers help provide young persons with a new look at authority. The experience of most children in trouble with authority has been with aggressive, powerful, and sometimes abusive authority. Working with the young person through nonauthoritative relationships or, at least, somewhat voluntary authority, might provide him with a new perspective of the entire community power structure. It may help him eventually to accept the establishment.

Volunteers can place an emphasis on local and neighborhood problems. A volunteer program must be flexible, rather than trying to operate under rigid criteria. The interjection of humanitarian values and judgment into the volunteer-child relationship tends to be more functional than does the "by the manual" approach when working with young people. A caseload of one permits individual attention and an individual relationship. The informal and flexible approach in volunteer programs on a one-to-one basis is essential for meaningful relationships with children in trouble.

Implementing Programs

Translating the philosophy of and need for volunteer programs into social action demands coordinated effort. Personalities are more important than any other factor in implementing volunteer programs. Keeping the judge and court personnel informed is a basic essential in the process. Keeping the police, schools, civic groups, church groups, and the general public informed is also essential. Effective communication is basic to the implementation of any social program, particularly one aimed toward assisting children in trouble, an objective that involves probably more people than any other single social objective.

Judge Eugene A. Moore of Pontiac, Michigan, wrote to Judge G. Bowdon Hunt of Bartow, Florida, as follows:

> There is no "right way" to set up a volunteer program. Some programs are court sponsored. Some are non-court sponsored. Some volunteers serve as probation officers. Others serve as aides to probation officers. The local needs of your own community must be assessed by you and the court, and what program develops will depend largely on these needs. While there is a great deal of material printed and made available that can be of assistance to you, you and your neighbors are best able to evaluate your community and determine what its needs are. No one can dictate to you how to develop a program to meet these needs.

Dr. Jackson C. Dillon, Los Angeles psychiatrist, suggested the following steps in the establishment of a juvenile court volunteer program:

> Step 1: Obtain informed consent and sanction from judges and county probation officer.
>
> Influential volunteers to approach the court with proposal for a volunteer program.
>
> Provide orientation and interpretive experience for the responsible officials; i.e., visit to a successful, ongoing program, participation at a regional training institute, consultation with national leaders, or etc.
>
> Step 2: Recruit cadre of interested volunteers who will initiate pilot program.
>
> Step 3: Interpret new program to probation department staff and other agencies; involve them in training and consultation roles for volunteers to establish proximity, reduce stereotypical fantasies of the volunteer, and gradually develop new "super professional role" for the professional staff.

Step 4: Develop a full-time coordinator for the project, either volunteer or staff member, who will assume an administrative-planning role on equal status with other leaders in the organization (Ira Schwartz). The coordinator will recruit, train, advocate for, and create appropriate roles for volunteers. Also, he will participate in organization planning and development to create a new volunteer component for each program unit. Involved together from the outset, volunteer and professional can develop a creative partnership. Special consideration should be given the "new volunteer" because his needs are different from the professional and from the traditional volunteer.

Step 5: Seek funding for volunteer coordinator and staff. (Possible sources: LEAA grant, private foundations, public solicitation, etc.)

Step 6: Expand volunteer services: Initial efforts should be directed to one-to-one relationships with selected probationers, donated services of professionals, recreational activities, etc. After program is accepted, other more innovative services can be considered. Goal should be to involve as many citizen participants as possible (even for minimal assignments) to develop an informed, involved community. Prevention programs utilizing chiefly volunteers should be stressed.

Many faculty members at the conferences said repeatedly to "start small," particularly Judge Keith Leenhouts and Judge William Sylvester White. After a small cadre is trained and established in a program small enough to be controlled and supervised, then the additional volunteers can be assimilated gradually by the original nucleus of workers. In any case, it appears to be risky to expand prematurely. A small beginning with gradual expansion appears to work best.

Support of Judges

Support by the judge of the juvenile court and his staff, particularly his chief probation officer or chief counselor, is a prerequisite for successful operation of a volunteer program. In many cases, the judge or his chief probation officer takes the leadership in establishing the volunteer program. In many other instances, however, the suggestion has to come from interested sources outside the court, such as the PTA or other groups interested in children. In any case, a volunteer program cannot move without the support of the juvenile court judge and his staff.

Many judges, chief probation officers, and probation staff are apprehensive about volunteers in the juvenile court. Without real authority and control over the volunteer, there are certain political risks involved as far as the judge is concerned, and there are professional risks in terms of possible damage to young people in trouble or a form of sibling rivalry as far as the chief probation officer and his staff are concerned. These have to be allayed before a volunteer program can succeed. One of the best ways is to have a juvenile court judge already convinced of the value of volunteers talk positively about them to the judge who is not yet convinced. Another way is to start the program on an experimental basis and let the results convince the judge and the staff. Sometimes the judge is convinced sufficiently by other judges and programs that he will initiate the program, himself. Judge James Gulotta of New Orleans says that judges are really "crying for help" but are circumspect. Volunteer programs need to develop trust as far as judges are concerned.

When the judge or his staff initiates the volunteer program, it is important to make certain that the program functions in accordance with the desires of the judge. As experience is gained, many judges have expanded their concepts of the functions of the volunteers. As a judge gains confidence and trust in the volunteer program, he will expand its function. On the other hand, if a judge becomes disillusioned by a volunteer program that is either ineffective or does not function according to his desires, then the volunteer program can be in trouble. Close communication with the judge and his staff is essential. No judge likes to be surprised and have to explain something about which he was unaware to a significant member of the community.

When the volunteer program is initiated by the PTA or other groups outside the juvenile court, it is important to gain the support of the judge and his staff, particularly the chief probation officer or chief counselor, before moving ahead with the program. The judge must be kept informed and involved, if possible, while the chief probation officer or counselor must similarly be involved. How this is to be accomplished may vary from court to court. For example, the judge and his chief probation officer in a full-time juvenile court can be involved simultaneously, or the judge can be approached first. In many part-time juvenile courts, or where a probate or county judge or other part-time arrangement exists where the judge may devote only a fraction of his time to juvenile cases, it is important that his chief probation officer or counselor who works full-time on juvenile cases be contacted initially along with the judge. Where there is neither a full-time judge nor a full-time probation officer or counselor, then the part-time judge must be contacted for the purposes of initiating court staff on a volunteer basis. Several courts in rural areas in various parts of the country function on this basis. In any case, the person primarily responsible and who has the authority in juvenile cases must be contacted and his support obtained before a volunteer program can function adequately. Active support is important, as compared with passive permission or grudging tolerance.

Resistance and apprehension on the part of the juvenile court judge and his chief probation officer or counselor generally emerges from two sources. First, the activity of the volunteer on the job may be to the detriment of the court by failure to perform effectively or, on the other hand, good performance may be threatening to the staff. There may be a threat that the volunteer is "taking over" the function of the probation officer or counselor, or that the volunteer may "show up" unfavorably the chief probation officer or counselor by doing a better job than he in some areas. Second, neither the judge nor his chief probation officer or counselor has any real control over the activities, gossip, or "news releases" of the volunteers. The volunteer is not an "officer of the court" and any relationship between the volunteer and the court is, in fact, strictly voluntary.

Volunteer programs do, in fact, alter the role of the probation officer. They also increase his effectiveness. Without a volunteer program, one person tries to be all things to all juveniles. A volunteer program permits an amplification of services, a diversification of services, more humanization of services because of the volunteers' one-to-one caseloads, enhanced support in the community, and an antidote to the increased and pervasive impersonalization to bolster the self-esteem of the child, the volunteer, and the court staff.[17] The probation officer with a volunteer program has greater power and effectiveness in his work. He has more resources to tap and more people to help him do his job effectively. With this increased power, of course, comes increased responsibility. While this threatens some probation officers, the majority of them are already committed to the field of juvenile correction and view the volunteer program as a significant breakthrough.

Interpreting the services of the volunteer program and its potential to the judge and the chief probation officer is basic to acceptance and support. This service and potential service can be shown as an extension of the protectiveness of the court. It can also be interpreted constructively as a source of citizen participation in which information about the problems, needs and services of the court can be disseminated throughout the community.

The advantages and disadvantages of volunteer programs have been well documented in the literature.[18] Some of the advantages have been listed as follows:

1. Volunteers increase the amount of total court contacts with court clients, thereby giving more information, more service, and maintaining direct contact with children.

2. The child in trouble can have frequent contacts in a meaningful way with a person he considers to be influential, the volunteer being a father figure or mother figure with a caseload of one, making it an exclusive relationship for the child.
3. The economic advantage is that a court without adequate funds to hire a staff can profit immensely from the use of volunteers.
4. A volunteer program takes some of the probation load of the regular staff.
5. Volunteer programs facilitate community involvement and help to educate the public regarding the objectives, problems, and needs of the juvenile court.
6. Volunteer contacts with probationers are less threatening than contact with paid court staff, and children will sometimes respond better to persons not "paid off" by the court.
7. Volunteers provide the court with additional sources of information and a different viewpoint with regard to the juvenile.
8. The use of college-age volunteers or even younger volunteers indigenous to the neighborhood lessens the age differential between the child and his volunteer court contact, and a more relaxed atmosphere can produce better communication.
9. The court may act as a training ground and selective recruiting agency for people who may desire to enter the correctional field as a career.

Some of the disadvantages of volunteer programs have been listed as follows:

1. A volunteer program does cost money or its equivalent in staff time, because of training programs and the supervision needed that must be done by the court staff.
2. In cases of ineffective screening, a volunteer may create a negative image for the court and could have a negative influence on the child.
3. By involving an additional person with the child in trouble, extra communication problems are added in which the child may "play one staff member against the other" with the volunteer "in the middle," by clever manipulation.
4. Some staff people tend to become administrators of volunteer programs, rather than juvenile court counselors or probation officers, and so undergo a change in role as a direct result of the volunteer program.

Most judges consider that the advantages can outweigh the disadvantages, however, and regard many of the disadvantages listed as being controllable.

Most of the experts in the field of volunteer work in juvenile court think that agencies that serve youth should include volunteer workers because: (1) they help to maintain a friendly climate, (2) the volunteers themselves learn from the experience and become better citizens, (3) they help in propagating public understanding for the work of the agency, (4) they furnish greatly needed personnel, (5) they make it possible for the agency to expand its services without increasing its budget. Ways in which volunteers can assist in agency functions are listed and include such services as providing youth with models to emulate and supplementing agency functions that may not require specialized competence.[19]

The judge is always the boss. Where any differences occur between the person coordinating the volunteer program and the judge or his chief probation officer, discussions may occur to clarify the situation, but the judge remains the boss. Consistency in recognizing this will contribute immeasurably to the acceptance and active support of the volunteer program by the judge and his chief probation officer.

Judge Lindsay Arthur of Minneapolis, current president of the National Council of Juvenile Court judges, wrote in a letter to Judge G. Bowdon Hunt of Bartow, Florida, and past president of the council, the following concerning the need for volunteers in the juvenile court:

> There is so much to do for children in trouble, so much for both court personnel and for volunteers: We need to provide help without the involvement and cost and stigma of court proceedings; we need to see and be seen by children in trouble and to talk to them when they have been confined while awaiting court, or while locating mothers and friends and advocates; we need to explain what is happening and what will be happening so as to remove the fear of the unknown; we need to assure some children that they will be protected, and to assure others that the public will be protected; we need to substitute for missing fathers, inadequate mothers, rejecting and uncontrolling parents. Volunteers can do all of these.

PART III: RECRUITMENT AND ASSIGNMENT OF VOLUNTEERS

Recruiting volunteers can be accomplished in several ways. Volunteers generally come from civic organizations, church groups, persons already in "people-contact" occupations, retirees, and friends of volunteers. Presentations before organized civic and church groups, presentations and commercials in the newspapers, on the radio, and on television have elicited volunteers. Notices or advertisements in the news media, journals, civic club newsletters, and church bulletins have brought volunteers.

An advisory committee has been established in some places as a link to the community. These committees can help recruit volunteers. In addition, they serve as a contact source with the community for a variety of purposes, including the expression of community desires and values, generating employment and other service resources, and ameliorating potential conflict between the volunteer program and the court. Of considerable importance is the enhancing of understanding, coordination of effort, and reduction of conflict between the court and other agencies interested in children, such as the schools, the welfare department, and police.

It has been observed that the rewards of volunteer work can be very great, but it takes a dedicated, stable person who is conscientious and willing to become involved in helping children in trouble, many of whom have experienced many years of emotional trauma.[20]

There is wide difference of opinion about the selection and assignment of volunteers in the juvenile court. There is agreement that the volunteers who will have direct contact with children should be carefully selected and trained. The differences of opinion relate to the question as to whether all people who volunteer can be used somewhere in the program other than in direct contact with children. The resolution of this issue has been accomplished in different ways in many juvenile court volunteer programs in America.

There is no doubt that those persons with personal and other difficulties that might damage children more than help them have to be eliminated from contact relationships with the children. Some of these persons may be sadistic and power-oriented people who want to exhibit their superiority over others. Some volunteer organizations have found sexual deviates of various types making application to contact children. Other people "feed off" people, particularly less adequate people, to maintain themselves emotionally in neurotic-interaction life style. All these people and others may do more damage to children in trouble than good. Consequently, the selection of assignments for volunteers, if they are to be used in the program, must include identifying those persons who can and cannot constructively work with children.

Some experts in the field of volunteer work in juvenile courts have indicated that they could use somewhere anybody who volunteered. Those persons who cannot work with children can be used constructively elsewhere. For example, there is much clerical work, including typing, filing, serving as receptionist, or answering the telephone that has to be done around the juvenile court. A volunteer can serve as a coordinator of employment, canvassing the community for jobs and referring available jobs to the chief probation officer or other designated persons. Writing news releases, writing requests for grants from governmental agencies and private foundations, keeping books, writing monthly or other periodic reports, and many other functions need to be done in a juvenile court for a volunteer program, without having contact with children. Consequently, volunteers who cannot work with children can be used in other areas.

Separating persons who can work with children and those who cannot takes some professional assistance. Consequently, a volunteer psychiatrist, psychologist, or social worker might well be available to help make the judgment. Too frequently, however, the judgment is made after an unfortunate experience in which a child was damaged. Usually, the volunteer has reached an age at which his pattern of past experiences can be assessed. In any case, it is important to separate those persons who can work with children in order to implement a successful volunteer program.

Why People Volunteer

People volunteer because they care. They are emotionally committed to somebody or something. Anthropologists and biologists indicate that the species *homo sapiens* is naturally a herding or gregarious group. This is why early man traveled in tribes, rather than alone. Man has a basic need to invest emotionally in other people. This explains the monogamous marriage vows of most societies, the permanence of relationships, and the predictability of credit ratings. Man does base his life style on trust, faith, and confidence in his fellow man. This is called socialization. Persons who do not so live are called anti-social. This basic need to invest emotionally in others has given rise to the historical legends about the Good Samaritan; the virtues of faith, hope, and charity; the Eternal Verities of the True, the Good, and the Beautiful; and the belief that man is, indeed, his brother's keeper.

The specific motives for volunteering, or the specific ways in which this basic need to invest emotionally in others is manifest, may vary quite widely. Some may have a genuine interest in the welfare of other people, while others want to use other people for their own emotional needs. The need for man's concern for others is equally strong in either case, but is not equally beneficial to his fellow man. This is why screening of volunteers is so important where children in trouble are concerned. The separation has to be made as to whether the motivation for volunteering is conducive to a constructive and helpful one-to-one relationship between the volunteer and the child, or whether the volunteer will use the child for his own emotional needs. After that separation is determined, there is still a twilight zone where a volunteer can be helpful to a child with other than the exactly correct motivation or can be damaging to the child with the right motivation.

The best volunteer is motivated by sincere humanitarian interests. Some of the best volunteers have indicated that their reward is that they could do more for somebody than anybody else could, thereby combining humanitarian and competitive motivations. Some of these people have had social problems in their own backgrounds or in those of their families, which give greater meaning and understanding to them concerning the problems of others. Their humanitarian motivations are compensatory or reactive, which makes them work harder with others in whom they have interest.

Personal interest in the field of corrections, education, or the helping professions is also a constructive motivation. Many high school and college students interested in psychology, education, social work, or other forms of helping people have used volunteer service as a means of acquiring experience and sophistication in working with people. Others have been identified with a hobby or special interest, such as weight-lifting, music, chess, or some other activity, and enjoy passing on their interests to children in trouble by teaching and association. Many volunteers become "missionaries" for various reasons.

People need to be needed. Consequently, a middle-class housewife whose children have grown and who has become bored with club work may gain satisfaction from working as a volunteer with a child in trouble. Many retired persons are similarly motivated.

Many businessmen who begin to question the merits of their philosophical focus on the dollar and material wealth have frequently used volunteer service, if only through philanthropic activity or civic club projects, as a way of becoming involved in the resolution of social problems. Many of these businessmen have volunteered in juvenile court and other programs as a way of enhancing the meaning of life for them.

On the other hand, some motivations are not conducive to helping children in trouble. Most obvious are homosexuals and people who need to demonstrate superiority and control over somebody else. Cold and controlling people who attempt to dominate social situations are damaging to growing personalities. Sadistic, masochistic, and otherwise disturbed people who want to use people to meet their own emotional needs must be carefully screened out of volunteer programs where they will be in direct contact with children in trouble.

In summary, volunteers work to fill emotional needs that include humanitarian motives, to fill unproductive time spans, to promote causes or activities, and to gain experience in working with people. It is for this reason that so many potential volunteers are available that an active and energetic program leader can obtain all the help he can supervise or handle. Leaders who have difficulty in finding volunteers simply have not tapped the available resources.

Training Volunteers

All volunteers need training. There have been many approaches and the training depends in part on the personnel available for the purpose. In general, approximately 50 percent of the training period should be devoted to general education, such as psychology, social problems, communications, report writing, and public speaking.[21] Approximately 25 percent should be devoted toward supportive social sciences, such as social welfare, family, abnormal psychology, black culture in America, the culture of poverty, and juvenile delinquency. Approximately 25 percent should be devoted to social service technical subjects, such as interviewing skills, group leadership skills, and social change skills. In addition, there should be some field experience outside the training classroom with an experienced volunteer.

There are generally three approaches inherent in any position in the criminal justice system, including the volunteer in the juvenile court. All jobs in this field have investigative, counseling, and enforcement components. Without authority, of course, the volunteer approaches these tasks in a subtle and low-key manner, although they are background phases of working with children in trouble. Some of the basic characteristics and competencies in this field that must be considered in training programs are:[22]

1. Ability to understand and withstand provocative behavior without becoming punitive.
2. Development of objectivity in accepting relationships with all clients in a nonjudgmental manner, without either punitive or sentimental emotional involvement.
3. Competence to accept an inmate or person on the caseload without personal involvement, with neither punitive nor sentimental views, much the same as a physician views a patient. This does not mean complete detachment.
4. On-the-job counseling techniques.
5. Ability to say "no" with reasons when necessary, and to say "yes" with equal reason.
6. Sensitivity to pathological behavior, as compared with normal random behavior, sufficient to permit intelligent referral to professional staff.
7. Ability to assess strengths of an individual, to determine what the treatment team has to build on in the treatment of an offender.
8. Making referrals to all staff, community resources, and other specialties with some sophistication.
9. Ability to use tact to avoid creating or aggravating problem situations.
10. Ability to use tact to ameliorate developing problem situations.
11. Willingness to augment and support the therapeutic community and the therapeutic process in the institution and the community programs.

12. Ability to observe and accurately record
    a. Individual behavior:
       Pathological behavior needing referral to professional staff.
       Escape, manipulation, or other suspicious behavior in which the safety and security of the institution or community may be concerned.
    b. Group behavior:
       Beginning of disturbance.
    c. Miscellaneous behavior:
       Incidents that might be recorded that may crescendo into major difficulty or be part of an organized illicit activity.
13. Ability to assess the community-reintegration model, including attitudes toward the returning offender.
14. Constructively interpret administrative decision, actions, and procedures to inmates, probationers, and parolees.
15. Serving as upward communicator from the inmate body to the administration, and from the probation and parole caseload to the judge and field services supervisor, with the view toward improving correctional services.
16. Maintaining discrete silence on some critical issues and "classified" information to maintain
    a. staff morale.
    b. inmate and caseload morale.
    c. good public relations.
17. Capability of exerting external controls on individuals who need containment with physical force, or firearms when necessary, without using more force than the situation actually requires.
18. Knowing specific procedures that might be modified or elaborated in the in-service training program of the correctional agency or institution—such as classification procedure, pre-parole planning, probation and parole revocation hearings, and procedures at similar level.
19. Knowledge of the civil and constitutional rights of prisoners, whatever their status, and the incorporation of that knowledge into the supervisory process.
20. Knowledge to interpret the system of justice—including laws of arrest, judicial procedure—and the total correctional process of probation, prison, and parole, together with knowledge of revocation hearing procedure and pardon procedure.

Training the volunteer is essential. Knowledge of the complex organization and procedure of the juvenile court, attitudes consistent with the helping professions, and the development of skills in working with people and in oral and written reporting are all basic to effective functioning of the volunteer. Volunteers can be trained at various times: (1) during screening of applicants, (2) after the screening, (3) orientation, (4) traditional training classes before assignment, (5) small group discussions, (6) contact with the staff, (7) large group meetings, (8) periodic in-service training programs, and (9) through direct supervision.[23] Training is a continuing process. Films, slides, television and videotapes, tours of institutions and programs, lectures and panel presentations, and assigned reading are all part of the training. Training would not be complete without counseling-supervision of professional juvenile court counselors or probation officers regarding the child under supervision during the supervisory or coordinating contacts of the volunteer with the court.

Checklist

Steps in developing a volunteer program in the juvenile court:

1. Develop an interest in volunteer programs by becoming aware of the need.
2. Acquire sufficient knowledge so that you can talk about it intelligently.
3. Talk to the juvenile court judge.
4. Talk to the chief probation officer and the court staff.
5. Recruit volunteers by word-of-mouth, lectures, and news media.
6. Select from applicants the volunteers to work with children. Others may be used for functions other than contact with children, such as office work.
7. Train volunteers in the objectives of the juvenile court, how it is to be achieved, pertinent legal concerns, and general understanding of human behavior and how it can be changed.
8. Supervise—or coordinate—the volunteers to get optimum results from them.
9. Know when to terminate a case and assign a new one to the volunteer.

PART IV: COORDINATION OF VOLUNTEER PROGRAMS

The coordinator of volunteers has the supervisory function over the volunteer program, himself being under the supervision of the judge and the chief probation officer. Since volunteers have no tangible identification with the court in terms of salary, their function is voluntary and without authority. Consequently, they have to be coordinated, rather than supervised.

A coordinator of volunteers is necessary to make a volunteer program function effectively. In many places, this coordinator of volunteers is a full-time worker paid by the juvenile court. In other places, he may be a full-time volunteer without pay. Experience has indicated, however, that better services can be expected from a full-time paid coordinator of volunteers.

The coordinator of volunteers has the function of recruiting, selecting, training, and supervising the work of the volunteers. Depending on the size of the court, he may have one or more assistants. He must keep the judge and the probation officers informed in order to coordinate efforts and reduce suspicion and apprehension. The volunteer augments and supports work of the probation officer, so this communication is necessary.

Liaison with schools and law enforcement is an important phase of coordination. Liaisons with the community, particularly part-time employment resources and other agencies interested in children, are also important for the effective functioning of a volunteer program. The juvenile aid bureau of the police department is an important group with which to establish and maintain contact. Some smaller cities have a single juvenile officer, while some larger cities may have a hundred or more officers assigned to working with juveniles.

Financing is an important part of any program—including a volunteer program. As previously mentioned, a volunteer program does cost money or its equivalent in staff time, because of training programs and the supervision needed that must be done by court staff. In addition, there are other incidental expenses in working with children, such as tickets to the ball game, a baseball and bat, dinner at a nice restaurant, a much-needed pair of shoes, and other incidentals. While many hold that these are not legitimate expenses for tax funds, the fact remains that they are realistic expenses for the volunteer. The coordinator of volunteers frequently handles the funding problems by private donations, grant requests from governmental agencies and private foundations, getting the volunteer program adopted as a project by a civic club, and other means. The judge includes the salary of the coordinator of volunteers in his budget request to the county commission, but the coordinator, himself, frequently has to "scratch" for other funds.

The coordinator of volunteers must maintain close liaison with the judge and the chief probation officer. He must also maintain close liaisons with all his volunteers, over whom he has no real authority. Consequently, it takes a competent person who relates well with people to serve as a coordinator of volunteers. He must provide almost inspirational leadership, to coordinate the motivations of the people who volunteered to assist with the needs of the children in trouble within the guidelines of the juvenile court. Supervision of volunteers is the most important part of coordinating volunteers, even though it is called "coordination" rather than "supervision," because of the unpaid and nonauthoritative nature of volunteers and volunteer programs. Frequent consultation about cases and their progress is essential. Supervision is incorporated in all phases of relationships with the volunteers, including the training procedure. There are several basic principles that can be taught in one evening class or one daytime session:

1. *Listen* to the child. Nothing can be learned about another person when somebody else is talking.
2. *Accept* the child as he is without being judgmental. Nobody tries religiously to be bad, and everybody wants to be accepted and loved. Deviant behavior is a failing attempt to resolve personal and social problems. Rejection aggravates the problem.
3. *Give the child a meaningful relationship with an adult he can trust,* probably for the first time in his or her life. Socialization is based on faith, trust, and confidence. Without experiencing trust of adults, no child can possibly be socialized.
4. *Develop the capacity to withstand provocative behavior,* since children who think they are "picked on" tend to fight back by baiting and taunting authority. Faced with the usual hostile response, the child's negative relationship with authority. Faced with the usual hostile response, the child's negative relationship with authority will be reinforced. An accepting and non-reaction to hostility will give him a "new look" at authority and enhance the socialization of a child in conflict with authority.
5. *Don't give advice,* because people asking for advice are "shopping" and compare opinions of various people. It is much more effective to respond with questions about what other factors are present and what would happen if various alternatives were taken. Advice places the counselor in the position of being "an S.O.B." if the child fails or encounters further problems while following advice. Most important, the advice is not "his," and he is not committed to it. Rather than having thought through his problem with the questioning and suggesting help of his counselor, he is "following instructions" as from a cookbook or manual, simply hoping the advice works.

Giving Direction

Direction of the volunteer program must be worked out among the judge, the chief probation officer or court staff, and the coordinator of volunteers. Together, they must identify: (1) the primary problems in the community and in the court; (2) the interested persons in the community and in the court; (3) the target people, whether only juveniles who have come to the court or children in trouble in school or elsewhere; (4) the goals of the court and the volunteer program; and (5) the delivery agencies or resources available in the community.

Volunteer probation officers in other countries have functioned even longer than those in the United States, and many have worked out their directions. For example, the Japanese volunteer program practically "professionalizes" the volunteer by treating him similar to paid workers; they place a premium on community service; they try to pair probation officers with volunteers in more even proportion than in America; they make use of retirees and semi-retirees, consider confidentiality most important, and place the volunteer on a high level of prestige because he is providing service as a contribution to the community and his fellow man.[24] This approach and generalized role of the volunteer provides direction to his efforts. Similar status recognition can be provided the volunteers in the juvenile court by making them feel that they belong to an "exclusive club," with a certificate issued by the court that could be framed and hung on the wall and a wallet identification card. For a variety of reasons, it is well that these certificates and identification cards have expiration dates and can be reissued, sometimes selectively, as they expire.

Supervision of casework and other relationships between the volunteer and the child in trouble is most difficult. The best aproach appears to be a "staffing," as is done in mental hospitals and mental hygiene clinics. Once a week or at other designated periods, a volunteer may present his case to the staff, including the chief probation officer, the probation officer or counselor working with the case, and the coordinator of volunteers, as well as other members of the staff and volunteer groups. Questioning what he did, why he did it, and what he should do results in an ability to assess the competence of the volunteer as well as providing an educational experience for the volunteer and other members of the staff.

Providing direction to a volunteer program is as important as providing guidance for children. A completely laissez faire administration of the volunteer program results in much wasted effort. On the other hand, a rigid and regimented administration that functions "by the manual" negates the advantages of a volunteer program. Decisions mutually agreed upon and transmitted with supporting reasons and prognostication as to the effects of actions taken appears to be the most effective way of providing direction to the volunteer program. In this manner, everyone will be going in the same general direction with full knowledge of the rationale supporting the policies.

The Young Person

The volunteer's relationship to the young person in trouble is essentially that of an adult friend. His primary mission is to provide the young person with a meaningful relationship with an adult he can trust. Generally, the relationship provided by the volunteer is the first time young people in conflict with authority have had this experience. The volunteer gives the young person a "new look" at authority, one that is accepting and supporting of him. Dr. Tom Kennedy, psychiatrist from Meridian, Connecticut, has said at two of the conferences that youngsters will "parentalize" the volunteer.

This relationship may be resented by the child's parents, which makes their constructive involvement important to reduce hostility and enhance socialization. Dr. Kennedy says that resentment by parents is normal because of guilt. Effectiveness, too, always draws jealous attacks by threatened people. Respect shown parents by volunteers by "passing the time of day," by asking their advice, and by supporting to the child the right things they have done will go far toward gaining parental cooperation. It is just as difficult to be 100 percent wrong all the time as it is to be 100 percent right all the time.

Judge Wilfred W. Nuernberger of Lincoln, Nebraska, has provided a list of suggestions used in the volunteer program in Lincoln, originally developed in the Howard Juvenile Court in Kokomo, Indiana, as follows:

> We realize fully that working with juveniles cannot be reduced to "cookbook" form. Much will always be left to your own good judgment. Every case is unique and cannot be handled exclusively in terms of specific rules.
>
> Respect is the keystone in working with a juvenile. The youngster will be open to you when he respects and trusts you, as he has been able to deceive many people. You must be different. You must be honest. Never make a promise or threat that you cannot back up. You will begin to make some progress when he realizes you are honest with him and are not easily deceived. Within this general framework, here are some guidelines well worth your thinking about as points of departure around which to build or organize your own personal experiences working with juveniles.
>
> 1. *Keep in contact with the child.* Whatever your volunteer job, be prepared to invest some time with the child. We recommend a minimum of one visit a week. Occasional contacts are unlikely to make the kind of impression we need.

Keep in contact not only with the child but with the office. Reports you will fill out on each contact with the child are extremely important in keeping the office fully advised. Please file and return these reports fully and promptly by the 5th of each month. Come in and see us as frequently as you can with your ideas, reports, problems, and suggestions. We are here to help, too.

2. *Patience.* Don't expect overnight miracles. When things have been going wrong for years for a child, they cannot be corrected in a few weeks, or months, or even years. Indeed, the positive impact of your work may not give decisive effect until long after you have stopped working with a youngster; you may never see them.

    It takes time. Even if slow progress is visible, there will be frequent setbacks.

3. *Be ready for such setbacks.* Be patient and have the ability to deal with your own disappointment and heartbreak. That does not mean you cannot show anger under control—as a normal human would respond to "bad" behavior. But do not vent your frustration and anger on the child. It's a very easy trap to fall into, even unconsciously. Although we all like to achieve success with a child, remember he does not owe it to us, he owes it to himself.

4. *Give attention and affection.* The child you are working with may never have known really sustained attention and affection, and he may not know how to handle it in a normal way; i.e., he may tend just to sop it up hungrily without giving in return.

    For one thing, don't expect overt and explicit thanks and gratitude from the child or his parents. Even if the child feels it, he may not know how to express and communicate it and may actually be embarrassed by it. Though your work is not rewarded by specific "thank you's," it is, in the long run, appreciated, probably more than you or we shall ever know.

5. *Be prepared to listen and to understand what your child says.* Maybe it's easier for you to do most of the talking, even to "preach," but the chances are that the child has had plenty of this before and hasn't responded to it. What he very likely hasn't had is an adult who will hear him out, really listen to what he has to say. What the child has to say may shock you in its difference from your own set of values and standards. Try, then, to think of it in terms of its causes objectively, without either judging or condoning.

    Sometimes, one of the child's problems may be communication with adults. This is not because they haven't "talked at" him but because they haven't "listened" to him enough. Too much talking on your part is more likely to break communication than enhance it.

6. *Be a discerning listener.* Listening does not mean you have to believe everything you hear. Some of these youngsters are skilled manipulators and have come to believe that stretching the facts a bit is an effective life style (they may not even know they do it). Much of this too, will just be letting off steam, getting things off their chests, and within limits, this is a good thing.

   Don't be a naive, all-believing listener. Check the facts, whenever you can; see how well what the youngster tells you accords with reality. When it doesn't, it is frequently good to let him know this, kindly, but firmly; i.e., "reality test" for him. As he comes to know that you expect accuracy (within his means to achieve it), maybe he'll respect you more because you expect it.

7. *Don't pre-judge.* Keep an open mind on the youth when first getting to know him. Avoid forming fixed and premature opinions until you have done a lot of discerning listening and gathered all the background information you can.

8. *Respect confidentiality, utterly and completely.* Whatever you know or surmise about a youngster is under no circumstances to be divulged to, or discussed with, anyone but a person authorized to receive this information.

   Violations of confidentiality are not only highly unethical, they are a sure way to destroy a relationship with the youth. Related to this, be cautious and judicious about asking probing personal questions, especially early in the relationship. The response may be only resentment. It is not a good idea to assume the youngster wants to hear you discuss your personal life in lieu of his.

9. *Don't rush it,* but as the relationship develops, you can encourage the youngster to think about himself, his actions, goals, etc., and from that knowledge, plan together more constructive activities from which he will derive a measure of self-respect and success. Many of your youngsters have done almost no careful thinking about themselves in a planful, forward-looking way. They seem almost to run away from self-awareness.

10. *Be sure you discuss with the office and understand thoroughly your particular volunteer role* before beginning work. Know its possibilities and its limitations.

11. *Present your ideas clearly, firmly, simply.* Mean what you say and be consistent. Never make a promise or proposal unless

you have thought it through first and are fully prepared to back it up. The child will test you, "call your bluff," and see if you will consistently deliver as promised, either as rewards or in backing up the limits you set. Be serious about the limits when he tests you and the rewards when you've promised them and he has delivered. All of this is an important part of his learning to trust you—which generally will come slowly.

Don't let the child down, even in apparently small things, like *showing up for appointments and being on time.* If you don't show responsibility as a model for him, you cannot expect him to learn it for himself.

12. *Be supportive, encouraging, friendly, but also firm.* Respect and friendship will be far more solid with both of you if the child knows that, at the same time, you appreciate and respond to efforts at self-improvement. You should be firm, honest, and objective in disapproving where it is warranted.

13. *Be a good behavior model for the child.* One of the best things you can do is to become, in your own behavior patterns, a good model for the youngster. If your own dress, language, and behavior is not standard, you can scarcely expect it from him. Chances are that he has had enough "bad models" already; give him a good one.

14. *Avoid being caught in the middle.* You can be liaison between the child and his ward, but be careful not to get caught between the child and his parents, or the child and his teachers, especially in some way which will be used by the child against his parents, or vice versa. They may happen when you succumb to the temptation to be liked by the child at all costs. The child may "use" you in the conflict with authority. Your relationship with the child's parents may be a sensitive area. Whenever possible, work with the parents and the child, but do not put yourself in a position where it is you and the parents against the child.

Remember that your young friend has other important relationships as well as yours—his parents, peers, teachers, etc.

15. *Positive reinforcement.* Many of the youth do have a great deal of acceptable behavior. Rarely does anyone thank them or reward them for when they are right. They need your praise and reward to encourage this acceptable behavior.

16. *Be yourself and care sincerely about the youngster.*

Mrs. Donna Messacar has provided a list of suggestions to volunteers used in the Friends In Action program in Middletown, Hamilton County, Ohio. They are:

1. Above all, be yourself!
2. Keep your appointments, remember that you are dealing with a young person who may already have been let down too many times. If you make plans and don't keep them, let him know in plenty of time and give an honest reason.
3. Give your relationship time to unfold. This young person may be experiencing a completely new kind of relationship. What may seem like a simple courtesy to you, such as returning a phone call, may have to become a learned response from him. At the onset, you may have to "push" the friendship just to keep it going.
4. Develop an appreciation for the young person in his own life situation. Judging him by your own standards is, at best, unfair. He will come to feel this judgment as criticism of himself. You have offered your friendship; as a friend you can only point out alternatives for more satisfying behavior.
5. Listen to the young person. At first, he may be reluctant to talk about his situation. However, as he learns to trust you, he will probably open up. It is important to him to be listened to and to be heard. Listen to themes in conversations. What repeats itself may very likely give you a clue as to what is bothering him.
6. Use appropriate language. Don't pick up the young person's vernacular. To use language that isn't part of you can label you as a phoney. At the same time, don't leave the impression you don't understand the four-lettered words. There is language understandable to the young person; don't use words that are beyond his comprehension, speak simply and directly.
7. Become a friend that a young person can count on. He may live with crisis much of the time. He may be accustomed to being overcome by crisis and may expect to be defeated. You are in a position to stand by him at a time when he really needs a friend, and you may be able to help him overcome the situation.
8. Maintain control of your feelings—you must remain the stronger person. It is important that you be able to feel *with* the young person, but to feel *like* him will make him feel you are as powerless as he is.

9. Be willing to learn from situations. As part of our humanity we cannot always predict just how an activity or situation will be accepted. Moods and feelings change and with time we can respond to situations in varying ways. When an activity that seemed like a great idea falls flat, try to evaluate just what went wrong, and then store that knowledge for future planning.
10. Avoid feeling irritated when the young person fails to comply with your suggestions. At the onset of your relationship, discuss certain minimums and then calmly insist that they be met as part of your relationship. For instance, you might make it clear to the young person that you expect him to keep your appointments or else call you.

In summary, the volunteer's primary contribution is to provide the young person in conflict with authority a meaningful relationship with an adult he can trust. While education and training in human behavior, counseling and interviewing techniques, and other useful supporting tools are essential, the successful volunteer has to find out how best to use himself in the relationship. Mr. Ray Sharp of Pontiac, Michigan, has indicated that mistakes can damage young people, but new volunteers will make them—it is the only way people learn some things. Theoretical considerations are always in the background, but the volunteer has to work in the concrete and practical, rather than in the abstract. Young people see competence and effectiveness in terms of tangible results.

Urban and Rural Differences

Throughout the entire project, judicial concern for children in trouble—the evaluations, both written and verbal—frequently indicated that most of the information was imparted by experts from urban areas for use in urban areas and that the rural areas had been neglected. Conversations with some of the experts indicated that this might be true of recruiting and screening efforts, the type of administration of a large program, and the availability of community resources, but the relationship of the volunteer with children in trouble was the same. There would be cultural differences, of course, between urban and rural children, but the volunteers would be from the same area and/or culture in either case. Some volunteer workers from rural areas have viewed the hundreds of volunteers in the Chicago area, for example, as compared with the three or four in a rural area. A quick computation of the size of the populations shows that there may not be much difference in the ratio of volunteers to population and this sometimes favors the rural area.

Two-thirds of the population of the United States lives in urban and suburban areas that occupy 2 percent of the land, while one-third lives in rural areas on 98 percent of the land. While there are differences in the density of population in the rural East and the rural West and Mountain areas, this ratio provides some index of the vast distances that characterize some of the rural areas. The differences found in the rural areas emphasize great distances and lack of community resources. These have to be counteracted in rural areas with the identification of volunteers in the specific area of the child in trouble and the use of such local welfare and family resources as might be available. There is greater word-of-mouth recruitment and informal supervision in rural areas than in urban areas.

Problems that are present in rural areas: (1) dispersed population or low population density; (2) transportation; (3) low availability of work sites; (4) low level of existing human and social services; (5) multiplicity of rural county governments, fragmented districts, such as welfare districts and county agricultural agents' districts; and (6) political problems that arise from relations with established political and service groups, particularly in the rural South, where "programs from outside" are viewed with apprehension and reserve.[25]

A formal program is practical in an area of 30,000 population, or within commuting distance of population centers of at least 10,000.[26] When the population density is less than 10 persons per square mile, formal programs must give way to recruiting individuals who live in the area as volunteers. There were 5,600,000 non-whites in the rural population in 1960. It is generally more successful to match racial and ethnic background of the volunteer with that of the child. Conditions may qualify that concern. Poverty is more prevalent in rural areas, also, than it is in urban areas—the poverty level being 17 percent in central cities, 12 percent in urban areas outside central cities, 25 percent in rural nonfarm areas, and 33 percent in farm areas.[27] The poverty level is always a consideration in any program.

In the rural areas, there is greater need for volunteers than in the urban areas, because the great distances prevent the probation staff from supervising or even visiting young people in trouble as frequently as is possible in urban areas.[28] Volunteers in rural areas are needed because of the general lack of any professional personnel within a 50-mile radius in many regions. The volunteers fill the gaps, substituting for professional assistance. Further, they provide services in accordance with the customs and culture of the area they serve.

Volunteers in urban areas are needed because of inner-city and ghetto problems. Volunteers from indigenous groups, particularly black inner-city populations, can be much more effective than a white social worker with a master's degree wearing a coat and tie.

In large, urban-centered probation departments, young adults who are themselves ex-offenders can be utilized by probation departments as the "front line" officers, both paid and volunteer, who would be in frequent and intimate contact with our juvenile offenders.[29] The traditional probation officers would act as supervisors, but from "behind the lines." These indigenous ex-offender volunteers should operate out of neighborhood centers. The advantages would be to reduce the gap between generational, racial, ethnic, social, and educational differences between the professional probation officer and the client.

Ongoing Evaluation

Evaluation is the "bookkeeping" of any social program. Any program, including the volunteer program, should not be learned on a "faith, hope, and charity" basis. Adequate records should be kept as to what was done, when, why, and the results.

Nearby colleges and universities can provide assistance in evaluation. In many cases, graduate students are available in sociology, psychology, and other disciplines who will provide evaluation services as part of their supervised study. Anyway, ongoing evaluation is essential.

The court volunteer program should be rewarding to the court, the probationer, the volunteer, and the community.[30] To do this, any program must involve: (1) training and orientation so the people involved will know the objectives, techniques by which they are achieved, and what to expect; (2) finding out needs, desires, and fears for the court, the probationer, the volunteer, and the community; (3) specifying goals as operationally as possible and mutually determined; and (4) developing a system of constant feedback to determine whether the program is affecting everyone involved as favorably as possible. This feedback is essential to ongoing evaluation of the volunteer program.

Results of volunteer programs have been shown to increase significantly the effectiveness of probation.[31] It significantly increases socialization and decreases the repetition of offenses. Success may be related to the frequency of contacts that enhance relationships, rather than a specific type of counseling or a particular person.

Dr. Ernest L. V. Shelley of Lansing, Michigan, emphasizes the importance of evaluation of volunteer programs. He says:[32]

> It is very important that any program be evaluated so that we know what it is accomplishing and how well it is accomplishing it. This does not always have to be sophisticated research. Frequently, just good data regarding the total program tell much of the story. Some suggestions would be:
>
> 1. Use volunteer high school students or college students to gather data such as statistics from the files about both the children and the volunteers.
>
> 2. Many of the evaluation programs can be done as good term papers or master's theses by students in nearby colleges and universities.

3. The court staff should identify its major evaluation needs and then lay these before the faculty of nearby colleges and universities, suggesting that they either carry forward this research themselves or direct graduate students in doing it.
4. It is well to have a master plan of evaluation, so that the total picture gets taken care of and that reseachers can see where their part of the work fits in.
5. In starting a new program, it is highly desirable to bring in college or university faculty to advise as to the best ways of evaluating those things which you want evaluated in the program. Thus, the kind of evaluation you need and want can be built in from the very beginning.
6. Even if the program has been started without any evaluation built in, bring in these people to advise you as to how you can initiate it.
7. Be sure that the data which are a result of evaluation get communicated to staff, to judges, to volunteers, and to the community.

CONCLUSIONS

One of the primary conclusions of examining the volunteer program, both existing and potential, is that it appears to be the only method of obtaining the manpower needed to cope with the problem of children in trouble in modern America.

The impact of court volunteers has been a reduction in institutionalization rates, reduction in repeat offense percentages, and a lessening of antisocial attitudes. Volunteers function effectively as the court's ambassadors and educators in the community. The volunteer's impact on professional roles and structures in the courts has produced profound changes in these roles. First, the probation professional profits from enhanced interaction with additional professionals brought in as volunteers. Second, the leadership of the high-quality court volunteers challenges the probation officer professionally as never before. Third, the volunteers have been effective allies in improving pay scales, which helps the profession to attract and retain high-quality people.

Another important impact of volunteers on professional roles: When volunteers take over a number of cases which do not require the attention of the professional, he now has a chance for direct work with probationers, which is ideal in two senses. First, having been relieved of part of his caseload by volunteers, he can concentrate better on the fewer probationers remaining as his direct responsibility. Second, this reduced caseload may be composed largely of the probationers he deliberately selects to work with, as those who are most likely to benefit from his professional attention.

The volunteer movement in American juvenile courts is one of the most promising movements relating to children in trouble to have developed in recent years. It is the only way apparent to work with children in whom social stability or emotional maturation has not been achieved. It will not be achieved in the juvenile court with one worker for every 150 children brought to its attention. It must be accomplished by involving volunteers.

Court volunteer programs can contribute in two ways. First, amplification of services: For each hour of the probation officer's time spent in volunteer supervision, ten to twenty hours of volunteer service output can be received by the probationer (amplified via the volunteer). Second, diversification of services: In the area of direct contact with probationers, volunteers can bring many competencies and skills to bear on problems as needed.

Volunteer programs tend to lessen the distance and enhance communication between socioeconomic classes, thereby supporting democratic ideals. In a totalitarian state where "everything is G.I.," the contributions of volunteers are less significant.

The PTA is a "natural" organization for the purpose of generating volunteers and volunteer programs. It is also a strong and widespread organization. Judge Gullata of New Orleans has said that the PTA is the standard by which other people-oriented organizations are measured. Their interest in children provides the motivation for a strong organization to be effective.

Stability in the past was achieved by external coercion, while today it is being achieved by internal cohesion.[33] A quick review of the history of the family indicates that the internal controls provide the "social gyroscope" within people, rather than technological and physical limitations. This means that the socialization process for juvenile delinquents in the 1970s must be achieved by person-to-person relationships that can transmit the values of our culture to unstable people, in order to develop the internal cohesion necessary for stability. This is the challenge that faces the PTA, the juvenile court judges, the schools, and all of America. The volunteer program appears to be the most adequate response.

NOTES

1. *Task Force Report: Corrections* (Washington, D.C.: The President's Commission on Law Enforcement and the Administration of Justice, 1967), p. 1.
2. Ibid., p. 97.
3. Ibid., p. 1.
4. *Juvenile Court Statistics, 1968* (Washington, D.C.: Office of Juvenile Delinquency and Youth Development, Department of Health, Education and Welfare, 1970), p. 3.
5. Loc. cit.
6. Loc. cit.

7. *The National Missing Youth Locator,* vol. 1, no. 1 (Hayward, California: NMYL Publishing Company, January 1971), p. 3.
8. Ivan H. Scheier and Leroy P. Goter, *Using Volunteers in Court Settings: A Manual for Volunteer Probation Programs* (Washington, D.C.: Office of Juvenile Delinquency and Youth Development, HEW, 1969).
9. *The Use of Volunteer Probation Counselors for Misdemeanors: A Special Demonstration Project* (Denver, Colorado: The County Court, 1968), p. 24.
10. Loc. cit.
11. Letter from Mrs. Lillie Herndon, Columbia, South Carolina, August 14, 1972.
12. Paul Wiers, *Economic Factors in Michigan Delinquency* (New York: Columbia University Press, 1944).
13. Thomas P. Monahan, "Family Status and the Delinquent Child: A Reappraisal and Some New Findings," *Social Forces* 35 (1957):250–58. See also Fritz Redl and David Wineman, *Children Who Hate* (Glencoe, Illinois: Free Press, 1951), pp. 55–56, 113–121; and Ruth S. Cavan, *Juvenile Delinquency* (Philadelphia: Lippincot, 1962), Chapter 10, "The Family Setting of Delinquency," pp. 11–127.
14. C. S. Hewitt and Richard L. Jenkins, *Origins of Maladjustment* (Springfield: Illinois State Department of Health, 1944).
15. Ivan H. Scheier and Judith A. Berry, *Serving Youth as Volunteers* (Boulder, Colorado: National Information Center on Volunteers in Courts, February 1972), pp. 15–17.
16. Jewel Goddard and Gerald D. Jacobson, "Volunteer Services in a Juvenile Court," *Crime and Delinquency* (April 1967), pp. 337–42.
17. Scheier and Barry, op. cit., pp. 7–10.
18. Gordon H. Barker and Ronald R. Matson, "A Volunteer Probation Officer Manual," *Volunteers in Court: Collected Papers* (Washington, D.C.: Youth Development Delinquency Prevention Administration, 1971), pp. 54–57.
19. R. W. Tyler, "The Role of the Volunteer," *California Youth Authority,* vol. 18, no. 4 (Sacramento: California Department of the Youth Authority in conjunction with Stanford University, 1965), pp. 15–23.
20. Mrs. Theresa Yancey, Cook County Juvenile Court Augments Service," *Source,* vol. 1, no. 4 (publication of the Illinois Information Center on Volunteers in Courts), p. 3.
21. *Guide for Associate Degree Programs in the Community and Social Services* (New York: Counsel on Social Work Education in Cooperation with American Association of Junior Colleges, 1970), pp. 19–20.
22. Vernon B. Fox, *Guidelines for Corrections Programs in Community and Junior Colleges* (Washington, D.C.: American Association of Junior Colleges, 1969), pp. 18–19.
23. James Jorgensen and Ivan H. Scheier, *Training the Volunteer in Courts and Corrections* (Metuchen, New Jersey: Scarecrow Press, 1972).
24. Albert G. Hess, "The Volunteer Probation Officer in Japan," *International Journal of Offender Therapy,* vol. 14, no. 1 (1970), pp. 8–14.
25. Michael Munk, *Rural Youth-Work Programs: Problems of Size and Scope* (New York: New York University Manpower Training Series, Summer 1967) pp. 41–43.
26. *Rural Youth in Crisis* (Washington, D.C.: United States Bureau of Census, 1964), p. 5.
27. Op. cit., p. 9.
28. Edwin B. Cunningham, "The Role of the Parole Advisor," under the Section "Use of Volunteers in Parole," in Charles L. Newman (ed.), *Sourcebook on Probation, Parole and Pardons* (3rd ed.; Springfield, Illinois: Charles C. Thomas, 1968), p. 327. Originally published in *Federal Probation,* vol. 15, no. 4 (December 1951), pp. 43–46.
29. T. P. Thornberry, "Ex-Offenders in Community Based Probation," *Prison Journal,* vol. 48, no. 2 (1968), p. 23–25.
30. Unpublished paper by Ann Waldo, Director of Youth Opportunities, Boston, Massachusetts, delivered in Boston, November 17–19, 1971.

31. Gerald Rosenbaum, James L. Grisell, Thomas Koschtial, Richard Knox, and Keith J. Leenhouts, "Community Participation in Probation: A Tale of Two Cities," *Proceedings of the American Psychological Association, 77th Annual Convention*, Washington, D.C.: (1969), pp. 363–64.

32. Original statement prepared by Dr. Ernest L. V. Shelley for this presentation.

33. Unpublished paper by Judge G. Ross Bell, Birmingham, Alabama, presented to the conference at Chicago, September 13–15, 1972.